T4-AEC-744

MONTGOMERY COLLEGE LIBRARY
GERMANTOWN CAMPUS

*ISSUES OF
POLITICAL
DEVELOPMENT*

SECOND EDITION

ISSUES OF POLITICAL DEVELOPMENT

Charles W. Anderson

Fred R. von der Mehden

Crawford Young

PRENTICE-HALL, INC., Englewood Cliffs, New Jersey

Library of Congress Cataloging in Publication Data

Anderson, Charles W.
   Issues of political development.

   Includes bibliographical references.
   1. Comparative government. 2. Underdeveloped areas – Politics and government. 3. States, New – Politics and government. I. von der Mehden, Fred R., joint author. II. Young, Crawford, joint author. III. Title.
JF60.A53 1974   301.5'92   73-13963
ISBN 0-13-506410-4

© 1967, 1974 by PRENTICE-HALL, INC., Englewood Cliffs, New Jersey

All rights reserved.
No part of this book may be reproduced
in any form or by any means
without permission in writing from the publisher.

Printed in the United States of America

10 9 8 7 6 5 4 3 2 1

Prentice-Hall International, Inc., *London*
Prentice-Hall of Australia, Pty. Ltd., *Sydney*
Prentice-Hall of Canada, Ltd., *Toronto*
Prentice-Hall of India Private Ltd., *New Delhi*
Prentice-Hall of Japan, Inc., *Tokyo*

Contents

Preface to the Second Edition   vii

Preface to the First Edition   ix

Introduction   1

PART ONE

THE ESTABLISHMENT OF POLITICAL ORDER
Nationalism and the Problem of Cultural Pluralism   13

CHAPTER 1
The Developing State and Its Cultural Components   15

CHAPTER 2
Social Change and Cultural Pluralism   28

CHAPTER 3
The Activation of Cultural Conflict   62

CHAPTER 4
Crises of Cultural Pluralism: Biafra and Bangladesh   79

CHAPTER 5
Nation-Building: Coexisting with Cultural Pluralism   101

PART TWO

THE MAINTENANCE OF POLITICAL ORDER
Stability and the Problem of Political Violence   111

CHAPTER 6
The Problem of Political Violence   113

CHAPTER 7
Civil Strife in Burma   125

CHAPTER 8
"La Violencia" in Colombia   136

CHAPTER 9
Domestic Violence in Africa: Zaire   147

PART THREE

THE PURPOSE OF POLITICAL ORDER
Development and the Problem of Political Ideology   167

CHAPTER 10
The Meaning of "Revolution" in the Developing World   169

CHAPTER 11
Socialism as a Program for Development   198

CHAPTER 12
Political Ideology and Development Policy   252

Index   271

Preface to
the Second Edition

Our overall impression in accounting for the events that have taken place in the politics of the developing world between 1965 and 1973 is one of essential continuity rather than striking change. The issues we focused on in the first edition – national integration, political order, and the role of government in the developmental process – still appear to be among the central concerns of politics in these regions. New political movements and regimes have been established in various countries; here and there the public debate on development has shifted perspective; the configuration of perennial problems has changed in some nations; and recent research has caused us to revise earlier interpretations. However, we have not seen any general trends in the pattern of events of this most recent period in the third world that cause us to characterize the processes and problems of change in a new way. Once again, what impresses us most is the fundamental variety and heterodoxy of the responses of the African, Asian, and Latin American nations to the issues of political development, and the diversity of the problems that have to be resolved in the name of political development.

Perhaps the more significant change that has taken place between the first and second editions of this book is not that which has occurred in the developing nations themselves but rather the different perspective that people in the so-called advanced nations now bring to the study of developing societies. The politics of the advanced and the developing worlds simply seemed more categorically different seven years ago than it does today. In the early 1960s such issues as cultural pluralism and political violence seemed to distinguish the politics of Africa, Asia, and Latin America from those of the more stable societies that we identified with modernity. Now it is more apparent that national integration and political order are universal political issues. Similarly, ideology, and particularly revolutionary or radical ideology, seemed hypothetically a more characteristic factor in the politics of the developing world against the background of the assumptions of a decade ago, when it was widely believed that an "end of ideology" had occurred in the politics of the West, than it does in the light of the "new politics" of Europe and North America of the late 1960s. Changing great power relations, and particularly, the waning of the Cold War, have made a difference in the politics of the developing world, but this has also meant a difference in the way the issues of development are understood by the people and the leaders of the great powers themselves.

In the early 1960s, economic prosperity and abundance was a consensually postulated objective of development policy — the difference was that the industrial nations had achieved it and the developing world had not. The renewed public debate in the West on the quality of life afforded by industrial society and the emergence of concern for the environmental consequences of economic growth has affected our conception of the goals of the developmental process. Once again, the changing perspective in the advanced world is more striking to us than any definitive trend in the politics of the developing continents. In some places, there has been a response in development ideologies to the questioning of the goals and achievements of industrial society. However, for much, if not most, of the developing world, the objective of economic growth is still persistent and central, an attitude perhaps characterized by the tone of the debate at the 1972 Stockholm conference on world environmental problems and the plea of the Brazilian delegate to "send us your pollution."

In preparing this second edition, we have tried to remain aware of the shifting interpretations of the global problem of development. However, we have been fundamentally concerned to remain consistent with our objective in the first edition — to portray the issues of development as they are defined and dealt with by the leaders of the developing nations. Basically then, this edition represents an updating and revision to account for political events and changes during the seven-year period since the completion of our original analysis.

Preface to the First Edition

This book is about three political aspirations that seem to be common to all emerging nations and the problems that the leaders of these states must resolve if these aspirations are to be fulfilled. The first goal is nationalism, the formation of viable political communities. The related problem is cultural pluralism, the diversity of life that may prevent men from seeing their fellow citizens as "we" rather than as "the others."

The second political aspiration is stability, and the problem is one of civic disruption and violence. At issue is the maintenance of political order in a functioning, but imperfect, political community.

The third aspiration of emergent nations is "development," that wonderfully open and ambiguous term that may connote no more than the desire to achieve material well-being but may also imply a utopian vision of a desirable social order in the future. In discussing the aspiration to development, we focus on the problem of ideology, the fashioning of a context of ideas that will describe what the nation wants to achieve and how it is going to get there. At issue is what the political community will be used for, what the "togetherness" of the nation implies.

In choosing these three topics to exemplify the issues of political development, we are suggesting that these problems are indeed fundamental ones, for they deal with the establishment, maintenance, and purpose of political life itself. These are "classic" questions of politics. The fact that they are to a large extent academic questions in modern, industrialized societies, while at the heart of the political process in many emerging nations, may constitute the definition of the distinction between politically "developed" and "developing" societies.

This book is also something of an experiment in comparative political analysis. It is based on close collaboration and extended dialogue between three "area specialists," for each of us has done most of his professional work in one of the developing continents — Anderson in Latin America, von der Mehden in Asia, and Young in Africa. Our method was essentially inductive. We started with no theory of comparative politics, but rather with the distinctive characteristics of politics in our own regions, and inquired of the others whether such characteristics were indeed general phenomena. We tried to use our very ignorance to positive advantage, proposing only that which seemed distinctive of our regions and accepting only that which fit our regions as we understood them. We tried to avoid an *a priori* model of what developmental politics is all about.

In spite of the fact that, as research on the developing world goes, this was a relatively low-cost venture, we have incurred numerous debts of gratitude to many people. Each of us, of course, would first of all acknowledge the wisdom and patience of those who told us about their nations and taught us about their way of life, in Africa, Asia, and Latin America, long before we invoked their guidance and counsel in the discussions that led to this book. Second, we would cite the hard work and insight of those graduate students who worked with us in the seminar in which these ideas were sifted and winnowed. We are grateful to Myron Weiner, who read the manuscript and offered invaluable comments. We would also acknowledge financial support from a grant made by the Center for International Studies and Programs of the University of Wisconsin from funds provided by the Ford Foundation. For typing and secretarial services, we commend Mrs. Theodore Bast, Mrs. Florence Meland, and Mrs. Elmer Dalyrimple. Finally, we collectively and individually recognize the support of Jean, Audrey, and Becky, who kept our lives in order while we sat in our smoke-filled room and pondered universal truth. Needless to say, we alone are responsible for errors of fact and judgment, though they were probably the fault of the other two guys.

CHARLES W. ANDERSON
FRED R. VON DER MEHDEN
CRAWFORD YOUNG

Introduction

The sudden entry of Africa, Asia, and Latin America into the mainstream of world politics has been one of the most far-reaching consequences of World War II. Once again, the pace of history had outrun the accumulation of knowledge. As new and urgent problems posed for and by the "developing nations" (itself a newly coined phrase) pressed upon the world's attention, a nearly total void in social and especially political science was revealed. Sedate prewar debates among colonial officials and missionaries over administrative or evangelical methods in Africa and Asia have left their traces on the library shelves, and the ethnographic cataloging of subject peoples was well advanced. But there was very little else — and Latin America was almost totally ignored. No university offered a course in the politics of developing areas or the economics of underdevelopment.

The picture, in some ways, is very different today. A torrent of publications has filled the libraries. Whole new subfields of history, political science, economics, sociology, and even psychology have developed. The necessity of grappling with novel data has compelled social scientists to cast about for new approaches: historians have learned to scientifically exploit oral tradition in pre-literate societies, economists have re-examined classical axioms in the light of pre-industrial environments, psychologists have (barely) begun to seek culture-free standards of comparative measurement of human behavior. And political scientists have experimented with conceptual frameworks capable of sustaining meaningful comparative analysis of nearly one hundred diverse political units, having in common only varying degrees of poverty and, in the majority of cases, the newness of their national sovereignty.

The research explosion occasioned by the social scientist's discovery of the developing world has led to important breakthroughs in each of the disciplines affected. Briefly, one might suggest three consequences of the confrontation with the developing world that deserve special mention. First, there has been a virtual avalanche of detailed studies of particular countries or regions. The mind fairly reels before the task of synthesizing this heterogeneous bombardment of materials into a coherent statement about this "new world" of international concern.

Second, one happy outcome of the separate endeavors of the different social sciences has been the partial subversion of the tyranny of disciplinary boundaries. In the past, knowledge had been staked out and title registered to different sectors by the various departments. Trespassing outside one's own intellectual territory was strongly deprecated. However, it was quickly discovered that this artificial compartmentalization of the quest for understanding was peculiarly inappropriate to the study of developing areas. The emergence of the area studies approach has made a major contribution to interdisciplinary exchange of information, concept, and method. The one discordant note in this development has been the tendency to substitute continental for departmental barriers to communication. Area specialization tended to focus upon Latin America, or Africa, or the Middle East, or Asia, and only rarely upon developing areas as a whole. Clearly requisite, then, was the third accomplishment of this postwar period in the study of developing areas – the formulation of a set of universal, generalized propositions and theories about the process of "development" as a whole.

Although progress in the study of developing areas is indisputable, few would contest the statement that a long road lies ahead before we can consider that the state of knowledge is adequate to our needs. For the authors, the most attractive point to be probed further lies in the gap between universal theory and discrete experience.

We have become accustomed to speaking about the "problems of the developing nations" as though it were really possible to encompass the lives, cultures, and diverse circumstances of two-thirds of the people of the world in one set of concepts and propositions. However, even as we engage in such sweeping generalization, we normally feel a bit uneasy. We continually remind ourselves that, given the diversity and complexity of the problems, "there are many exceptions." There is a strong temptation to retreat from soaring abstraction into minute particularism.

Our point is not that universal abstraction about the developing nations is pointless, nor that the detailed discussion of any of these eighty-odd nations is trivial. Rather, it is our suggestion that some helpful things can be said about the problems of political development at the levels of both generality and particularity but also that, although certain things can be said at a particular level of abstraction, other things cannot. We also suggest that much of the discussion about the developing nations has been less than careful to distinguish the intellectual utility of various levels of argumentation. Hence, it is very

Introduction 3

helpful to have an abstract model of how a postulated state of "underdevelopment" may pass into a postulated state of "development." It is quite another thing to insist that everything that happens in a developing nation must somehow fit into such a model. At the same time, each proponent of a theory of development has had to face the fact that his own particular background lies in one nation or area; inescapably there is some tendency to universalize the contours of the region he knows best.

Such considerations led us to the conviction that some part of the difficulty of our discourse on the developing nations is due to the fact that very little has been done in social science research between the levels of universal theory and of case study. We have not exploited the utility of other levels of generalization and abstraction. Furthermore, we have been peculiarly uninterested in linking together particular cases and theoretical generalization.

It is to this "middle range" of theory on the problems of political development that this book is dedicated, and particularly to that type of theory that is derived from the inductive examination and classification of discrete cases — "the discovery of similarities and the explanation of differences," to use Roy Macridis' phrase.

To illustrate more clearly the distinction we make between "universal" development theory and the particular "middle range" of abstraction we will pursue, and to get a better impression of the utilities and limitations of each, let us compare these two approaches to the study of political development in greater detail.

THE NEW SCIENCE OF DEVELOPMENT

The past generation has seen the growth of what might be called a "science of development." The use of the singular is not totally inappropriate. Despite the fact that the postulates and theories of this field have not been completely synthesized, there is a remarkable degree of agreement on the fundamental content of the field. Almost all practitioners understand the same basic concepts and have a similar sense of the importance of the most significant relationships.

The science of development is interdisciplinary in character. Economics, sociology, anthropology, and political science have all contributed to the framing of a body of related propositions about what happens to a society in the process of modernization and, to some extent, how that process may be fostered. The assumption is that a number of related things do happen, and must happen, to the culture, institutions, values, and organization of a society *en route* from the predominance of village-level subsistence agriculture and traditional patterns of culture to urbanized, industrialized, rationalized society.

Economics, of course, has been the queen of the development sciences. Our most generally acceptable definition of the "developing nations" is basically an economic one: these are the poor nations of the world, characterized by levels of income and productivity markedly below those of the industrialized nations. For economics, the key questions of development are both to explain why the gap between rich and poor nations exists and to describe the process by which growth may most effectively be generated in an underdeveloped country. The question becomes one of determining the most effective ways to replicate those processes that gave birth to the industrial revolution in the Western nations. The essential task of the developmental economist is to dissect advanced, industrial society, asking why growth was generated here and then seeing how those institutions and processes might most logically be stimulated in the poorer nations.

As the science of development was pursued, it became increasingly apparent that economic growth is interdependent with certain sociological and psychological changes in individuals and in societies. The equation works both ways. Economic development seems to require certain social institutions and social values and attitudes; conversely, economic development produces marked changes in social systems and in the way men view their lives and their relations with other men. The passage from village to urban life, with all of the complex implications of that change, is perhaps the most apparent example of such a social correlate of industrialization, but there are many others.

The sociologist speaks of the passage from "traditional" to "modern" society, a movement related to the level of economic development, which involves a complex set of changes in the organization of the society and in man's perspective on his society. There is a movement from identification with primary groups to identification with secondary groups, from social norms in which status is derived from inherited place in the order (ascription) to the function that one performs in society and how well one performs it (achievement). It is a movement toward more complex, highly differentiated and specialized social institutions and social roles. Life becomes less viewed as a whole, less diffuse, within the setting of the village and traditional agriculture, and man sees himself as a specialist in one aspect of life, dependent upon other specialists for other activities.

The political scientist, similarly, has sought to outline the character of a political order compatible with the modernization of social institutions and the achievement of economic development. Modern society requires a different sort of political order, one serviceable to a much expanded notion of the relevant community, as the scope of social life changes from the order of the village to the order of the nation. Government must provide means for the expression of the new demands and interests wrought by change; mechanisms must be devised for reconciling and coordinating diverse groups.

The confrontation with the developing areas has involved a quite thoroughgoing reappraisal of that field of political science usually known as comparative government. Traditionally, the content of this field has involved little more than disconnected country-by-country analysis masquerading under the comparative label. Little effort was made to develop a common frame of analysis capable of making systematic comparison between polities.

With the publication of the Almond and Coleman study, *The Politics of the Developing Areas*, a first step was made toward more fruitful comparative discourse. Even here, we might note that the comparison in fact was elevated only one degree; analysis was extended to a continent-by-continent basis rather than country by country. Since then, a number of important contributions have been made – by Easton, Pye, Binder, Huntington, and a number of others. In each case, stimulating insights have been added to the theory of political development. These studies, however brilliant, all reveal a disconcerting gap between the ambition to propose a universal theory and the inadequacy of the empirical underpinning. All students of political development become quickly aware of the many aspects of their subject that are covered inadequately or not at all. With so many of the factual building blocks of sound theory missing, it would be unreasonable to expect the resultant superstructure to be completely sound. This observation by no means suggests that tentative speculation in the direction of the universal hypothesis is unrewarding; at the same time, it would be rash indeed to expect complete success.

The assault upon the unknown has been launched from a different direction by a growing number of quantitatively-oriented political scientists. Karl Deutsch has no doubt been the leading prophet of this movement; he has called for a search for more rigorous comparison by expressing the characteristics of a political system on ordinal scales, thus rendering the data subject to mathematical manipulation and computer processing. Banks and Textor, and Russett et al. have made interesting experiments in carrying out the Deutschian prescription. Elaborate codifications have been attempted on a wide range of attributes of developing states and quantitative data amassed on variables that could be considered significant indicators of the character of a new nation. We feel there is some promise in this approach, although there are also serious shortcomings. At worst, it can result in a series of summary judgments based on inadequate or nonexistent information, given a specious precision by their numercial expression. At its best, however, quantitative indicators can provide a useful auxiliary analytical tool to supplement other methods.

The comparative study of developing areas came into its own almost simultaneously with the blossoming of the "behavioral persuasion" in American political science. The study of American politics itself has been the stronghold of the behavioral school, and there has also been a marked impact on comparative politics. By now, the behavioral perspective has been well integrated into the intellectual traditions of the discipline; no longer does "behavioralism" generate furious debate, or divide departments. We might add, however, that the new dimension to political analysis added by the behavioral orientation has yet to be fully realized in the study of the developing nations. Many gaps remain in our basic understanding of the structure and functioning of the political institutions — and such knowledge as has been cumulated is constantly rendered obsolete by the sheer pace of change. The basic data infrastructure provided by a thorough, reliable census is frequently missing. Such powerful research instruments in the behavioral armory as the sample survey are exceedingly difficult to apply in many countries.

The "science of development" is relatively new. Although its intellectual progenitors can be traced back well into the eighteenth century, it is fundamentally a product of social science speculation and research since the end of World War II. In some fields, particularly political science, most of the work has been accomplished in less than a decade.

Partly because of its very newness, the science of development is far from perfect. Many of the things we say about the "process" of development today may appear quite preposterous a generation hence. Nonetheless, the effort is not to be dismissed lightly. This linking together of the approaches of a variety of social science disciplines into a common theoretical framework will probably be recognized as one of the major achievements of twentieth-century social science.

However, the "science of development," like all intellectual tools, must be used with discretion and care. Like any intellectual apparatus, it is apt to be quite misleading when applied indiscriminately. It should be remembered that the propositions and theories of this science are concerned with the *process* of modernization, with the hypothetical passage from a status defined as "underdevelopment" to that of "development." They are not designed to account in detail for the manifold circumstances of all the nations of Africa, Asia, and Latin America. The science of development is concerned with the relationships among a specific set of variables — those associated with the introduction of technology and scientific patterns of thought in a society — or with the social and political prerequisites to modern forms of technological and economic organization. The science of development does not pretend to take account of the peculiarities of culture, of diverse forms of social organization and political and economic life, established in the nations presently described as "developing" or "emergent."

Hence, when used in a certain way, the science of development would seem to predicate a rather unilinear pattern of modernization and change. There is something rather deterministic, rather Hegelian, about the propositions of the science of development when it is used incautiously. One sometimes derives the impression of a drab cultural uniformity emerging in the world as nations in the process of change are "forced," by the logic of the modernization process itself, to adopt the social norms and social systems "requisite" to economic and political modernization.

Furthermore, an unsophisticated application of the science of development can lead to some rather ethnocentric conclusions: that which is "developed" is that which resembles the existing institutional structure of North

America or Western Europe. Quite clearly, it is one thing to argue that "institutional differentiation" is characteristic of "modernizing" societies and quite another thing to suggest that a political system in which the executive, legislative, and judicial branches of government are separated is more developed than one in which they are not. We should be very careful about the teleological propositions implicit in our notions of development. We do have a problem of cultural perspective. It might be remembered that for many of the people of the developing world, "acquisitiveness" is an attitude of mind that indicates a far lower level of development in the individual than "peace," "serenity," or "harmony with the order of nature."

None of this denies the utility of the science of development when used judiciously. No careful social scientist has claimed that societies in which "acquisitiveness" is highly valued are better than those in which it is not. Rather, all the social scientist is saying, or is entitled to say, is that the value of "acquisitiveness" has been associated with the historic emergence of certain forms of economic and technological organization, and that there are good reasons for believing that certain forms of economic organization presuppose that the members of society place a high value on being acquisitive.

DIVERSITY AND COMPARABILITY IN THE DEVELOPING WORLD

The approach of this book is fundamentally different from that of the science of development as we have described it above. Our problem is not one of defining the process of modernization or of ascertaining how political development might be achieved. Rather, our objective is to capture and convey the diversity and heterogeneity of the experience of the developing nations in confronting some of the problems that all of these nations have in common. Our aim is to indicate the range of experience of the developing nations, to catalog the vividly distinctive ways in which similar problems are defined and attacked from the various perspectives of the different cultures, beliefs, and political systems of Africa, Asia, and Latin America.

We will not delineate a "pattern" or "process" of political development in this book, nor will we attempt to present a series of "stages" of political evolution. Our inquiry has persuaded us that political change in the developing world is not apt to be a unilinear progression, but that it is apt to take a wide variety of forms. To put this another way, we are less inclined to see the leaders of the developing world as the instruments of some type of relentless "process" of modernization, and we are more inclined to see them as individuals engaged in a complex process of problem-solving. We focus on the common problems that such leaders confront, but we are particularly concerned to portray the diversity of response to these problems: the innovations, the creative patterns, the essential "newness" of much of the political life of these societies.

This book, then, represents a commitment to a genuinely comparative approach to the study of the politics of developing nations, one that transcends both the traditional country-by-country approach or the more recent continent-by-continent approach. It represents an effort by three people to pool the resources of their individual area specializations — Anderson on Latin America, von der Mehden on Asia and Young on Africa — in the interest of making a general statement about the political problems that affect all of these areas of the developing world. For the purposes of our collaborative effort, each individual played two roles. Each was a "universalist," suggesting propositions and ideas that might apply to all the emerging nations. Yet each retained a vested interest in his own group of states and would not accept any general proposition until it could be hammered into a form that fitted the conditions of politics in this region.

Our commitment to an eclectic approach to political analysis led us to experiment with a wide variety of techniques. On the quantitative side, we have sought to find statistical indices for measuring the nexus between ideological input and policy output in our discussion of developmental socialism. With some misgivings, we present several scales of cultural pluralism, which we feel may assist in summarizing in tabular form some of the important determinants in assessing the significance of cultural pluralism in different developing political systems. We have also ransacked the findings of historians, anthropologists, sociologists, economists, as well as political scientists who have written on Africa, Asia, and Latin America, to equip ourselves with the widest possible range of descriptive data, to be analyzed by more conventional, inductive means. All of this material has been passed through a largely unconscious filter of what might be simply labeled as "political intuition" acquired by us in our separate field explorations in many of the countries of the three continents that have been our canvas. We make no special claims for the reliability of our judgments, much less for any peculiarly "scientific" validity of our own conclusions.

We begin with three themes that we feel are crucial to an understanding of the problems of the developing nations: nation-building in the context of cultural pluralism; sustained domestic violence; and the widespread ideologies of revolution and socialism in the context of the aspiration to economic development. These are common issues of political development, natural topics wherever the "third world" is discussed. Each of these topics implies a problem that will confront political leaders in developing nations. Each is concerned with a phenomenon of political change — with the dynamic rather than the static properties of the political systems of these nations.

It should also be admitted that, in part, this choice of topics was dictated by our desire to make maximum use of our own particular experience and specialization. Thus, the section on nation-building reflects Young's interest in ethnicity in politics and the effects of cultural pluralism on nationhood in Africa. Von der Mehden has long had a research interest in the ideologies of the developing nations; the chapter on revolution, as well as the assessment of the causes of political violence, reflects this concern. Anderson has been particularly involved in the problems of politics and economic development; the chapters on socialism derive from this interest. All three of us have research interests in countries plagued by persistent internal violence — Anderson in Colombia, von der Mehden in Burma, and Young in Zaire.

The three major themes considered — nation-building, domestic violence, and the ideologies of revolution and socialism — have a common relationship to the overall problem of political change. In examining the issue of nation-building, for example, we start from the uncontroversial proposition that Afro-Asia, in particular, is dominated by new states that face agonizing problems in winning the full commitment of their citizenry which is taken for granted in most Western societies. In equipping the state with a mystique of nationhood, the new leaders face intense competition from diverse forms of subnational loyalties, which we have referred to as cultural pluralism. These loyalties may be based upon race, ethnic identity, language, caste, religion, or region; they have in common the capability of evoking sentiments in men very similar to those described as nationalism. What seems to us crucial to know is the direction of change. Are subnational loyalties giving way to the imperatives of nationalism, as many seem to assume? Our evidence suggests to us that this is not the case in Africa and Asia. Both national identification and subnational loyalties are growing stronger as modern communications and education penetrate and the self-enclosed, small-scale, rural subsistence communities are progressively eliminated.

The "participation revolution," the social mobilization of many layers of population that were previously isolated and inert, is a prerequisite for development but also produces new and heightened forms of subnational differentiation. At the same time, we have found it particularly intriguing to contrast the dynamics of cultural pluralism in Africa and Asia with the dramatically different pattern of change in Latin America. Although three-fourths of the Latin American states have the ingredients of cultural plurality in sizable Amerindian or Negro populations, subnationalism of the type that besets Africa and Asia has never been a serious problem. The reasons for this difference seem to us to shed significant light on the nature of cultural pluralism.

Internal violence or disintegration of the state are the ultimate sanctions for the failure of nation-building. Order except in conflicts between states is taken for granted in the industrial world, yet there is no reason why it should be an assumed characteristic of a political system. We feel that a careful, searching scrutiny of three of the instances where prolonged internal warfare has occurred can illuminate the conditions that may lead to a dissolution of public order, the characteristics of persistent violence within a political system, and the discontinuities produced by the habitual resort to force and coercion, not just by the state but by various actors within the political system. In this section, we have varied our procedure of inductive examination of as many cases and examples as we could secure data for; because large-scale, sustained violence is a relatively restricted phenomenon, we have relied upon the careful exploration of one case in each of the three developing continents. Limitation of the number of cases examined has permitted far more detailed consideration of the nature of internal warfare in concrete settings; on the other hand, it also limits our ability to generalize.

Finally, the rise to self-assertion of the developing world has naturally been accompanied by an acute awareness of the common characteristic of poverty which is the very definition of underdevelopment. The growing disparity between the "have" and "have-not" nations in the world has generated various ideologies of discontent, most of which can be subsumed under the twin themes of revolution and socialism. Our concern with these formulations has been at two levels. First, we have been interested in revolution and socialism as ideas. What do leaders of developing nations mean to say when they proclaim their commitment to revolution, or socialism, or both? In both instances, we have found a wide diversity of usage. The rhetoric of revolution runs from the institutionalized commemoration of a historical discontinuity in the life of a nation, now firmly embedded in the national identity, to the sporadic call for liquidation of incumbent regimes by small and insignificant groups of dissidents. And socialism runs the gamut from Marxist-Leninist orthodoxy to the subtle humanism of Senghor. However, especially in the case of socialism, we have found certain common themes. Socialists of the developing world have preoccupations very different from those of the classical socialists of the Western world. Redistribution makes little sense in states that have only poverty to share. The working class and labor movements can hardly assert social leadership in countries where they barely exist. Socialism in much of Latin America, Africa, and Asia seems to be preoccupied with development and social harmony, not redistribution and class struggle.

Secondly, we have sought to unravel the connective threads between ideological commitment and policy choices. In the case of socialism, we have looked for ways to measure the extent to which a conscious articulation of socialist ideology contained imperatives that altered the decisions of governments. With the exception of the Marxist-Leninist states and a handful of others, our evidence indicates that the policy impact of developmental socialism is smaller than its ideological prescriptions might suggest. Put another way, we might conclude that a given policy in many cases can be equally justified in terms of the tenets of developmental socialism and the postulates of the liberal, free enterprise economy.

Our aim in this volume, then, is at once ambitious and limited. We have wanted to explore collaboratively several important themes of comparative politics, on a truly comparative basis spanning the whole developing world. We feel that the continuous dialogues among us during the years this book was in gestation have permitted an effective aggregation of the more limited specializations of each one of us. At the same time, we are very conscious of our joint shortcomings. The Middle East and South Asia in particular are important areas in which none of us has undertaken field research. And we are equally aware that the topics we have chosen to discuss represent only a small sampling of the significant political phenomena in the developing world. If these essays are found to have made some contribution to an understanding of the dynamics of political development, within these limitations, we shall be more than satisfied.

PART ONE

THE ESTABLISHMENT OF POLITICAL ORDER:
Nationalism and the Problem of Cultural Pluralism

CHAPTER 1

The Developing State and Its Cultural Components

The Royal Commission appointed in 1964 to inquire into the problems posed by the duality of language and culture in the Canadian Confederation issued a solemn warning to the nation in its preliminary report:

> We believe that there is a crisis, in the sense that Canada has come to a time when decisions must be taken and developments must occur leading either to its break-up, or to a new set of conditions for its future existence ... The signs of danger are many and serious.[1]

The gravity of the challenge to Canada's survival was underscored in 1970 when terrorists committed to Quebec separatism kidnapped a British diplomat and a provincial minister, murdering the latter.

Even more startling was Britain's slow descent into the maelstrom of subnational conflict in the neglected province of Ulster. The United Kingdom for generations had served as the implicit model of the "developed" political system; scratch the surface of many theories of political development, and beneath the abstractly formulated description of the ideal type of the mature, industrial polity, the classic outlines of Westminster are apparent. The underlying pathology of the polarity in Northern Ireland between Protestants and Catholics came to public view in about 1968. The dreary cycle of unrestrained mob action and intimidation and murder by small terrorist groups on both sides required by 1971 the full-scale military occupation by the British army and direct rule from London. So total was the impasse generated by cultural conflict that in 1972 few could discern even the dimmest outlines of a political solution.

[1] Quoted in "Report on Canada," *The Economist*, July 10, 1965, p. xxvi.

Both of these political communities, nations of long standing, ranking in the vanguard of modern, industrial civilization and far-removed from the ascriptive norms of a traditional world, find themselves confronted with an identity crisis. Nor do they stand alone in what were thought to be the securely integrated polities of the North Atlantic world. Belgium experienced a major constitutional crisis in the 1960s, in redefining the relationships between Fleming and Walloon, in which the cost of failure might have been the breakup of the state. Black riots in a number of American cities, and militant self-assertion by Chicano and American Indian groups challenged the comfortable premises of the "melting pot" in the United States. Noteworthy, if less traumatic, symptoms of cultural conflict appeared in France, Switzerland, Yugoslavia, the USSR, and Spain.

These examples are highly relevant to our consideration of the challenge to nation-builders posed by the widespread fact of cultural pluralism in the developing areas. They alert us to the fact that history is not unilinear, that "progress" and "modernization" are not necessarily correlates of national integration, despite the widely-held assumption of such an automatic relationship in much of the literature of development. Scholarly discourse on nation-building is peppered with arresting and facile vocabulary of the "take-off" genre, with the unspoken premise that "communalism," or "tribalism," or "primordial sentiments" are a transitional phenomenon rather than a permanent feature of the political landscape. Characteristic of this point of view is the following statement by a particularly able student of nationalism, Karl Deutsch:

> The dynamic processes of social mobilization and cultural assimilation ... are thus likely to be more powerful in uniting or destroying an emerging people or a newly-established state than are the mere static facts of the multiplicity of tribes or languages within its territory....[2]

What we shall endeavor to show is that neither "tribe" nor "nation" is a "static fact." Social mobilization and cultural assimilation take place simultaneously on different levels. Terminal loyalty may well come to reside in the existing state, or in some cultural component smaller than the internationally recognized territory, or indeed vacillate between one and the other. Far too many variables are involved to make safe predictions about the future of the majority of developing countries in their quest for a securely integrated national identity; success is neither impossible nor inevitable.

Our present objective, then, is to assess the nature of the problem of cultural pluralism. We need first to consider the origins of the existing state system in Africa, Asia, and Latin America. What basis existed for the

---

[2] Karl W. Deutsch and William J. Foltz, eds., *Nation-Building* (New York: Atherton Press, 1963), p. 6.

establishment of the territorial entities which are now called upon to win the overriding loyalty of peoples who happen to reside within their boundaries? Upon what bases do nonterritorial patterns of solidarity arise? What types of situations activate subnational loyalties? At what point does cultural pluralism lead to the demand for dismantling the political community? What formulas have been uncovered to cope with cultural pluralism? These are the primary issues examined in the present volume.

Two terms we will invoke frequently in this discussion require definition: "cultural pluralism" and "nationalism." Definitions cannot be patented, and a considerable diversity of usage prevails; all we aspire to is clarification of our own meaning.[3] By cultural pluralism we mean the existence within a state of solidarity patterns, based upon shared religion, language, ethnic identity, race, caste, or region, which command a loyalty rivaling, at least in some situations, that which the state itself is able to generate. By "nationalism," we mean the assertion of the will to constitute an autonomous political community by a self-conscious group, whether or not the group coincides with a recognized state.

THE ORIGIN OF THE STATE

At a superficial level, states of the developing world share a fundamental uniformity in international law; they are all recognized as sovereign entities, as terminal human communities within which the formal institutions of government are acknowledged to hold the legitimate monopoly of ultimate coercion and sanctions. But beyond this, the picture is one of great diversity. States differ in their historical origin, in the nature of their relationships with the colonizing powers during the imperial era, in the character of the independence movement and power transfer process, and in the cultural characteristics of race, language, or religion, which may be explicitly or implicitly asserted as the basis for the state. The nature of the state defines the environment of cultural pluralism. It is therefore appropriate to begin by exploring the various types of states.

A first category is made up of states that are the lineal descendants of colonial administrative divisions, where power devolved to the settler elite. This

---

[3]The concept of cultural pluralism is generally attributed to J. S. Furnivall, *Colonial Policy and Practice* (Cambridge: Cambridge University Press, 1948). In a subtle and interesting discussion, M. G. Smith proposes that the term be reserved to situations involving a "formal diversity in the basic system of compulsory institutions," a definition somewhat too restrictive for our purposes. "Social and Cultural Pluralism," *Annals of the New York Academy of Sciences*, 83, Art. 5 (January 20, 1960), 768. On nationalism, the abundance of the literature has produced a plethora of definitions; see especially Rupert Emerson, *From Empire to Nation* (Cambridge: Harvard University Press, 1960); Hans Kohn, *The Idea of Nationalism* (New York: The Macmillan Company, 1945); Royal Institute of International Affairs, *Nationalism* (New York: Oxford University Press, 1939); Carlton J. H. Hayes, *Essays on Nationalism* (New York: The Macmillan Company, 1933). For a sociological perspective on cultural pluralism, see Tamotsu Shibutani and Kian M. Kwan, *Ethnic Stratification: A Comparative Approach* (New York: The Macmillan Company, 1965).

is the characteristic pattern in Latin America; the only other major example is South Africa (with qualifications[4]) and (temporarily) Rhodesia. In the former Spanish realms, preexisting Indian structures were significant to the extent that the two principal Vice-Royalties (Lima and Mexico City) were seated at or near the former capitals of the two major Amerindian empires, the Aztec (Mexico) and Inca (Peru). Spanish suzerainty was at first assured simply by substituting Spaniards for Aztec and Inca and maintaining the lower ranks of the preexisting hierarchy for an interim period. Over the three centuries of Spanish rule, with many local variations, the relatively small number of Spanish settlers succeeded in imposing themselves as a quasi-feudal caste, abetted by often shrewdly conceived patterns of intermarriage into Indian lineages. The settler culture served as the unquestioned basis for the newly independent communities; those who did not belong to it were nonparticipants. The effective political community gradually enlarged itself by absorbing the culturally distinct outsiders into the settler-elite culture. This will be discussed in more detail at a later stage; for the moment, we may suggest that the problem of "artificiality" is of a different order in Latin America than elsewhere in the developing world. There was a period of unscrambling, with the dissolution of the Central American Federation, the collapse of Gran Colombia (including Ecuador, Panama, and Venezuela), and the appearance of Uruguay. Thereafter, national identity never posed the same kind of problem that it has in much of Asia and Africa.

A second category of states includes a string of island republics around the world, formerly under British or French rule, where both metropolitan settlers and indigenous population were overwhelmed by slave or indentured labor brought in from Africa, China, or India to work in mines and on plantations. These include Haiti, Jamaica, Trinidad and Tobago, and Singapore, as well as scattered microcosmic communities such as Mauritius and Fiji. Acute problems of cultural pluralism may arise in such polities, either through the importation of distinctive groups of subjects, as in British Guiana, or through the survival of a significant number of original inhabitants, as in Singapore and Fiji. Although cultural groups may seek to control the state (i.e., the Chinese in Singapore), the state is not historically identified exclusively with any one of the communities. In this sense, the state *qua* state may be considered as culturally neutral.

A third group of states are traditional kingdoms that experienced a period of colonial rule, ranging from a shadowy protectorate (Nepal, Laos) to relatively direct administration (Morocco, Madagascar, Burma). Numerous examples of this form may be cited; in addition to those already listed, Cambodia, Sri Lanka (Ceylon), Egypt, Tunisia, Rwanda, Burundi, Zanzibar, Madagascar, Lesotho, Swaziland, and Botswana, fall into this classification. In many of these examples,

---

[4] The existence of independent Boer republics in part of what is today South Africa, prior to the brief British subjugation of the entire area, makes this case somewhat different from Latin America.

although the legitimation of historical prescription remained, the polity had been substantially secularized and transformed by the colonial experience. In many, the monarchy itself had been subverted (Madagascar, Burma, Sri Lanka, Rwanda), or the seeds of its destruction sown (Zanzibar, Egypt, Tunisia). In a number of them, the traditional monarchy had been associated with the overlordship of a given cultural group, such as the Merina in Madagascar, the Arabs in Zanzibar, the Watutsi in Rwanda, and the Arabs in Morocco. In those where the colonial occupancy had been thorough, the resultant secularization of politics had rendered difficult the simple restoration of the traditional pattern of authority.

Fourth, we may distinguish an important group of states to whom the "artificial" label is most appropriate; these were born of the colonial partition of Africa and, to a lesser extent, Asia. These territories owe their boundaries to imperial competiton rather than to the reduction of an existing kingdom to colonial status. For the most part, precolonial political systems in these areas were much smaller in scale. In any given territory, a number of traditional monarchies were absorbed within the new boundaries, as well as the numerous societies, especially in Africa, which lacked centralized institutions. Thus the present unit has no historical sanction. However, unlike the first category, the demand for self-government is made by the indigenous population, although generally under the leadership of an elite which derives its prestige and authority from success according to the norms imposed by the colonizer.[5] The state is culturally neutral in the sense that it is not associated with any given cultural grouping, although there may be one dominant group, as in the case of the Wolof in Senegal. However, the absence of historical legitimacy for the polity, and the diversity of self-conscious cultural units incorporated within it, greatly complicate the task of creating an integrated loyalty to the territorial state. An elite that has achieved power by coalescing opposition to the colonial occupant is faced with the paradoxical duty of engineering loyalty to the territory carved out by the colonizer. Examples of this type would include most sub-Saharan African states, Indonesia, and the Philippines.

A fifth major category is composed of traditional states that never fell under prolonged colonial occupation. Geographical situation or sheer luck sheltered these kingdoms from absorption into any European empire. Into this class would fall Thailand, Afghanistan, Iran, Yemen, and Ethiopia. In some cases there have been brief occupations (Iran, Ethiopia) and, in most, border alterations and extensive European involvement short of imposition of colonial rule. The absence of direct foreign rule in these states has delayed the impact of social

---

[5]This ignores the small number of African cases where self-government demands were formulated at an earlier stage by the settler population, on the assumption that autonomy was possible with power largely restricted to settler groups. Rhodesia is the last surviving example of this transitional stage in the development of pressures for termination of direct colonial tutelage.

change upon customary institutions and given a rather different stamp to the type of nationalism that has emerged. Even where the traditional monarchy has not survived intact (Thailand, Yemen, Iran), the historic basis for the state has remained. In general, the social mobilization that diffuses territorial nationalist sentiment and cultural subnationalism is much less advanced in these political systems.

Finally, there are a handful of residual cases that do not fit into any of these categories. The breakup of the Ottoman Empire and British World War I Arab policy left in its wake the Hashemite kingdoms, Jordan and Iraq, more or less fabricated to reward those who had rendered wartime services. The contemporary international order requires that territory be organized into recognized states; to do this, petty monarchs were awarded (or permitted to seize) territory ranging beyond the ambit of any traditionally justifiable claims (Saudis in Saudi Arabia, Senussi leaders in Libya). Religion has been the organizing basis of several emergent territories (Islam generally in Pakistan, the Wahabi and Senussi Islamic sects respectively in Saudi Arabia and Libya, Judaism in Israel). A sense of linguistic-ethnic identity served as a basis for unifying former British and Italian Somaliland, an entity which had never been united under a common administration in either the colonial or precolonial era. Finally, we may note three states whose *raison d'être* was as a homeland for the dispersed (Israel, Liberia, and Sierra Leone). In the Israeli case, ancient history offers a sanction for the geographical zone designated as the homeland. In Liberia and Sierra Leone, returned slaves were precariously planted on the West African shore in arbitrarily selected locations. In Israel, those returning have numerically submerged or physically expelled those who had supplanted the children of Israel after the diaspora two millennia ago, and the identity of the returned Jews is the permanent basis of the state. In the African instances, the Liberian Americo-Liberians and Sierra Leone Creoles were relatively few in number, and a conscious effort to revamp the basis of the state has been necessary, to afford an honorable place to the overwhelming indigenous majority.

CULTURAL DIFFERENTIATORS I: RACE

The networks of social solidarity which we term cultural pluralism are of different sorts. "Pluralism" in the past has often applied primarily to the "racial" category,[6] differentiating European and African in Africa, Iberian-mestizo and Indian in Latin America, Malay and Chinese in Malaysia. But this would seem to unduly restrict the scope of the discussion; we would suggest that

[6] This was the main thrust of the treatment in a symposium, International Institute of Differing Civilizations, *Ethnic and Cultural Pluralism in Intertropical Communities* (Brussels, 1957).

the primary bases of cultural solidarity with political relevance are — in addition to race — ethnicity and language, religion, caste, and region. These categories are not entirely discrete; as will be seen, some of the most extreme examples of cultural solidarity are founded upon an identity deriving from more than one common factor.

Race is a highly relevant consideration in producing a keen sense of differentiation among men. As a basis of social differentiation, the instant recognition of variance in skin pigmentation, hair color and consistency, and facial characteristics are the key elements. Although "race" is today largely discredited as a scientific concept, the dynamics of cultural pluralism rest upon subjective human sentiment, not the detachment of the scientific laboratory. A sense of pronounced racial identity seems to emerge only in multiracial settings; there was no common sense of being "African," "European," or "Indian" (Western hemisphere) prior to the creation of multiracial communities by the population movements of the imperial age. Europeans transplanted to an overseas environment quickly perceived the indigenous population, however diverse, as simply "natives" — "Indians," "Africans," etc. A set of stereotypes, usually pejorative, developed, implying a cultural sameness to the colonized. In reaction, the subjugated began to develop a genuine sense of racial identity. No doubt the most striking example of this phenomenon is the emergence of the idea of Pan-Africanism. What is at bottom a sense of racial identity, which grew out of the brutal confrontation with the European world through slavery and colonialism, has developed an elaborate ideological superstructure, which posits underlying cultural oneness beyond the common coloration and historic experience. Racial separation has often been buttressed by legal and social barriers, especially in the colonial context but surviving in such post-independence situations as different land tenure patterns for Indians in Central America and the Andes and the whole rigid edifice of apartheid in South Africa.

CULTURAL DIFFERENTIATORS II: ETHNICITY AND LANGUAGE

The ethnic and linguistic criteria are not in all cases synonymous but may be considered together. This type of identity is usually labeled "nationality" in the European context. The binding link between members of such groups is an awareness of common culture, common ancestry, shared history, and generally a common language. In many cases, the myth of kinship, of the mystic bonds of blood relationship, is present.

The ethnic or linguistic identity may have quite diverse origins. Solidarity may cohere around a traditional authority system, as in the case of the Barotse in Zambia, the Lunda in southeastern Zaire, or, historically, the Inca in Peru. In these instances, the traditional kingdom was originally superimposed upon an amalgam of ethnic groups. The ethnic loyalty may belong to a group growing out of the interpenetration of immigrant and indigenous cultures; examples of this are the Guaraní in Paraguay and the Swahili of coastal East Africa. Or ethnicity (ethnic identity) may be the recent diffusion of cultural self-awareness among linguistically related peoples who had previously lived in dispersed, autonomous communities, such as the Nigerian Ibo or the Zaire Mongo. A unified identity may develop among people formerly owing their loyalty to a series of kingdoms, as with the Malays. Or the common language, perhaps only recently endowed with a genuine literary and cultural tradition, may be the core of the solidarity system, as in India.

CULTURAL DIFFERENTIATORS III: RELIGION AND CASTE

Religion is a third major basis for identity and cultural cohesion. Politically relevant religious affiliation is restricted to the world's great religious configurations: Islam, Buddhism, Hinduism, Judaism, or Christianity, or one of the particular sects or rites of these, or one of the messianic or prophetic syncretic religions which arise in reaction to the penetration of one of these into an area previously dominated by particularistic cosmologies. The latter, so-called "animist" religions are in general too local, and too inseparably related with small-scale traditional systems, to be important to the present discussion.

The profound hold that religion is capable of exerting upon man's emotions and imagination render these cleavages pecularily intractable. Common religion can produce both militant cultural identity and a sense of sacred mission. Where religion regards the sacred and secular realms as inseparable, coexistence of different religious communities within the same state is peculiarly difficult. Often certain aspects of religious membership are of high visibility to the community at large. There may be public observance of certain rites or festivals. The Muslim may be seen at his daily prayers; the Catholic is highly conspicuous on Ash Wednesday. The Jew will close his shop to celebrate Passover or Yom Kippur. Religious taboos, especially dietary, may also provide a specialized marketplace and a frequent reminder of differentiation. In some cases, a man's name will identify his religion.

Cleavages internal to a major religion can be of great significance. This is particularly true of Islam, where a breakdown in the political kingdom tended strongly to acquire religious significance; conversely, antagonism between different rites or tariqa (brotherhood) had immediate political repercussions. In Iraq and Yemen, the conflict between Sunni and Shi'ite Muslim is of prime importance. In Sudan, political competition outside the non-Muslim south has in good measure reflected the contest between the descendants of the followers of the Mahdi (Umma party) and the supporters of the Khatmia sect. The French were ultimately able to isolate and crush Abd-el-Kader's epic rebellion in Algeria (1830-1848) by demonstrating its linkage with the Qadiriyya order, thus separating the rebels from the majority of the population, who did not identify with this tariqa. Although Indonesia is 90 percent Muslim, entirely different views of the appropriate relationship of religion to the new state have been held by Dār ul-Islam, Masjumi, Partai Sarekat Islam Indonesia, and several smaller parties.

Perhaps because the classic divisions of Christianity lie outside the historical experience of the developing world, these have played a lesser role. The Protestant-Catholic cleavage may become important in some parts of Latin America and has been of great relevance in Uganda, with the former ruling Uganda People's Party (UPC) being also dubbed "United Protestants of Canterbury," and the opposition Democratic Party (DP) as "Diini Ya Paapa" (Pope's Religion). However, this is exceptional. Syncretic sects, largely inspired by Christian symbols, have been of occasional importance as agents of politically significant divisions in independent states; Cao Dai in Vietnam and Alice Lenshina's Lumpa Church in Zambia are contemporary examples.

Although Buddhism is divided into two major rites — the Hinayana (Thailand, Cambodia, Laos, Burma), and the Mahayana (Sri Lanka, Nepal, Tibet, Mongolia, Japan) — the fact that this division does not occur within territorial boundaries makes it irrelevant to the present discussion. More important is the existence of sects within Buddhism in several predominantly Buddhist countries (Thailand, Cambodia, Vietnam, Sri Lanka) which have been a significant source of social cleavage. Hoa Hao in South Vietnam is an example of this type of sect, identified with a given region. In Sri Lanka, there are three major sects, closely identified with given castes in Sinhalese society.

Caste is a fertile source of social cleavage in a rather restricted universe; only in India, Nepal, and parts of Pakistan can a caste system be considered a crucial element of division within the polity. Caste is also visible in Sri Lanka and within Indian immigrant communities in Malaysia and East Africa. A stratified social system, with endogamy required within each stratum, may also be found among several ethnic groups in Mali and especially in Senegal; the pattern is most highly developed among the Wolof, the largest ethnic group in Senegal. However, this type of caste is far less elaborate than that of India and is more permeable to the leveling influences of modernization.

CULTURAL DIFFERENTIATORS IV: REGIONALISM

Finally, regionalism must be briefly noted as a significant type of subterritorial solidarity. Few, if any, examples in the developing world compare in intensity or durability to the North-South division in American politics.

Regionalism, in most of Afro-Asia especially, seems to pale into insignificance before the more pressing ethnic or religious cleavages. However, there are examples worthy of mention. Administrative divisions, or provinces, at times generate a degree of loyalty separate from identification with the national territory, even when they do not overlap any other cultural entity. For example, in Zaire, Katanga (since renamed Shaba) did achieve a measure of regional identification, abetted by its experience of secession, especially among the peoples in the southern portion of the former province. Kwilu, a colonial district, was of sufficiently compelling magnetism to serve as the basis for Zaire's most effective mass nationalist party in 1959-60. Casamance in southern Senegal, although ethnically diverse, has always felt a pronounced local identity. In Indonesia, Sumatra and other outlying islands have given evidence of regional self-assertion in reaction to the appearance of Javanese domination. Sabah and Sarawak, on northern Borneo, are clearly imperfectly integrated into the Malaysian nation. In the confused kaleidoscope of Laotian politics, one may discern residual regional loyalties revolving around the traditional Lao principalities of Champassak, Vientiane, and Luang Prabang. It will be noted that a theme that runs through most of the examples is geographic remoteness from the political centers.

Latin America constitutes a rather special case in this category. Regionalism became deeply embedded in the larger polities during the nineteenth-century era of caudillos, imperfect or nonexistent communications, and central administration whose orbit often did not extend far beyond the seat of government. This development has been especially pronounced in Venezuela, Mexico, Colombia, Chile, Brazil, and Central America; to a lesser extent, it has occurred in Ecuador, Peru, Bolivia, and Argentina. In Peru, until recently, the trans-Andean Amazonia region could be conveniently approached only up the Amazon River through Brazil. The tendency to regional loyalty was strongly reinforced by the circumscribed horizons of the hacienda system which characterized much of rural Latin America.

The nature of the regionalism phenomenon in Latin America is ably summarized in a recent study of Venezuela:

> A powerful force which shaped the lines of Venezuelan political development is regionalism. ... For one thing, in the last half-century, with only a brief interlude in 1945-48, the military barracks of the Andean state of Táchira have furnished all the presidents of Venezuela. ... The pre-eminence of Táchira in national politics has naturally given rise to bitter jealousy in the people of other regions and states, but so strong has been the military power of the men of Táchira that little progress has been made in breaking their hold over the government.
>
> Regionalism also manifests itself in cultural and economic ways. For many years there was considerable cultural rivalry between the aristocratic families of Caracas and those of Cumaná. A

similar rivalry persists to this day between Caracas and the Andean city of Mérida, which considers itself the intellectual and cultural superior of the capital city, being the seat of a great university and the home of many distinguished families. There are few common interests between the proud families of the Andes and the rough *Llaneros* of the great plains. Their economic interests, coffee for the former and cattle and oil for the latter, help to accentuate the differences.[7]

Regionalism also manifests itself in a sense of cultural and economic distinctiveness. The Brazilian of the *gaucho* heritage of Rio Grande do Sul finds the life of the *carioca*, of Rio de Janeiro, distinctly foreign. The citizen of the Department of Antioquia, in Colombia, invidiously compares his driving, practical spirit with the cold, aloof intellectuality of the Bogatano. The people of the highlands of Colombia, Ecuador, and Venezuela have much more in common with each other than each has with his coast. Similarly, the distinctive economic interests of coffee-producing highlands and cattle-ranching *llanos*, as in Colombia or Venezuela, of arid, impoverished north and thriving, industrial south, as in Brazil, help to accentuate loyalties that rival the nation.[8]

BADGES OF CULTURAL IDENTITY

Thus solidarity patterns similar to nationalism may develop around a variety of foci. Nation-builders, seeking to secure the loyalty of the citizenry for the state alone, face serious competition. For somewhat different reasons, race, language, and religion especially are capable of generating an intensity of identification that can eclipse all other issues — or absorb other conflicts and translate them into communal hostility. Racial consciousness, facilitated by its extreme visibility, creates its own stereotypes of cultural differentiation. Language, as the medium of social communication, simultaneously creates networks of intensive social communication but also discontinuities where the linguistic frontiers are contained within a given territory.[9] Religion, by positing a divine or supernatural imperative for communal identity, removes differentiation from the plane of human rationality or debate. Conflict can become invested with a mandate from heaven and be pursued as a holy duty.

[7]Leo B. Lott, "Venezuela," in Martin C. Needler, ed., *Political Systems of Latin America* (Princeton: D. Van Nostrand, 1964), pp. 243–44.

[8]We should note that our categories, although separately derived, largely overlap those suggested by Clifford Geertz in his illuminating essay, "The Integrative Revolution: Primordial Sentiments and Civil Politics in the New States," in Geertz, ed., *Old Societies and New States* (New York: Free Press of Glencoe, Inc., 1963), pp. 112–13. The Geertz categories are assumed blood ties, race, language, region, and custom.

[9]This issue was first given systematic theoretical formulation in Karl Deutsch's brilliant study, *Nationalism and Social Communication* (Cambridge: MIT Press, 1953).

The dimensions of the cultural pluralism problem are further expanded by the tendency of sources of differentiation to intertwine. An immigrant community will bring not only its language but its religion; thus, for example, the Tamils in Sri Lanka are differentiated from the Sinhalese majority not only by their linguistic identity but by their Hinduism, in contrast to Sinhalese Buddhism. In a multicultural region, the diffusion of Christianity and Islam has often proceeded through the successive permeation of whole ethnic groups. For example, in Malawi the Yao, a trading people in close contact with East African coastal Islam, became largely Muslim in the last century, creating a new basis for differentiation from most other Malawi peoples. The Harar in Ethiopia have been intimately identified with Islam since their sixteenth-century assault upon the Christian Amharic kingdom. In Burma, two-thirds of the Christians are from the Karen group; in Indonesia, Protestant missionaries were most successful among the Batak of Sumatra and among Celebes and Molucca Islands groups.

One common charasteristic of cultural clusters within developing states is the high visibility of differentiation. Both in-group solidarity and the sense of differentness from other groups feeds upon instantaneous recognition. "Racial" features are perhaps the most conspicuous differentiating factor. However, language is almost as effective. The first phrase uttered identifies an individual as either "one of us" or "one of them." Not only does the person involved become duly noted as an "X" or a "Y" to his interlocutor, but he is instantly enveloped in a whole syndrome of stereotypes. These exist at all levels; a recent survey in Poona, India, found a striking correlation in the characteristics attributed to other regional groups by university students and slum housewives. For both groups, "Gujeratis" were "fat and spineless."[10] Similar findings have been reported in a number of African studies and in Latin America with regard to perceptions of the "Indian."

A characteristic costume is another major badge of cultural identity. Indeed, in Latin America the Indian is in part defined by his dress. One reason why cultural pluralism is a less severe problem here is that the Indian can shed his identity almost literally by changing his clothes and speaking Spanish. Zaire Muslims can generally be identified by their long robes after the East African coastal fashion. In countries with core nationalities, like Burma and Thailand, one nation-building technique (of doubtful efficaciousness) has been encouraging minorities to wear the "national dress" associated with these nationalities. In the 1920s Reza Shah sought to suppress the distinctive headdress that Arab tribes of southwestern Iran proudly wore, seeking to impose the substitution of the Iranian pahlavi hat. In other circumstances, the manifesting of differentiation has been achieved through bodily markings. In precolonial Africa, many clans or ethnic groups branded identity upon their

---

[10] Selig S. Harrison, *India: The Dangerous Decades* (Princeton: Princeton University Press, 1960), pp. 103–10.

members through distinctive facial scarring, tattoos, or patterns of filing the teeth. The Sikh in India is identifiable by his uncut hair, bound up in a turban. The saliency of distinctiveness assures a daily reinforcement of both the sense of identity with the group of which one is a member and its uniqueness with regard to other groups.

CHAPTER 2

*Social Change and
Cultural Pluralism*

If cultural pluralism only would hold still, nation-builders would have a simpler task. The very crux of the drama of nation-building is that modernization and social change transform not only individual and nation, but also the cultural groups that stand between. A failure to give full recognition to this fact has obscured the perspectives of both scholars and nation-builders. Our very vocabulary is tainted. In an otherwise excellent essay, Clifford Geertz chooses the term "primordial sentiments" to cover the diverse forms of cultural pluralism. But as he himself recognizes, "one common developmental tendency does stand out: the aggregation of independently defined, specifically outlined traditional primordial groups into larger, more diffuse units whose implicit frame of reference is not the local scene, but the nation — in the sense of the whole society encompassed by the new civil state . . ."[1]

In short, the crux of the role of cultural pluralism lies in the simultaneous development of both national and subnational solidarities to previously unmobilized populations. It is thus more a "modern" than a "primordial" phenomenon. To seek understanding of cultural pluralism, we must turn to the dynamics of differentiation, the unfolding process of interplay among different levels of social identity. Through a close examination of the emergence of subnational loyalties, we may begin to establish some baselines for fixing at least the general direction of change.

An encyclopedic compilation of all examples is obviously beyond the scope of this survey. We propose to give particular attention to the forms of cultural plurality that play the largest role — ethnic-linguistic and religious — by examining a range of examples, with the choice partly determined by availability

---

[1] Clifford Geertz, ed., *Old Societies and New States* (New York: Free Press of Glencoe, Inc., 1963), pp. 153-54.

of data and partly by a desire to illustrate the diversity of the phenomenon. The very special pattern of evolution of loyalties among the Amerindians of Latin America merits particular attention for the insight that it yields regarding the range of possible outcomes in the symbosis of modernization and cultural differentiation.

AFRICA: ETHNICITY AND NATIONALISM

In Africa, cultural pluralism has generally been labeled "tribalism." It is worth pausing briefly over the intellectual history of this term. Only with the emergence in Europe of systematically racist stereotypes of Africa did the term "tribe" come into general use. Previously, travelers and missionaries simply spoke of kingdoms and peoples. By the time colonial administration began in earnest, the image of the "tribal" African was well established. With the beginnings of a new, educated elite in the towns, the label of "detribalized" African was coined. To the early generation of administrators and anthropologists, this person was a kind of hybrid, removed from his natural habitat. Bumptious and believed to be totally (although superficially) Europeanized, the educated African was "cut off from his own people," following the "detribalization" metaphor to its logical conclusion. In somewhat amended form, the myth of detribalization had great appeal to the new African himself when the hour of nationalist self-assertion came. His right to the mantle of leadership was reinforced by the hypothesis that he was shorn of ethnic reflexes, easily able to speak the inarticulate desires of all the peoples of the territory. A new generation of scholars, highly sympathetic to the aspirations of African nationalism, looked naturally for the factors of cohesion rather than for elements of potential discord. "Tribalism" was a retrograde force of merely historical interest; the future belonged to the "detribalized." The inevitable urbanization and industrialization would create a social system dominated by economic classes on the Manchester model. "Class formation," wrote one distinguished anthropologist, "tolls the knell of tribalism."[2]

In fact, the transcendent obligation of resistance to the colonizer did largely obscure the vitality of ethnicity as a basis of social solidarity. Only in the cold dawn of independence did the potency of this factor begin to become clear. African leaders were soon to share the anguish well expressed by Nehru commenting on the tenor of testimony and debates of the Linguistic Provinces Committee, on which he served in 1948:

> The work of sixty years of the Indian National Congress was standing before us, face to face with centuries-old India of narrow loyalties, petty jealousies and ignorant prejudices engaged in mortal

[2] D. F. McCall, "Dynamics of Urbanization in Africa," *Annals*, No. 98 (March 1955), p. 158.

conflict and we were simply horrified to see how thin was the ice upon which we were skating. Some of the ablest men in the country came before us and confidently and emphatically stated that language in this country stood for and represented culture, race, history, individuality, and finally a sub-nation.[3]

Several writers have noted the link in Africa between the urban environment and new forms of ethnicity. A reductive process takes place in the town; the intricate ethnic mosaic of the countryside becomes simplified to a manageable number of ethnic categories. A sense of membership in a group significantly expanded in scale from the clan and lineage system of the very localized rural "tribal" community develops. This phenomenon has been most thoroughly studied in the Copperbelt towns of Zambia, by social scientists associated with the Rhodes-Livingstone Institute. Ethnicity was tested by the construction of an ingenious scale of social distance. It was found that town-dwellers display their ethnic origin in the language they use and in their way of life, which enables others "immediately fo fit their neighbors and acquaintances into categories which determine the mode of behavior toward them." According to the Rhodes-Livingstone study:

> For Africans in the Copperbelt "tribe" is the primary category of social interaction, i.e., the first significant characteristic to which any African reacts in another. Frequently relationships never penetrate beyond this and tribes appear to one another to be undifferentiated wholes.... There is a constant flow of newcomers into the towns from the various rural districts from which the Copperbelt draws its labor supplies. They are not immediately absorbed into the prestige system which could possibly supply an alternative principle of social interaction. Instead their own ethnic distinctiveness which they took for granted in the rural areas is immediately thrown into relief by the multiplicity of tribes with whom they are cast into association. Its importance to them is thus exaggerated and it becomes the basis on which they interact with all strangers.
> ... The more distant a group of peoples is from another, both socially and geographically, the greater the tendency to regard them as an undifferentiated category and to place them under a general rubric such as "Bemba," "Ngoni," "Lozi," etc. In this way, from the point of view of the African on the Copperbelt, all tribes other than those from his particular home area tend to be reduced into three or four categories bearing the label of those tribes who, at the coming

---

[3] Quoted in S. Harrison, "The Challenge to Indian Nationalism," *Foreign Affairs* 34, No. 4 (July 1956), 621.

of the European, were the most powerful and dominant in the region.[4]

THE MYTH OF THE "BANGALA"

An extreme example of the urban ethnicity phenomenon is represented by the "Bangala," of Kinshasa (formerly Leopoldville), Zaire. There is, in fact, no traditional, rural society which calls itself "Bangala." But for both Belgians and Zairiens, the reality of "Bangala" was unquestioned ethnological dogma. The origins of this myth are particularly intriguing and have much to suggest about the lack of primordiality of much cultural pluralist sentiment.

The first non-African visitor to the region from which the "Bangala" were believed to come was the versatile explorer-cum-journalist Henry Stanley. He noted what struck him as "unquestionably a very superior tribe," located in a string of villages extending ten miles along the Congo River banks.[5] Thus the Bangala were born. Stanley's glowing account led to designation of this area as the site of an outpost of King Leopold's Congo Free State. The first Belgian commandant of this post, Camille Coquilhat, gave credence to the fireside tales spun by a village chief, who claimed control of a huge tract of rain forest; Coquilhat estimated there were 110,000 "Bangala," a substantial increase from Stanley's string of villages.[6] The Belgian commandant was highly disconcerted, however, when informed by the chief one day that he was not a "Bangala" after all, but that this label applied to a people further down the river.

The small area within range of Coquilhat's station assumed special importance when it became the first place where Zairiens could be recruited for service outside their immediate region. In the early years, many of the Congo Free State's auxiliary troops and the bulk of the river steamer crews were secured in this zone. Their European commanders, who by and large were not overly concerned with ethnographic precision, considered them indiscriminately as "Bangala," and the label was quickly accepted. As one early Free State officer wrote:

---

[4]J. Clyde Mitchell, *The Kalela Dance* (Manchester: Manchester University Press, 1956), pp. 28-29. On the subject of ethnicity in Africa generally, see especially Ronald Cohen and John Middleton, eds., *From Tribe to Nation in Africa* (Scranton, Pa.: Chandler, 1970); Leo Kuper and M. G. Smith, *Pluralism in Africa* (Berkeley: University of California Press, 1969); P. H. Gulliver, *Tradition and Transition in East Africa* (Berkeley: University of California Press, 1969); Victor Olorunsola, *The Politics of Cultural Sub-Nationalism in Africa* (Garden City, N. Y.: Doubleday & Co., 1972); *Journal of Asian and African Studies* 5, 1-2 (January-April, 1970), special issue on "The Passing of Tribal Men in Africa."

[5]Henry M. Stanley, *Through the Dark Continent* (New York: Harper & Bros., 1878), II, 301-2.

[6]Camille Coquilhat, *Sur le Haut-Congo* (Paris: J. Lebegue et Cie., 1888), p. 202.

Take a contingent of workers engaged aboard the steamers, or workers in the state posts along the Congo River, choose them from all the tribes of the area; they all become Bangala. They will tell you ... "We are Bangala." Even if they belong to hostile groups, while out of their areas they will unite.[7]

The "Bangala" were accorded official anthropological recognition when an entire volume was devoted to them in 1907 in the first ethnographic survey of Zaire peoples. Attached to the volume was the inevitable map, ascribing to the "Bangala" a vast empire of 80,000 square miles in the central Zaire. However, the first Protestant missionary in this area lodged an immediate protest:

In a work published in Brussels the term Bangala is made to cover a vast area. . . . This includes a dozen or more different tribes, talking as many distinct languages, having various tribal marks, possessing in many instances very different customs ... among whom there is nothing in common except their black skin and backwardness in civilization. . . . The natives themselves never used the name Bangala.[8]

To complete their ethnic identity, the "Bangala" were awarded a language. A river trading language, mainly derived from Lobobangi, but drawing upon many of the river dialects, was adopted by the army and administration for communicating with Africans; it was simplified and standardized, especially by removing the tonal elements difficult for Europeans to learn, and became known as Lingala, or language of the Bangala. Again missionary testimony is illuminating:

This heterogeneous mass (of Africans employed by the state) ... held communication with each other by means of the "trade language." The smartest of the natives in the towns adjacent ... quickly learned this jargon, and used it more or less fluently when communicating to State soldiers and workmen, and the white men hearing the natives of the neighborhood talking this lingo jumped to the conclusion that it was their own tongue in which they were conversing and thus called it the Bangala language, and by that name it was generally known on the Upper Congo.[9]

A nucleus of persons from this area settled at the post that later became Kinshasa. As the years went by, all those who arrived in Kinshasa from the upper river became labeled as "Bangala," especially by the Bakongo, who had arrived

---

[7] Quoted in Cyr. Van Overbergh, *Les Bangala* (Brussels: Institut International de Bibliographie, 1907), p. 55.

[8] John H. Weeks, *Among Congo Cannibals* (London: Seeley, Service & Co., 1913), pp. 61, 65.

[9] Weeks, *Among Cannibals*, pp. 48–49.

from the other direction. The distinctiveness of the migrants from the upper river was reinforced by their use in town of Lingala, rather than Kikongo, the Bakongo language. A major ethnic federation, Liboke-lya-Bangala was organized, composed of some forty-eight affiliated tribal associations. When political competition first was introduced, European and African alike were long accustomed to analyzing Leopoldville society in terms of a Bakongo-Bangala duality. One major Zairien political figure, Jean Bolikango, linked his fortunes to the reconstitution of a *grande ethnie Bangala;* significantly, he was born in Kinshasa, of Ngombe parents.

THE COMING OF SELF-AWARENESS
IN SEGMENTARY SOCIETIES: THE MONGO

Another interesting Zairien example of the evolution of ethnicity lies in the gradual emergence of self-awareness among the Mongo. Unlike the purely urban "Bangala" case, there is an identifiable culture cluster that could reasonably have been labeled by ethnographers as related in language and custom. Curiously, in contrast to the Bangala, the Mongo had no early anthropological advocates; the initial wave of ethnographic studies made no mention of the Mongo as a people, and they do not appear on early maps. The Mongo are characteristic of many peoples of the tropical rainforest throughout the world's equatorial belt in that there was never any central political structure in this segmentary society nor any evidence of ethnic self-consciousness predating colonial penetration. However, throughout the Mongo area a common legend of origin is found — that all are descended from the first ancestor Mongo.

Among the pioneers of Mongo nationalism, three Belgian missionaries and an administrator occupy a place of honor. The latter, Georges Vanderkerken, published in 1940 a massive tome on the Mongo — including a map. Two of the four publicly urged the formation of a special Mongo province, and all called for the fusion of Mongo dialects into a single language, to be rendered adequate for purposes of modern education and administration. A large part of the new Mongo elite drew inspiration as students from contact with the missionaries. The missionaries also produced a journal, widely read by young Mongo intellectuals, devoted to articles on Mongo culture and history.[10]

By the 1950s the new Mongo elite was ready to stand on its own feet; a Mongo association (Fedequalac) was founded in Kinshasa. Articles asserting the virtues of Mongohood began to appear in Zaire publications. Characteristic was

---

[10]It is more than coincidence that all four were Flemish; a striking parallel exists between what they sought to achieve for the Mongo — unification of language and people — and the demands of the growing Flemish nationalist movement in Belgium.

an extended study of Mongo custom and tradition by a leading Mongo intellectual, Antoine-Roger Bolamba, who wrote:

> More than persons of other races (ethnic groups), the Mongo are proud of their land, their past, and their language. ... If we defend our name, it is not by egoism or mistrust, but because it suits us .... The Mongo ... group occupies a vast stretch in the central basin of the Congo. ... In the history of our ancestors, we are told that no neighboring group was our master; nearly all were inferior to the Mongo. Therefore, we are discontent when people try to degrade us.[11]

The message of Mongo identity was transmitted from the Kinshasa elite back to the major regional town in the Mongo area, Mbandaka (formerly Coquilhatville). When local elections were first organized in 1958, it quickly became a political creed, as disunity among the Mongo majority permitted the election of a burgomaster from the "alien" Ngombe. In 1960, the prospect of the first general elections of the country led to the creation of the *Union des Mongo,* a political party that sought to unite all of Mongo country. This desire greatly accelerated the already perceptible diffusion of Mongo self-awareness to the rural areas, where previous loyalties had always been much more circumscribed – to village and clan. For a brief period, from 1962 to 1966, the Mongo were awarded their own province; during that period, they had their first period of political unification in history. Provincial institutions were harnessed to the task of propagating the doctrine of Mongohood. Although this was halted by President Mobutu's sharply centralizing reforms of 1966, Mongo identity remains a significant factor in the modern scene.[12]

THE TONGA: IDENTITY FORMATION AND ASSIMILATION

The Tonga group is to be found in the southern region of Zambia, numbering about three hundred thousand, with another fifty thousands odd in neighboring Rhodesia. The crystallization of an active sense of cultural identity among this linguistic group, linked with the processes by which strangers were incorporated into the society, offers further insight into the dynamics of ethnicity.[13]

[11]"Vie coutumes et moeurs des Mongo de l'Equateur," *La Voix du Congolais* (April 1958), p. 373.

[12]For a more extended discussion of ethnicity in Zaire, see Crawford Young, *Politics in the Congo: Decolonization and Independence* (Princeton: Princeton University Press, 1965), Chapter 11.

[13]This section is drawn primarily from Elizabeth Colson's excellent monograph in Cohen and Middleton, eds., *From Tribe to Nation*, pp. 35–53.

Until the late nineteenth century, the largest social unit was a neighborhood or local rural community which shared ritual shrines and the expectation that disputes would be peacefully settled by agreed norms and procedures. However, there was no formal set of offices. Beyond the neighborhood, relatively stable relationships, cemented by intermarriage, were maintained with an orbit of nearby neighborhoods. Within this zone, travel was relatively safe; beyond it, even if a man was still in Tonga-speaking territory, he was an alien and traveled at his own risk.

Both structure and, ultimately, unity were imposed upon the community by the colonial administration and by patterns of change associated with it. Headmen were designated for the neighborhoods; the Tonga linguistic zone was organized into three administrative divisions. A railroad was built through their district, which both facilitated movement of strangers into Tongaland, and for some Tonga, provided a pathway to the new urban centers. It was during the colonial period that Tonga-speakers began to be aware of their broader identity as Tonga.

The crystallization of Tongahood was accompanied by a process of incorporation of non-Tonga into Tonga culture. Oral tradition as well as the records of early travelers demonstrate that some neighborhoods, which a century ago were not Tonga-speaking, have now been wholly absorbed into the new Tonga identity. Further, many of the strangers who immigrated individually via the railway were also incorporated. One significant exception to the incorporation process was the small communities of Ndebele from Rhodesia, who had come as auxiliaries of the Christian missionaries. These groups, apparently, considered themselves superior both in their own right and by virtue of their close association with the missionaries; this self-image made incorporation into Tonga society obviously impossible.

While within Tongaland, assimilation was occurring, without, Tonga self-awareness was fuelled by a growing consciousness of other collectivities in Zambia. With the formation of competitive political parties in the 1950s, nascent ethnicity was sharply politicized. One of the major African parties, the African National Congress, was led by a politician from a closely related language group, Harry Nkumbula; the ANC was viewed as a party that spoke for Tonga interests. The movement that became dominant in Zambia, however, the United National Independence Party, was perceived as dominated by Bemba-speakers from the northern part of the country.

At the same time, new identity patterns were not confined to the all-Tonga level. The three administrative divisions created by the colonial administration, Plateau Tonga, Valley Tonga, and Toka-Leya, also served as the basis for significant cleavages. In the context of a national political party conflict, the Tonga subdivisions could unite around ANC against "Bemba domination". However, in more local conflicts, the subdivisions were a basis for alignment. Colson cites the example of a 1957 petition from elders of one Valley Tonga area, who indicated that a Plateau Tonga technical assistant posted in their area was unacceptable. Give us a man from any other part of Zambia, they said, only a Plateau Tonga is unacceptable.[14] And yet the concept of a "Valley Tonga", like Tongahood itself, does not extend back beyond the colonial period.

EMERGENT KRUHOOD

The Kru in Liberia are another interesting example of the mechanisms by which modern ethnic identity is consolidated. The Kru, traditionally, were organized into a substantial number of autonomous, small town settlements and discernible regional subgroups, primarily along the coast of Liberia. They never shared a common political organization, and bitter rivalries existed among different Kru groupings. However, their strategic location on the coast brought them into early contact with the outside world, and by the nineteenth century a regional tradition of deck crew service on coastal shipping and as stevedores was developing.

A vital step in the evolution of a unified Kru identity was the gradual growth of a Kru community in Monrovia. The Liberian capital has never had an urban administration per se, and the new townsmen were forced to provide their own social services and mechanisms for regulation of internal conflict. Government until very recently was entirely an affair of the small Americo-Liberian minority (roughly 25,000 in all of Liberia), for whom the rest of the population, collectively designated as "tribal peoples," were not of great concern. Thus, in 1916, the area of Monrovia in which the Kru immigrants had congregated was incorporated as "Krutown," under the effective control of a new body established to serve Monrovia Kru, the Kru Corporation.

Although the Kru Corporation was founded to meet urban needs, it gave structural acknowledgment to the traditional subunits of the Kru. Seven councilors serve as the governing board, each representing one of the major subdivisions. The "governor" of Kru Corporation was the first man who could, in a sense, speak collectively for all the Kru. In the 1930s, Kru pride was stirred by the organization of an all-Kru football (soccer) team. When in 1945 old Krutown was inundated to enlarge Monrovia's port facilities, the Kru Corporation bought and administered the land reserved for New Krutown. In the words of the one serious student of urbanization in Monrovia, the Corporation "has a peculiar significance in that it can draw on the loyalty of the local members of all the Kru *dako* (subgroups), which makes it a new phenomenon in Kru social organization, and an important one, since the Monrovia Kru are today the largest cluster of Kru in the republic."[15]

---

[14]Cohen and Middleton, eds., *From Tribe to Nation*, p. 50.
[15]Merran Fraenkel, *Tribe and Class in Monrovia* (London: Oxford University Press, 1964), p. 82.

The occupational specialization in the maritime-stevedoring sector has also been of prime importance in Kru self-awareness. Many Kru Corporation councilors and governors first achieved prominence as heads of boat gangs or deck crews. The seafaring tradition gives the Kru the distinctiveness of familiarity with faraway places; they are proud of their "colonies" of Kru sailors clustered in London, Liverpool, and New York. The Kru Corporation treasury is fed by seventy-five cent dues which Kru deck-hands pay on completion of each journey. When a wage dispute broke out in 1958 between shippers and stevedores, it was Kru Corporation that stepped in to hire a lawyer to defend the interests of the dockers. Regular unions are as yet nonexistent in Liberia, which is still a living reminder of paradise lost for employers. This common occupation is important in Kru social cohesion in Monrovia. "The degree of tribal solidarity it implies is particularly interesting since traditional Kru social organization involved a very high degree of local autonomy, and there was no mechanism for cooperation between the various *duko*."[16]

Liberia is rapidly changing, under the impact of unprecedented economic expansion founded primarily on the development of its rich iron ore deposits. The new attitude of Americo-Liberians toward the rest of their countrymen, sponsored by the late President William Shadrach Tubman and stimulated by the exigencies of the Pan-African era, has provided the Kru with opportunities for upward mobility. Many have moved into the civil service, where they may even form a majority. But the evidence does not suggest that a growing integration into a Liberian framework necessarily means the end of Kruhood. On the contrary, it has been found that among the new student generation, "tribalism is particularly strong, because in the context of the high schools and the universities young people reared in their exclusive ethnic groups are often confronted with one another for the first time, and deep-rooted prejudice runs riot."[17]

These four African examples make clear that there are many roads that lead to ethnicity; obviously we have explored only a few. What is general is the development of solidarity patterns extending over wider ranges of humanity than ever before – integration, but on a subnational scale. The inarticulate loyalty to the little community is being supplanted by a wider range of identity. We have stressed examples where militant identity is a very recent phenomenon; in other instances, such as the Bakongo of Congo-Brazzaville, Zaire, and Angola, or the Baganda of Uganda, self-awareness was already firmly rooted at the

---

[16] Fraenkel, *Tribe and Class*, p. 83. Another interesting example of the role of occupational specialization in interaction with ethnicity is found in the structure of the cattle market in Ibadan, involving Hausa from the North and Yoruba indigenous to Ibadan. Today, a rigid convention has emerged that restricts butchering to Yoruba, and cattle-droving to Hausa, although formerly members of both groups were found in both functions. Abner Cohen, "The Social Organization of Credit in a West African Cattle Market," *Africa*, 35, No. 1 (January 1965), 8–19.

[17] Fraenkel, *Tribe and Class*, p. 188.

beginning of the colonial period. However, even in these instances, important changes have taken place as social change and ethnic competition have intensified subnationalism.

What we have described is obviously only part of the story. Nationalism of the territorial variety is very much a reality; indeed, in a number of African polities, it seems to far overshadow the importance of ethnicity. In some cases, the very situation of an ethnic group will predispose it toward territorial or even transterritorial perspectives. For example, the Malinke, beginning in the fourteenth century, became dispersed as traders all along the interior West African trade routes; their trading communities outside the Malinke homeland in present-day Mali became known as Dioula. They have thus been knitted into a broader world by the trans-Saharan trade and the Islamic faith. It is accordingly not surprising that the Malinke and Dioula played a crucial role in party-building on a West African scale and remained until the end fervent supporters of a greater Mali.[18]

The heart of the matter is, then, that ethnicity and nationalism are both an intimate part of the process of social change. We would suggest that the most likely outcome in the middle run is the consolidation of both ethnicity and territorial nationalism in much of tropical Africa, with a gradual absorption of the very local loyalties of the countryside into both identities, and a disappearance of ethnic groups whose scale is too small for an efficacious defense of ethnicity within a territorial political arena. These loyalties are not mutually exclusive; Jomo Kenyatta first became known to the world in the 1930s through his book, *Facing Mount Kenya,* a passionate assertion of Kikuyu cultural values. As Kenya's first president and the best-known nationalist leader, he symbolizes the Kenyan nation. Nor is the relative saliency of national and ethnic levels of identity always the same; in Zaire, ethnicity was far less visible as a political determinant in 1970 than it had been in 1960, whereas in Nigeria the reverse was true. The intricate relationship between these two identity patterns will lie at the very core of the postindependence political process.

ETHNICITY AND LANGUAGE IN ASIA

In Asia, recognizably similar patterns of ethnic-linguistic identity may be found. However, the different nature of the state system in much of Asia situates ethnicity and linguistic nationalism in a distinctive environment. The majority of Asian states are built around a core nationality with outlying minorities (Iran, Burma, Thailand, Cambodia, Laos, Vietnam, and, to some extent, Sri Lanka). Centralized kingdoms had a much wider range of effective

---

[18]Thomas Hodgkin and Ruth Schachter Morgenthau, "Mali," in James S. Coleman and Carl G. Rosberg, Jr., *Political Parties and National Integration in Tropical Africa* (Berkeley: University of California Press, 1964), pp. 219-21 and *passim.*

authority than was the case in most of Africa; there is a greater continuity between pre- and postcolonial state organization. Many of the minority peoples were little touched by modernization; in Laos, Vietnam, and Burma, especially, the "hill peoples" were subject to only minimal colonial contact. We may note in passing that those who did become closely involved with the colonial system, through designation as a source of heavy recruitment for the colonial army (Ambonese in Indonesia, Karens in Burma) or missionary activity (Karens, Toba Bataks in Indonesia), have become keenly conscious of their own distinctiveness from the dominant culture. To illustrate the dynamics of ethnicity and linguistic nationalism in Asia, we may explore Indonesian, Indian, and Kurdish examples.

In the Indonesian case, ethnicity patterns closely parallel to the African examples may be observed, especially on the outer islands. In Java itself, modernized identity among the ethnic Javanese has been largely fused with territorial Indonesian nationalism. But for the average villager outside Java, and among minority groups in Java, ethnic loyalties, according to a valuable study of the identity problem in a series of Indonesian local communities, "take priority over allegiance to any region not coterminous with his ethnic area."[19] Many of the same factors are operative here as in Africa and are important variables: the degree of Christianization; the extent of population pressure on rural land, forcing a surplus into the towns; a social organization that casts out the young and ambitious. The modernizing social nexus, creating awareness of a wider self through competitive urban contact with others, is again central to the process:

> Ethnic awareness is intensified by interethnic contact, and ethnic loyalties come to the fore only when the members of the group recognize common interests vis-à-vis others. It is notably those ethnic groups whose members during the last half century of Dutch rule were most mobile and most avidly in pursuit of scarce ends in the larger society which are outstanding today for ethnic loyalties bordering on chauvinism....
>
> Such ethnic groups are not only exposed to other peoples, they are thrown into competition with them. Under the colonial regime, and in the independent republic as well, Ambonese, Minangkabau, Minahassans, and to a lesser extent, Toba Bataks have, along with the strategically situated Javanese, been disproportionately successful aspirants to positions of higher status in the modern, national and urban sector of society. But competition has been intense, frustration not uncommon, and the process has sharpened not only ethnic loyalties but also ethnic animosities.
>
> ... The urban job hunter is quick to resent the disproportionate employment of other groups, and almost as quick to rely on ethnic favoritism within his own. Toba Bataks and Minahassans, who fifty years ago were barely aware of one another, today play out bloody feuds in the streets of Djakarta.[20]

[19] G. William Skinner, ed., *Local, Ethnic and National Loyalties in Village Indonesia,* Yale University Cultural Report Series (New Haven: Yale University Press, 1959), p.5.

[20] Skinner, *Loyalties,* pp. 7-8.

The capacity for effective social action within an ethnic framework is, however, sharply restricted by the geopolitics of the Java-outer-islands duality. The most important single group in Indonesia is the ethnic Javanese, who are, moreover, strategically situated at the political core of the country. There is widespread resentment in the outer islands at Javanese domination of the system. At the same time, the geographic dispersion and ethnic fragmentation of the outer islands have impeded unified "anti-Java" action. The rise of political parties has not played the same role in consolidating ethnicity as in many African states; parties have been based primarily upon other types of ideological and religious cleavages.

INDIA AS A CULTURAL COMPOUND

India is a veritable laboratory of diversity; linguistic, religious, and caste cleavage have all played a crucial role in defining arenas of conflict. On close examination caste and language have proved to have similar boundaries and have even been mutually reinforcing. Religion, on the other hand, split the country on different lines, and moments of intense luminosity of religious cleavage tend to eclipse awareness of linguistic differentiation. The magnitude of the nation-building problem was clearly revealed by the findings of a survey in both north and south India showing only 8 percent of the people demonstrating nationally oriented loyalties.[21]

Indian linguistic clusters have a far longer history than do African ethnic groups. By the twelfth century, the major regional languages had not only scripts, but scholars and literatures. An alien tongue had been used as a language of administration since the thirteenth century, when Persian supplanted Sanskrit in most of what is now India. Neither the Moguls nor the British gave recognition to linguistic frontiers in determining administrative boundaries. Indeed, a major event in the crystallization of Indian nationalism was the protest against the partition of Bengal in 1905, a move taken by the British Raj in reaction to protonationalist disturbances in Bengal, partly based on Bengali linguistic solidarity. Evidence for the growth of linguistic sentiments may be seen in the Congress Party decision in 1920 to organize on the basis of linguistic sections. However, linguistic cleavages paled into relative insignificance for the next quarter century as the rapid rise of the Muslim League polarized India into two religious communities, resulting in a transcendent conflict that culminated in the holocaust of 1947, with its five hundred thousand dead and 12 million refugees. So greatly did the religious communalism dominate the scene that the decision in 1947 to make Hindi the official language for all of residual India within ten years met with relatively little objection in non-Hindi areas.

[21] Joseph W. Elder, "National Loyalties in a Newly Independent Nation," in David Apter, ed., *Ideology and Discontent* (New York: Free Press of Glencoe, Inc., 1964), pp. 77-92.

However, linguistic tranquility was not of long duration. The excision of Pakistan removed the Hindu-Islam conflict from the center of domestic preoccupations. The cry for linguistic self-determination and the redrawing of provincial frontiers on this basis began to echo from all corners of the subcontinent. The language of the independence movement had been English; this was the lingua franca of the new Indian elite, with which they had faced the dual battle against British rule and Muslim separatism. Looking backward, a Committee on Emotional Integration, composed of scholars designated by the government to seek escape from the morass of linguistic divisiveness, recalled with evident nostalgia the days of unity of purpose:

> Indians from all parts of India, no matter how sharply divided they might otherwise be, felt a sense of solidarity with one another in their common humiliation and frustration and their desire to achieve their freedom. The English language brought them together on a common platform and evoked their inherent feeling of "Indianness".... The country stood as one man against the British. Loyalty to the nation put all other loyalties in the shade.[22]

Though the shared use of the English language and spirit of nationalism unified the elite at the top, a contrary process was underway at other levels. In the view of a careful but pessimistic scholar, "The independence movement and Independence have activated millions who are, in their linguistic behavior, doing what comes naturally — expressing a new mass social consciousness through their own languages."[23] The social mobilization of low-caste masses, extension of literacy — in the regional languages — to millions of persons, has vastly expanded the dimensions of the linguistic problem, by multiplying the number of participants. Whole new mechanisms of communication have developed to cater to this market — films, pulp literature, regional newspapers — all in the regional languages. As in the old Austro-Hungarian Empire, language was a relatively unimportant matter as long as the small regional elites were enclosed in a cultural world entirely separate from the vernacular-speaking peasantry. But when the elites switched from the German of the Hapsburg court to the regional languages, and when new groups began to participate in the network of social and political communication, the situation was radically transformed and the Austro-Hungarian framework no longer viable.

Further, the regional languages appear to face diminishing effective competition from all-India languages. There are only about 3.6 million persons literate in English in India; standards of English instruction are declining. By 1955, Bombay University noted that most of its entering students had received

[22] *Report of the Committee on Emotional Integration* (Government of India, Ministry of Education, 1962), p. 3.

[23] Selig S. Harrison, *India: The Dangerous Decades* (Princeton: Princeton University Press, 1960), p. 55.

their secondary as well as primary education in a regional tongue.[24] Education is a regional prerogative; the central government cannot stop the states from adopting local languages for university instruction as well.

On the other hand, Hindi, the designated national language, has grave defects. Although approximately 40 percent of the population are Hindi speakers, the balance, especially in the Dravidian linguistic zone of southern India, have developed an intense antagonism toward the language, as evidenced by the serious rioting that took place in 1965 when a deadline (in effect postponed indefinitely) for the full adoption of Hindi as national language approached. The problem is further complicated by the fact that there is no consensus over what Hindi is. Purists demand a return to the Sanskrit sources; others prefer a standardization of the Hindi of the marketplace or varying degrees of Urdu admixture. Village Hindi is a diverse series of dialects, often mutually unintelligible, and far removed from the Hindi of the towns. Beyond this, there are major subgroups under the Hindi category, such as Rajasthani, Bihari, and Punjabi.

Linguistic awareness has been kept in the forefront of public attention in the years since independence by the twin issues of the national language and the creation of linguistic states. Nehru fought desperately to keep provincial boundaries on a nonlinguistic basis, but it was a losing battle. The issue was joined in 1950, when widespread rioting forced the government to accede to the creation of a Telugu-speaking state in Andhra. In 1953, a States Reorganization Commission was established; the mere existence of the Commission unleashed a veritable chain reaction of linguistic claims, as groups were formed up and down the land to formulate demands, discuss linguistic grievances, and prepare petitions and memorials. Some 152,250 documents were submitted to the Commission.[25] In 1956, on the basis of the Commission's report, a major reshuffling of provincial boundaries took place; this was followed in 1960 by the collapse of the last remaining great experiment in a bilingual state in Bombay, with the partition into Gujarat and Maharashtra provinces. Assam subsequently further exacerbated animosities by declaring itself a unilingual state, in violation of the national rule requiring bilingual facilities in any state in which more than 30 percent of the population did not speak the major language.

Caste has been an important factor in Indian politics; the very process of politization of caste has, in significant ways, contributed to the alteration of its content. Nothing is more intimately associated with the image of ageless and unchanging India than its caste-based structure; consequently, nothing so dramatically underscores the ubiquity of change and dynamic nature of cultural pluralism than the visible transformations in the caste system in recent decades.

---

[24] Harrison, *India: Dangerous Decades*, p. 69.

[25] Naresh Chandra Roy, *Federalism and Linguistic States* (Calcutta: Firma K. L. Mukhopadhyaya, 1962), p. 203.

For a long time, caste in India was associated with four major categories, Brahmans (priests, scholars), Kshatriyas (warriors), Vaisyas (merchants) and Sudras (artisans, servants), with a large residual category of despised castes ("untouchables"). This classification appears to derive from a study of caste through the "sacred sociology" of the Hindu classical texts. Only recently has the caste phenomenon been the object of empirical inquiry, which has clearly demonstrated that the operative unit is the subcaste (*jati*), within which rules of endogamy, right behavior, and mutual loyalty are enforced. These latter are localized and innumerable; in any given community there are normally a number of *jati*, with a locally recognized hierarchical ranking. Rarely did *jati* extend across a linguistic frontier, although the caste system was everywhere (except in remote "hill tribe" areas).

Within the framework of modernization and social change, caste became one of the idioms of group competition. Subcastes could improve their position in the social scale by adopting some of the rituals and practices of higher castes; this practice has been labelled "Sankritization" by the ablest student of caste, M. N. Srinivas.[26] At the same time, for many purposes of group competition and especially in the urban or political realm, the *jati* was too small a unit to operate effectively. Accordingly, caste associations appeared that linked "more advanced sections of similar jatis . . . to upgrade the position of the caste in the social hierarchy. They pressed for the extension of privileges and rights by adopting the attributes and emulating the behavior of higher castes and by turning to the state for recognition of their claims."[27]

At the very top of the caste hierarchy, castes with a literary tradition had tended to have first access to English schools and, in turn, entry into the modern roles in administration and industry. These higher castes, many under the Brahman label, sought to preserve their early lead in the services and professions. In the words of the Committee on Emotional Integration:

> It is pertinent to remark in this connection that what often appears as a conflict between different castes is at bottom only a struggle among the educated people for obtaining jobs and political power . . . . Individual failure and frustration tends to be translated into caste terms and the result is the increase in tension and bitterness between the different sections of society.

The committee goes on to observe that the increased power in the hands of local self-governing bodies paradoxically created a major new arena of caste conflict: elections to village *panchayats* (councils) heighten caste feelings

---

[26] M. N. Srinivas, *Caste in Modern India* (Bombay: Asian Publishing House, 1962).

[27] Lloyd I. Rudolph and Susanne Hoeber Rudolph, *The Modernity of Tradition* (Chicago: University of Chicago Press, 1967), p. 31. This excellent study offers a thorough exploration of the modern political role of caste.

through electoral invocations of caste loyalty. The traditionally dominant castes struggle to preserve their hegemony, the others to overthrow it through the new principle of majority rule.[28] Harrison concludes, "Far from dissolving under the impact of economic change, therefore, caste is, if anything, stronger than before."[29]

Finally, the nature of the federal system in India should be mentioned. The states have substantial powers, and state governments are a major arena of political conflict and competition. This imposes a peculiar strain on the dominant Congress party. Nationally, it bears the responsibility for nation-building. Yet the provincial branches of Congress are forced to contend in a very different environment, where they must embrace the particular local causes or perish. Thus, in the 1957 elections, Congress found itself fighting "Communists in Kerala, Bengal, and Andhra; against communal religious parties in Punjab, Uttar and Madhya Pradesh, and Rajasthan; against tribal unions in Assam and Bihar; against ethno-linguistic fronts in Madras, Maharashtra, and Gujerat; against feudal-prince restorationist parties in Orissa, Bihar, and Rajasthan; against the Praja Socialists in Bombay."[30]

India's diversity has come into sharper focus since independence. Any sober assessment must surely conclude that there is no basis for expecting an early reduction in the emotional potency of subnational solidarity. With linguistic states now a reality, and both educational policy and civil service being inexorably reshaped by this fact, there is every reason to suppose that linguistic loyalties will become more firmly rooted. At the same time, the remarkable achievements of independent India become the more extraordinary when set against the overwhelming challenge of cultural diversity. By 1972, India had conducted five national elections on the basis of universal suffrage, absorbed millions of refugees bequeathed by the 1947 partition, survived – indeed, was probably unified by – two wars with Pakistan and the Chinese invasion of 1962. Its self-confidence as a nation was enormously buoyed by the successful outcome (from the Indian point of view) of the Bangladesh crisis and by renewed economic growth in the late 1960s after a period of stagnation early in that decade.

TRANS-TERRITORIAL ETHNICITY: THE KURDS

The Kurd case illustrates the particular situation of an ethnic-linguistic group, situated as a minority in each of four distinct states (Syria, Iraq, Turkey, and Iran), each of which is defined in terms of a core nationality that ascribes an

---

[28] *Report of the Committee on Emotional Integration*, p. 20.
[29] Harrison, *India: Dangerous Decades*, p. 102.
[30] Geertz, *Societies and States*, p. 141.

alien role to the Kurds. This situation has led to a Kurdish self-awareness founded upon the dream of an independent Kurd republic — an aspiration that has made them suspect to the ruling groups in all four sovereignties. The Kurds have been involved in major insurrections in Turkey, Iran, and, most recently, Iraq; Kurdish nationalism feeds upon the reverberation of perceived oppression from one Kurd community to another. In 1870, a traveler in Iran could write that town-dwelling Kurds were ashamed of their origins; those days are long past. The Kurdish self-consciousness has been further stimulated by the development of militant nationalism among the dominant groups in the four states. Cultural pride is gratified by the belief that Kurd history can be traced back forty-two hundred years to the ancient Medes. The great majority of Kurds are Sunnite Muslims, particularly important for the group in Iran which confronts the dominant Shi'ite Iranian culture. The bitter revolt against successive Arab nationalist governments in Iraq during much of the 1960s has been a continuing stimulant to Kurdhood. Thus religion, a shared sense of persecution and resentment at minority status, a sense of historic uniqueness, and the impact of intensified nationalism in surrounding zones have brought Kurd nationalism a long way from the cultural shame of a century ago.[31]

THE CULTURALLY UNCONSCIOUS: LATIN AMERICAN INDIANS

The pattern of correlation of social change and intensification of ethnic-linguistic differentiation in Asia and Africa must now be matched against the strikingly different sequence in Latin America, where modernization seems to be producing increased cultural (if not always social) integration. Latin American census data indicates that five states have 30 percent or more of the population classified as Indian (Mexico, Guatemala, Peru, Ecuador and Bolivia); six others are predominantly of mixed population, with the Indian component prominent in the mixture (El Salvador, Honduras, Nicaragua, Colombia, Chile, Paraguay). The mystique of the Indian heritage, or *Indigenismo*, is salient in the national ideology of Mexico, Guatemala, Peru, Bolivia, and Paraguay. When we note that the apostles of *Indigenismo* have been white or mestizo intellectuals, and not the Indians themselves, we are perhaps very close to the heart of the paradox.

Latin American states, it will be recalled, differ from most Afro-Asian examples in that they are dominated by the Iberian culture of the Spanish (and Portuguese) immigrants or culturally-assimilated mestizos. By the time of independence, Indian communities had already been overwhelmed, dispersed, or destroyed in the majority of Latin American polities. We may accordingly focus our main attention upon three primary Indian clusters, the Meso-American

---

[31] See the useful review of Kurd nationalism in Richard W. Cottam, *Nationalism in Iran* (Pittsburgh: Pittsburgh University Press, 1964), pp. 65–74.

complex of Mexico and Central America, the Andes republics, and the special case of Paraguay.

There are two ways in which a militant Indian identity might have emerged to challenge the traditional basis of Latin American nations. On the one hand, a trans-ethnic Indian nationalism might have arisen, comparable to the supra-ethnic African nationalism that successfully disputed European supremacy in most of that continent. On the other, Indian ethnicity might have crystallized, founded upon historic linguistic groupings or precolonial Indian states, comparable to Tonga, Mongo, or outer island Indonesian examples described earlier. By ransacking history, we can find some sparse evidence of incipient ethnicity among the Indians. In the contemporary period, the role of the Guaraní myth in Paraguay deserves close attention. We will first explore these cases, then turn to the more important question of why in this age of rapidly extending social mobilization there has been no emergence of either militant Pan-Indianism or ethnic nationalism among the Quechua of the Andes republics, the Maya of Guatemala, or the five major language groups in Mexico.

TABLE 2-1
Latin American Population, by Racial Group (in percent)

Country	Amerindian	African	White	"Mixed"[1]	Asian	Unspecified
Argentina (1960)[2]	0.6 (Overwhelmingly white, but exact proportions unknown)					
Bolivia (1950)	63	–	37	–	–	–
Brazil (1960)	1.5	11	61.7	26.5	0.6	0.2
Chile (1960)	3.2 (Overwhelmingly mixed, but exact proportions unknown)					
Colombia (1961)	1.2	4	20	74.8[3]	–	–
Costa Rica (1962)	0.6	1.9	87.3	(Included with white)	0.1	–
Cuba (1953)	–	12.4	72.8	14.5	0.3	–
Dominican Rep. (1950)	–	11.5	28.1	60.4	0.0	–
Ecuador (1961)	30.4	5	10	49.6	–	5
El Salvador (1961)	0.4	–	5	94.6	–	–
Guatemala (1959)	53.6	–	–	46.4[4]	–	–
Haiti	(Overwhelmingly African, but exact proportions unknown)					
Honduras (1960)	5.5	2.1	1.2	91.1	–	–
Mexico (1960)	8.8	–	10	81.2	–	–
Nicaragua (1960)	2.9	10	17	70.1	–	–
Panama (1960)	5.8	13.3	11.1	69	–	0.7
Paraguay (1960)	3.8 (Overwhelmingly mixed, but exact proportions unknown)					
Peru (1961)	46.7	0.5	–	52.1	0.7	0.1
Uruguay	(Overwhelmingly white, but exact proportions unknown)					
Venezuela (1960)	1.5	8	20	70.5	–	–

Source: Compiled from *Statistical Abstract of Latin America,* 1965 and 1971 editions, Center of Latin American Studies, UCLA.

[1] "Mixed" category includes Indian-white (Mestizo), African-white (Mulatto), and African-Indian (Zambo).

[2] Dates refer to census year.

[3] Approximately 57 percent Mestizo, 14 percent Mulatto, 3 percent Zambo.

[4] "Ladinos."

THE TWILIGHT OF INCA

Historical data are particularly appropriate in the Latin American case in that a prime differential factor, especially with relation to Africa, is the depth of the colonial experience. The date of 1492 is familiar to every schoolchild; what is perhaps less readily remembered is that a permanent settlement in what is now the Dominican Republic was established forthwith and that the first revolt had already taken place before the sixteenth century began. Spanish rule was already three centuries old when independence was achieved in the early nineteenth century. Intensive Indian-Hispanic culture contact, then, has far deeper historic roots than acculturation in Asia and Africa, where effective colonial administration and intensive European contact, with few exceptions, began only in the nineteenth century.

There were in the New World, as in Africa and Asia, many instances of primary resistance movements by indigenous groups, combatting initial conquest or seeking to throw off the foreign yoke as soon as the ambitions of the conqueror to remain and rule became clear. Indeed, especially in the case of the Araucanians in southern Chile, primary resistance was protracted and bitter. But this type of reaction is not comparable to resistance in the name of a new nationalism, integrating elements of indigenous historic identity with portions of the culture of conquest.

The annals of Latin American Indian history record only one major uprising in which syncretic elements are visible: the revolt of Tupac Amarú II in Peru in 1780-81. The Spanish under Pizarro had decapitated the Inca Empire and substituted their own rule for that of Inca or the Emperor. Among Indian states, the Inca had been exceptional not only in the degree of sophistication of its organization, but in its assimilative features; not only loyalty to Inca, but the language of empire, Quechua, were diffused over a broad swath of both highland and lowland Andes. Thus both the remembered glories of the old state and a common language over a wide area provided a mobilization potential much wider in orbit than was the case in most Indian areas.

José Gabriel Condorcanqui, better known to posterity by his Imperial Inca title of Tupac Amarú II, was fully assimilated into Spanish culture. He had been educated in a Cuzco secondary school, spoke fluent Spanish, and wore the velvet breeches and beaver hat characteristic of the Hispanic elite of the vice-royalty of Peru in the eighteenth century. And he was also a descendant of the last crowned Inca Emperor, Tupac Amarú I, executed in 1571.

Abundant material cause for resistance was present. Through peonage, conscription, and other means, in many areas virtually the entire Indian population was reduced to chattel labor in the mines and textile plants. Thus when Tupac Amarú II seized and executed a Spanish district official, proclaimed himself Inca, and raised the standards of insurrection, many flocked to his banner. For a time, Tupac Amarú II enjoyed one success after another, and Spanish authority crumbled in a large sector of the highlands. However, the tide soon turned, and the rebellion was crushed before it could become consolidated, before Tupac Amarú II could make clear precisely what his goals were or what kind of an Inca state he wished to restore. The repressive measures that followed showed clearly that the Spanish took very seriously the threat of a resurgent Incahood. An (unsuccessful) effort was made to suppress Quechua, and all surviving members of the Inca royal house were hunted down and assassinated.[32] The shock wave of the revolt seems to have reverberated throughout the Andes. In 1781, a rumor spread in highland Colombia that a descendant of the last Chibcha Emperor Zipa had been proclaimed prince of Bogotá. This led to Indian riots, the like of which had not been seen before or since in the former Chibcha zone. This movement seems literally to have been a last gasp for Chibcha identity; the use of Chibcha language is reported to have entirely ceased by 1795.[33]

ETHNICITY ON THE AMAZON: THE TUPI

Another form of Indian ethnicity that has marked parallels with African cases was found among the Tupí of the Amazon valley up through the nineteenth century. The Tupí were, like the Mongo, a culture cluster rather than a politically organized people. Tupí was a series of related dialects, spoken by the coastal peoples of Brazil whom the Portuguese first encountered when they arrived in the New World. Observing that Tupí dialects were found all along coastal Brazil, missionaries concluded that this was the Indian language. For the same reasons and with the same fervor as missionaries in Africa, they set to work distilling a unified language out of the diverse dialects and stabilized standard Tupí by reducing it to writing. This *lingua geral* was then used as the language of instruction and especially of evangelization for all Indians.

The principal zone in which Indians survived was the Amazon basin; elsewhere they were overwhelmed by Europeans and African slaves. The Amazon prior to the rubber boom at the beginning of the twentieth century had only very sparse immigrant settlement. It remained a preserve of the Jesuits and the Tupí culture which they fostered. Tupí was quickly adopted as an Amazon *lingua franca* and spoken not only by Indians, but also by mestizos. Had isolation from the rest of Brazil continued, it seems entirely plausible that Tupíhood could have produced unified social and political behavior in the Amazon.

However, such was not to be the case. The assimilationist predispositions of Portuguese colonial philosophy led to strong inducements being offered for intermarriage and mestization. By the nineteenth century, few "pure" Indians

[32]Philip Ainsworth, "The Rebellion of Tupac-Amaru II, 1780–1781," *Hispanic American Historical Review* 2, No. 1 (February 1919).

[33]Orlando Fals-Borda, *Peasant Society in the Colombia Andes: A Sociological Study of Saucio* (Gainesville: University of Florida Press, 1955), pp. 236 – 37.

were left along the main river and accessible tributaries. In the mid-eighteenth century the Jesuits were expelled, and all instruction was required to be in Portuguese rather than Tupí. Although, as late as the mid-nineteenth century, it is estimated that the upper river was still entirely Tupí-speaking and the lower river bilingual, today Portuguese has almost completely supplanted Tupí.[34]

THE INDIAN BASE OF PARAGUAYAN NATIONALISM

Paraguay presents the most intriguing case of interpenetration of Indian and Hispanic cultural identity. Asunción is the only Latin American capital where an Indian language is widely spoken – and not just by an ignorant peasantry newly arrived in the city as a badge of illiteracy, but proudly, almost militantly, by all strata of society. Indeed, Paraguayan national identity is partially founded upon the mystique of the Indian heritage – and the first to insist on their Guaraní origins are Paraguayan intellectuals. A leading scholar of Amerindian cultures cogently describes this phenomenon:

> The belief that the Paraguayan peasant is a Guaraní Indian has been fostered by the intellectual and educated Paraguayans, who have made it the principal symbol of a cultural nationalism that, in turn, has been used to further political nationalism. Some years ago, when visiting Asunción, I had occasion to observe the intense feeling attached to the Guaraní myth. Certain of Paraguay's leading scholars told me at length of the superior features of the Guaraní culture and language. I was privileged to attend a meeting of one of the country's outstanding scholarly societies, the Academia de la Cultura Guaraní, which is devoted to recording and publicizing the merits of what all leading citizens take to be the basically Guaraní way of life of Paraguay's rural population.[35]

The history of Guaraníhood is particularly illuminating. The Guaraní were a series of segmentary, seminomadic communities, occupying the fertile forest and grassland that extend in a 120-mile arc radiating from Asunción, where 95 percent of the present Paraguayan population dwells. Spanish settlement began in 1534, when a military force arrived in search of precious metals. The presence of silver seemed to be proved by the possession of some silver ornaments by local Indians; it was some time before the disappointed soldiers discovered that these emblems originated in the Andes deposits which Pizarro had already laid hands upon. The 350 Spaniards thus had to turn to agriculture to survive.

---

[34]The best study of Amazon culture is Charles Wagley, *Amazon Town* (New York: The Macmillan Company, 1953).

[35]Julian Steward in his introduction to Elman R. and Helen S. Service, *Tobati: Paraguayan Town* (Chicago: University of Chicago Press, 1954), p. ix.

On the La Plata delta, the hostility of local Indian groups was such that no small settlement could be secure. Accordingly, what is now Argentina was not settled until several decades later. But the Guaraní were not initially opposed to the small Spanish force. It was possible to remain, but urgent to render the situation secure by rapidly establishing relations with the far more numerous Indians. A thousand miles from the sea, the precarious colony of sixteenth-century Paraguay was literally years away from help.

The small band of Spanish soldier-agriculturalists took Indian wives. The pattern of Indian intermarriage seems to have been perspicacious and individual Spaniards became fitted into the Guaraní kinship system by marrying into senior lineages. By the middle of the sixteenth century, Spaniard and Guaraní regarded each other as kinsmen. Unlike the Mexican or Peruvian situations, the Spanish added to the local society such elements of statehood as overall political, military, economic, and religious institutions. Within a very short space of time, the lower-class Hispanic culture represented by the soldier-settlers had all but supplanted the previous Indian patterns. However, at the same time, the Spaniards learned Guaraní. The mestizo offspring emulated the cultural norms of their fathers and learned to speak in the idiom of their mothers. Thus a remarkable cultural fusion took place, Hispanic in most elements but Indian in language.

This initial pattern survived over the years precisely because of the isolation of Paraguay as a backwater of empire. Once Madrid learned that Paraguay was no El Dorado, very few European immigrants followed the first band. For that matter, the Paraguayan image among the potential immigrants has not greatly improved to this day. Those choosing Latin America as a new home were attracted by the more inviting prospects of Argentina, Chile, Uruguay, Brazil, Colombia, Mexico, or Cuba. True, Paraguayan history also records the picturesque episode of the Jesuit domain in even remoter Paraguay, but the permanent sociocultural legacy of this exotic and paternalistic earthly kingdom of God (1609–1767) was very small; the mission towns disintegrated after the expulsion of the Jesuits, and the Indians who had lived under communal Jesuit tutelage dispersed.

Thus, when independent Paraguay began its search for national identity, the Guaraní myth was ready at hand. Unlike other Latin American countries, Paraguay teaches its Indian tongue in the schools. The new generations learn in the classroom that they are Guaraní and that the Guaraní were a unique Amerindian group, superior to other Indians. For Paraguayan nationalists, Guaraníhood is what makes Paraguay distinctive. Spanish is not questioned as the language of official administration, but Guaraní is accorded loving nurture as a vehicle of cultural identity.

Guaraníhood is thus comparable in some respects to the examples of ethnic-linguistic identity cited in Africa and Asia. The "moi commun" of Guaraní solidarity is not the resurgence of a precolonial social pattern; there never was a Guaraní state or nation. It is a network of cultural solidarity born of the colonial contact and the social transformations that resulted. It is unique in the strong element of cultural fusion involved. In Africa and Asia, indigenous cultures emulated and eventually internalized some of the norms and practices of the culture of the colonizer. There was never, however, the type of total interpenetration and fusion that characterizes Guaraní.

It is vital to stress that within the Paraguayan framework Guaraníhood is an integrative, not a pluralist, form of ethnicity. The orbit of the Guaraní myth is coterminous with territorial Paraguay. Unlike most Afro-Asian examples, state and ethnicity coincide. The Guaraní myth is in fact a highly efficacious instrument of nation-building. The Hispanic-Indian duality of the Paraguayan past is transcended in the unitary mystique of Guaraníhood.

THE SILENT MAJORITY IN PERU

Peru would seem to be a logical site for Indian nationalism, and yet nothing of the scale of the Tupac Amarú revolt of 1780-1781 has recurred. Monolingual Indians are almost without exception locked into precarious and poverty-ridden existence in the *altiplano*; there has been periodic restiveness, notably in the 1870s and again about 1900. On the latter occasion, there was renewed talk in some zones of a revival of Inca.[36]

Some 45.9 percent of the population was classified as Indian in the 1940 census. Of these, the vast majority speak a single language, Quechua (which covers the entire Andes area of Ecuador, Peru, and Bolivia, except for a pocket of Aymara-speakers around Lake Titicaca and La Paz). Yet despite the desire of mestizo Peruvian nationalist thinkers like Haya de la Torre to incorporate the Indian heritage into an Indoamerican national culture, there has been a general assumption that this process would take place through assimilation of the Indian into the dominant Hispanic culture, with the Indian past relegated to the national museums. Unlike Guaraní, Quechua is not taught in the schools, although it is estimated that in the sierra, which is 80 percent Indian, "Quechua is predominantly spoken and the majority of the Quechua speakers know no Spanish."[37] The mestizos of the sierra are generally bilingual. Despite the considerable radius of dispersion of the language, until three decades ago it had not been adequately reduced to writing and to grammatical analysis so that it could be suitably taught in a classroom.

A study of Muquiyauyo, a mining town in the Peruvian Andes, provides useful insight into the failure of Quechua nationalism to coalesce.[38] The first

[36] Edward Dew, *Politics in the Altiplano* (Austin: University of Texas Press, 1969), pp. 22–28.

[37] Moises Sáenz, *Sobre el Indio Peruano y su incorporación al medio nacional* (Mexico City: Secretaria de Educación Pública, 1933), p. 242.

[38] Richard N. Adams, *A Community in the Andes* (Seattle: University of Washington Press, 1959).

Spaniards found two local groups of Indians in the valley in which the town nestles, one indigenous, the other a group of colonists settled by the Inca Emperor when the area was incorporated into the Inca domain in the mid-fifteenth century. The Spaniards took part of the surrounding lands for Church and settler and awarded some tracts to traditional Indian social groupings, the *ayllu*, each headed by a cacique. Control over the Indians was assured by placing Spaniards at all hierarchical levels above the *ayllu* and by using the caciques as intermediaries. Supplementing this was the *encomienda* system, by which the Indian groups were placed under the jurisdiction of individual Spaniards for "protection" – and for whatever labor could be squeezed out. Subsequently, most Indians were organized into *reducciones* (Indian townships) and settled in the flatlands at the valley bottom; out of one of these the present town of Muquiyauyo has grown.

With the introduction of the *reducción,* the Indian was removed from any land to which he might develop mystic ties of ancestry. By the nineteenth century, the separate Indian officials were declining; in 1886, the last cacique disappeared, and with him the final vestige of Inca organization. In 1904, communal lands managed by the Indian community were divided up into individually registered plots, removing a major focus of Indianhood. The tradition of separate religious fiestas for Indians and mestizos quietly terminated as well. In 1905, 70 percent of the births recorded were listed as Indian. In 1940, the percentage had fallen to 45, and since 1943 all have been entered simply as mestizo. Nearly all the towndwellers in Muquiyauyo now speak Spanish. Only a few women use Quechua in preference to Spanish. Dress styles are also becoming standard throughout the town as growing numbers of Indians silently drop the distinctive Indian costume. Thus, all three of the formerly crucial identifying variables – landholding, language, and dress – are ceasing to demarcate the Indian and mestizo groups.

In Muquiyauyo an interesting survey was taken of the ability of knowledgeable permanent residents of the town to identify as either Indian or mestizo a group of 457 persons, whom the judges all knew personally. The judges agreed that persons could not be identified on the basis of physical appearance. They were able to agree on 14 percent of the names as mestizo and 49.1 percent as Indian; however, there was disagreement on 36.9 percent. The lines between the two primary groups in Peruvian society are clearly becoming increasingly blurred. Because of its relative proximity to Lima and its nearby mines, Muquiyauyo is more integrated into the modernizing national culture than are many of the Andes settlements. However, the direction of change observable here seems to suggest the pattern likely to prevail elsewhere.[39]

Although the dominant trend seems to run toward the gradual weakening of ethnicity as a basis for cultural and political differentiation in Peru, there have

---

[39] Adams, *Community in the Andes*, pp. 82–92.

been, in the recent past, intriguing sort-run countercurrents. One study of the radical agrarian movement that was prominent in the nation during the late 1960s suggests that the appeal of such peasant revolutionary leaders as Hugo Blanco was more effective in "traditional" communities where the legacy of Indian institutions and culture was more nearly intact than in those areas that had become more closely integrated with the modern sector of Peru. The explanation suggested is that the more modern, "integrated" peasant farmer finds individualistic options more plausible in resolving his problems, such as migration to the cities, land purchase, or protest and litigation through parties, interest groups, the courts and local government institutions. The radical appeal to collective action seemed more suggestive in communities where Indian culture was more nearly intact and where national institutions and the processes of modernization had penetrated least.[40]

Interestingly, the radical nationalist military regime that assumed power in Peru in 1968 has, as part of its populist lexicon, given an important place to Indian symbols. A policy directed toward altering the balance of privilege and benefit toward the nether strata is necessarily directed at the Indians. Symbolic recognition of this fact is the designation of Tupac Amarú as the official national hero of the new regime.[41] At the same time, it is important to note that the ruling officers are drawn from the Hispanic-mestizo cultural strata; symbol manipulation is on behalf of the depressed Indian populations, rather than by them directly. For that matter, as we have seen earlier, Tupac Amarú himself was genetically Indian, but culturally mestizo.

MAYA AND LADINO IN GUATEMALA

Guatemalan Indian communities are still a majority of the country's population. In the Western highlands of this Central American state we may find part of our answer to the puzzle of nonemergence of Indian nationalism. Guatemala's Indians are classified under a number of ethnic labels; however, they are for the most part related to the Mayan culture. Curiously, in contrast to the Afro-Asian pattern, the impact of colonial rule and incorporation at the bottom of an Hispanic society has pulverized the Indian groups rather than unified them. Loyalty is localized and coheres only around the nuclear family and village (*municipio*). Each village has come to be differentiated in terms of dialect, patron saint, costume, and occupational specialization. Neighboring villages are isolated even in their continuity. To the outside observer, the differences are small; to the villagers, they are infinite. The villages are nearly endogamous. An Indian from any other village is an outsider, a "foreign Indian."

[40] Howard Handelman, *Struggle in the Andes: Peasant Political Mobilization in Peru* (unpublished Ph.D. dissertation, University of Wisconsin-Madison, 1971).

[41] *The New York Times*, October 5, 1972.

Not only is there a nearly total lack of communications between villages, but what is particularly striking is the virtual isolation of each nuclear family. Aside from the religious confraternities devoted to a highly ritualized worship of local saints, there are no associations, no group activities, no interpersonal social communication. This point is expressed in a case study of one (modernizing) community:

> There are no opportunities in the ordinary life for protracted personal interaction with nonkinsmen, nor any associational structures based upon the premise of like interests or upon ideas of fellowship or sport. . . . The temporary grouping of men into civil or religious offices, such as the *cofradias* (societies of worshippers of a given saint) or the group of young civil police who serve for a year, is so stylized and custom controlled in most of its aspects that personal knowledge of the individuals with whom one serves is nearly impossible.[42]

In short, the rural Indian village is enveloped in a profound silence.

The Indian society is not, of course, immutable, but the way in which it interacts with the modern economy is particularly pertinent to our discussion. There is a constant process of attrition, a crumbling of the human edges of the village society, a handful of individuals who change their cultural clothing. The Indian is distinguished from the Guatemalan variant of the mestizo, the "Ladino," by his dress, by mother tongue, and usually surname. By changing these, he will be recognized as a Ladino by both groups. The relative facility of this exchange of cultural identity is beyond any doubt a crucial part of the explanation for the failure of Indian nationalism to develop. A new identity which will provide admission into the modern, national culture is no farther away, in a manner of speaking, than the corner clothing store.

Thus, the ardent and the ambitious, the men who in other cultural contexts have provided leadership for both national and subnational groups, are silently drained away from the Indian community. The fascinating chronicle of the careers of three prominent trade union officials in one Indian town well illustrates this point. The union, organized in 1944 by the workers of a cotton textile plant which had been located in the town since 1876, had made a marked impact on the local Indian community. It provided for the first time a basis for communication between townsmen based on common interests. Union office provided broadened horizons and entirely new opportunities for the leaders. All three had occasion to visit Guatemala City on a number of occasions, and two received trips abroad, one to Moscow. However, as a result of their experience, they ceased to be Indians. They became Ladinos and were seen as being from the local community, but not of it.[43]

---

[42]Manning Nash, *Machine Age Maya* (New York: Free Press of Glencoe, Inc., 1958), pp. 56–57.

[43]Nash, *Machine Age Maya*, pp. 82–91.

Thus, in Guatemala, the difference between Ladino and Mayan, between Guatemalan and Indian, is the difference between the universalist and the particularist, between a world-oriented perspective and a village-centered view. The cry for *Indígenismo*, for reverence of the Indian component of the nation, arises not from the Indian lower strata of Guatemala, but from the predominantly Hispanic upper-clsss Ladino intellectual.[44] The village communities are too fragmented for a reaction in the name of Mayanism; the Ladino-Indian boundary is too blurred and the Ladinization process too simple to permit the emergence of a racial consciousness akin to Africanism.

MEXICO AND THE MYSTIQUE OF THE INDIAN PAST

Of all the nations of Latin America, Mexico has certainly been most self-consciously preoccupied with the Indian. *Indígenismo* was a central theme of the Mexican Revolution and is today securely embedded in Mexican national identity. However, invocation of Mexico's indigenous heritage was hardly the product of the Indian community of the nation. Ironically, the country's first Indian President, Benito Juárez, is remembered in Mexican history for his efforts to "liberate" the country from its traditional past and to move Mexico toward constitutionalism and economic liberalism. In fact, the liberal policies of Juárez's "reforma" mark the real beginning of the alienation of communal Indian lands in Mexico, creating a grievance that was to become a major factor in mobilizing peasant support for the Revolution of 1910.

The advocates of *Indígenismo* in post-1910 Mexico were almost entirely members of the dominant Hispanicized community, although some were of mestizo racial background. The muralists – Rivera, Orozco, Siqueiros – contributed to the mystique, as did composers (Chávez) and authors (Vasconcelos). Research in archeology and anthropology was officially endorsed and enthusiastically supported. The agrarian reform of the Revolution took on its "distinctive Mexican character" from the effort to reconstitute the Indian communal, or *ejido*, lands.

What was at issue, of course, was not so much *Indígenismo* as Mexicanism. For the nationalized elites of Mexico, long departed from Indian culture themselves, this was a search for the distinctive roots of national identity; it was a search for the Mexican *Volk*. The subtlety of the process is missed if one identifies it only with a romanticizing of Mexico's Indian heritage. What was more at stake was the blending of Indian with Western themes into a unique "Mexicanness." Hence, Chávez's music is an adaptation of Indian themes to the Western symphonic form. Mexican ballet is a working together of the classic Western dance with the Indian moods. Vasconcelos writes of the Indian but also

---

[44]See, for example, the anguished plea on behalf of the Indian by the conspicuously Iberian J. Fernando Juárez Muñoz, *El indio guatemalteco*, 2 vols. (Guatemala, 1931, 1946).

of the "cosmic race" that will come from the blending of all world racial groups in the Latin American. And the Mexican Revolution was to be the *ejido* system *and* industrialization, constitutional democracy *and* the expression of Indian society.

THE "INDIAN" BECOMES A "BOLIVIAN"

A striking example of this phenomenon may be found in the Bolivian Revolution of 1952. The Revolution, to a large extent, was fought in the name of the Indian mass base of the society. The active political mobilization of the Indians, who fought against the landlords and divided the estates into private parcels even before governmental authorization for such action, gives this Revolution its distinctive tone and significance. Nonetheless, the Bolivian Indians did not fight for "Indianness." Rather, after the Revolution the term "Indian" fell into disuse. It was considered to have disparaging implications. The "Indian" was now to be regarded (and he regarded himself) as a "campesino" (a rural dweller or farmer). Referring to the psychological transformation wrought by the Revolution, Robert Alexander writes:

> One interesting aspect of this psychological change was an alteration in the popular vocabulary. Antexana explains this in the following words: "From that moment the word 'Indian' disappeared and was wiped from the language to become a relic in the dictionary. Now there existed the 'peasant.' The worker of the countryside had been given land and liberty in all of its aspects. 'Indian,' a feudal concept, was the serf of an epoch which had disappeared...."[45]

Although this symbolic transformation is significant, it is also apparent that many of the reform measures carried out after the Revolution of 1952 had the effect of stabilizing and strengthening the cultural distinctiveness of different sectors of the population. The peasant farmer, secure in title to his own land as a consequence of agrarian reform, tends to retain many features of his traditional way of life, to resist further efforts at assimilation. He has been relatively resistant not only to entreaties from La Paz to become a more active participant in the political and economic processes of national life, but he has also been skeptical of appeals to radical political activism, as Che Guevara discovered in his ill-fated effort to establish a rural base for revolution in Bolivia in 1967. The peasant farmer is more apt to retain use of Indian languages and Indian cultural characteristics than are members of other occupational groups. In contrast to the relative autonomy of the way of life of the beneficiary of the Bolivian agrarian

---
[45] Robert Alexander, *The Bolivian National Revolution* (New Brunswick, N.J.: Rutgers University Press, 1958), pp. 75–76.

reform, one recent study comments on the socialization process that takes place in the mine camps of the nation. The new recruit to the mines is ridiculed by his peers for his Indian language, customs, and habits. He becomes the object of a socialization and communications process, conducted in Spanish, that reflects the concerns of nationally-oriented trade union and political leaders.[46] While the assimilation of the peasant to Bolivian national life and the culture of the Spanish-speaking sector of the society continues, the pace has been slower than in other occupation groups.

Whereas structural reform has perhaps sharpened, or at least stabilized, patterns of cultural differentiation in Bolivia, the consequences in terms of national political cohesion appear a bit paradoxical, particularly in comparison with certain African cases. While the peasant retains a strong diffuse loyalty to the national government that gave him land, the more culturally integrated and assimilated miners and factory workers of Bolivia have been prone to discontent, protest, and political radicalism.

RELIGION AND SUBNATIONALISM

Finally, we may take brief note of transformations in the character of religious communities, although here the pattern seems less general. Obviously, religion is only a basis of differentiation in polities where more than one major religion is present or salient cleavages within the dominant religion exist. It has been primarily in Asia that religious cleavage has played a prominent political role. In Latin America, nearly all the pious are Catholic. In Africa religion did not sharply demarcate African from European at the elite level; the new leadership was in most territories at least nominally Christian, thanks to the close relationship between missions and educational opportunity. And in many of the predominantly Muslim areas, leading marabouts and prominent Islamic figures had been assiduously and usually successfully wooed by the colonizer, who found them valued intermediaries in instructing the faithful in the virtues of civil obedience to the colonial order. In reward, missions (and therefore for a long time Western education) were excluded from these zones. Thus, nationalism and ethnicity were generally secular. We find in a state with an overwhelming Muslim majority, such as Senegal, that Leopold Senghor, a Catholic, has dominated politics for two decades. He has been able to maintain an intimate relationship with the leading Muslim notables, who are leading pillars of support in the countryside. Indeed, Senghor's principal rivals during his period in power have all been Muslims, who have been unable to crack Senghor's reservoir of rural Muslim support. In Chad as well, Protestant Pierre Tombalbaye presides, albeit uneasily, over a predominantly Muslim state. Dissident groups, who

[46] John H. Magill, *Labor Unions and Political Socialization in Bolivia* (unpublished Ph.D. dissertation, University of Wisconsin-Madison, 1972).

sustained a sputtering revolt during the late 1960s, did not overtly couch their resistance in religious terms. A non-Muslim president would have been inconceivable in the Islamic states of the Middle East or Asia.

In Asia, two phases in the development of religious solidarity may be distinguished: first, religion as an early stage in nationalism; and second, religion as an aspect of postindependence political competition. With the exception of the Phillipines, religion did sharply distinguish between colonizer and colonized. In Burma, Indonesia, and Pakistan, consciousness of religious distinctiveness marked the first stage in an awakening national consciousness. However, in both Burma and Indonesia, secular leadership rather quickly supplanted the religious figures, and neither Buddhism nor Islam was at the forefront when independence came. In Pakistan, religion was postulated as the unifying basis of nationhood, linking the noncontiguous Punjabis, Sindhis, and others of West Pakistan with the Bengalis of East Bengal. Once the unifying focus of the Muslim-Hindu competition within the Indian independence movement was removed, Islam proved wholly inadequate as the raison d'etre of a united Pakistan.

In the post-independence phase, the most notable development is the politization of Buddhism in Sri Lanka and Vietnam. In both cases, Buddhism confronts religious competition — in Sri Lanka, the secularism of the coastal elite and the Hinduism of the Tamil; in South Vietnam, the zealous Catholicism of the Diem regime and some of its successors and the social problems resulting from relocation of a million Catholic refugees from North Vietnam. Clearly the upsurge in militant Buddhism is related to the crystallization of a sense of distinctiveness of one segment of the population as opposed to others.

The rise of political Buddhism in Sri Lanka is particularly instructive on both similarities and differences in religious and other forms of self-awareness. The impact of the outside world on the coastal areas had been far more intense than in the more inaccessible uplands. Availability of modern education was much greater, presence of Christian missions more visible, the ethos of the coastal elite more secular, and its social structure less traditional. The lowland Buddhist temples had generally lost their lands and thus their source of wealth. The spread of modern education in the lowlands, and the secular values it inculcated, were seen as a threat to the status of the monks, who in the lowlands had been increasingly overshadowed by the new elite. In the uplands, however, the Buddhist monk continued to be esteemed as the wisest man of the village, whose advice was to be sought on diverse problems. Tamil laborers brought in from South India to work highland tea plantations were a particularly intrusive group. In some regions south of Kandy, they had come to outnumber the indigenous Sinhalese population. As Tamil numbers increased, they were seen as a threat both by the Sinhalese peasant, who feared being forced from his land, and by the Buddhist clergy, resentful of an alien, encroaching, Hindu population.

Unlike Burma, Buddhism was not salient in the low-keyed Sri Lanka nationalist movement. It was not until after independence that more militant Buddhist expression appeared, symbolized by the formation of the All-Ceylon Buddhist Congress as a pressure group, along with work for the improvement of Buddhism. In 1954, the Congress appointed a Buddhist Committee of Inquiry, which studied ways and means of strengthening Buddhism. In early 1956, shortly before national elections, the report was issued, with sweeping recommendations for the elevation of Buddhism in Sri Lanka. The state was called upon to offer its full support to Buddhism. The report also demanded the recognition of Sinhalese as the national language to supplant English without granting equivalent status to Tamil. The Sinhalese-only policy which was subsequently adopted automatically improved the status of the Buddhist orders vis-à-vis the English-speaking coastal elite, through replacing the language in which the monks had little facility with one in which they taught. Finally, the report called for a national Buddhist council, to nurture Buddhist institutions, and the assurance of more ample material support for the temples and orders.

The Buddhist monks played a key role in the bitterly fought 1956 election, between the coastal elite United National Party of Sir John Kotelawala and S.W.R.D. Banderanaike's Sri Lanka Freedom Party. They were able to deliver much of the rural and lower middle class vote that unseated Sir John. We may note the importance of the overlap between Buddhism and other social cleavages — the rural resentment at the relative prosperity of the more developed and detraditionalized coast, the Sinhalese antagonism towards the encroaching Tamils. Howard Wriggins gives pertinent summation to the sources of renascent Buddhism:

> The Buddhist revival was a complex phenomenon. No doubt it was encouraged by the desire of Ceylon's secular politicians to ensure themselves of the Buddhist majority vote. But it was more than this. . . . It represented a rural, fundamentalist reaction to the city's worldly ways, a middle and lower-class protest against the wealthy and influential elite who had been educated by a foreign curriculum away from Sinhalese social ways and religious practices. . . . In one sense, it looked to the past, casting back to the times when Buddhist monarchs ruled a realm that was believed to have been happy and serene, the perfect embodiment of the Dhamma. In another sense, it was revolutionary. The attempt consciously to alter relations between laity and Sangha and between the individual and his faith in an effort to counter denationalizing Western influences, has no historical model in recent centuries.[47]

---

[47] W. Howard Wriggins, *Ceylon: Dilemmas of a New Nation* (Princeton: Princeton University Press, 1960), p. 210.

Libya offers an interesting example of changing patterns of religious solidarity as the basis for the polity. Nationalist resistance to Italian rule was led by the Senussi Islamic brotherhood, which is particularly strong in Cyreneica, in eastern Libya. The collapse of Italy in World War II left the United Nations with the task of establishing some form of independent government for what was then an utterly impoverished society, before the oil revenues had begun to flow. The new state was, in effect, built around the Senussi sect, and its leader Mohammed Idris established as monarch — even though his religious writ had never run in Tripolitania in the west or Fezzan in the south. When the aging monarch was overthrown in 1969 by young officers led by Colonel Qadafi, the Senussi basis for the state was abandoned. In its place the military regime invoked a puritanical attachment to Islam, which was asserted as a passionate central element in Libyan identity.[48]

Lebanon represents a limiting case of the institutionalization of religious cleavage as the very basis for the organization of the state. Autonomy for separate religious communities was a long-standing principle of Ottoman administration; however, in the transition from Ottoman dependency to independent state, important changes occurred. In the eighteenth and nineteenth century, in the Mount Lebanon core of historic Lebanon, civil war between the Muslim-related Druze sect and Maronite Christians broke out, with the Druze winning the upper hand. When France acquired control in 1920, substantial new areas were added to what is now Lebanon, mainly Sunnite Muslim in population. French rule offered special educational advantages, in practice, to the Christian populations. In 1943, with independence in view, a compromise between Muslim and Christian was reached, whereby Christian support for independence was traded for assurance that Muslim leaders would forego their goal of unity with Syria. By 1960, a parliamentary formula had been reached that instituted rigid confessional quotas; thirty seats were reserved to Maronite Christians, eleven to Greek Orthodox, six to Greek Catholics, four to Armenian Orthodox, one to Armenian Catholics, one to Protestants, one to other minorities, twenty to Sunnite Muslims, nineteen to Shi'ite Muslims, and six to the Druze community. It is, in addition, an entrenched principle that the president is a Maronite, and the prime minister a Sunnite. One of the prices of constitutional segmentation in the inordinate cost of altering it to reflect any changes that may occur. No census has been taken since 1932, because of the fears of the destabilizing effect of recalculating quotas.

When set beside the emergent role of Beirut as commercial entrepot and Middle Eastern financial center, religious segmentation has had the intriguing effect of producing a liberal economy at sharp variance with the socialist policies of neighboring Syria and Egypt. In effect, segmentation and the cultural security

---

[48]For a vivid portrait of the extraordinary intensity of Colonel Qadafi's religious commitment, see the long interview transcribed by Edward R. F. Sheehan in *The New York Times Magazine*, February 6, 1972.

it has provided has as its price sharp limitations on the central role of government. To complete the picture, the distinctive economic path followed by Lebanon must be attributed not only to structural immobilism but also to its congruence with the interests of the large and growing mercantile elite centered in Beirut.

There is, then, a vast diversity of causal factors and patterns of development of cultural pluralism. Rupert Emerson's observation that the very success of nationalism in binding men together has as its counterpart "its intensification of their sense of separation from those on the other side,"[49] can be applied, *mutatis mutandis*, to cultural pluralism. In the European context, with a substantial overlap between state and nation, the rise of nationalism has been reflected in tensions in the international order. In the developing world, this same order of conflict has been in good part internal. To carry the comparison a stage further, we may suggest that nationalism in Europe was both a cause and a result of the modern phenomenon of total war — confrontations where entire national communities are pitted against each other. The network of social communications, through the spread of literacy and the advent of the industrial age, came to incorporate entire populations. The accelerating diffusion of a similar capacity for social communication throughout the world is producing the same results, yet with an original twist given by the superimposition of the grid of modernization upon polities in which important internal cultural discontinuities existed or developed. Cultural confrontations without precedent have occurred in many developing polities; in contrast, there has been a striking absence of conflict at the international level.[50]

---

[49] Rupert Emerson, *From Empire to Nation* (Cambridge: Harvard University Press, 1960), p. 329.

[50] Even the most striking exception, the recurrent Indo-Pakistani conflicts partially reinforces the hypothesis. The Kashmir dispute is a continuation of Muslim-Hindu confrontation which began on a large scale with the rise of nationalism in former British India.

CHAPTER 3

The Activation of Cultural Conflict

We have suggested that social transformation in Africa and Asia is producing new forms of cultural nationalism, mobilizing large numbers of previously nonparticipating members of the political community around some type of identity, which in itself is often new in scope and concept. The history of cultural pluralism in the developing world suggests that this is the central tendency, the long-term trend. But the pattern is not unilinear; it has proceeded by jerks and starts, in interaction with other forms of conflict and consensus within the political community. It is now appropriate to look more closely at factors productive of short-term vacillations in the general pattern. Most culturally plural polities pass through phases of acute tension along the cultural axis of differentiation; at other times, cultural antagonisms are relatively quiescent. On the basis of post-independence politics, we propose to suggest some of the recurrent classes of conflict that seem most likely to activate cultural division.

Every actor in the political community, no matter how unimportant, has a multiplicity of potential foci of social solidarity. The appropriate role is prescribed by the nature of the situation – or more precisely, by the actor's perception of the situation. This point can be best elucidated by a diagram. Taking arbitrarily an urban Mongo from the groups we have selected for discussion, we may represent his potential solidarity roles in terms of a series of concentric circles (see Figure 1).[1]

---

[1] A comparable schema has been produced by M. Fortes and E. E. Evans-Pritchard, eds., *African Political Systems* (London: Oxford University Press, 1940) and Fred G. Burke, *Local Government and Politics in Uganda* (Syracuse: Syracuse University Press, 1964). The idea of multiplicity of roles, of course, is closely related to the concept of multiple-group affiliation developed by David Truman and others of the group theorists in the American field.

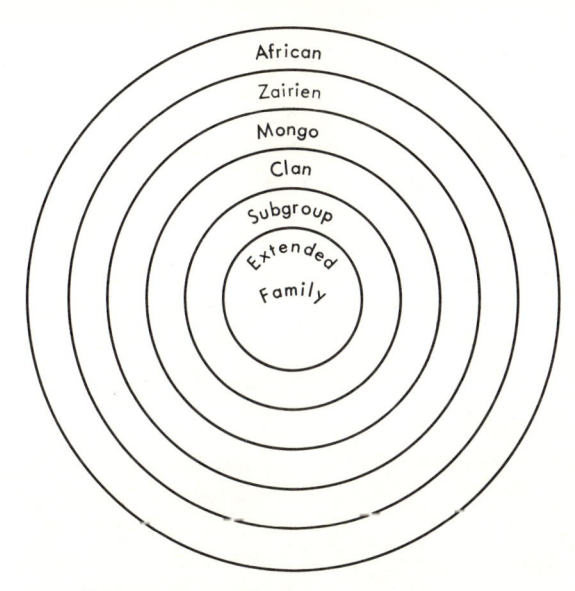

FIGURE 1

Concentric circles labeled from innermost to outermost: Family, Extended, Subgroup, Clan, Mongo, Zairien, African.

Many of the problems of daily life will be confined within the first two circles of solidarity – the extended family or the subgroup. A dispute may involve members of one extended family or subgroup with another over a question of bride-price, or a place for a kinsman in school or the civil service, or an accusation of witchcraft, or a competition for local chieftaincy. In this instance, the range of solidarity is restricted to the extended family or subgroup itself.

Moving out a step, we may encounter a dispute between two clans over land rights, or the slaughter of game in another clan's hunting preserve, or the proportions of representation on a local council. In these instances, solidarity would crystallize within the third ring of the circle; this ring would become temporarily a social wall separating "we" from "they." In the traditional, rural world, virtually all conflict would involve one of these three identities.

In the outer rings, we find solidarity roles most likely to come into play in an urban environment, although perhaps experienced in vicarious form by the villager when the daily truck passes through with news of what has happened in town. In Mbandaka, as we have seen, the Mongo conflict role came to the fore in 1958 when control of the town council and the burgomaster post were at stake. When a Ngombe "stranger" won the latter job, Mongohood became the appropriate frame of reaction; the inner circles for the moment were effaced, and Mongo stood united in their indignation at this affront to the group. However, when a Colonial Minister visited town to learn African views of appropriate future arrangements, Mongohood momentarily dissolved, and the Zaire ring came into play. And when the situational referent was an overt expression of racial contempt by a European towards Africans generally, or discrimination at the local hotel, or access to the senior ranks of the civil service, racial identity came into focus. It is pertinent to note that a feedback of situation to solidarity occurs; the more frequently and intensively a given circle is activated by perceptions of situation, the more deeply ingrained in the social consciousness of the actor this circle becomes. The colonial situation produced a relatively high number of situations for the urban Mongo in which the outer two circles were involved. The dialectic of decolonization and the nature of postcolonial domestic conflict in the early 1960s threw the Mongo circle into sharp relief. After President Mobutu seized power in 1965, competitive electoral politics were eliminated, ethnic provinces regrouped, and the provincial arena as an autonomous stage for resource allocation terminated. Thus situations wherein the Mongo role was salient as a referent for social interaction and conflict were greatly reduced. Accordingly, Mongohood was a less pervasive cue for social action.

This illustration of the interaction of situation and pluralism, however useful, has some defects; especially in coping with the modern sector of society, too many types of conflict are left out. In particular, the market-place also creates its patterns of social solidarity, founded on common occupational or economic interest. By somewhat amending our imagery, we can perhaps propose a closer approximation to the full range of possible social roles.

Figure 2 suggests the process of external challenge, perception, and role selection, depending on which prism of the actor's social personality serves to relate him to the situation. In the Ibo case, which we will consider in more detail in the following chapter, social identity was important at several different levels. The traditional, rural unit was the village group. More recently, regional identities had crystallized around major centers of administrative divisions (for example, Onitsha or Owerri). Social competition within the all-Nigerian frame had produced a powerful Ibo-wide solidarity system, reflected both in the rise of an Ibo association, the Ibo State Union, and massive Ibo alignment behind the first comprehensive nationalist movement, the NCNC. Within the context of anticolonial struggle, the Ibo were in the forefront of aggressive opponents to continued British rule; subsequently, when the political forces in independent Nigeria seemed from their perspective to be aligned in an anti-Ibo front, they rallied behind the idea of Ibohood to fight a bitter struggle for separation. In religious terms, Christian evangelization had been intensive, with Catholics holding the upper hand in a heated competition with Protestant missions. Religion, although generally not of high saliency, did differentiate Ibo from the other two very large subnationalities, Yoruba and Hausa-Fulani, the latter wholly Muslim, and the former divided between Islam, Protestant, and African independent churches of Protestant antecedents. Ibo had migrated in large numbers to towns, both within and without Iboland. Especially in other parts of Nigeria, they were to be found in a wide range of occupational roles, from workers, to traders, to clerical and professional functions. On occasion Ibo workers reacted strongly to occupational strata solidarity norms. For example, a

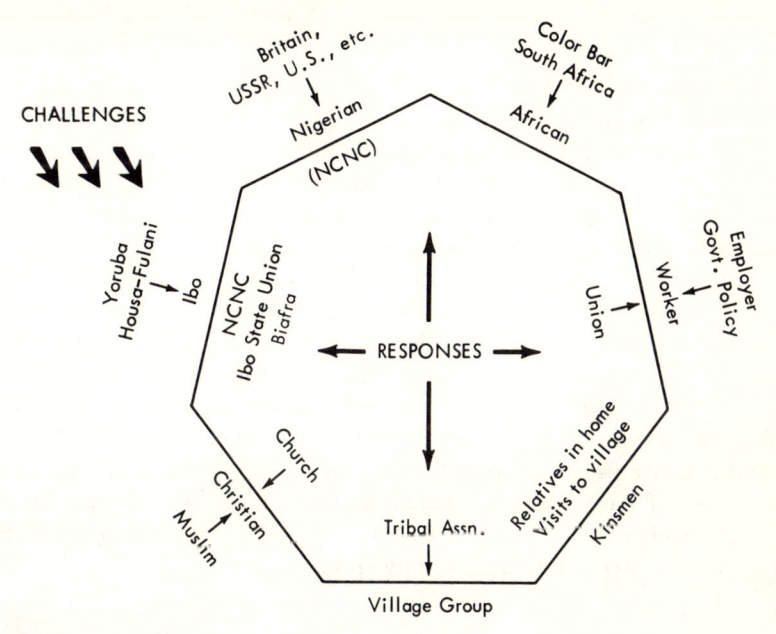

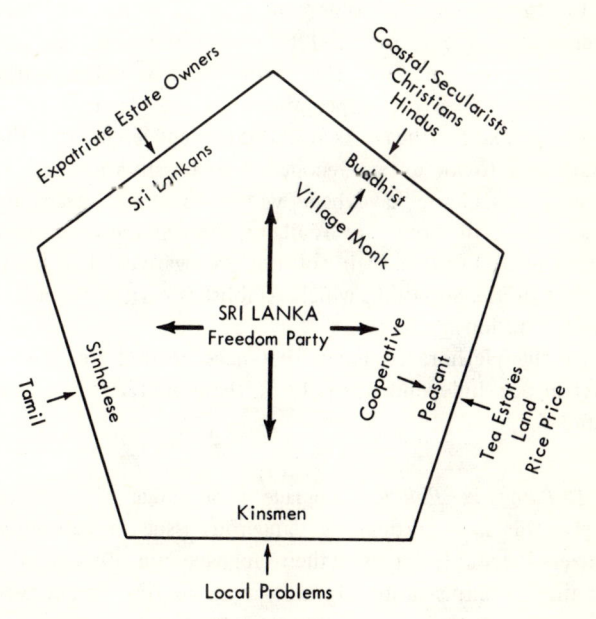

FIGURE 2
Role and Identity, Nigeria and Sri Lanka

bitter dispute arose in 1963 over the nonimplementation by a government in which the Ibo political elite played an important role of a report by a blue-ribbon commission on wage policies, recommending substantial rises. In this context, Nigerian workers and their unions achieved a unity of purpose never before seen; situational cognition was almost entirely nonethnic, and a surprisingly effective two-week general strike was called.

In the Sri Lanka case also illustrated in Figure 2, we may note the range of social roles held by a Sinhalese peasant. Although ethnicity is important, it is by no means the sole or necessarily the most significant status set. In a setting where rural stratification and land rights are more salient issues than in Eastern Nigeria, and in particular where the most prosperous form of agricultural production, tea, is frequently managed by nonindigenous estate holders, conflict roles that derive from the structure of the rural economy are more significant. The success of the Sri Lanka Freedom Party, beginning with its first national electoral triumph in 1956, may be largely attributed to its success in aggregating the solidarities latent in virtually all of the peasant roles.

NATURE OF CONFLICT SITUATIONS

In considering the types of conflict situations that render cultural differentiation salient, we need to return briefly to our earlier discussion of varying bases for the state. The environment in which conflict situations arise partially determines the expectations of the participants. To cite but one example, in most Southeast Asian states (except Singapore), the overseas Chinese population is to an extent reconciled to its situation as a minority. Even in Malaysia, the Chinese have been willing to accept discrimination in favor of Malays in the civil service: in Thailand, the Chinese have resigned themselves to extensive restrictions in their cultural prerogatives. The basis of the state is a given fact of the situation, which establishes certain boundaries to conceivable cultural aspirations.

Of the plethora of issues that have created frequent arenas of cultural conflict in post-independence politics, there are five which seem to us especially widespread:

1. Language Policy. Language is a badge of social identity. Not surprisingly, this is a particularly dangerous issue in culturally plural societies. Colonizers inevitably imposed their language as a convenient vehicle for modern and central administration. Except in Latin America, however, the colonizer failed to provide the educational means for full linguistic assimilation. Most new states, then, have faced a serious problem of a postcolonial language policy. Official multilingualism is simply too burdensome. Retention of the language of the colonizer is felt by many to be a tacit admission of cultural poverty. And the choice of one non-European language, associated with a particular cultural group, can be explosive.

Not all Afro-Asian states are afflicted with this problem. For the wide swath of Arab-speaking states, language has not been a serious difficulty (except in the non-Arab parts of Iraq and Sudan). In most core culture states, the choice has been obvious, even if it has provoked resistance when too zealously imposed on outlying minorities (Thailand, Burma, Iran). Some multicultural states have been able to adopt (Indonesian in Indonesia, Swahili in Tanzania) or to promote actively (Sanga in the Central African Republic, Nyanja in Malawi) a culturally neutral lingua franca without creating serious political problems. The bulk of African states have tacitly retained the language of the colonizer while paying occasional lip service to the principle of a national language. The most serious linguistic disorders have been in India and Sri Lanka, where decisions to impose Hindi and Sinhalese respectively led to grave disturbances.

2. Localization of Civil Service. Especially in Africa, civil service posts represent the most desirable employment opportunities available, both for the educated elite and, at lower levels, for the growing numbers of primary school graduates. In Africa there has been a general tendency to adopt salary levels in the civil service strongly influenced by the pay scales deemed necessary in the colonial epoch to recruit qualified personnel in Europe — rates competitive with professional salaries in developed industrial societies. Acutely sensitive about measures implying invidious racial distinctions in the terminal colonial period, colonial governments generally conceded the same privileges to the senior African civil servants that were accorded to expatriates. After independence, the considerable salary disparity between senior and junior civil service levels was usually reduced by raising the floor rather than by lowering the ceiling. Accordingly, civil servants are in general well remunerated in contrast to pay scales in alternate lines of employment. In a number of countries the government is by far the largest employer.

Further, the bureaucratic legacy of the colonial systems has meant that the field administrators are highly visible authority-holders, inheriting at least part of the prestige and wide discretionary authority of the old District Commissioner. Thus the ethnic identity of those exercising authority over the rural population is crucial; especially in Africa, the cry "we A's do not want to be ordered around by that B" is heard up and down the continent. At the same time, governments preoccupied with the integrity of the state and integration of the polity are reluctant to restrict assignment of central personnel to their ethnic homelands where the alchemy of local attachments may transform the administrator from representative of central authority to spokesman for parochial grievance. Indeed, the dominant trend appears to be toward systematic scrambling of administrative personnel, so that persons are posted deliberately outside their home area.

In Asia, where the problem was compounded in several instances by colonial practices of recruiting heavily from minority areas, the dominant groups quickly sought to reverse this situation after independence. Thus, in the early years of independence, localization of civil services has two catalyzing aspects: the very rapid allocation of thousands of desirable positions in a context in which the cultural distribution stands out, and the placement of individuals of one cultural grouping in authority roles with relation to others.

3. Electoral Competition. In a polity where political party divisions are absorbed into cultural cleavages, an election becomes a cataclysmic confrontation between communities. Modernizing elites throughout the developing world widely share a philosophic commitment to the idea of democracy (however much they may diverge on the practical implications of the term, especially the restraint on power and protection of the right to dissent). The crucial value that is distilled from "democracy" is majoritarianism. And when the major cleavages of society follow cultural contours, elections translate cultural plurality through the mechanism of majority rule into hegemony of one group over another. The haunting fear of this development is the most compelling argument for the single party system adopted by most African states; where the military does not hold power.

The introduction of majoritarianism in Rwanda and Zanzibar led directly to a dissolution of traditional social relationships. In Nigeria, Zaire, India, and Indonesia, national elections have been severe tests for the very survival of the polity. In extreme cases, such as the Congolese elections of 1960 or the Nigerian elections of 1964, the campaign takes on the character of a cultural census and precipitates intense antagonisms. In Colombia, the close correspondence between partisan affiliation and family, community, or regional identity led to a long and tumultuous civil strife. One might also note the regional basis of the Liberal (León) and the Conservative (Granada) partisan conflict in Nicaragua.

4. Resource Allocation. Developmental socialism is a doctrine widely adopted in Asia, Africa, and Latin America. Even where socialism per se is not salient, the central government generally enjoys a decisive voice in critical decisions of resource allocation within the polity. Scarcity of resources is the distinguishing characteristic of underdevelopment; accordingly, the choice of site of a major new industrial project, the route of a new road or railway, or the price established for an agricultural commodity may frequently be perceived as conferring particular advantages on one or another cultural group. One fascinating example involves the competition between the cities of Quito and Guayaquil in Ecuador. Despite their very different needs and characteristics, it is essential that national authorities apportion programs and facilities equally between them. Hence, if Guayaquil receives four garbage trucks, Quito will almost certainly demand the same.

5. Educational Policy. In most developing countries, the diffusion of social awareness has reached a point where both rural and urban populations are keenly conscious of the relationship between educational opportunity and social mobility. Thus access to education is a critical issue, and policy decisions that tend to culturally define educational opportunities provoke violent reactions. There are many points at which cultural pluralism and educational policy intersect. The choice of language of instruction may give what appears to be an unfair advantage to those for whom this is a maternal tongue. Identification of the schools with a given religion may virtually require parents to choose between renunciation of their faith and lack of education for their children. Regional differences in the density of the school network may operate a silent but highly effective selection of the future elite. One particular cultural group may contribute a disproportionate number of schoolmasters and then be suspected of favoritism in admissions and grades. Scholarships for university study domestically or overseas may be thought to be awarded on cultural criteria; few Ministers of Education have not heard this charge raised against them. The payoff in prestige and material prospects from education is so high that the unsuccessful are bound to be bitter and quick to find an explanation in cultural partisanship.

A number of other less salient causes of cultural conflict might be listed, but these seem the most important. What characterizes all these types of conflict is the perception of the dispute in terms of cultural identity by large numbers of persons. Adoption of another group's language as official, disproportionate recruiting of civil servants to replace the departing expatriates from one group, loss of an election to a party dominated by a different group — all of these pose a threat to the social identity and tend to produce a visceral, emotional, and violent response dictated by the profound instinct for cultural self-preservation.

SECESSION, SEPARATISM, AND IRREDENTISM

The ultimate political consequences of cultural pluralism are, of course, breakdown of the polity through the withdrawal of a segment of it, either to become independent or to join another territory. Table 3-1 records major instances of separation, important secession movements, and irredentism, covering the terminal colonial period and postindependence life span of former colonial territories and the twentieth century for states without a colonial past.

With 150 years of postindependence history, it is clear that separatism is largely an issue of the past in Latin America. In large measure, the problem was confined to the original separatism in the early independence period from the four vice-royalties and four captaincies general that were the organizational

TABLE 3-1
Separatism, Secessionism, and Irredentism

Separation		Important Movements Demanding Secession			Irredentism	
Separating state	Former parent state	Secessionists	Parent state	Cultural group	Parent state	Proposed affiliation

Latin America

Guatemala Nicaragua Honduras El Salvador Costa Rica	Central American Federation	(Threat frequently occurs in political rhetoric of larger polities where regionalism is strong, but not a serious or sustained demand)				
Panama	Colombia					
Venezuela Ecuador	Gran Colombia					
Paraguay Uruguay	Argentina (La Plata Vice-Royalty)					
Texas California	Mexico					
Jamaica Trinidad & Tobago	West Indies Federation					

Asia

Singapore Pakistan Bangladesh	Malaysia India Pakistan	Ambonese Sumatrans and to some extent Outer Islands generally	Indonesia	Arakanese (Muslims) Shans	Burma Burma	Pakistan Thailand
		Karens Kachins Shans Arakanese	Burma			
		Sabah Sarawak	Malaysia			
		Bengal	Pakistan			
		Naga Kashmir	India	Kashmir (Muslim)	India	Pakistan
		Tibet Sinkiang	China			
		Pathans	Pakistan			

TABLE 3-1 (continued)

Separation		Important Movements Demanding Secession			Irredentism	
Separating state	Former parent state	Secessionists	Parent state	Cultural group	Parent state	Proposed affiliation
		Azerbaijan Kurdistan Khuzistan Qashqais Gilan Khorasan	Iran	Kurd	Turkey Iraq Syria	Kurdish State
				Armenian	Iran Turkey USSR	Armenian State
Middle East						
Syria	Unified Arab State			Arab	Syria Iraq Jordan Libya Yemen Sudan	Unified Arab State
Africa						
Mauretania Senegal Mali Niger Guinea Ivory Coast Upper Volta Dahomey Gabon Congo-Brazzaville Central African Republic Chad	Afrique Occidentale Française	Touareg Sanwi (Agni) Ashanti Northern Islamic Chieftancies Eastern Region Northern Region Katanga Sud-Kasai	Mali Ivory Coast Ghana Chad Nigeria Cameroons Congo	Ewe West Cameroons Bakongo	Ghana Nigeria Angola Congo-Brazzaville Zaire	Togo Cameroons Bakongo St.
Senegal	Mali	Buganda	Uganda	Ubangi	Zaire	Central African Republic
Rwanda Burundi	Ruanda-Urundi	Bahr el Ghazal, Upper Nile, Equatorial Provinces	Sudan	Baamba-Bakonjo	Uganda	Zaire
Zambia Malawi	Federation of Rhodesia and Nyasaland	Darfur Eritrea	Sudan Ethiopia	Ogadan (Somali)	Ethiopia	Somalia
				Northeast Frontier District	Kenya	Somalia

structure of the colonial system. Paraguay and Uruguay broke away from Argentine in the La Plata region, Ecuador and Venezuela from Nueva Granada (Colombia, ending Bolivar's dream of "Gran Colombia"). Central America seceded from Mexico and subsequently fragmented itself into five states. Among the causes of this early tendency to fragmentation were geographic barriers, effectively preventing a sense of community from developing. In the Andes and Central America, for example, traditional regional antagonisms, suppressed under the colonial system, opened up in the independence period. The political cleavages of the day sometimes precipitated secession if the "dominant" part of a political unit was controlled by enemies (e.g., the battles of Conservatives and Liberals contributed to fragmentation both in the Andes and Central America). Finally, the localism of the independence movement itself was a factor; its organizing focus was often the *Cabildo*, or town council, the one institution of local government in the colonial system.

Although there were frequent threats of secession in the nineteenth century, these usually resolved into battles between federalists, seeking a larger measure of regional autonomy, and centralists, identified with the capital or "center" of a viable political unit. Thus, the chronic conflict between Buenos Aires and the provinces in Argentina, or between Mexico City and the hinterland, frequently was focused on the proper definition of federalism, without recourse to the ultimate sanction of secession. The only examples of separation since the early period are that of Panama from Colombia in 1903 and Texas and California from Mexico, none of which can be entirely explained with reference to domestic circumstance. A sort of informal secession has been practiced in some parts of Colombia, where small areas, under Marxist ideology, effectively maintained their independence from national control for a number of years. Even today, the threat of secession is occasionally heard and remains a tactical weapon for dissident regions.

In Asia, separators and secessionists are minority groups in outlying areas, especially in states where a core nationality exists that makes periodic assimilationist gestures. The existence of prominent ideological cleavages in the Asian context, often cutting across the cultural divisions, tends to blur the edges of separatist movements. This has been particularly marked in Burma, where since independence there has been an intricately structured series of rebellions, in which ethnicity, religion, and Communism overlap and interact in a complex way, as analyzed in our study of violence. The Marxist-Leninist ideological commitment of some Asian groups who might otherwise be tempted by separation also sets Asia apart. For example, the Pathet Lao movement in Laos has relied heavily on antagonism of hill peoples toward the Mekong Lao in its recruitment of partisans. Ever since Laotian independence, there has existed in effect an autonomous Pathet Lao state in Phong Saly and Sam Neua provinces. However, the ideological imperative is eventual control of all Laos, not legalization and consolidation of the separate zone as an independent state.[2] In a somewhat different context, the almost wholly ethnic Chinese rebellion in Malaya, because it was waged in the name of Marxism-Leninism, articulated its goals in universalist terms rather than expressing goals directly related to the identity of the rebels — for example, partition into separate Chinese and Malay states. Of course, the most spectacular Asian example of secessionism was the revolt of former East Pakistan, and its conquest of independence as Bangladesh in 1971. We will examine this case in some detail in the following chapter.

Although the Middle East has its share of arbitrary political units, such as Libya, Iraq, and Jordan, the fact that the most salient identity has been supranational, rather than subnational, also places the Arab world into a special category. The two Arab states that include a substantial non-Arab population, Iraq and Sudan, have both faced long and bitter struggles to maintain their present boundaries. In the Sudan instance, southern Sudanese dissidence which first became overt with a mutiny of southern troops in 1955 on the eve of independence (achieved in 1956) coalesced by 1963 into sustained civil war, which was settled only in 1972 on the basis of substantial regional autonomy to the non-Arab southern provinces, and integration into the national army (and thus remunerated employment) for a large fraction of the guerrilla forces. Iraq, as noted earlier, has had sporadic periods of open warfare between Kurdish forces and the Iraqi army; in the early 1970s, a phase of truce and cautious cooperation had again begun. Lebanon, it is true, is one of the world's most culturally divided states, but the cleavages between Sunnite, Shi'ite, and Druze Muslims, Maronite, Greek Orthodox, Greek Catholic, and Armenian Orthodox Christians are not wholly geographical and therefore cannot be resolved by the simple expedient of fragmenting the polity — although occasional separatist rumblings have been heard from the Druze sect concentrated on Mount Lebanon itself. Particularly unstable are the successor states to the colonial protectorates around the fringes of the Arabian peninsula — South Yemen (replacing Aden Protectorate), Oman, and the United Arab Emirates in the Persian Gulf. In South Yemen, the duality between the secular Marxist nationalist elites of Aden town who control the institutions of government, and preside over a bankrupt microeconomy, and the traditional sheikhs who command the largely nomadic rural population could not be more extreme. On the Persian Gulf, the tortuous negotiations to establish a tenuous federation among the nine petty but oil-rich emirates are an extreme case or particularism, although all are Arabs. In the end, Bahrein and Qatar went separate ways, despite the apparent self-interest of the rulers in achieving a common political organization.

[2] We have omitted from this discussion three cases of territorial scission which are a direct result of the "cold war": the two Koreas and two Vietnams and the de facto independence of Taiwan from China. Also, the Soviets briefly toyed with secessionism in Iran, encouraging temporarily a Gilan split-off after World War I and Azerbaijani and Kurd states in 1946.

The case of Palestine, now a stateless nationality, is in a category of its own. The state of Palestine was created under British mandate after World War I; substantial communal autonomy was accorded to the component Arab and Jewish communities. After World War II, no accommodation proved possible between the demands for a Jewish homeland state and Arab claims that Palestine should be preserved as a bicultural entity. In 1947, the United Nations recommended partition, but the issue was removed to the court of arms. Israeli forces defeated the Arab army, and the new state of Israel was launched in 1948, with frontiers substantially larger than those provided for in the UN partition scheme. Massive Jewish immigration, and the flight of the bulk of the Arab population of former Palestine utterly transformed the human geography. The portions of Palestine not absorbed into Israel were administered by Jordan and Egypt, and Palestinian refugees gathered in camps in all surrounding Arab lands. The 1967 war saw another defeat of Arab armies, the occupation of the remainder of former Palestine, plus Sinai (Egypt) and the Golan Heights (Syria) by Israel. In the wake of these setbacks, Palestinian nationalist movements became more militant, and adopted new strategies of international terrorism, such as the spectacular wave of aerial hijackings in 1970, and the kidnapping of part of the Israeli Olympic team in Munich in 1972. At least in the short run, the diminishing prospect of fulfillment of its goals only reinforced the intensity of Palestinian nationalism, fed by the festering frustrations of the refugee camps. Support for Palestine and antagonism toward Israel became in the last two decades the most salient referent of Arab nationalism.

The quest for political realization of the cultural dream of Arab unity remains a constant vector in Middle Eastern politics. A succession of federations, leagues, and groupings of states has been proclaimed in execution of this principle. Each in turn has foundered upon the fragmenting impact of ideological factions, monarchical prerogatives, personality differences, fears of non-Arab or non-Muslim populations, and regional divergences. The most serious experiment to date in Arab unity was the United Arab Republic linking Egypt and Syria from 1958 to 1961. When Syria seceded in 1961, uneasy over Egyptianization of the union, Nasser chose not to endeavor military repression, whose outcome in any case would have been uncertain. Yet the unitarian impulse remains, with Colonel Muammar Qaddafi of Libya in the early 1970s emerging as the most ardent spokesman. That Arab unity remains a meaningful moral imperative is perhaps illustrated by the remarkable fact that subsidies provided to the Egyptian Arab Republic by oil-rich Kuwait, Saudi-Arabia, and Libya after the disastrous 1967 war closed the Suez Canal have more than compensated Egypt for the loss of the estimated $180 million yearly canal revenues.

As might be expected, the specter of separatism looms large in Africa. Few African leaders are entirely free of the haunting fear of either an ethnic or regional secession movement or the demands of ethnic groups straddling frontiers to rejoin their brethren on the other side of the boundary. The reality underlying these fears was demonstrated by the magnitude of the tragedy of the Nigerian civil war, from 1967-70, which we will explore in the following chapter. The actual separations to date are simply a result of terminating administrative integration of a number of territories that had been carried out under colonial auspices (Afrique Occidentale Francaise, Afrique Equatoriale Française, Ruanda-Urundi, Federation of Rhodesia & Nyasaland).

The seriousness of the problem is reflected in the vigor of reaction to instances of it; the Katanga effort to separate from Zaire was fervently condemned in part because if one separator "got away with it," the risk of contagion was considerable. The Organization of African Unity in its inaugural meeting in Addis Ababa in 1963 firmly proscribed territorial revisions, even when, in the case of Somali-inhabited zones of Kenya and Ethiopia, the principle of self-determination might thereby be compromised. The wall of hostility to separatism anywhere under any circumstances received its most severe tests in the Southern Sudan and Biafran cases. In the former instance, the grievances of insurrection, founded upon allegations of racial, cultural, and religious oppression of the black, non-Muslim south by the Arab, Muslim north, struck some responsive chords, yet the Anyanya insurgents received precious little aid and comfort from other African states, except on occasion from Ethiopia and Zaire in retaliation for Sudanese toleration of arms traffic to their own rebels. In the Biafran instance, despite a skilled diplomatic effort and the emotional backdrop of the 1966 Ibo pogroms, and predictions of genocide, only Tanzania, Zambia, Ivory Coast and Gabon gave diplomatic recognition to the short-lived Ibo state. The great majority of African states cast their support with Nigerian unity.

In silent antithesis to the catalogue of instances of separatism are the many cases where it has not emerged, despite the existence of cultural pluralism in the polity. Self-consciousness at a subnational level is clearly a necessary but not a sufficient condition to activate secessionist demands. There are certain specific types of situations that seem to catalyze separatist potential, to actualize latent fragmenting forces. Above all, the perspectives of the potential separatists must comprehend the fragmenting act as within the realm of feasible political action. Separation, in short, must have not only sociological logic, but practical application.

Distance from the center is a first obvious consideration. Traditionally, areas on the periphery of precolonial states in Africa and Asia could regard separation as a political option whenever a weakening of the center provided the opportunity. Those close to the royal court could only hope to change the ruler at the center. Similarly, in a large state like Indonesia or Zaire, the Ambonese or Katangans could envisage withdrawal from the system as an obvious option, which was simply not available for an area in the central part of the country.

A coincidence between geography and cultural plurality is essential. In polities like Malaysia, Lebanon, Rwanda, or Burundi, where the major subnational groups are more or less dispersed throughout the territory, partition was not a real alternative. Only a formula for toleration and reconciliation (Lebanon), or an uneasy coexistence (Malaysia), or outright hegemony of one group (Rwanda) can resolve the conflict (however unstable such resolutions may be). The recurrent crisis in Burundi well illustrates this point. The two major components of the population are the Watusi and Bahutu, although each of these broad categories contains complex subdivisions. Both groups are found throughout the country, speak the same language, but otherwise retain a sense of cultural distinctiveness, within the context of a stratified society with the Watusi dominant (although less completely so than in neighboring Rwanda). The first post-independence governments had participation from both groups, although there was a clear Watusi center of gravity. An abortive coup by Bahutu army and gendarmery officers in October 1965 led to bloody reprisals decimating the Bahutu elite and sharpening the pattern of Watusi control. In 1972, an obscure scenario of conspiracy led to assaults on a number of Watusi, followed by overwhelming reprisals on Bahutu that left a death toll estimated by the government at 50,000, and by foreign observers as high as 120,000.

A serious weakness of the Karen autonomist movement in Burma was the partial dispersion of the Karen community; an important portion of the group were cohabitants of the lowland plains with the ethnic Burmans. This led to the tactical uncertainty of the Karen army in 1949-1950, the confused assault on Rangoon itself, and vacillation between apparent efforts to reconstitute Burma on a basis more favorable to the Karens and creation of an independent Karen state.

Economic arguments may be used by separators to rationalize withdrawal but are rarely accepted as persuasive grounds for renouncing fragmentation by determined secessionist movements. Katanga and the Indonesian outer islands, for example, accused Kinshasa and Java respectively of preempting for their own benefit the economic contribution of the dissident regions. The option for secession by Eastern Nigeria was partly sustained by the belief that newly-developed oil resources would assure the prosperity of the new state. But the possible economic deprivation that might result from the withdrawal of a poor zone from a more prosperous territory seems to have had negligible influence in situations like Nagaland, the Shan States of northern Burma, or the three non-Arab provinces of southern Sudan. Rwanda cheerfully bore the economic price of disengaging itself from the Belgian Ruandi-Urundi trust territory, administratively headquartered in the somewhat more developed Burundi portion of the tandem.

There are in the lives of states occasional cataclysmic moments when what appear to be decisive and perhaps definitive options have to be made. At the apocalypse, the latent separatist must suddenly make his choice; the circumstances that led up to the fundamental reappraisal of the basis of political community may well provide the occasion for attempting to opt out, and the prospect that another chance to act may never come. This is especially true at the time of power transfer or in its immediate aftermath. It was at this juncture that Pakistan split from India, that Rwanda separated from Burundi, that the old administrative federations in French tropical Africa dissolved. The breakdown of central institutions in Zaire immediately after independence gave Katanga its chance to try to secede. Similarly, the unsuccessful secession of the Ambonese archipelago as the South Moluccas state followed immediately upon the heels of the Dutch-Indonesian settlement of 1949, before the new Djakarta government could make effective its sovereignty in the area. The Somalis in Kenya, who had been more or less quiescent under colonial administration, saw the change to the control of an African government as an entirely different matter — the signal for insurrection. Leopold Senghor and his associates in Senegal perceived in August 1960 that a scheme to convert the Senegal-Soudan federation into a unitary state was imminent and that immediate withdrawal was the only alternative to Bamako-dominated integration.

The structure of the international state system makes postcolonial secession a perilous adventure, except by mutual consent, as in the case of Singapore's withdrawal from Malaysia or Nasser's acceptance of the Syrian withdrawal from the UAR. The Katanga episode, as well as the collapse of the Soviet-sponsored Kurd and Azerbaijan states in northern Iran in 1946, clearly showed that survival in the world complex of states is ultimately dependent on securing international recognition. Autarchy may have been possible for the Soviet Union, but it is not viable for a small, weak territory in the developing world. The climate of "world opinion," especially among Afro-Asian states, is strongly hostile to separatist states. The overall world balance makes it unlikely that sustained patronage would be available from a major world power. Symptomatic of this were both the Katanga and Iranian examples. Katanga wanted desperately to be a Western client state, but the United States felt it had too much to lose elsewhere in Africa to encourage these overtures. In Iran, the Soviet Union rather quickly abandoned the Kurd and Azerbaijan republics in portions of Iran that the Red Army had occupied during World War II. The likely cost to the Communist movement elsewhere in Western Asia was out of proportion to the gain to the Soviet bloc of these two small states.

Prospects for successful separation would be vastly improved if it either could be immediately followed by attachment to a recognized state, or at least patronage of a neighboring nation. This could simultaneously solve the international recognition problem, and also provide military protection for the separators. The indispensable role played by India as midwife to Bangladesh independence is illustrative. Not only was Indian military intervention decisive in defeating Pakistani forces in East Bengal, but the powerful sponsorship of India assured diplomatic status as well as emergency assistance during the travail of birth and early consolidation of the fledgling state.

The serious difficulties in achieving full separation has led to a search for formulas for internal autonomy or the restructuring of the state so that cultural plurality will not be threatened by enforced assimilation. Federalism is thus a popular constitutional creed among potential separators. In Ghana, Nigeria, Zaire, Uganda, Kenya, Libya, Burma, India, Indonesia, Venezuela, Mexico, Argentina, Colombia, and Brazil, federalism has either been adopted or strongly demanded by a cultural or regional group or groups. Another formula has been the internal reconstruction of the state through redrawing provincial boundaries to coincide with cultural differentiation. The formation of linguistic states in India is one spectacular example. In Nigeria, breaking of the old three regions into twelve states has transformed cultural politics in important ways. Institutional recognition was thus given to the "minorities," or diverse groups representing the third of the population not accounted for by the three giant subnationalities of Ibo, Yoruba, and Hausa-Fulani. No longer simply eclipsed by the most numerous groups, they have played a much more visible role in Nigerian politics since 1967.

Finally, in extreme cases autonomist aspirations can be achieved by the simple expedient of internal withdrawal from the political system. Remote areas satisfied with a near-subsistence level of economic activity can simply cease obeying central authority, without overt secession. Central efforts at coercion are often rendered difficult by the terrain. This phenomenon is probably far more widespread than we can be aware, since by definition such silent internal withdrawal is unlikely to be reported, and the remoteness of the areas make it also likely that it will be unseen. This has clearly happened in Colombia, Zaire, and Burma. Certainly, the Indian cultures of Guatemala or Peru may be said, in some sense, to have simply "not recognized" the authority of either the Spanish conquest or of the independent Latin American states. Other states with weak administrative capacities and traditions, such as Indonesia, Chad, Niger, Ethiopia, Liberia, and Laos, are likely to encounter instances of this form of local withdrawal. Lucian Pye suggests persuasively that countries like Burma and Indonesia are able to tolerate for protracted periods the loss of administrative control of large regions, as long as the center is not threatened. On the other hand, a government with high administrative standards in the maintenance of law and order, as in Malaysia, cannot tolerate even localized insurrection.[3]

---

[3] Harry Eckstein, ed., *Internal War* (New York: Free Press of Glencoe, Inc., 1964), pp. 165-66.

CHAPTER 4

Crises of Cultural Pluralism: Biafra and Bangladesh

The ultimate failure of human society is measured by warfare. In the resort to the arbitrage of the mailed fist, witness is borne to the incapacity of man to find peaceful resolution of his differences in the social forms he has created. Particularly is this so for the holocaust of civil war. Perhaps the international arena remains resistant to the crafting of authoritative peace-maintaining mechanisms. But the state, defined in terms of its legitimate monopoly of force, surely has as its first charge the preservation of internal peace.

In this light, two epic instances of failure in the ultimate mandate of the state bear examination, the Nigerian civil war of 1967-70, and the Bangladesh war of independence in 1971. Not all internal wars derive from cultural pluralism, in the developing world or elsewhere. Neither in the Chinese nor the Vietnamese revolutions did factors of ethnicity, race, religion, or language play a significant part. But the tensions secreted by cultural diversity do, if unreconciled, have a massive destructive capacity; these two cases represent well the potential for human tragedy in pluralism turned malignant.

The outcomes of these two recent internal wars, of course, stand in total contrast. Bangladesh is a sovereign state, its destiny forever severed from Pakistan. Biafra, on the contrary, belongs to history, no doubt to be viewed by future generations of Nigerian schoolchildren as a necessary step toward One Nigeria, like the Civil War for Americans long after the event. Both crises can be conveniently analyzed within the framework that we have suggested in the preceding chapters. Crisis often lays bare the inner workings of societal conflict, which may be much harder to discern during periods of tranquility. On this premise, we will explore the antecedents, proximate causes, and dynamics of these two secessionist movements.

BIAFRA

On May 30, 1967, Colonel Odumegwu Ojukwu, Oxford-educated, son of a Nigerian millionaire, declared that the former Eastern Region of Nigeria was constituting itself as the independent state of Biafra. Six weeks of uneasy calm followed, as both sides steeled themselves for the struggle. On July 6, Nigerian president General Yakubu Gowon gave the order for federal forces to enter Biafra, marking the beginning of a bitter thirty-month conflict, which will now enter the history books as the "War of Nigerian Unity."

Although the Ibo were the dominant ethnic group in the Eastern Region, somewhat more than one third of the population was of different origin, with the Ijaws of the Niger Delta, the Ibibio and related Efiks of the coast, being the largest of the other groups. Events soon made it clear that the secession had the support only of the Ibo. In the first year of the war, federal troops slowly occupied most of the non-Ibo areas in the south. The Ibo heartland of Biafra was cut off from the sea, and, unless international assistance could be secured, the ultimate outcome could hardly be doubted. But the cause of Ibo nationalism generated intense loyalty, and enormous sacrifice was made. The conviction — widespread — that genocide lay at the far side of surrender certainly reinforced the resolve to struggle. How was it possible that ten million people would commit themselves to a battle to the death in the name of an identity that almost none of them would have claimed a century ago?

As with the Mongo and Tonga cases discussed earlier, Ibohood is a novel identity, which has grown out of the dynamics of modernization. The label appears to originate during the slave-trading days, primarily as a designation used by Europeans to identify those speaking related dialects originating in hinterland eastern Nigeria. There is no myth of common ancestry uniting Ibo-speakers. Indeed, until very recently, a number of Ibo-speakers, notably in the Onitsha area, denied they were "Ibo," contending rather they were descended from subjects of the prestigious Benin kingdom. To this day, there has been no generally accepted standardization of the Ibo language; language has been singularly absent in the symbols of Ibo identity. The operative social and political unit was the village group; the sole precursor of pan-Ibo identity was the Aro Chuku trading community, whose possession of an oracle of extraordinary supernatural power ("the long juju") made possible free and safe movement throughout the region. The key to colonial occupation of Iboland was the capture and destruction of this oracle by the British in 1902.

Initially, the Ibo had an exceedingly negative stereotype in the eyes of the colonizer. They were unfavorably compared to the aristocratic culture of the Muslim emirates of the Hausa-Fulani areas of the north, as well as the Yoruba kingdoms and nascent Yoruba professional elite of the west and Lagos. One psychologist has argued that the exceptional competitive impulses exhibited by many Ibo subsequently were a consequence of an awareness of this pejorative stereotype, a new synthesis of traditional norms and Westernizing values of material progress, and a socialization process that internalized these new norms in the younger generation.[1] Others have argued that the traditional culture itself was open and competitive in the social sphere, with economic success rewarded by access to high traditional status.[2] An unusually high population density, which forced young men to seek opportunities in towns, is another explanation.

Whatever the merits of these arguments, the facts are unmistakable. As colonial occupation became more thoroughly implanted in Iboland, especially after World War I, a veritable Ibo diaspora to all the major cities in Nigeria began. Christian missions, after a slow start, swiftly spread, linked as they were to the schoolhouse which was the ultimate measure of mobility. Young Ibo in towns became aware that especially the Yoruba, but also smaller groups of the eastern coast, Ijaw and Ibibio, had a tangible educational lead over them. In rural areas, Ibo communities competed with each other, in the intensive striving to "get up", individually and collectively. The status of the community was revealed in its artifacts of modernity — a school, a dispensary, a road, perhaps a church.[3] From this dialectic of competitive modernization came swift Ibo social mobility, and crystallization of Ibo self-awareness.

Above all it was the movement to towns that fostered the idea of Ibohood. In the urban setting Ibo became conscious of the similarities of language and custom throughout the Ibo area, and of their distinctiveness from other people. As late as the 1930s, the process of identity-formation was still in a relatively early stage; it is given interesting summation by one of the first anthropologists to undertake field work in Iboland. Although her field research was in the early 1930s, her book was published much later; she notes that it was only after completing her study that she began to realize the significance of emergent Ibohood:

> There is no doubt that an increasing number of educated or sophisticated Ibo-speaking people are coming to use the name both about their whole people and their language and with a more or less clear idea of the unit to which the name refers. The name, in fact, is becoming a symbol of unity....
>
> As with most peoples, in fact, the Ibo feel the bonds between them most closely when they are confronted by foreigners. Two men from whatever part of Ibo-speaking country when they meet in Lagos or in London will call themselves brothers. Increasing

---

[1] Robert A. Levine, *Dreams and Deeds: Achievement Motivation in Nigeria* (Chicago: University of Chicago Press, 1966), pp. 87–88.

[2] Simon Ottenberg, "Ibo Receptivity to Change," in William R. Bascom and Melville J. Herskovits, ed., *Continuity and Change in African Cultures* (Chicago: Phoenix Books, 1959), pp. 130–42.

[3] On the Ibo awakening, see Victor C. Uchendu, *The Ibo of Southeast Nigeria* (New York: Holt, Rinehart and Winston, 1965); David B. Abernethy, *The Political Dilemma of Popular Education* (Stanford: Stanford University Press, 1969).

sophistication is bringing a clearer notion of belonging to the whole unit of Ibo-speaking people. At home, however, people will count themselves as belonging to their village group, will recognize the neighboring village-groups as people with whom they trade and marry, and will say of the people beyond a radius of about seven miles: "The people of that place are very wicked."[4]

Politization of emergent Ibo ethnicity began in Lagos, where the growing numbers of Ibo intellectuals began in the late 30s to challenge the dominant position of the older Yoruba elite. Ethnic factionalism lay just below the surface in the major political movement of the epoch, the Nigerian Youth Movement. The Ibo movement to towns had given rise to a wide range of voluntary associations built around locality groupings.[5] In 1936, the first effort at pan-Ibo organization was launched in Lagos, with the founding of the Ibo Union (Lagos). The objectives of the movement in creating and consolidating Ibohood were given clear statement at the inaugural meeting:

> Brethren, this is the day and the hour when the Ibos of Nigeria should rally together ... (and) sink all differences — geographical, lingual, intellectual, moral and religious, and unite under the banner of our great objective — the tribal unity, cooperation and progress of all the Ibos.[6]

Departing from the core of the Ibo Union (Lagos), Ibo leaders sought to enlarge their base by federating all of the numerous locality associations into a single organization; this effort culminated in the launching of the Ibo Federal Union in 1944, rebaptised the Ibo State Union in 1948.

At this same time, Nnamdi Azikiwe, later to become the first President of independent Nigeria, flamboyant and dynamic, had emerged as the most aggressive and articulate spokesman of Nigerian nationalism. He was the leader of the first major political party that claimed to operate nationally, the National Convention of Nigeria and the Cameroons (NCNC). Ibo rallied massively behind the new movement, as did many other Nigerians in the 1940s. However, grumbling began to be heard, especially among Yoruba, that the NCNC was actually a diabolical instrument of Ibo chauvinism. Some apparent validation for this perception came from the overlapping roles of leaders in the NCNC and pan-Ibo movements. Azikiwe's leading preindependence rival, Chief Obafemi Awolowo, made telling use of occasional statements of ethnic pride by Azikiwe, as suggested in the following passage from his autobiography:

---

[4] M. M. Green, *Ibo Village Affairs* (London: Sidgewick and Jackson, 1947), pp. 6-7.

[5] For an excellent case study of these vigorous associations, see Audrey C. Smock, *Ibo Politics* (Cambridge: Harvard University Press, 1971); Chinua Achebe offers a vivid fictional account of one of these in *No Longer at Ease* (London: Heinemann, 1960).

[6] James S. Coleman, *Nigeria: Background to Nationalism* (Berkeley: University of California Press, 1958), p. 340.

Besides, in spite of his protestations to the contrary, Dr. Azikiwe was himself an unabashed Ibo jingoist. And he gave the game completely away when he said inter alia in his presidential address to the Ibo Federal Union in 1949, as follows:". . . It would appear that the God of Africa has specially created the Ibo nation to lead the children of Africa from the bondage of the ages. . . . The martial prowess of the Ibo nation at all stages of human history has enabled them not only to conquer others but also to adapt themselves to the role of preserver. . . ."

Awolowo concluded:

> It was clear from these statements and from the general political and journalistic maneuvers of Dr. Azikiwe over the years that his great objective was to set himself up as a dictator over Nigeria and to make the Ibo nation the master race. It would appear according to his reckoning that the only obstacle in the path of his ambition was the Yoruba intelligentsia, and these must be removed at all costs. . . . I am implacably opposed to dictatorship as well as the doctrine of *Herrenvolk* whether it was Hitler's or Dr. Azikiwe's.

A major activity of the Ibo Federal Union, and the many local Ibo associations, was the promotion of education; educational opportunity was by now widely perceived by all as critical to the competitive position of the group in the new postwar Nigeria. Competition also required the spread of the new ethnic consciousness back to the rural areas, a task also enthusiastically pursued by the ethnic associations. David Abernethy gives able summary to this twin process:

> What was the best course of action open to the urban migrant who was acutely concerned lest his ethnic group fall behind others in the struggle for wealth, power and status? Certainly the rural masses had to be informed of the problem. If the masses were not aware of their ethnicity, then they would have to learn who they really were through the efforts of "ethnic missionaries" returning to the homeland. These "missionaries" would also have to outline a strategy by which the ethnic group, once fully conscious of its unity and its potential, could compete with its rivals. . . . The gospel of ethnicity and the gospel of education were thus mutually reinforcing. Educational schemes sponsored by the tribal unions fostered ethnic consciousness in the rural areas; a heightened sense of ethnicity, in turn, facilitated the spread of education.[8]

In the Ibo case, Ibo Federal Union general secretary B. O. N. Eluwa undertook a number of tours of Iboland in 1947-1951; he reported that, at this point in time, many villagers could not even imagine all Ibos.[9]

[7] Obafemi Awolowo, *Awo* (Cambridge: Cambridge University Press, 1960), p. 172.
[8] Abernethy, *Dilemma of Education*, p. 108.
[9] Abernethy, *Dilemma of Education*, p. 110.

Thus, a short two decades before the proclamation of Biafra, Ibo identity formation, well advanced in the towns, was still very incomplete in rural areas. The 1950s were a period of constant political organization and activity, as a formula for independence was pursued. Elections in 1951, 1953, 1954, 1956, 1959, and 1964 for regional and national legislatures meant that electoral politics were constantly salient. Grant of effective African self-government at the regional level first, added to the significantly different administrative traditions of the three great regions of east, west, and north, meant that before a Nigerian national government was formed, dominant political movements reflecting the major subnationalities had been entrenched in the state machinery at the regional level. The ethnic idiom became built into the lexicon, and hence the perception of politics. Faced with alleged Ibo dominance in the NCNC, Awolowo rallied many Yoruba behind the Action Group (AG). In the north, the Northern Peoples' Congress (NPC), closely linked to the traditional hierarchies of the Hausa-Fulani states, was a riposte to the incursions of both southern Nigerian parties.

However, electoral competition should not be seen as simply a three-actor ethnic game. In each of the three regions, the dominant subnationality accounted for only approximately two-thirds of the population, with smaller groups comprising the remainder. Competitive modernization also produced new forms of ethnic awareness among these groups, sharpened by pervasive fears that Nigerian independence would result in their permanent subordination to the larger groups. One outlet for these fears was the demand for creation of new regions, which would move the "minorities" out from the shadow of the dominant groups. The other was the tendency for minority areas to serve as an electoral base for a dominant party from another region. Thus the AG sought to win support in non-Ibo areas of the Eastern Region; the NCNC became dominant in non-Yoruba areas of the Western Region, and both parties competed in the non-Muslim, non-Hausa "Middle Belt," or southern zone of the Northern Region.

Secondly, we must recall that ethnicity at the level of the Ibo, Yoruba, and Hausa-Fulani cultural groupings was superimposed upon, but did not obliterate, lower levels of identity, in the same manner illustrated for Mongo and Tonga in Chapter 3. Within Iboland, competition between Onitsha and Owerri Ibo was frequently strong. In any given urban center in eastern Nigeria, factionalism was likely to cohere about conflicting interests of "sons of the soil", who were indigenous to the neighborhood, and immigrant Ibo from other parts of Iboland. Rivalry between Catholics and Protestants was also significant. In the sprawling Yoruba city of Ibadan, fierce political competition occurred between Ibadan Yoruba, and those from other Yoruba subunits, in particular the commercially successful Ijebu Yoruba who were strongly represented in the AG leadership. So strong was this animosity in the 1950s that the Ibadan Yoruba entered into electoral coalition with the NCNC against the AG. The idea of

Yoruba unity, like Ibohood, was primarily an artifact of contemporary social and political competition. In the north, within the Hausa linguistic zone, the operative units were the separate Hausa-Fulani states, such as Kano, Sokoto, Zaria, and others; common language, a shared understanding of Islam, and the symbolic preeminence of the Sokoto emirate provided latent predisposing factors upon which northern political unity was constructed to meet the requirements of politics in the modern Nigerian arena.

Such then was the cultural amalgam upon which the giant state of Nigeria was launched into independence in 1960. We must again stress that social and political conflict is not solely explained by cultural pluralism. In particular, nascent social class differentials were also a fertile source of conflict. One outstanding student of Nigerian politics, Richard Sklar, has argued that we should primarily interpret Nigerian politics in terms of emergent class conflict, with the institutions of the independent state being the vehicles for what he terms "the rising class" of politicians, teachers, civil servants, traders, and intellectuals.[10] The regionalization of Nigerian politics thus gave the "rising class" a vested interest in ethnicity, as a basis for their own power. We would reformulate this proposition to suggest that the ethnic perception of politics had become so pervasive that a strong tendency existed for the articulation of conflict in ethnic terms, whatever its roots.

The formula for independence was a coalition between the NCNC and the NPC, with Azikiwe given ceremonial precedence as president, and a northern leader, Sir Abubakar Tafewa Balewa, more effective political power as prime minister. A series of events dissipated the euphoria of Nigerian independence in the first half-decade of self-rule; most important among these were the 1962-63 census dispute, the 1964 federal elections and 1965 Western Region elections, the two coups in 1966, and Ibo massacres of May and September-October 1966.

In the context of a Westminster electoral system allocating power on the basis of numbers, and the ethnic patterns of politics, the explosive potential of a census is self-evident. The first postindependence census began in 1961, with the knowledge by all that the new figures would serve as a basis for redistribution of parliamentary seats for the federal elections due in 1964. The results of the 1961-1962 count were never published, but became generally known in 1962; these figures showed the southern regions, which together had 83.5 percent of the total population of the north in the previous 1953 census, had now moved into a majority. The northern population was said to have increased by 33 percent, whereas the south had gone up by over 70 percent, with many areas of the east purported to have doubled in numbers. These results were attacked as preposterous. Northern leaders in particular were convinced the southern totals were fraudulently inflated; so intense was the storm that there seemed no recourse but to scrap the enumeration, and redo it from scratch.

[10]Richard Sklar, *Nigerian Political Parties* (Princeton: Princeton University Press, 1963.)

The second census, published in 1963, reversed the outcome of the first, with equally remarkable alterations in Nigerian demography. The north this time showed a 70 percent increase, the west more than doubled, and the east had grown by only 50 percent. An overall population of 55 million was recorded, which involved a nearly 7 percent per annum growth since 1953, a pace of increase that is demographically impossible – although the question remained whether Nigerians were undercounted in 1953, or overcounted in 1963. More important, to the Ibo, it implied manipulation of population figures to produce permanent minoritization.

At the same time, the northern party, NPC, had achieved an absolute majority in the federal legislature through carpet-crossing and was no longer dependent on its NCNC coalition partner. The NCNC leaders joined with one wing of the AG (now split) and other smaller formations to construct a broad electoral coalition for the 1964 elections, under the label "United Grand Progressive Alliance", or UPGA. Even with the new census results, UPGA organizers calculated that, in a free electoral competition, they might secure a majority by sweeping the southern constituencies and winning some seats in the minority areas and urban zones of the north.

But tensions in the Nigerian polity were simply too high for free elections. The incumbent political class on all sides had too much at stake in wealth, power, and status. The NPC dominated counter-alliance, the Nigerian National Alliance (NNA), had no intention of permitting UPGA to win seats in the north. In the spiral of fraud, intimidation, thuggery, and violence, it becomes impossible to discern who has struck the first blow; each contestant was convinced that he was taking measures only in self-defense.[11] The NNA, with superior resources at its disposal, emerged triumphant. Indignant UPGA backers spoke of the breakup of Nigeria, but a tenuous national coalition, including some NCNC figures, was reconstructed in the early days of 1965.

The last hopes of effecting political change in Nigeria through the electoral system evaporated in October 1965, when regional elections took place in the Western Region, by this time governed by a splinter of the old AG which had become wholly dependent on northern backing. If the UPGA alliance could win power in the west, all of southern Nigeria's regional institutions would be joined in a front against northern domination. So far was the Lagos regime discredited by this time by corruption and ineffectiveness, as well as the feared conservative northern domination, that there could be little doubt as to the outcome of an openly conducted election in the west – so little doubt, indeed, that the incumbents backed by Lagos intervened even more extensively than in 1964 in fixing the results.

The decomposition of the first Nigerian republic was by this point far advanced. Various conspiracies began to take form, and rumors multiplied. In

---

[11] For a richly insightful, fictionalized account based upon these elections, see Chinua Achebe, *A Man of the People* (London: Heinemann, 1966).

January 1966, many believed that the northern leadership intended a preventative coup of their own, to complete their control over the Lagos institutions. In the event, in the early morning hours of January 15, 1966, a cabal of army majors struck, to cleanse Nigeria of corruption, reaction, and tribalism. There is little evidence to support the thesis that the coup was an Ibo conspiracy, although six of the seven majors and nineteen of the twenty-three second echelon leaders were Ibo. There is no reason to doubt the genuine commitment to a radical reform of Nigeria, and reinforcement of its unity, which the majors proclaimed as their objective. Indeed, the coup was welcomed throughout the country with rejoicing, or at least benevolent neutrality, so far discredited was the federal government. But aspects of the coup's composition and tactics soon gave rise to suspicions of ethnic factors.[12]

Apparently, the coup-makers intended to neutralize the federal government and four regional governments, and remove the top command of the armed forces. In the event, the coup was successful in obtaining initial control only in the north, and partially in Lagos and the Western Region. The northern prime minister, Balewa, and regional premier Sir Ahmadu Bello (the most powerful man in the first republic), as well as the Western Region premier were killed, as were a number of senior officers. Of the seventeen army officers of lieutenant colonel rank and above, seven were killed (and more apparently slated for execution, but could not be apprehended on the night of the long knives). None of the seventeen was Ibo, but only one was killed while denying access to a Lagos armory to the conspirators. Six of the eight others, including four of the five northerners, were killed.

But the coup aborted, and the commander-in-chief, J. T. U. Aguiyi Ironsi, himself an Ibo, rallied the garrisons by the late morning of January 15 and forestalled the assumption of power by the majors. The surviving members of the federal cabinet simply abdicated, and a military regime under General Ironsi took over. The Ironsi regime enjoyed widespread initial support, especially in the south; a new departure toward One Nigeria seemed possible.

But the initial momentum quickly evaporated, and ethnic tensions escalated to more dangerous levels. General Ironsi was certainly not an Ibo chauvinist; indeed, he had probably been slated for execution by the majors. But he was ineffectual, and his regime came to be seen as serving Ibo interests. When in May 1966, twelve promotions to lieutenant colonel to replace the dead officers were announced, nine were Ibo. In fact, none was promoted over officers more senior in date of rank than himself, but this did not diminish the psychological impact. Many of Ironsi's inner cabinet of advisors were Ibo. The army was not exempt from these tensions; the great majority of enlisted ranks were northern. The troops had been initially confused, then many outraged by

---

[12] Of the many accounts of the 1966 coups, we find the most cogent and best-informed to be that of Robin Luckham, *The Nigerian Military* (Cambridge: Cambridge University Press, 1971).

what they saw as the ethnic selectivity in the massacre of senior officers. Control of Ibo officers over northern troops became tenuous.

On May 24, 1966, General Ironsi decreed the abolition of the old regions, and the recasting of Nigeria as a unitary state. Almost immediately, the north exploded, with a first wave of killings of Ibo in several cities. At this point, the deaths ran in the hundreds, and thousands fled back to the Eastern Region. These disorders were accompanied by a cry for nothern secession. However, Ironsi partly retreated on the unification edict; Colonel Odumegwa Ojukwu, military governor of the Eastern Region, reassured the refugees and urged them to return to the north.

Two months later, on July 29, the decomposition of the military structure reached a new low, with a second, loosely organized coup, organized this time by northern officers. Vengeance was levied in full measure for the January murders. General Ironsi was seized and assassinated; assaults were mounted against Ibo officers and men in garrisons throughout the country. Of 39 officers killed, 27 were Ibo, and the rest other southerners. Of the 171 enlisted men recorded as casualties by Robin Luckham, all but a handful were Ibo.[13] On this occasion, the hierarchy of the security forces, guarantor of the integrity of the state, was all but pulverized. The ranking officer, Brigadier B. A. O. Ogundipe, declined to assume command; as a Yoruba, he felt there was no way to impose his authority – at the moment of decision, he was stunned when an ordinary sergeant declined to obey his order until he could consult his northern captain. The next-in-line, Yakubu Gowon, a Christian northerner from a small "minority" group, was sufficiently acceptable to northern elements in the army to assume power – in the eyes of many, merely to preside over the dissolution of Nigeria. Remaining easterners in the army had fled back to their region; northern elements among the army garrison there were removed. The merest breeze would suffice to tumble the tottering Nigerian edifice.

It was at this point that the top leadership of what became Biafra made the decision for secession, although it was not carried out until nine months later.[14] Secession was also seriously urged in the north, and even, or occasion, in the west. Constitutional talks with "leaders of thought" were organized in September 1966, to see what could be salvaged. Eastern and northern delegations arrived with briefs for exceedingly loose confederation, with the west ambivalent.

All parties were faced with an agonizing recalculation of costs and benefits of at least a relatively united Nigeria. One major segment of Nigeria quickly realized that it would lose heavily, and incur unknown but possibly grave risks in the hypothesis of separate Ibo, Yoruba, and Hausa-Fulani independent or

---

[13] Luckham, *Nigerian Military*, p. 76.

[14] The former head of the Biafran civil service, N. U. Akpan, offers convincing evidence on this point in his memories, *The Struggle for Secession 1966–1970* (London: Frank Cass, 1971), p. 71.

loosely confederated states; this was the "minority" third of the population. Their intervention at a critical stage in the debates, when the sands seemed to be running out on a united Nigeria, was decisive. The northern delegation swung sharply away from their confederal position, leaving the east isolated. The polarization of the east versus the rest was completed when, as the talks were coming to a close, a new wave of Ibo massacres broke out in the north. This time the magnitude of the tragedy was far greater; estimates of the dead ran from six to thirty thousand. As many as one million refugees streamed back to the eastern region. The traumatism of these events in a culturally polarized atmosphere can hardly be exaggerated. A former senior (non-Ibo) Biafran official describes the overpowering emotional impact on himself and the large crowd at the sight of maimed, dazed people emerging from one of the refugee trains — with the most unspeakable sight of all a naked woman stumbling from a carriage, holding aloft the severed head of her murdered child.[15]

Ethnic mobilization of the Ibo was now virtually total. Hardly a lineage had not lost a member in the northern massacres. Negotiations to acquire arms were quietly begun. Ibo faculty and students from Ibadan and other universitites returned to the east, as evangelists of secession. The road to secession had one last detour, with a momentarily euphoric conference of military leaders at Aburi, Ghana in January 1967, which gave rise to a short-lived accord on a very confederal formula. However, this accord quickly foundered on divergent interpretations of the agreement, and the conviction of many Nigerian officials that far too much had been conceded. Secession and civil war were now only a matter of time.

The troubled year before secession showed remarkable fluctuation in positions as ethnic perception of arena and situation went through kaleidoscopic changes. For Ibo, the January coup seemed to usher in a new age with unity, equality, and social competition by the merit system, which would assure a comfortable niche for the Ibo elite. In the north, confusion gave way to a growing feeling that the balance was altering to the fundamental disadvantage of all northerners. The July coup participants were from all parts of the north, not only the Hausa-Fulani areas. By September, however, a sharp divergence in perspective had arisen between the Hausa-Fulani and "minorities" in the north, with the latter drawing back from rearrangements of Nigeria that risked permanent hegemonic overrule by the Hausa-Fulani elites. A similarly strong position was taken by non-Yoruba in the midwest; their intervention had the effect of changing the perspectives of the Yoruba as well, toward reaffirmation of Nigeria. In the final months before the secession, the arena came to be seen in increasingly bipolar terms, simply as a conflict between the Ibo and the rest. Thus it was that, although eight months before the Biafran secession ambivalence about the desirability of Nigerian unity was profound in west and north as well as east, when General Ojukwu's declaration of independence was

[15] Akpan, *Struggle for Secession,* p. xii.

made on May 30, 1967 the remainder of Nigeria swung behind the war of reconquest; only the Midwest hesitated.

The 1966-67 period also calls into fundamental question the widespread postulate concerning the integrative role of the military in culturally diverse polities. We must not overlook the likelihood that the tensions of cultural conflict in the society at large will be reflected within the armed forces, and the possibility, demonstrated in the Nigerian instance, that they may shatter its hierarchy. In the words of an informed student of Nigerian military politics:

> We are then left with a situation where the officers of a certain tribal group become but the armed wing of a tribal political group, fighting against a similar combination of tribal group politicians and officers of the opposing tribe. The old political conflict is then fought out again, but the medium of conflict is no longer political maneuver, manifestos, votes, and speeches, but rather violence, with an immense advantage to the side which strikes first. This is a situation of lawless confrontation, analogous to some models of international affairs; it has its own inherent logic towards pre-emptive strikes and treacherous violence.[16]

None of those who made the critical decisions when the secession was declared and civil war launched could have had much notion of the human costs of a civil conflict. Indeed, many in the east were spoiling for a rumble with the "Hausa," who were deemed responsible for the pogroms. Federal leaders stated that a fortnight blitzkreig would do the job; Ojukwu was felt by his colleagues to be a morbid pessimist in believing that three months would be necessary to secure the secession.[17]

In the event, the war lasted more than thirty months. Rather quickly, Biafra was reduced to a landlocked Ibo redoubt, shorn of its minority areas both by federal military action, and the remorseless logic of distrustful relations with the non-Ibo minorities. Although non-Ibo minorities shared in the tragedy of the northern pogroms, and the intensely emotional reaction to them, even at moments of maximum eastern solidarity the attitude toward secession was at best ambivalent. When the war started, relations quickly deteriorated. Ibo suspected — with good reason — the fidelity of the minorities to the Biafran cause; each advance of federal forces through minority areas was said to be abetted by minority fifth columns. These accusations of sabotage of the Biafran cause were frequently followed by reprisals against minorities still within the Biafran lines. The most costly of these was exacted against Ijaw villages outside Port Harcourt, after the federal army had ousted Biafran forces from this key

---

[16] M. J. Dent, in Robert Melson and Howard Wolpe, *Nigeria: Modernization and the Politics of Communalism* (East Lansing: Michigan State University Press, 1971), p. 368.

[17] Akpan, *Struggle for Secession,* p. 90.

port. It is no accident that, in the aftermath of the civil war, the one place in the Nigerian federation where it was absolutely unsafe for Ibo to return was in the Port Harcourt zone.

Within the Ibo heartland, however, the passions that had led to the desire for vengeance on the north gave way to a chilling fear that the ghastly carnage of the north would be repeated in Biafra itself. The spector of genocide was a chimera, but few Ibo could be persuaded of that fact during the struggle itself. After expectations of a quick and easy victory faded, the only hope was that prolongation of the struggle would eventually mobilize world opinion against Nigeria and impose a settlement from outside.

On the Nigerian side, the prosecution of the war brought a level of unity that had never before been known. The breakup of the old regions into twelve states, which led to General Ironsi's downfall and death the year before, was proclaimed by General Gowon in May 1967, and accepted without a whimper. The "minority" groups were offered a degree of security and participation in the affairs of the republic that had never previously been known; the idea of "Nigeria" penetrated far further into the periphery of the polity than it ever had before.[18] The Nigerian army, a modest five-battalion force of ten thousand men on the eve of the crisis, swelled to two hundred thousand — and remained at that level after the war. The power relationship between the center and the component states was radically altered, which in turn necessarily affected the perspectives of political actors as to choices available in the interaction between national and subnational roles and identities.

With the collapse of the Biafran regime in January 1970, the war came to a sudden end. Many, impressed with the overwhelming solidarity of the Ibo people during the dreary months of isolation and defeat during the latter stages of the war, had made dire forecasts of an endless guerilla battle that would follow the end of organized resistance. But neither partisan struggle nor the oft-forecast genocide ensued. Beside the many lives lost, the Ibo elite had lost heavily — their wealth, their positions in public bureaucracies. With surprising swiftness, however, the spirit of rejuvenation began to return. Small numbers of Ibo traders ventured back to the north to recover their sequestered properties. Communities reconstituted themselves; the economy began to recover. Ibohood has not died, but its perspectives have altered. The complex prism of hope and fear through which the future is contemplated is firmly set within the Nigerian frame; whether this is seen as a confining prison or a larger stage for the fulfillment of Ibo talents, there is not, at least in the immediate future, any alternative. That simple but basic fact is perhaps the most fundamental point of departure for assessing the pattern of social identity and political change in post-civil war Nigeria.

[18] Ronald Cohen provides fascinating detail on the integrative impact of the civil war on the hitherto isolated 1,000-year-old Kanuri-speaking Muslim state of Bornu, in northeastern Nigeria in Melson and Wolpe, *Nigeria,* pp. 559–75.

BANGLADESH

The Bangladesh insurrection enters history as an independence struggle rather than a secessionist revolt. The reasons for the different outcome relate primarily to the contrasting structure of force, in particular the crucial Indian intervention. Whereas a momentarily successful separation in Biafra was crushed by Nigerian forces when it could not secure sufficient international backing, central power that had made a pre-emptive strike to anticipate a secession in East Bengal was ousted with the decisive backing of external force.

The genesis of Bangladesh lies in the formation of Pakistan itself, which in turn was born of the complex process of emergent nationalism interacting with a decolonization founded on the principle of deriving power from majority rule in a continent of extraordinary cultural diversity. The forces we have cited throughout this section — competitive modernization, politization of communal identities through the electoral process, shifting patterns of saliency of alternative foci of identity dependent upon varying definitions of the socio-political arena — gave rise in turn to the Muslim League and Pakistan, and the Awami League and Bangladesh.

Although Islam first reached the Indian subcontinent in 712 A.D., its period of major expansion was several centuries later; its high water mark was during the Mughal empire, a Muslim dynasty centered in north India in the period just prior to British rule. There were some pockets of Muslims to be found throughout India, but the two major concentrations were in the northwestern region, which is now West Pakistan, and in East Bengal. There were major differences between these two Muslim communities; in the West Pakistan area, Persian influences were strong, and contacts with the major world centers of Islamic learning were far closer.

Bengal came under Muslim rule in the thirteenth century. Over the following centuries, conversion to Islam was widespread, with many of its converts found in the depressed lower castes; it is certainly no accident that Bengal had both a high degree of conversion to Islam, and the highest concentration of lower castes and untouchables in the subcontinent. Thus, Bengali Islam prior to British rule was at once a religion of the ruling elite and of depressed rural populations.

During the nineteenth century, a new pattern of polarization began to emerge between Hindu and Muslim in the Indian subcontinent. With the introduction of Western education, and a gradually enlarging set of new professional and administrative roles becoming available, a modern elite took form, heavily recruited from Hindu ranks. In the richly stratified Indian society, recruitment into modern roles was concentrated at the upper levels. Whereas the occupational traditions of a number of the Hindu upper castes, such as the set of castes often labelled Brahman, were quite congenial to modernization, Muslim elites found the Islamic world view, with its traditions of learning and piety, wholly satisfying. Western education was suspiciously tinged with Christianity. The English school, quite often under religious auspices, was a veritable Trojan horse of deculturization. During this period, only in exceptional cases did lower caste Hindu or poor rural Muslims, less assimilated to the "great tradition" of Islamic observance, have any opportunity for access to schools, and hence social mobility. The Muslim disadvantage was above all in Bengal.

Thus by 1881, of the 37,000 Indian students enrolled in English secondary schools, only 363 were Muslims.[19] By this time, the first voices began to be raised in the Muslim community, calling for acceptance of secular education, on pain otherwise of being locked into subordinate roles in the new institutions. At the same time, the Muslim leader who first urged Westernization, Sir Syed Ahmad Khan, also was the first to forecast the ultimate outcome of the dialectics of competitive modernization. In 1867, he made his prophetic remark: "I am convinced that the two communities will not sincerely cooperate in any work. Opposition and hatred between them, which is felt so little today, will in the future be seen to increase on account of the so-called educated classes.[20]

In the late nineteenth century, the first timid steps began to be taken toward eventual self-government. Indians were admitted to the Indian Civil Service, and the first electoral bodies established by the Morley-Minto reforms. Congress was formed in 1885, initially as a moderate, reform-oriented caucus of the new Indian elite. The prospective introduction of the electoral principle helped stimulate the foundation of the Muslim League in 1906; Muslims demanded — and were granted — separate Muslim and Hindu voting rolls in the 1909 reforms. As the pace of political change quickened, Muslims came to realize the high costs of remaining encased in the cocoon of traditional piety. Their growing fears are well expressed by a former Prime Minister of Pakistan, describing the forebodings produced by the prospect of representative government:

> ... The fact is the Muslims were greatly outdistanced by the Hindus in practically every field of social and economic endeavor, and the Hindus had come to regard this state of inequality as their birthright, due to them by virtue of their superior education, social status, and economic strength. They were determined to maintain and, if possible to improve, their position by means of political power. Prospects of democracy thus intensified the struggle between Hindus and Muslims. Democracy is rule by majority, but if the majority is fixed and hereditary, and also enjoys the privileges of superior education, greater economic and administrative power, control over the press, and talent and money for political organization, the minority is doomed forever to a position of subordination.[21]

[19] Chaudri Muhammad Ali, *The Emergence of Pakistan* (New York: Columbia University Press, 1967), p. 7.
[20] Ali, *Emergence of Pakistan*, p. 9.
[21] Ali, *Emergence of Pakistan*, p. 11.

Bengal was the first major center of British overrule in India, former Prime Minister Jawaharlal Nehru noted that it had a clear half-century of British rule before it spread over other areas, and produced the first groups of English-educated Indians who "gave the lead to the rest of India in cultural and political matters, and out of whose efforts the new nationalist movement ultimately took shape."[22] By the beginning of the twentieth century, nationalism in Bengal was becoming uncomfortably aggressive for the British, even developing a small but highly visible terrorist wing at its extreme fringes. Further, although nationalism did not speak for Hindu interests, in the 150 years preceding the turn of the century, Bengal had been transformed from Muslim hegemony to Hindu predominance, under British overrule, in virtually all sectors of the economic realm, from urban commerce to rural land ownership. In 1905, on the ostensible grounds that Bengal had become an unwieldy unit, it was divided into two provinces. The still inchoate Muslim opinion appeared to favor the partition, especially in the areas that now have become Bangladesh, where the numerical preponderance of the Muslims was greatest; in their eyes, this would diminish the position of the great Calcutta-based Hindu merchants and landlords.

However, articulate nationalist opinion, primarily Hindu, strongly opposed the partition, as a cunning scheme to weaken the nascent nationalist movement. When the British retreated in 1911 and reunified Bengal, many Muslims feared that nationalist grievance as a cloak for Hindu interests would always carry the day.

After World War I, the creaking machinery of decolonization began to grind slowly forward. For a period in the interwar era, there seemed a real possibility that a secular nationalism committed to a single India might win the adhesion of all. To such a vision much of the Congress leadership was devoted. But the heightened self-awareness of religious, linguistic, and caste communities inevitably produced an ongoing process of calculation and recalculation of hope and fear, gain and loss, as the image of independent India gradually assumed form and content. At the 1930 Congress of the Muslim League, presided over by a renowned poet, the fateful call was first made for a separate, Muslim state – although at this point only in northwest India, and not including Bengal. A decade later, at Lucknow in 1940, the Muslim League officially – and, in the event irrevocably – committed itself to partition. However, significantly, the Lucknow Resolution declared that "... the areas in which the Muslims are numerically in a majority as in the north-western and eastern zones of India should be grouped to constitute independent States in which the constituent units shall be autonomous and sovereign...."[23] The reference to "independent states" in the plural partly reflects the absence of specific thought as to what partition would mean; it is nonetheless significant in foreshadowing the lack of cohesion of Pakistan as a nation.

[22] Jawaharlal Nehru, *The Discovery of India* (London: Meridian Books, 1966), p. 314.
[23] Ali, *Emergence of Pakistan,* p. 38.

As the final negotiations immediately after World War II began to determine the shape of independent India, the Hindu-Muslim conflict became the transcendant issue, eclipsing virtually all else. The degree of polarization on this axis of differentiation was reflected in the nearly complete sweep of Muslim seats by the Muslim League in elections in 1945-1946. In mid-1946, the first communal rioting pitting Muslim against Hindu occurred. The thousands of casualties that resulted from these almost uncontrollable conflagrations demonstrated the gravity of the situation and the totality of the impasse. Although a desperate last effort was made in 1946 to find some formula for the preservation of one India, by March 1947 the Congress leadership had given up hope of averting Pakistan. The dual birth of India and Pakistan in August 1947 was accompanied by the communal holocaust that took the lives of countless thousands and produced twelve million refugees, as both Hindu and Muslim fled minority status. The massacres and population movements were concentrated on the West Pakistan side; nearly ten million Hindus remained in East Pakistan, whereas in the remainder of India sixty million Muslims stayed.

Pakistan took its first steps as a nation in extraordinarily difficult circumstances. The apparatus of a state had to be created from scratch, with the most minimal of means. The great majority of the Indian Civil Service was Hindu. Even within what became Pakistan, much of the economy had been dominated by Hindu traders and merchants; in East Bengal, this also applied to landholding. Although their removal offered new opportunities for social mobility for Muslims, in the short run their skills were difficult to replace. And, within the Muslim community, modernization had been very imbalanced; Punjabis were disproportionately represented in the new elite that assumed the levers of command. The great, charismatic figure of the Pakistan movement, Mohammed Jinnah, died within a year of independence; as a Bombay Gujerati, Jinnah was outside of the east-west duality in Pakistan, and his loss was a heavy blow to the new state.

With the powerful, aligning force of the communal conflict with the Hindu removed, it was not long before a new dialectic of regional tension within Pakistan set in. The two regions were separated by 1,000 miles of India. The Islamic basis for a united state was precarious from the outset, as the religious traditions in East Bengal were quite distinctive. In particular, Bengalis did not share the commitment to Urdu as an element of Islamic identity which was strongly felt in West Pakistan. And it was around the issue of a national language that the first serious confrontation between East and West Pakistan took place.

Urdu is a varient of Hindi, written in Persian script and heavily influenced by Persian and to some extent Arabic which the ruling Muslim elite of the Mughal empire had developed. Even in West Pakistan, it was not a mother tongue for very many; according to the 1951 Pakistan census, only 7.2 percent of the total population of the country spoke it, compared to 54.6 percent of the Pakistani population who spoke Bengali (the latter figure reflecting the demographic predominance of East Pakistan).[24] But it was viewed as a central symbol of the new nation by West Pakistani elites, who sought to establish it as the sole official language. The peak of the Urdu-only campaign was in 1952; when disorders broke out in East Pakistan, led by rioting students at Dacca University, the Karachi government backed down and conceded official status to Bengali as well. But de facto efforts to promote Urdu continued.

The flight of Hindu landlords from East Bengal permitted a de facto land reform, with former tenants acquiring rights over the small plots of land they occupied; this reform by default provided short-run benefits to rural Muslims. However, the administration created in East Pakistan was heavily dominated by Punjabi and other non-Bengali personnel; in all of the Indian Civil Service in 1947, there was only one Bengali Muslim, a representative measure of the near-total absence of Bengalis who could fill modern roles.[25] A novel problem of social disparity, which escaped the notice of most analysts of Pakistani politics until the crisis broke in 1971, grew from the influx into East Bengal of nearly one million Muslim refugees from north central India, who were collectively known as "Biharis," although not all were from that province. Many of the "Bihari" refugees were comparatively skilled; as the economic and bureaucratic infrastructure of East Pakistan took shape, Biharis became increasingly visible as a new elite.

Bengali dissatisfaction with Pakistan remained close to the surface throughout the first two decades of independence, but did not coalesce as an active movement. Perhaps part of the explanation lies in the greater voice Bengal might expect to have when a democratic constitution was finally elaborated, and power allocated at the center on the basis of majority rule; here the numerical preponderance of East Bengal would work to its clear advantage. Independence was achieved without a constitution, and the early years of independence saw interminable labors towards the elaboration of a basic law, accompanied by a swift succession of ineffectual regimes. However, the very top Bengali political elite did participate in the endlessly dissolving political cabals in Karachi and shared in the benefits of periodic access to high office. Parliamentarians elected under British India, with swiftly diminishing credibility, were eager participants in a process by which, in the words of one analyst, successive prime ministers had "the daily task of rounding up at various prices sufficient supporters in the legislature to remain in office."[26] But clear evidence of the extent of the decomposition of the Jinnah movement came when regional elections were held in East Pakistan. The Muslim League, party of Pakistani independence, was crushed by the Bengali-oriented Awami League in 1954.

[24] Karl von Vorys, *Political Development in Pakistan* (Princeton: Princeton University Press, 1965), p. 90.
[25] Khalid Bin Sayeed, *Pakistan: The Formative Phase* (Karachi: Pakistan Publishing House, 1960), pp. 298–301.
[26] Von Vorys, *Development in Pakistan*, p. 124.

By 1958, Pakistan seemed on the verge of chaos. In the East Pakistan Assembly, the Speaker was assaulted, the Deputy Speaker killed, and the national flag desecrated. The army, under General Ayub Khan, took power, and dissidence for a time was quieted. A period of swift economic growth followed, which at the national level gave restored self-confidence and probably, combined with the evident superior force of the army, dampened discontents. But Bengali grievances remained. The benefits of economic growth, it was felt, were concentrated in West Pakistan — and those that were conspicuously successful in the east often were not Bengalis. Throughout this period, the hostility to India that was an important common denominator of nationhood revolved about issues that primarily affected West Pakistan: Kashmir, the division of the Indus basin waters. The brief and inglorious war of 1965 was also fought in the West.

In 1966, Bengali discontents were crystallized into a "six point program", propounded by Sheikh Mujibur Rahman, General Secretary of the Awami League. Rahman's Six Point Program catapulted him to the first rank of what had been an ineffectual array of politicians. The six points were a platform for virtually complete autonomy, conceding only foreign policy and defense to Karachi. East Bengal would have a separate currency, sole powers of taxation, and its own militia.

In 1967, Rahman and thirty-four Awami Leaguers were charged by the Pakistan government with an elaborate conspiracy, involving secret contacts with India to gain backing for a guerrilla force; this is the earliest indication of the possible emergence of an organized uprising, although the charges were never fully proved. However, rioting broke out in early 1969, with demands for Rahman's release from prison and acceptance of the Six Point Program. With troubles in West Pakistan as well, General Ayub Khan turned over power to another army commander, General Yahya Khan, in March 1969. The latter immediately promised national elections with universal suffrage.

After some delays, the promised elections were held in December 1970, with Sheikh Mujibur Rahman's Awami League winning 80 percent of the vote, and 167 of the 169 East Pakistan seats, thus assuring Bengali antonomists an absolute majority in the all-Pakistan constituent assembly, which was to draft a new constitution. This sweeping triumph reflected the powerful attraction of the Six Point Program and, at a minimum, total Bengali autonomy. Bengali sentiments had been intensified the previous month when typhoon-borne floods had killed 200,000 persons. East Pakistanis believed that the Karachi government was laggard and indifferent in its response to this national disaster.

West Pakistan was not prepared in the last analysis to accept the degree of antonomy that the Bengalis claimed via the Six Point Program. Efforts at negotiation apparently came close to success at one or two points, but in the end the viewpoints remained irreconcilable. In March 1971, a civil disobedience campaign paralyzed East Pakistan; then on March 25, the Pakistani army, heavily dominated by West Pakistanis, which had been quietly reinforced, undertook a violent crackdown. Although in the short run, by dint of a merciless, ill-disciplined terrorism, a precarious order was restored in the urban centers, the scale of the repression sundered the last tenuous links of attachment to Pakistan. At this juncture, only the immigrant "Biharis" were willing to cooperate with what was no longer Pakistani administration, but a military occupation. Thus three-quarter million Biharis, as intermediaries for the Pakistan army, became indelibly stained with the sins of the repression.

After the initial shock, a real guerrilla force rapidly came into being, the "mukti bahini" (freedom fighters). Little is yet known about the sociological contours of these groups, nor how much of a nucleus existed prior to the Pakistani repression. What is clear is that the crucial support elements of sanctuary and supplies became available from India after March. The magnitude of the Pakistani repression had touched every corner of the land; this specific catalyst, added to the generalized Bengali grievances that had festered since independence, meant that a virtually inexhaustible pool of young men was available, and the complete backing of the population was assured.

Ten million refugees streamed into India as a result of the hostilities. This was an intolerable burden; on one border West Bengal already had population as high as any in India. On the other border in Assam and other more sparsely settled areas to the northeast a Bengali influx that threatened to swamp the local linguistic community was radically unacceptable. For this reason alone, India had a high stake in a resolution of the crisis. To this inducement must be added the inescapable attraction of splitting Pakistan and the emergence of a secular state in East Bengal that would have more cordial relations with India.[27]

The following nine months were a nightmarish impasse. The mukti bahini could make West Pakistanis insecure everywhere but could not defeat their well-equipped army. Finally, in December 1971 the Indian army intervened. This no doubt inevitable move decisively altered the relationship of force. Now the Pakistani army, cut off from resupply, unable to secure the intervention of any foreign protector, faced a hopeless struggle. The invasion required only a week to bring about the surrender of the Pakistani army units. The proclamation of Bangladesh independence followed immediately, with widespread international recognition coming swiftly. Thus was born the world's eighth most populous nation, and the third biggest in population of the postwar new nations.

THE SECESSIONS COMPARED

In what ways do the similarities in causation and contrast in outcome instruct us on the politics of cultural pluralism? What significance lies in the birth of Bangladesh and the death of Biafra for the developing world? These two

---

[27]Marcus F. Franda, "Population Politics in South Asia," Parts I–III, in American University Field Staff, *Fieldstaff Reports*, 16, Nos. 2–4 (1972).

complex dramas, presented in only the most summary form here, deserve much more extensive study and certainly will receive it. Let us restrict ourselves here to a few conclusions, which relate these crises to the general comparative analysis that preceded.

To begin with, the rapid acceleration to the pace of social change, in which even over a single generation groups can visibly alter their collective standing, is a critical factor. Since the beginning of this century, the Ibo had moved from an almost wholly rural collection of local societies to a mobilized, partly urbanized collectivity with a sizable elite, and a much vaster group of primary school leavers prone to urban migration. It is certainly not implied that all Ibo had altered their social standing. However, a sufficient number had done so to create a generalized image, both in their own minds and in the eyes of their competitors, so that the "Ibo" ranked highly in the economic scale. In the case of the "Biharis," the creation of a new status group in East Bengal had been even swifter. Over a longer period, between the eighteenth and twentieth centuries, Muslims in Bengal had dropped from politically dominant status to a situation of crippling handicap in ability to furnish personnel for modern roles.

Secondly, both cases illustrate the process of crystallization and politization of social identities. Ibohood is an entirely novel, but no less meaningful, matrix of loyalty. Although a sense of membership in the Muslim community clearly preexisted contemporary politics, nonetheless it was given a new intensity by the political conflict over the future of India and the creation of Pakistan; the high saliency of communal identity caused it to affect a much wider range of social interactions than had previously been the case.

Thirdly, most members of the political community have multiple identities. This point was illustrated earlier in the Ibo case. In Bengal, the structure of conflict during the debate over decolonizaiton of the Indian subcontinent put forward all of India as the arena, and the Hindu/Muslim duality as the most salient cultural conflict. After 1947, Pakistan was the arena, and religion was not a significant differentiator. However, linguistic community was, and Bengali identity served as the orienting cognitive focus for most actors in Bangladesh.

Fourthly, the conflicts arising from differential access to economic and social rewards (or social class) are frequently perceived in ethnic or communal terms. The animosity to Ibo immigrants in other parts of Nigeria was generally related to a partly false perception that they were extraordinarily advantaged in the distribution of economic benefits. The Ibo determination to secede, in reaction, came at a moment when they had concluded that other groups in Nigeria were determined to exclude them on a systematic basis from the places to which individual merit would give title. In Bangladesh, Muslims had felt in colonial Bengal that they had become a deprived community relative to Hindu Bengalis, owing to British policies. After the creation of Pakistan, the same group found themselves, this time as Bengalis, still disadvantaged, now with relation to Punjabis and Biharis.

Although both roads led to secession, the routes were quite different, and of course the ultimate outcome in total contrast. In the case of Biafra, a chain of historical circumstance had placed the region in control of its own security forces; it could therefore proclaim secession, and endeavor to make it stick. The Bengalis were never in control of the apparatus of government or administration in East Pakistan and were never well-represented in the army officer corps, as were the Ibo at one point. Resistance, when it came, was through the guise of a guerrilla movement, rather than a regular army as in the Biafran instance. Conversely, it is more difficult to decisively defeat a guerrilla movement, especially one as broadly based and even spontaneous as the mukti bahini, when they have external support and places of sanctuary. Thus, once the federal army had defeated the Biafran forces in Nigeria, all resistance collapsed. In Bangladesh, despite the initial advantage of control of the machinery of government and overwhelming force, the Pakistani army could not win. Finally, the elementary fact of contiguity was critical. Iboland — once events demonstrated that the minorities in the Eastern Region felt more secure in the Nigerian Federation than in Ibo-dominated Biafra — was isolated and landlocked. This, added to the anti-secessionist ideology that is strong among African states, greatly diminished the effectiveness of such international assistance as was received. In the Bangladesh instance, Indian intervention was both crucial and sufficient.

One may also note the different dialectic of conflict. The final act of Bangladesh independence began with a military repression of the Bengali populace so severe and undiscriminating that a gap of animosity became an unbridgeable chasm of hatred. In the Biafran instance, although pogroms directed mainly against Ibo did occur in the north and were a major precipitant of secession, the federal army was never in a position to crush the idea of secessionism in the bud, as Yahya Khan tried to do. They had rather to carry out a classical invasion of the separated region. Although the conviction that this operation would lead ineluctably to genocide reinforced Ibo determination to maintain the struggle well beyond the point when hopes of victory could be seriously entertained, reality was very different. Although the record of the Nigerian army was not without blemish, on the whole the occupation of Iboland was carried out with restraint. The most striking fact is a degree of reconciliation that few would have believed possible in so short a time at the height of the hostilities.

Both Biafra and Bangladesh are extreme cases, but we would suggest that the latter is the most exceptional of all. Despite the strains placed upon the polity by cultural diversity, successful separation requires a wholly exceptional combination of circumstances and forces, likely to occur only in very rare cases.

CHAPTER 5

Nation-Building: Coexisting with Cultural Pluralism

By way of conclusion, we return to the question of nation-building. Prolonged immersion in the multifold problems of cultural pluralism would seem to lead to gnawing doubts about the viability of the territorial state system, especially in parts of Asia and Africa. And yet we feel that such pervasive pessimism is unwarranted; we need again to stress that, however imposing the dimensions of the challenge, they have been inevitably distorted by the analytical technique of extrapolating from the totality of social and political life of these polities those phases related to the cultural pluralism question. Manifestations of cultural pluralism, however important, are only part of the picture. Focus on this dimension leaves other forms of conflict and consensus unanalyzed. For example, social and economic class are often crucial factors. In Latin America in particular, this factor is probably more important than the problems discussed here.

Even within the framework of our analysis, we should emphasize that the evidence does not necessarily suggest an inexorable heightening of cultural tensions within the polity. There are several salient trends correlated with the general process of social mobilization. Awareness of territorial affiliation, and often deepening identification with it, is unquestionably increasing. The rise of national independence movements doubtless created a situational context more favorable to the reinforcement of territorial sentiment than the immediate postindependence situation; yet in most polities the long-term trend may well be toward a growing legitimation of the state as nation.

Simultaneously, social mobilization is creating transformed, enlarged, and thus "modernized" subnational cultural identification. Realistically, there seems no basis for assuming that this pattern will change; however, the sentiments of national and cultural identification are not mutually exclusive – except in situations that require the actor to choose between roles. There are a number of instances where national identification seems to be diffusing more rapidly than cultural pluralism. In Indonesia, for example, one of the rare achievements of the Sukarno regime was the strengthening of a national sentiment beyond Java into the outer reaches of the archipelago. In Ghana, Guinea, Zaire, and Tanzania, headway in promoting national identity has been rapid. In Latin America, a unique formula has been evolved to transform the latent challenge of culture pluralism into a positive symbol of national identification, through the Guarani myth in Paraguay and the ideology of *Indigenismo* in Mexico.

To complete our survey of cultural pluralism, we will examine some of the formulas that have been found by nation-builders to cope with the problem of multiple loyalties. The categories we propose are not entirely discrete; some overlapping is evident. However, they are suggestive of the range of policy alternatives open to render cultural pluralism compatible with territorial survival.[1]

FEDERALISM

The first temptation of Western observers in contemplating the problem of plural cultures is to turn to a legal-institutional formula for coping with it. For this reason, the federalist solution has labored in many areas under the stigma of identification with the colonizer. To the new nationalists, especially at the terminal colonial epoch when the problems of independence seemed easily soluble and cultural pluralism an invention of the colonial powers, the interest of the colonizer in creating federal forms was a diabolical divisive scheme, and the interest in minority rights seemed a hypocritical plot to weaken the central governments of new states. To date, federalism has generally been a formula negotiated between colonizer and colonized as a basis for power transfer. In Indonesia, the Dutch tried unsuccessfully to create a federal state. In Burma, a federal structure was accepted by Burman nationalists because of the hesitations of the Karens, Chins, Kachins, and Shans about remaining within the Burmese framework. Had they not received satisfaction, at that point, they could have seceded under British protection. However, Burmese practice has not been particularly federal, the constitutional promise of a right to secede has not been respected, and since the military takeover in 1962 all federal pretense has been abandoned.

In Africa, federalism was a battle cry of political opposition groups in Ghana and Kenya. It was the de facto result of the collapse of the highly

---

[1] Although the first edition of our book was in press when it appeared, we are struck by the common themes in the following list with those suggested as "normal political processes" for coping with subcultures in Western Europe by Robert A. Dahl, in *Political Oppositions in Western Democracies* (New Haven: Yale University Press, 1966), pp. 358-59.

centralized institutions of colonial Zaire and has been a useful mechanism for the uniting of East and West Cameroons, which since World War I had been under different colonial jurisdictions. In Uganda, federal status had to be given Buganda as the price of averting secession, though the ruling group abolished the federal constitution in 1966. Nigeria, India, and Malaysia are the outstanding cases of federations that were genuinely desired by the countries concerned at the time of independence. In these instances, federation has probably attenuated the cultural confrontation at the central level; on the other hand, it has established provincial political arenas where cultural politics are certain to be paramount. The military coup in Nigeria in January 1966, and the civil war that eventually followed, have completely altered the content of the original federalism, although the term continues to be applied to describe the country's constitutional arrangements. The division of the three old regions into a dozen states has significantly attenuated the former tri-polar cultural confrontation between Ibo, Yoruba, and Hausa-Fulani, by removing the structural formula that institutionalized it. In Libya, federalism succeeded so well that within a decade it could be dropped in favor of more centralized government. At the time of independence in 1952, there was real doubt whether even federalism gave sufficient rein to the regional particularism of Tripolitania, Cyreneika, and Fezzan.

In Latin America, federal forms probably made some historic contribution as a therapy for regionalism in a few of the larger states. However, the relevance of federalism is diminishing as the states become better integrated; in any case, federal norms have been generally honored in the breach. Finally, federalism by itself has proved inadequate to paste together such disparate and dispersed territories as the former British West Indies.

REPRESENTATION

Probably the most widespread and effective formula for coming to terms with diversity is through frankly recognizing it in the allocation of authority roles. This is simply what has been called the "balanced ticket" in ethnically conscious areas of the United States, especially New York and New England, or what has been labeled "ethnic arithmetic" in West Africa. An effort is made to distribute the visible leadership functions within the state in some rough proportion to the strength and self-consciousness of the primary cultural groups within the polity. Lebanon is probably the extreme case. The president is, by institutionalized tradition, a Maronite Christian; the prime minister, a Sunnite Muslim; and the chairman of Parliament, a Shi'ite. In this way, the primary groups have a psychic assurance that their communal interests are being defended, that there is no risk of the state being converted into an engine of hegemony of one cultural group over another.

In many states, in addition to his functional role, the office-holder is simultaneously a representative, a delegate of a given group; for example, in rural Congo-Brazzaville in 1964, a local crisis brought the minister of foreign affairs hurrying in to resolve the conflict. This should have been a functional responsibility of the minister of interior; however, it was more effective to settle the issue by relying on the ethnic representative from this area in the central government. When the national language issue was at its peak in India in 1965, Prime Minister Shastri found it expedient to designate a non-Hindi speaking leader from the "Dravidian" south to seek a compromise solution.

CULTURAL NEUTRALISM

This implies an assiduous separation of the central state and its leadership from any cultural identification. This is at once most logical and most frequent in Africa, where the majority of the states have no core culture. Leaders like Nyerere of Tanzania will scrupulously avoid word or deed that would link them with their ethnic background. Symbolic embodiments of the state – such as flags and anthems – must not be linked exclusively with any cultural subgroup. Language policy may be of particular importance in this connection. In the Philippines, it is necessary that the national language designed ultimately to supplant English be designated "Philipino," and not Tagalog, from whence it derives. In Indonesia and Tanzania, Indonesian and Swahili are effective national languages and valuable integrating devices because these trading lingua franca are not associated with particular groups. By contrast, Nigeria is forced to retain English as its national language because the most obvious alternative, Hausa, is far too identified with the north and can readily imply "northern domination."

IDEOLOGY

The vigorous inculcation of an integrative ideology has in some cases proved instrumental in nation-building. The twin themes of revolution and *Indigenismo* have been vital for Mexico; revolution as a metaphysical idea, linked with nationalism, has doubtless helped bind Indonesia together. Haya de la Torre's effort to weave the spell of "Indoamerica" has had an important impact on reform efforts throughout Latin America. African socialism has been invoked in a number of states as an ideology of integration.

ASSIMILATION

States with a core culture are frequently tempted to end the cultural pluralism problem by absorbing the differentiated groups. In another era, before the self-awareness of many cultural groups had become intense, this method was no doubt highly efficacious; indeed, this has been a continuous process throughout the world. In Latin America, the process was so far along before the era of social mobilization and the participation revolution began that there can be little doubt that it will eventually succeed. But few culturally plural societies today have high rates of intermarriage; endogamy within each cultural group is the rule, in contrast to the Latin American past. We might say that a few hundred intermarriages between Spaniard and Indian in sixteenth-century Paraguay were decisive in producing an assimilated, single national culture today. Once a cultural subnationality has achieved self-awareness, assimilation is likely to encounter bitter resistance, as was found in the instances of Burmese and Thai efforts to impose the language, dress, and religious practices of the core culture on the outlying minorities. Similarly, Sudanese moves toward the imposition of Arabic and Islamic culture on the non-Arab south provoked a generalized insurrection. The 1972 truce in Sudan was founded upon assurances that English, as the language of education for southerners, could remain, and that the southern three provinces would have sufficiently broad autonomy to guarantee against imposed Arabization or Islamization.

ENCAPSULATION

Some types of minorities, if not too numerous, can be dealt with by weaving a cocoon of restrictions about them, setting them apart from the national community but tolerating their continued presence. This has been a frequent fate of Chinese minorities in southeast Asia and of the Indians and Pakistanis in East Africa. In a sense, this could be described as the present status of unintegrated Indians in the Andes and Central America (and, for that matter, North America).

EXPATRIATION

The extreme solution for cultural pluralism is the physical removal of the differentiated groups either by expulsion from the territory or, in a few cases, by extermination. Probably the most spectacular examples of this tactic have occurred outside the developing world — the Greek-Turkish population exchanges after World War I, the Polish expulsion of several million Germans living in the areas annexed east of the Oder-Neisse — or, in more ghastly form, Hitler's "solution" of the "Jewish problem" through genocide. Often the expatriation has been the decision of the cultural group that felt threatened, rather than enforced by the government concerned. Cultural pluralism in independent Algeria was reduced by the voluntary exodus of 90 percent of the one million Europeans; the departure represented a judgment by the Europeans that their

TABLE 5-1
Types of Cultural Pluralism

Country	Origin of State	Basis of State	Degree of Cultural Pluralism	Types of Cultural Pluralism
Latin America and Western Hemisphere				
Argentina	1	4	2	2, 5
Bolivia	1	3	3	1, 2, 5
Brazil	1	3	2	1, 5
Chile	1	4	1	2, 5
Colombia	1	3	2	5
Costa Rica	1 (6)	4	1	
Cuba	1	4	1	
Dominican Republic	1	3	1	
Ecuador	1 (6)	3	3	1, 5
El Salvador	1 (6)	3	2	1
Guatemala	1 (6)	3	3	1, 2
Haiti	2	4	2	(2)
Honduras	1 (6)	3	2	5
Jamaica	2 (6)	1	2	1
Mexico	1	3	3	1, 2, 5
Nicaragua	1 (6)	3	2	5
Panama	6	3	1	
Paraguay	1 (6)	4	1	2
Peru	1	3	3	1, 5
Trinidad & Tobago	2 (6)	1	4	1
Uruguay	1 (6)	4	1	
Venezuela	1 (6)	3	2	1, 5
Asia				
Afghanistan	5	2	3	2
Bangladesh	6	4	1	
Burma	4	2	2	2, 3a
Cambodia	4	3	2	1
China	5	3	2	2, 3a, 5
India	3	1	4	2, 3a, 4, 5
Indonesia	3	1	3	1, 2, 3a, 3b, 5
Iran	5	3	2	2, 3a, 3b, 5
Korea (North & South)	4	4	1	
Laos	4	3	2	2, 5
Malaysia	2 – 3	2	3	1, 2, 3a, 5
Nepal	4	2	2	2, 3a
Pakistan	6	4	4	2, 3b, 5
Philippines	3	1	4	(2) (3a)
Sri Lanka (Ceylon)	4	2	2	2, 3a, 3b, 4
Taiwan	6	3	2	5
Thailand	5	3	2	2, 3a
Vietnam (North & South)	4	3	2	2, 3a, 3b, 5
Middle East				
Iraq	6	3	2	2, 3b
Jordan	6	3	1	5

TABLE 5-1 (continued)

Country	Origin of State	Basis of State	Degree of Cultural Pluralism	Types of Cultural Pluralism
Kuwait	4	4	1	
Lebanon	3	2	4	3a, 3b, 5
Saudi Arabia	5	4	1	
Syria	3	3	2	2, 3b, 5
Yemen	5	3	2	2, 3b
Africa				
Algeria	3	3	2	2
Burundi	4 (6)	2	4	2
Cameroon	3	1	4	2, 3a, 5
Central African Rep.	3 (6)	1	4	2, 3a
Chad	3 (6)	1	4	(1) 2, 3a, 5
Congo-Brazzaville	3 (6)	1	4	2
Dahomey	3 (4) (6)	1	4	2, 3a, 5
Ethiopia	5	2	3	(1) 2, 3a, 5
Gabon	3 (6)	1	2	2
Ghana	3	1	4	2, 3a, 5
Guinea	3 (6)	1	4	2, 3a
Ivory Coast	3 (6)	1	4	2, 3a, 5
Kenya	3	1	3	1, 2, 3a, 5
Liberia	6	3	3	2, 3a, 3b
Libya	3	3	2	3b, 5
Madagascar	4	2	3	2, 3b, 5
Malawi	3	1	4	2, 3a
Mali	3 (4) (6)	1	4	2, 4
Mauretania	3 (6)	3	2	1, 2, 5
Morocco	4	3	2	2
Niger	3 (6)	1	4	2
Nigeria	3	1	4	2, 3a, 3b, 5
Rwanda	4 (6)	4	2	2
Senegal	3 (6)	1	3	2, 3a, 3b, 4, 5
Sierre Leone	3	2	4	2, 3a, 5
Somalia	3	4	1	2
South Africa	1	3	4	1, 2, 3b, 5
Sudan	3	3	2	1, 2, 3a, 3b, 5
Tanzania	3	1	4	1, 2, 3a, 5
Togo	3	1	4	2, 3a, 5
Tunisia	4	4	1	
Uganda	3	1	4	2, 3a, 3b, 5
United Arab Rep.	4	4	1	2, 3a
Upper Volta	4 (6)	2	2	2, 3a
Zaire	3	1	4	2, 5
Zambia	3	1	4	1, 2, 5

situation would eventually become intolerable under Algerian self-government, but it was not provoked by any overt Algerian act. Similarly, Pakistan became more homogeneous through the departure of seven million mainly non-Moslems in 1947. The uprooting was attended by a holocaust of violence but took place before the new Pakistan state could prove its ability to enforce toleration or, on the contrary, to pursue a policy of victimization of those outside the Islamic pale. The Bahutu revolution in Rwanda in 1959 led to the departure of over one hundred thousand Watusi, who feared a policy of vengeance from the new government. The conspiracies of a certain number of the exiles, aiming to restore the Watusi monarchy by a refugee invasion, rendered the situation of the remaining Watusi highly insecure. More deliberate policies of expatriation were pursued by the Burmese government toward the Indian minority, through application of vexatious restrictions on economic activities of this group, combined with exclusion from public employment. President Amin was more direct in abruptly expelling in 1972 the great majority of the Ugandan Asian community, who either had not sought or not been granted Ugandan citizenship. Thailand has been discreetly trying to repatriate a colony of approximately eighty thousand Vietnamese in northeast Thailand, of recent vintage and mainly sympathetic to North Vietnam. In the best of circumstances, expatriation is likely to be feasible only with immigrant groups who have a homeland that will receive them.

In the last analysis, the only alternative to success in learning to live with cultural pluralism is internal war. Some polities now visibly plural will no doubt succeed in rendering the national component of citizen identity paramount. But in many, including a number of the largest developing states, stable coexistence is the best outcome that can reasonably be expected. And all developing states are firmly locked into the present state system prescribed by the international order. Minor changes that can be insulated from great power confrontations may be feasible, but wholesale alterations are out of the question. This very fact suggests at least one compelling reason for tempered optimism: the twin progeny of modernization – cultural pluralism and nationalism – must find reconciliation, because the world offers no other choice.

KEY TO TABLE

Origin of State

1. Colonial administrative divisions, power transferred to European elite, modified metropolitan culture dominant.
2. Colonial administrative division, power transferred to non-European immigrant groups.
3. Colonial administrative division, power transferred to indigenous elite.
4. Traditional state with period of colonial subjugation.
5. Traditional state without period of colonial rule (Turkey not considered former imperial state).
6. Separatist state, fragment of disintegrated state, or other.

Basis of State

1. State without specific cultural referents.
2. State with core culture, though with some differentiated groups.
3. State with explicitly dominant culture, though may have some unintegrated groups.
4. State with explicit cultural referent, exclusive or without differentiated groups.

Degree of Cultural Pluralism

1. Homogeneous state.
2. Core, clearly dominant culture but significant minorities or other differentiated groups.
3. No majority culture, but one clearly salient culture.
4. Multiplicity of culture.

Types of Cultural Pluralism

1. Racial
2. Ethnic and/or linguistic.
3. a. Religious — two or more major religions.
   b. Religious — major cleavages within a major religion.
4. Caste.
5. Regionalism.

NOTES TO TABLE

States included in Table 5-1 are those recognized as independent and participating in the international system as of January 1, 1965 (except Bangladesh); microstates like Samoa are not included. Our definition of the compass of developing areas, here as elsewhere, has been the arbitrary regional delimitation of Latin America, Asia, Middle East, and Africa, despite the weaknesses of such an arbitrary selection of analytical boundaries. It is highly debatable whether, for example, Argentina, Uruguay, Chile, or South Africa should be labeled as underdeveloped countries. Judgments on categorization have been made on the basis of the most recent available census data, plus the standard "country studies" in cases where these are available; for analysis of the census material, we gratefully acknowledge the invaluable aid of our research assistant, Robert Darcy.

In any such taxonomy, the marginal cases abound. For this reason, we have hesitated to undertake any correlations of a quantitative nature. We are not sufficiently satisfied that our categories are adequately refined or that the data for a number of the classifications is satisfactory enough to make this type of analysis fruitful at the present juncture, although there is no reason that it could not eventually be undertaken. Particularly doubtful cases are enclosed in parentheses; for example, in Haiti it is not fully clear whether the Creole patois should be considered as a distinctive linguistic-ethnic group. Buganda was clearly the core of the Uganda protectorate when it was taken over by the British, but independence came to a government dominated by non-Baganda. Somalia is at once highly homogeneous in the widely diffused awareness of a single Somali nationality; at the same time, clan groups and loyalties play a role in the web of political conflict entirely comparable to that of ethnicity elsewhere in tropical Africa. And so forth. Despite all of these shortcomings, of which it is important that the reader be fully aware, we do feel that the table usefully condenses a large body of data amassed during our research, and is a suggestive indication of central tendencies.

PART TWO

THE MAINTENANCE OF POLITICAL ORDER:
Stability and the Problem of Political Violence

CHAPTER 6

The Problem of Political Violence

Violence as an aspect of domestic politics in the developing world has been front-page news in the postwar era. It does not take a close reading of *The New York Times* to be aware that contemporary examples of the use of physical force to attain political goals are not limited to the lesser-developed states. Violence in a variety of forms has been present as a political technique in every major region of the world. Political assassination has been perpetrated in Colombia, Hungary, Burma, Venezuela, Spain, India, South Vietnam, Zaire, Burundi, Iraq, and the United States, among others. Rioting in the streets has been experienced in Indonesia, France, South Vietnam, Japan, the Middle East, the United States, and within the student population of a number of Latin American states. Politically-oriented interethnic pillage and murder have taken place in as widely scattered places as India, Burundi, and Guyana. Guerrilla warfare in varying forms is an ever-present danger throughout the developing world, with states such as Burma and South Vietnam suffering through their third decade of this type of violence. Finally, open or undeclared civil warfare using regular armies or paramilitary groups has not been an unusual occurrence in the postwar world, with hostilities breaking out in Yemen, South Vietnam, Hungary, Burma, Indonesia, the Dominican Republic, and Cyprus.

Violence in the realm of politics has been complex in the forces that have given it birth and the techniques that have been used. It has been employed subtly, as in threats of reprisal in modern totalitarian systems, and through severe retaliation against an entire class or organization, such as the executions of political and economic offenders in China in the early 1950s or the near elimination of the Indonesian Communist Party in 1965–66. Violence may be an element rising out of the history and culture of a polity or the result of the reaction of an individual to a given set of personal circumstances. In order to understand more systematically the role of violence in the politics of the developing world, this section sets out to perform three major functions: (1) to consider the role of the "political culture" in fomenting violence; (2) to assess possible personal factors responsible for political violence; and (3) to analyze three cases of political violence in the postwar era.

An initial question to ask in assessing the role of violence in the newly formed states of Africa and Asia is if the phenomenon is unique to the postwar world or is a factor characteristic of new states over time. It is easy to draw examples from history of violence associated with the initial period of nation-building — the Whiskey and Shays Rebellions in early American history, the turbulence of the postindependence period in Latin America, the Riel Rebellion in Canada, English-Boer hostilities in South Africa, minority problems in East-Central Europe after World War I, and so forth. However, although it is obvious that the turbulence of contemporary Africa and Asia has its parallels in Europe and the New World, both areas do have examples of peaceful evolution to nationhood. At the same time, the actuarial tables for the dove of domestic peace in new states tend to show a short and precarious life.

The transitional period when the nation-building process is in its initial phase may be a highly traumatic one for the new state. It is necessary to establish new national loyalties and policies at a time when the administration is insufficiently trained, emotional euphoria from the independence movement pervades the attitudes of the political activists, and large sections of the population may still be politically unaware and economically impoverished. At the same time, these areas are in the midst of major economic and social changes that have impinged upon the developing world, including the shift to urban areas, the breakdown of traditional patterns, the growth of synthetic products to challenge older agricultural economies, and a multitude of other unsettling developments that have come with the "modernizing process."

In seeking to explain this prevalence of violence, one obvious place to look is the colonial experience and struggle for freedom of newly independent peoples. A few tentative relationships can be put forward:

1. Where a colonial regime governs in a society containing a politically aware stratum but will not allow nationalism a legal place, extra-legal revolutionary groups will tend to replace the moderates. This fairly straightforward hypothesis can be supported from a variety of examples, such as colonial Indonesia, Algeria, and, most forcefully, Vietnam. In the prewar Vietnamese case, the French administration suppressed moderate nationalists and at times used violent methods to repress those who sought open, peaceful paths to independence. The result was a revolutionary doctrine preaching violence as the only means to independence. According to Ellen Hammer, in her *The Struggle for Indo-China,* "By declaring political opposition illegal and subject to police reprisals, the administration left nationalists who desired action no alternative but to operate clandestinely, as revolutionaries."[1]

2. Within any colonial system there is the opportunity for the entrance of systematic or chance insults and humiliations to the "natives," whether actually perpetrated or erroneously perceived as perpetrated by the colonial rulers. The resultant environment of oppression may have a marked influence on individuals who perceive themselves as victims of mistreatment and may prepare the way for later demands for revolutionary change. This explanation may be exaggerated, of course. Thomas Hodgkin has put it well:

> We should abandon also the tendency to substitute psychological for sociological categories of explanation: the common practice of attempting to account for African revolutions in terms of the "humiliations," "frustrations," "traumatic experiences," and consequent "pathological states of mind" — arising from discriminatory treatment at the hands of the European ruling class — of a handful of Western-educated nationalist leaders. It is possible, of course, to apply such methods of explanation to other revolutions in the recent and remoter past. No doubt Cromwell, Jefferson, Robespierre, Lenin, Gandhi, Mao Tse-Tung all underwent, at one time or another, experiences of a comparable kind and reacted in comparable ways. No doubt, one could try to explain the rise of Islam in terms of the Prophet Mohammed's emotional reactions to his hostile reception by the Meccan Establishment. Indeed, this kind of thing is sometimes done. But I am skeptical of the value of this personal, psychoanalytical approach to history. It is not, primarily, the states of mind of individuals that need to be understood but the precise historical conditions which made it possible for these particular individuals, with their particular standpoints and attitudes, to emerge, and the character of the social movements in which they played a formative part and which at the same time helped to form them.[2]

At the same time, a myriad of examples can be drawn from personal statements and memoirs of nationalists to show the impact of personal insults on their revolutionary attitudes — always accepting the danger of divorcing these sentiments from the total environment of the individual. Nasser of Egypt resented the arrest of his uncle for organizing an anti-British demonstration, as a young officer smarted under the treatment of British officers, and stated that he was particularly drawn to violent action by the bloodless use of force by the British in 1942 when they forced the King to unseat an allegedly pro-Hitler premier. Among the surrendered Malaysian Communist insurgents interviewed by Lucian Pye there was considerable ambivalence toward the West and

[1] Ellen Hammer, *The Struggle for Indo-China* (Stanford: Stanford University Press, 1954), p. 79.

[2] J. Roland Pennock, ed., *Self-government in Modernizing Nations* (Englewood Cliffs, N.J.: Prentice-Hall, Inc., 1964), p. 62.

comparatively little contact with Westerners, but six party functionaries were apparently influenced by their personal relations with Europeans. In China a number of future Communists were enlisted through the May fourth anti-Japanese student movement and by general antiforeign sentiment. As one Communist Party functionary commented, "I had seen foreigners and received a bad impression of them because their attitude was arrogant. I contrasted their wealth with the poverty and backwardness of the Chinese and felt bitter."[3] No doubt, a relationship between preceived injury and an acceptance of revolutionary doctrine does exist, but it must be considered carefully within the cultural milieu as well as within a more systematic analysis of personal reactions.

3. Is there a relationship between the presence or absence of violence in the revolutionary struggle and the presence or absence of domestic political violence in the postindependence era? Violent colonial wars and postindependence turbulence do coincide in Burma, Vietnam, Indonesia, Algeria, and Syria; but the connection becomes fuzzy when we look at Israel, Tunisia, and Morocco. Certainly it can be argued that a prolonged armed struggle for independence can provide a foundation for future violence through the spread of arms among the populace, the formation of clandestine organizations, and the development of a multitude of personal frustrations.

4. It has been stated by some that the most dangerous course a colonial system can take is a fluctuating program of repression and concessions; this actual or perceived lack of continuity of policy leads to frustrations of a violent nature. It is argued that a policy of vacillation dashes hopes of moderates, aids revolutionaries in their projection of the colonial government as two-faced, and reminds the nationalists of their lack of control over their own destiny. There can be some doubt as to the general applicability of such a hypothesis. Colonial administration in general has been notoriously lacking in continuity of policy, and it is difficult to provide many cases offering clear evidence of a causal relationship between such policies and postindependence violence. In fact, one example of what colonial peoples perceived as a continuous and unbroken policy — divide and rule — has been blamed for much of the postcolonial friction that has developed.

An even more tenuous set of reasons for politically related violence revolves around the existence of a national or subnational culture of violence. This argument not only suffers from the usual deficiencies of national character studies but also from the extreme paucity of related evidence in the developing world. While making the reader aware of the caveats in this line of thinking, it is worthwhile considering the argument. Basically, the culture-violence-revolution syndrome can be broken down into three distinct sections:

First, it is stated that the culture of a particular people makes them prone

[3] Nym Wales, *Red Dust* (Stanford: Stanford University Press, 1952), p. 50.

to violent acts. The protagonist of this view may refer to a warrior culture (some tribal states or prewar Japan) or to a people with atavistic roots of violence (as Germany was characterized during both world wars). Several authors have commented upon various traditions of violence in the politics of developing states. Pye has asserted that "basic to the Burmese feeling about the tenseness of politics is the concern with violence that we have noted as such a fundamental part of Burmese politics."[4] Latin America's history of revolution has brought forward a number of cultural explanations. F. Garcia-Calderon stated that "both the Indian and the Spanish races which settled America were warriors and their spirit explains the disorders in these republics"[5] while an Argentinian scholar, Carlos Octavio Bunge, holds that Latin American revolutions "result from the habitual inactivity of the people who do nothing but accumulate bile."[6] Others refer to the heritage of Spanish culture − "the Spanish tendency to dissension and civil war for the sake of dissension and civil war" (Salvador de Madariaga),[7] or the natural harshness of the environment, as in Domingo Sarmientos' comment that, "From these characteristics rises in the life of the Argentine people the reign of brute force, the supremacy of the strongest, the absolute and irresponsible authority of rulers, the administration of justice without formalities or discussion."[8] None of these explanations appears entirely satisfying.

A second aspect of the culture argument is based upon the role that childrearing has upon the place of violence in the polity. Although certainly insufficient evidence is available in the developing areas to substantiate this relationship, the psychological dimensions of this sort of approach are highly suggestive. One nation where a number of authors have seen childrearing as having a role in patterns of national violence in Burma. There, the transition of the boy "from seeing indulgence to insistence on docile submission to elders" supposedly supplies a traumatic shock that leads to aggressive tendencies. Authors such as Everett Hagen also argue that like his Latin American or Javanese counterparts, the Burmese male must constantly prove his manhood. Pye asserts that due to the changing nature of his mother's treatment, "the Burmese may constantly seek warm and close relations, but unconsciously he tends to expect that he cannot control others in any positive fashion and that his actions are only likely to produce hostile responses."[9] Space does not allow a

[4] Lucian Pye, *Politics, Personality and Nation Building* (New Haven: Yale University Press, 1962), p. 166.

[5] Quoted in Donald M. Dozer, "Roots of Revolution in Latin America," *Foreign Affairs,* 27 (January 1949), 274–88.

[6] Quoted in Dozer, "Roots of Revolution," 274–88.

[7] *The Fall of the Spanish American Empire* (London: Hollis and Carter, 1947), p. 29.

[8] *Civilization and Barbarism: The Life of Juan Facundo Quiroga* (Buenos Aires: Editorial Santander, 1845).

[9] Pye, *Nation Building,* pp. 138–39, and E. Hagen, *On The Theory of Social Change* (Homewood, Ill.: The Dorsey Press, 1962).

full consideration of the points made by Hagen, Pye, and others. Their positions, although suggestive, are also highly controversial, and critics attack the paucity of evidence for statements made.

The third aspect of culture has related to military elites, and the male "subculture." The argument has been made that the value system of the military in some states is one that seeks immediate solutions and is incompatible with evolutionary parliamentary processes. For example, one American author on military affairs states that the military career "would permit an officer to take prompt, ruthless and effective action to accomplish his mission, with no thought — as the politician would be likely to have — to avoid unpleasant or unpopular measures."[10] However, there is no universality in military political values, and it is vitally necessary to analyze the values of particular national military establishments when discussing the relationship between values and doctrines of violence.

In the Latin American case, authors have pointed to the subculture of the male elite to explain the prevalence of violence in the area. Again, necessity for the male to prove his manhood is mentioned. This is epitomized by the cult of "machismo," a term that has been given wide pejorative currency in recent years in North America by women's liberation movements as connoting in a single term all of the most unpleasant aspects of male chauvinism. "Machismo" in its original Latin setting is the overt validation of manhood through conspicuously aggressive behavior, physically and sexually. Salvador de Madariaga states that over the centuries the Spaniards had acquired two definite and ingrained trends: "one, a man of quality, by fighting, acquires wealth more honorably and quickly than a meaner man of work; and two, a man of quality does not rest on his wealth, but goes on fighting as a matter of course, for of infidels to destroy, of wealth to acquire and honors to reap, there is no end."[11] Although statements of this sort have more poetry than evidence, they, like other aspects of the cultural approach, should not be rejected out of hand. The need for far more research in this field does not mean that such an analysis will not yield worthwhile results.

This leads us to the last major consideration in our search for why individuals or groups seek violent political solutions — the personal environment and perceptions of the individual or, as Lasswell has termed it, the "projection of personal conflict onto a public object." The basis of this set of arguments is that personality factors and personal orientation can lead to frustration and political alienation, which in turn will direct the individual toward violent political acts or antigovernment revolutionary solutions. Like so many of our previous points, these are but hopefully suggestive possibilities that cry for further detailed research. Examples are always available, but not in sufficient

---

[10]Trevor Dupuy, "Burma and Its Army: A Contrast in Motivations and Characteristics," *Antioch Review,* 20 (Winter 1960–61), 437.

[11]Salvador de Madariaga, *Fall of Empire,* p. 7.

number to verify the assertions made. Some possible reasons for deciding to use or accept violence as a political tool are outlined below.

REASONS FOR THE DECISION FOR POLITICAL VIOLENCE

Boredom, Restlessness, The Romanticism of Guerrilla Life

We have a number of instances, particularly in Southeast Asia, where young men have admitted joining a revolutionary organization because of the boredom of their peasant, urban, or school existence. In the Indonesian case the war left at loose ends many men who looked to the revolution as a romantic act. In Vietnam what little evidence we have suggests that being a guerrilla with the Viet Cong is considered a more romantic life than joining the regular government forces. Particularly in areas suffering from the disruption of war or the struggle for independence, youths may find that life in the village lacks the exhilaration and opportunities that they perceive to be available in guerrilla warfare against authority.

Alienation and Dissatisfaction with Personal Role and A Sense of Being Blocked from Improving One's Situation

There is some evidence to show that personal frustration with his status or prospects may lead an individual to seek higher status or an improvement of his prospects through antigovernmental activity. The blocks to individual growth may not be only personal but may relate to his ethnic, religious, or racial background.

The evidence to support this position is of three kinds: the makeup of Communist and other groups promoting violence, interviews with former revolutionaries, and statements or memoirs of those who have participated in revolution. In the first instance, a survey of Communist party membership provides some interesting leads. The role of deprived racial groups in Communist parties in the developing world shows a strong predisposition of depressed minorities to participate in antigovernment party activities. In peninsular Malaya, the party is composed almost entirely of Chinese, who have long felt persecuted. Similar roles have been played by the Vietnamese in the Communist parties of Cambodia and Thailand, hill peoples in the revolutionary Pathet Lao of Laos, the Arabs in the Israeli Communist Party, Bengalis in the outlawed Pakistani Communist Party, the Chinese community in the Communist movement of Mauritius, and African members of the revolutionary groups in South Africa.

Rare studies of the content of these revolutionary organizations are also illuminating. For example, a survey of some one thousand political inmates of a camp set up in the Netherlands Indies following an unsuccessful revolt in 1926-27 showed the following results: "... at a time when official statistics showed Javanese literacy to be under 6 percent, his sample was over 75 percent literate. However, what is interesting is that none had gone to an institution of higher learning and only 2.4 percent had received middle school training (only one graduated). The vast majority were from the lowest educational institutions in which they were unable to obtain sufficient training to place them in professional or technical fields where prestige and security were to be found."[12] Although there are numerous cases where intelligentsia have formed part of revolutionary groups, the general pattern is similar to the one given above — the bulk of the membership comes from those who are or believe themselves to be educationally, economically, or otherwise deprived.

Lucian Pye, in his study of surrendered communist-led insurgents in Malaya, found his interviewees articulating this frustration and alienation. He found that one of their deepest frustrations was that their schooling, in which they had such great hopes, was not sufficient to give them the social status they expected. At the same time he found that a feeling of Chinese racial superiority was central to the individual's relationship to the Communist Party. "The feeling of racial identity common to most of the SEP's (Surrendered Enemy Personnel) thus engendered the seeds of a kind of nationalism which, when fostered by the MCP (Malayan Communist Party), was hardly distinguished with racism."[13] Certainly more surveys of this type are necessary before any more than tentative conclusions can be made, but what we do not have shows a relationship between blocks to personal advancement and feelings of political alienation.

Isolated examples of these personal frustrations can be taken from the statements of national revolutionary leaders. These can do no more than illustrate a few cases where frustration happened to correspond to the growth of revolutionary doctrine (at least in the mind of the perceiver). A few examples follow:

"I was diligent and the teachers liked me. Once I asked a teacher to draw a picture for me but when it was finished a landlord's son asked for it and the teacher gave it to him instead. I fought with the student and the teacher punished me for that ... From then on I was inbued with a hatred for landlords." Following a discussion of his hard life, he went on: "I felt depressed and hopeless, and thought life offered no other way for the poor."[14] (Wang Shou-tao, Political Commissar in prewar China and later on Central Committee CCP)

---

[12] W. M. F. Mansvelt, "Onderwijs en Communisme," *Koloniale Studien,* 9 (1928), 202-25. The quote is from F. von der Mehden, "Marxism and Early Indonesian Islamic Nationalism," *Political Science Quarterly,* 73 (September 1958), 337.

[13] Pye, *Nation Building,* pp. 209-10.

[14] Wales, *Red Dust,* p. 77. There are a number of statements of this type among her interviews.

"Most of the people working in the tin mine were uneducated. I wanted to be a bookkeeper, but the only work I got was the same kind as those with no education at all got." (SEP interviewed by Pye)

Reconciliation of a Sense of Personal Inadequacy by Projecting the Blame on an External Object

Leading from the factor of personal frustration is the possibility that the affected individual will blame his troubles upon the evil acts of the imperialists or capitalists. These objects of his frustration are perceived as the forces that have led to his present state and, therefore, must be overturned. This conviction may lead to a sense of paranoia – a feeling that his world is inhabited by impersonal, threatening forces, conspiratorial by nature. These possible relations of personal problems and political perceptions do exist, but, given our present information, we have no way of ascertaining the extent to which the relationship is important in orienting an individual to violence and revolution.

Loss of Existential Meaningfulness, the Quest for It in Political Activity, and The Acceptance and Commitment to an All-explanatory World View

In a developing world where old traditions and values are being warped or destroyed, many individuals seek a new meaningful explanation of life or attempt to defend the old ways. To the former, the traditional religion appears inadequate, the advice of the elders not pertinent, and the traditional pattern of values unequal to the task of meeting the modern world. In this period of transition new revolutionary ideologies may appear to provide the needed world view and explanation of how the old ways can be quickly uprooted. However, in defining this category it is necessary to note certain differences between the Western world and the developing societies.

For example, in the West, Communism has become more "intellectualized" and its adherents less interested in the immediate use of political violence. Whereas Western ex-Communists have commented upon their search for a new meaning of life in terms of the "God that Failed," Pye asserts that Communists in Malaya "would characterize the same experience far more simply and directly as 'The Bastards That Cheated Me.' "[15] This is not to say that Communist doctrine in Afro-Asia is without intellectual content, but it can be stated that its supporters are more involved in action-oriented programs. In this period of transition, those interested in change are prone to violence, for it is often an accepted political tool among the traditional elements of society who see a danger to the old way of life from the new modernizing forces. Thus, religious

---

[15] Pye, *Nation Building*, p. 157.

groups may react against growing secularism, traditional oligarchies against the new middle-class elite, regionally-based ethnic groups against unity-minded leaders in the capital, and so on. Violence may come then not from the loss of existential meaningfulness of the individual but from a perceived danger to a group defending a pattern of values of long duration.

Quest for the Heroic Act, Immortality, or Being in Tune with the "Inevitable Force of Events"

The desire to be part of the flow of events, to take part in active politics has been noted as an important aspect of Italian and French Communist membership, at a time when these movements were still committed to direct action including violence. Not only is the flow of events supposedly impossible to stop, but it is exhilarating to take part in the process.

The more mundane aspect of this outlook is the belief in the efficacy of politics and participation among Communists in France and Italy. If they feel they are participating, their sense of their own value and worth as human beings is enhanced. In Malaya, Pye noted that to those he interviewed, politics was an elite activity and most of the surrendered personnel "indicated their belief that politics was the concern of those people who stood above the masses. If one became involved in politics, one would be establishing relations that would lead to elite status." As to the relation of politics to violence and revolution, he later states that the surrendered Communists "not only expected that physical violence was likely to be the final arbiter, but believed that hostility and aggressiveness were characteristics of political activities."[16]

Another aspect of this pattern of thought is the "heroic" or romantic aspect of taking part in revolution or guerrilla activity. In some areas of Southeast Asia young guerrilla revolutionaries have been looked upon as romantic, somewhat swashbuckling heroes. Again, one has only to look at some of the posed photos of Simbas in Zaire to see the efforts to strike heroic poses with rifles or pieces of enemy equipment and clothing. There is a difference between this and the more intellectual attraction to a philosophy of historic inevitability, but both can lead to support for revolutionary action.

Revolution as a Way of Life

Persistent instability may foster a situation in which rebellion and revolution are constants. This state of affairs can attract individuals to a revolutionary cause for two reasons. First, as in some nineteenth-century Latin American states, revolution can be the accepted pattern of political change. It can be taken as a more common cause of ameliorating grievances than free elections, and an individual would not need any personal traumas or aberrant

---

[16] Pye, *Nation Building*, p. 168.

experiences to cause him to seek a revolutionary cause. In the second instance, there are states such as Burma and Vietnam where various forms of guerrilla activity have taken place over a generation. The young man growing up in this environment may accept it as the only way of life, because he has experienced no other. War, tension, antigovernment views – all have been part of the "normal" pattern of existence. In an almost Orwellian world he knows no other way.

Simple Indignation, Frustration, or Fury at Injustice, Stupidity, and Tyranny

Unmet demands for agrarian reform, the rape of a daughter by a landlord, poor wages, political oppression or neglect, lack of food for the family, administrative inefficiency, graft or corruption, and a long list of actual or perceived personal injuries can lead an individual to seek redress.[17] If he does not believe that change can be obtained through peaceful evolution, he may turn to violent actions.

Terror, the Use of Force to Get Individuals to Aid Movements of Violence

Finally, a person may use violence out of fear for his own safety under pressure from Communists or others who demand his services. There is ample proof of individuals in Burma, Vietnam, and other areas of Communist insurgency being forced to commit acts of violence. This fear may arise out of seeing others punished for serving the government or from direct threats against the villager. The Communists have often stated that no one can be politically apathetic; in a guerrilla war, that means that those who do not support the movement must be against it.

All the points we have discussed may aid us in understanding why one person chooses violence while another accepts his fate in the face of injustice or tyranny. However, each one of these categories can only be suggestive. Case histories of particular revolutionaries may display different environmental forces influencing the decision to employ violence. In some cases only one of the many points previously alluded to may be pertinent; in others there may be a mixture of various forces.

When we aggregate these manifold causes of discontent and anger, we arrive at the notion of "relative deprivation" as a valuable concept summing the conditions for activation of violence. Political violence is a logical form of

---

[17] Alvin H. Scaff, *The Philippine Answer to Communism* (Stanford: Stanford University Press, 1955). Among the Huks and ex-Huk supporters interviewed by Scaff, 56 percent joined the Huk revolutionary movement over a desire for "land for the landless." A number also joined, they said, because they were forced to do so, a factor which may be of particular importance in guerrilla movements.

collective behavior when an aggregate of individuals is mobilized by the conviction that a large gap exists between goods and satisfactions they are accorded by the political system, and those that they could have reasonable right to obtain, in view of the resources visibly available in the society. In other words, the isolated hunting band in the Kalahari desert of Botswana in southern Africa, even though living on the very margin of survival, could hardly contemplate, even conceive of violent action directed towards a political system whose presence is barely felt. Conversely, an urban African in neighboring South Africa, although in absolute terms incomparably wealthier, has as his reference point the extreme affluence of the white ruling caste. The urban African further perceives that this disparity is maintained by a multitude of discriminatory devices, which serve rigidly to institutionalize inequality. In these circumstances, the propensity to violence is held in check only by the overwhelming coercive force of the South African state.

Departing from the core concept of relative deprivation, the question of when human groups have recourse to political violence is given brilliant exposition by Ted Gurr, in his recent study, *Why Men Rebel*.[18] Gurr's conclusion may serve as an appropriate introduction for our three case histories of political violence in Burma, Colombia, and Zaire:

> Political violence is episodic in the history of most organized political communities and chronic in many. No country in the modern world has been free of it for as much as a generation. But it is not an ineluctable manifestation of human nature, not is it an inevitable consequence of the existence of political community. It is a specific kind of response to specific conditions of social existence. The capacity, but not a need, for violence appears to be biologically inherent in men. The disposition to collective violence depends on how badly societies violate socially derived expectations about the means and ends of human life.[19]

---

[18] Ted Robert Gurr, *Why Men Rebel* (Princeton: Princeton University Press, 1971); for another especially valuable recent study on the causes of political violence, see Murray Edelman, *Politics as Symbolic Action* (Chicago: Markham, 1971).

[19] Gurr, *Why Men Rebel*, p. 317.

CHAPTER 7

Civil Strife in Burma

Violence and gentleness are two aspects of "Burmese nature" most often noted. Burmese and Europeans may differ on the pervasiveness of these characteristics, and scholars may debate the causes, but all note their presence. Almost all foreign observers of the Burmese political scene, such as J. S. Furnivall, Harvey, Pye, and Hagen, have made some sort of comment on the extent of crimes of violence and the prevalence of rebellion. Prior to World War II, when statistics were easier to gather, the following figures were compiled to show the former (the latter being daily proved by the continuance of rebellions since 1947).

> In England and Scotland, with a population over 40 million, there are on an average about 150 murders a year; in two districts of Burma, with a combined population of less than 1 million, the murders in 1927 numbered 139. In the United States, where social ties are looser than in England, the number of cases of murder and deliberate manslaughter even in the largest cities, taken as a group, is no more than 33 per million, whereas over the whole of Burma, including the most remote and peaceful areas, there are close on 40 per million. One district alone . . . with a population of only half a million, had 87 murders in 1927, as many as there are in Chicago with 3½ million and world-wide notoriety for gangsters.[1]

Whether or not Chicago deserves such notoriety, these figures are impressive. They became politically more meaningful when violence was practiced by groups against authority.

---
[1] J. S. Furnivall, *Colonial Policy and Practice* (Cambridge: Cambridge University Press, 1948), p. 138 *n.*

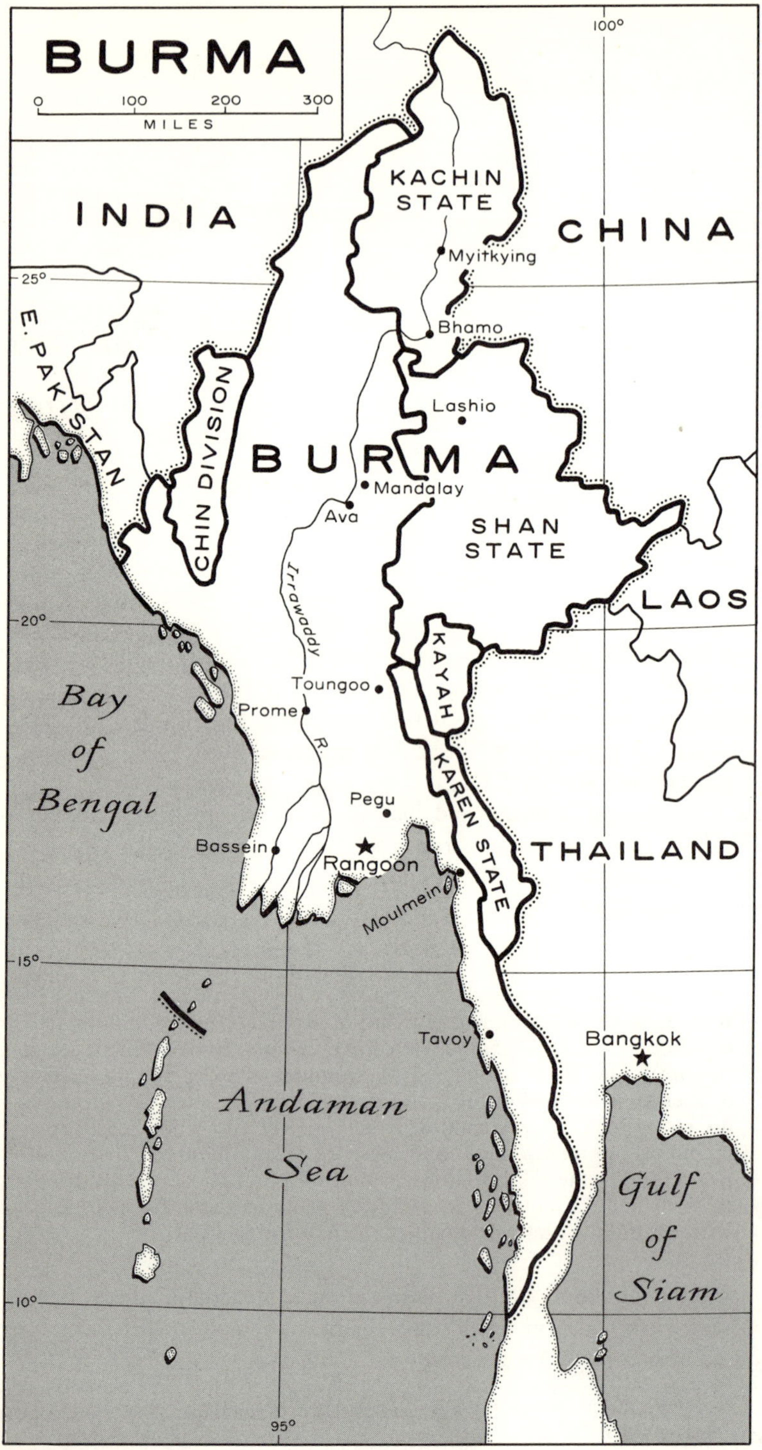
BURMA
0
100
200
300
MILES
INDIA
CHINA
KACHIN STATE
Myitkying
Bhamo
25°
E. PAKISTAN
CHIN DIVISION
Lashio
BURMA
Mandalay
Ava
SHAN STATE
Irrawaddy R.
LAOS
20°
KAYAH
Toungoo
Prome
Bay of Bengal
KAREN STATE
Pegu
Bassein
Rangoon
THAILAND
Moulmein
15°
Tavoy
Bangkok
Andaman Sea
Gulf of Siam
10°
95°
100°

A variety of explanations have been made through the years for the high degree of violence in Burma. These have ranged from cultural to psychological, each with its string of adherents and opponents. Basically, these explanations fall into four categories: (1) the Burmese tradition; (2) the impact of the British colonial system; (3) the impact of World War II and the nationalist movement; and (4) the role of family life in Burma. Briefly, each argument runs as follows:

1. Burma has traditionally been a country with a high degree of violence, beginning during the movement south from China centuries ago. Since that period, weak kings have practiced violence against possible contenders while maladministration allowed the growth of dacoity (banditry) which has become endemic to the country. When the country was strong, as it was at the turn of the nineteenth century, Burma launched aggressive wars of expansion against her neighbors. During such a period of military action, Burmese forces destroyed the old capital of Thailand in 1767. The first Anglo-Burmese War of 1824-26 resulted from a clash of imperial ambitions. Thus, goes the argument, Burmese history shows an aggressive culture that was prone to violence long before the entrance of the British. How much more violent she was than her neighbors or the colonial powers is open to serious question.

2. Other observers, among them Furnivall, tend to lay greater blame upon the British colonial system. First, it is argued, Burma was not conquered by the British in one campaign but in a series of wars that began in 1824 and ended in the annexation of the country in 1886. This piecemeal expansion had several consequences. It meant a long period of political tension and disruption not conducive to peaceful pursuits. Secondly, it gradually split both secular and religious authority. Part of Burma was ruled by traditional forms while other parts were under British control. In the religious realm, the Buddhist hierarchy lost control over areas under British rule, and the major stabilizing factor of religious authority over the many monks and monasteries was broken.

A second general consequence of British rule was the destruction of traditional secular authority in Burma proper. The British established direct rule in areas where the dominant Burman people lived, deposing and exiling the king, eliminating the former regional and local system of government, and putting in its place a system alien to the population. Thus, the colonial ruler left the population no longer bound by either the traditional secular or sectarian strictures of authority. This, it is asserted, was a major factor behind the breakdown of authority and growth of violence in colonial Burma.

Finally, it is argued that under British rule parental control began to lose its grip as the youth no longer saw their more traditional parents' models as the means for upward mobility within the colonial system. What was necessary was a European education, not monastery training; a knowledge of English, not Burmese; and a more European value structure, not the traditional pattern. More than most people in the developing world, the Burmese have clung to their former ways and values, but the presence of the British raj did inaugurate new strains on old political, religious, and family patterns.

3. More recent events also appear to have caused major conflict and resultant violence. During the 1930s, young nationalists[2] began to question British colonial authority as they denounced the Crown, burned the Union Jack, led strikes against the major university and in the oil fields, and generally attacked the legitimacy of the government. This period was followed by the successful Japanese invasion and occupation of the country. This occupation put the colonial system into further disrepute; more importantly, it broke the monopoly of the government over weapons. With Japanese arming of a new Burmese military and armies crisscrossing the country, it was now possible for disgruntled individuals and groups to take up arms almost at will.

Two further factors from the early postwar period may have been responsible for increased violence. First, a comparatively short time elapsed between the return of the British to war-torn Burma and the granting of independence on January 4, 1948. During that time the British found it extremely difficult to meet nationalist demands, pacify the country, and rehabilitate an economy wracked by war. Secondly, the country suffered from the loss of trained administrative leadership. Many British administrators did not return, and Burmans who had joined them in exile after the fall of Burma to the Japanese were not always welcomed back to their old positions. Far more unfortunate was the loss of the able leader of the nationalists, Aung San, who was assassinated in 1947. All these losses and disruptions have been pointed to as factors in the major outbreaks of violence following World War II.

4. The last general causal factor, and by far the most controversial, has been discussed in the preceding chapter. Briefly, it is that patterns in childrearing and interpersonal relations in Burma have led to a situation in which the individual male may vacillate between gentleness to violence. As we have noted, critics of this argument strongly deny its validity. Certainly more work is needed both in Burma and of a comparative nature before this sort of analysis can be fully accepted.

While various authors debate the relative merits of their respective analyses, we can at least accept the fact that Burma has gone through a series of national traumas and disruptions over the past century and a half, any or all of which might have led to a breakdown of authority. The three examples that follow will attempt to show the complexity and variety of the patterns of violence in Burma, and that violence itself may differ in its techniques, goals, and motivations within one state. They also illustrate the complexity of causes for a single act or set of acts of violence. Observers of Burmese politics (or of Southeast Asia in general, for that matter) have a tendency to explain issues and motivations in overly simplified single-cause explanations. Rarely is political life in the region so easily understood. Finally, it is hoped that the three examples, grouped over one generation, will show that acts of violence and attacks on

---

[2]For attitudes of young nationalists in this period see Richard Butwell's *U Nu of Burma* (Stanford: Stanford University Press, 1963).

authority tend to feed upon one another, leading to a continuing breakdown of law and order.

THE SAYA SAN REBELLION

The 1920s were years of growth and turbulence within the Burmese nationalist movement. New organizations were forming, religious leaders were actively participating in politics, economic problems were bringing new demands and grievances, and Burmese politics was in a transition period from more traditional elite politics, dominated by religious issues, to more modern secular, mass political action. To a degree, the Saya San Rebellion epitomized this transitional period.

Briefly, the rebellion broke out in 1930 in the Tharrawaddy District, a notably difficult area, under the leadership of Saya San, a former monk-politician. The rebels set up a jungle court, revising some of the trappings of the monarchy, and set forth to overthrow British rule. With 3,000 men at most and thirty rifles, the revolt was bound to fail, in spite of various tokens of invulnerability. Militarily the rebellion included a few pitched fights and a larger number of riots and guerrilla actions. Approximately 12,000 government troops were called in; by 1932 Saya San was captured and the revolt crushed.[3]

This summation of the events of 1930-32 can best be filled out by analyzing the asserted causes of the rebellion. Basically, they can be trimmed down to three: traditionalist, economic, and modern nationalist. In his history of Burma, John Cady called the revolt "a deliberately planned affair based on traditional Burmese political and religious patterns," and certainly the most fascinating facets of the rebellion center upon the "exotica" surrounding Saya San's court and actions.[4] The court itself attempted to copy the paraphernalia and ritual of the older monarchy while the leadership and followers depended upon oaths, symbols, and religious support. An example of those oaths, which were a mixture of animism and Buddhism, cries out:

> Do away with the heathens, oh Nats, so that our glorious Buddhist religion may prosper.... Hark! Ye Brahmans and Nats, King of Brahmas, Defender of Buddhism, and others. We swear we will not ill treat, nor destroy either the life or the property of the people who are members of the associations affiliated to the G.C.B.A. and the Galon Army as long as Burma does not attain freedom from the British yoke.... May we overcome the heathens speedily and may

---

[3] There is, as yet, no good book on this period, but for the military view see Ba Than, *Roots of the Revolution* (Rangoon: Directorate of Information, 1962).

[4] For information on this period see John Cady, *A History of Modern Burma* (Ithaca: Cornell University Press, 1958) and Fred R. von der Mehden, *Religion and Nationalism in Southeast Asia* (Madison: University of Wisconsin Press, 1963).

the arms and ammunition used by our heathen opponents and their servants turn into water or air or misfire and never attain their object.[5]

As its symbol the movement used the *galon*, a fabled bird that was able to destroy the *naga* or snake (read foreigner). Astrologers were used to choose the time of the revolt, and tattooing was employed as a means of gaining invulnerability. A story of the period states that after tattooing, the rebels once painted targets on their rear ends and waved them at the nonplussed government troops. These and other practices convinced some that the movement was of a primarily traditional character, not necessarily xenophobic in nature but generally a religiously, monarchically-oriented demand to return to the past.

A second line of argument held that the rebellion rose out of economic demands of the period. Tharrawaddy District had long been a center of agrarian agitation, as had much of lower Burma. The area had been hard hit by the depression, by Indian moneylenders, and by alleged overtaxation. Saya San was a dissident member of a radical monk-led nationalist organization, the Sao Thien G.C.B.A. With four district presidents of this group, he early pushed for antitax propaganda and action. These problems of taxation and land alienation to moneylenders tended to be overlooked by a government seemingly seeking more convenient excuses. Thus, while taking some tentative steps to aid the economic situation, the administration asserted that the spread of the rebellion "was due mainly to itinerant *phongyis* (Buddhist monks) whose preachings against the Government were helped by an unprecedented economic depression and a growing feeling of nationalism." The emphasis in the statement was, perhaps, somewhat misplaced.

Nationalism of the more modern type both helped and was aided by the rebellion. The growing consciousness in the Burmese of their national needs coincided with the development of a more aware nationalist leadership. Although the educated, urban nationalists did not actively engage in the movement, their previous agitation made the rebellion greater in the eyes of the administration than it actually was. Also, the urban nationalists were able to use the grievances of the rebels to put more pressure on the colonial regime. Various nationalist spokesmen used the rebellion as a means of aiding both themselves and their cause. As a result of this abortive, traditionalist movement, modern urban nationalism grew much stronger. As John Cady has expressed it,

> ... The perpetrators of the uprising breathed new vitality into Burmese nationalism simply by demonstrating the courage of their political commitment against impossible odds. The heat of their frenzied resistance welded a connecting bond, between the culturally disparate phongi-led masses and the Western elite.[6]

[5] Quoted in von der Mehden, *Religion and Nationalism*, p. 155.
[6] Cady, *History of Burma*, p. 318.

A far different type of violence erupted in 1938 when bloody communal riots broke out in various places in Burma. Again, the tendency has been to describe these developments in simplistic terms, overemphasizing economic, religious, or political causes. For example, the inquiry commission appointed by the administration held that "the real origin of the disturbances and the real cause of their protraction was, and is, political." The riots have been fully covered in the literature of Burma, but the effort here is to consider them as they relate to our thesis regarding the complexity of causation and techniques of violence and the cumulative effect of violence.

The riots ostensibly developed over the publication of a book by a Muslim, who took the opportunity to cast a number of gratuitous insults upon the majority religion, Buddhism. Although originally published without incident in 1931, its republication in 1936 was in time used by nationalist newspapers to attack the Indian minority in the country. This led to rioting with racial (Indian vs. Burman) and religious (Moslem and Hindu vs. Buddhist) aspects, resulting in some 240 killed, 1,000 injured, and 4,300 arrested. The rioters were frequently led by monks and directed primarily against mosques, Hindu temples and Moslem-Indian individuals and businesses. Compared to postwar communal riots in India and Pakistan, these disruptions were relatively minor, but they were indicative of deepseated problems and were another landmark in Burma's nationalist history.

Analyzing the complex causal factors behind the riots, we can refine these into three rather broad issues: (1) the challenges to Buddhism, (2) Indian economic power, and (3) political activities by nationalist politicians.

The British occupation had been a traumatic period for Buddhism in Burma. The religious leaders had seen their hierarchy disrupted, the educational system that had trained most Burmese boys usurped by Christian missionary schools, the faith endangered by missionary activity, the growing secularism of Western society and urbanization, and traditional values and family ties loosened. In this period of danger, the faithful saw their enemies as Westernization, Christian government and missionaries, and the Indian Muslim community. The last was disliked because of its proselytizing activities and the marriage of Burmese women to incoming Indian Muslims. Thus, one underlying factor of discontent was the wedding of general religious dissatisfaction with specific grievances against the Indian community. This was one reason for the presence of monks in the forefront of the riots. (We must also look to the tradition of religious influence in politics starting with the early period of the nationalist movement.)

The Indian community was held responsible for much of the economic suffering of the Burmese people. The depression had badly hurt the Burmese peasant, who found himself less able to hold onto his land, as well as the urban Burman, who had to face the competition of the Indian worker and professional. The competition between the Burman and Indian proletariat had led to bloody riots in 1930 in which perhaps three to five hundred were killed, and the following years saw an increase in this competition. It was in the rural areas that conditions were worst. Between 1929 and 1934 approximately two million acres of rice land in lower Burma came into the hands of Indian moneylenders, and by 1937 over 50 percent of the rice lands of lower Burma were out of Burmese hands. Over the years these conditions had led to bitter accusations against the Indian community; this animosity was at least partially responsible for the riots of 1938. In its generally excellent report, the "Riot Inquiry Committee" presented a long and cogent analysis of the history of the "Indian Problem" in Burma. It pointed out the omnipresence of Burman fears of Indian immigration and land ownership. When combined with religious fears and growing nationalism, the "Indian Problem" needed only a small spark to ignite into violence. The remarkable fact is that the violence was not greater.

The spark that ignited the riots came from the politicians of Burma, men who for personal and nationalist aims desired to move against the Indian community. Through their newspapers they made the anti-Buddhist book prominent, and in the pages of their papers they continued to inflame the populace against Indians. The Riot Committee was in turn castigated by the press for stating "it is, we think, fair to say that the newspapers ... continuously, if intermittently, sought to use them [Indian problems] for the political purpose of driving a wedge of prejudice and ill-feeling between the Burmese and Indian population of Burma." The Committee further charged nationalist politicians and organizations of taking advantage of the riots for their own benefit.[7] There seems sufficient proof of this charge, although the Committee probably cast its net too wide in some of its accusations. The riots of 1938 were probably a combination of all these factors, combining in different ways from region to region and playing upon the accumulated grievances of the Burmese population. However, "violent" Burma of the prewar days was to prove quite peaceful when compared to the developments in the postwar era.

Like other areas of Southeast Asia, Burma has been the scene of violence and political turbulence for a generation. Some of this violence was foreign-inspired, such as the vicious fighting that took place during World War II or the invasion of Kuomintang troops into northern Burma after their defeat by the Chinese Communists in 1949. However, since 1947 Burma has continuously experienced various forms of rebellion and civil war. The actors and techniques of insurgency have varied, thus differentiating Burma from most areas in the sheer variety of its violence. The history of these rebellions still needs to be written. When it is, it will probably be voluminous.

The character of the groups that have taken part in violent rejection of the authority of the Burmese government is complex but can arbitrarily be broken

---

[7]For a study of the riots see von der Mehden and Cady and especially the interim and regular reports of the riot committee published in Rangoon in 1939 by the Superintendant of Government Printing and Stationery.

down into three groups: Communist, ethnic groups, and military or paramilitary units. Since the eve of independence, the Communists have participated in antigovernment military action. They included two mutually antagonistic sections — the "Trotskyists," or Red Flag Communists, and "regular," or White Flag Communists, who probably numbered approximately twenty-five thousand men at the beginning. In spite of constant efforts by the government to seek peace terms, groups of Communist guerrillas still roam rural areas of Burma carrying out hit-and-run attacks. Their numbers are now probably somewhere between one and two thousand; many of their leaders have been killed or captured.

The second group of insurgents was composed of military units who went into open rebellion soon after independence. These included a section of the P.V.O. (a paramilitary organization composed of veterans who were not incorporated into the regular Burmese army) and two of the five fully equipped battalions of the Burma Rifles. These units went into the field in an effort to bring down the government or make it "reform" by force of arms. In time they either returned to the fold or merged with other insurgent units. Luckily for the Burmese government, they did not fully cooperate with the other rebels in the field.

The Communists and dissident military units chose violence for a variety of immediate and more deep-rooted reasons. Their immediate grievances were against what they felt to be an undesirable independence agreement between Burma and the United Kingdom and the unwillingness of the government to move to the left fast enough. It should be stated that many of the men in the military units were not aware of the ideological niceties of their officers' dissatisfaction but just followed their leaders. Beyond these immediate causes, we must look to the continuing role that violence had played in Burmese politics and, particularly, to the disruption of the country's political, economic and social life caused by World War II and the Japanese occupation. Many of these young men had known nothing but the violence and disruption of war with the status given the man with a uniform and rifle. After the war there was the chaos and instability of reconstruction, a period of transition from an unsure colonial administration to an inexperienced independent regime. In this situation it was difficult for the individual to return to the less exciting civilian ways, while the political chaos of the period made the possibility of an overthrow of the government inviting to those choosing to take the gamble.

The third element taking part in the rebellions almost broke Burma. In January 1949, the Karen minority, primarily Christian-led and including some of the best military units of the nation, broke and went into rebellion against the government in Rangoon. This period was the nadir for Rangoon, as the capitol was under siege for six weeks (during which time the civil service went on strike), Mandalay and other major cities fell to rebel forces, and the nation was in disarray. Again, the government was saved by a combination of poor military timing by the rebels, promises of the political leaders, and perhaps most importantly, the fact that the various rebel groups could not agree to cooperate and coordinate their political and military actions.[8]

Since 1950-51, when the rebel military was broken into small guerrilla units, other ethnic groups have gone into rebellion, although usually not in a highly coordinated action. These have included the Shans of northeast Burma, the Kachins of the north, and the Arakanese and Mons of the south – the last two not causing large-scale depredations. The reasons for the actions of these non-Burman groups are highly complex and tend to differ according to group. Generally, their grievances are as follows:

Demands for Autonomy

There is a general demand for more control of their own affairs. In the case of the Karens, many wanted full independence. Although officially pre-1962 Burma was a semifederal system, many of these peoples felt that it was more unitary in practice. The Karens, Mons, and Arakanese desired their own states with a large degree of autonomy.

Historic Differences

Behind the demand for control of their own affairs was a variety of antagonisms between the majority Burman population and the minorities. For centuries these people were isolated from the Buddhist Burman culture of the lowlands. When the British came, they maintained this separatism in the administration of the country, the formation of separate military units, and a fostering of close ties with the hill peoples. The result was that while nationalism flourished in Burma proper, many hill peoples continued to support the British raj in the hopes of maintaining their separate status. In addition, the articulate leadership of these peoples, particularly the Karens, tended to be Christian, thus driving another wedge between the Burmans and hill peoples. One can imagine the reaction of a Buddhist nationalist to the following statement by a Karen Christian leader: "The Karens are not ashamed or afraid to proclaim to the world publicly or in private that they owe what progress they have made, to the missionaries whom they affectionately call their 'Mother' under the protection of the British Government whom they rightly call their 'Father.' "[9] During the war the Karens and other hill tribes showed their "affection" by aiding the British while the Burmans at first supported the Japanese in hopes of gaining early independence.

[8] For the Burmese government position on the various uprisings see *Burma and the Insurrections* (Rangoon: Government of the Union of Burma Publication, 1949).

[9] San C. Po, *Burma and the Karens* (London: Elliot Stock, 1928), p. 58.

Local Leadership

It is a contention of the Burmese government that dissatisfaction is fomented by feudal leadership among some of the hill peoples. The government states that these leaders seek to reinforce their own political power and economic interests, which would be diminished under the more democratic regime in Rangoon.

There are a number of other causal factors behind these ethnic insurgents, as has been noted in Chapter 2, but suffice it to state here that each case must be viewed as both a separate conglomeration of grievances and needs and a reaction to the political environment of the nation.

Finally, a word regarding the techniques of violence attributed to the various types of insurgents is appropriate. In the first years of the post-independence period, violence took the form of full-scale war with the battles and sieges involving artillery, units at regiment and battalion strength, and some use of air power. This formal type of warfare largely ended in 1950 except for isolated actions against KMT and Karen units. Since that period operations have been of a guerrilla warfare nature with attacks on roads, villages, and other targets by groups ranging up to several hundred (the large-scale attacks are primarily by ethnic units). Recently, violence has taken the form of blowing up bridges or, rarely, a train, closing road and railroad traffic, kidnapping, assassination, stopping government functionaries such as census takers, and from time to time attacking police outposts or villages to obtain supplies or to eliminate certain villagers as an example. The last type of violence has recently been practiced primarily by Communist groups. The scale of guerrilla operations tends to vary over the years and seems to be related to government military and political activity.

The future does not appear to hold any prospect of real change. The insurgents have not been able to escalate into large units since 1950, and the government has been unsuccessful in eliminating the rebels. By the early 1970s, a virtually permanent impasse seemed to have been reached. The number of actual engagements was much less than two decades earlier. However, an estimated 20 percent of Burma was in the hands of Karen, Kachin, and Shan insurgents.

CHAPTER 8

"La Violencia" in Colombia

Throughout the first half of the twentieth century, Colombia was generally numbered among the most politically mature countries of Latin America. In 1941, John Gunther described Colombia as "one of the most democratic and progressive nations in the Americas."[1] Austin MacDonald's classic text on Latin American politics reports in the 1949 edition that "Colombia is one of the few countries of Latin America that can be fairly called a democracy. Its differences of opinion are settled at the ballot box instead of on the field of battle. . . . The democratic tradition is now well established."[2] In a 1945 survey of Latin American specialists by Russell Fitzgibbon, Colombia was rated the fourth "most democratic" nation in the region.[3]

From the perspective of the mid-1940s, Colombia appeared to be a nation that had overcome a nineteenth-century legacy of chronic civil strife and achieved stable, responsible government. The military had not intervened in politics since 1906, and high caliber civilian statesmanship — of the type exemplified by such presidents as Alfonso López, Eduardo Santos, and Alberto Lleras Camargo — seemed to be the rule. Civil liberties were generally respected.

The political process appeared to be based on peaceful alternation in office by the well-developed Liberal and Conservative parties. Furthermore, in a pattern quite unusual for Latin America at that time, these seemed to be true "mass" parties that effectively held the loyalties of the greater part of the

---

[1] John Gunther, *Inside Latin America* (New York: Harper & Row, Publishers, 1941), p. 161.

[2] Austin F. MacDonald, *Latin American Politics and Government* (New York: Thomas Y. Crowell, 1949), p. 377.

[3] Russell H. Fitzgibbon, "The Measurement of Latin American Political Change," *American Political Science Review,* 55 (September 1961), p. 518.

Colombian population. Identification with one of the major parties was characteristic not only of the urban political elites, but of the lower class and peasantry as well. And although the politically cynical might protest that the *peón* was apt to vote according to the political loyalties of his *patrón,* the politically sophisticated might well have replied that this method of mobilizing the vote was not far different in its implications for the political system from the "machine politics" of more advanced democracies. In general, the dependable following of each of the parties was so distributed that the urbane, sophisticated, middle class controlled the balance of power between them. From 1903 to 1930, the Conservative party was dominant. From 1930 until the late 1940s, the Liberal party controlled the government of Colombia. Not only did the two-party system seem to be the basis of stable, democratic government, but it seemed as well to provide for the national integration of a country with a pronounced tendency toward regional fragmentation. Geographic barriers and distinct historical experiences gave rise to strong local or regional attachments, and the political observer, circa 1945, might well have speculated that party identification served a useful purpose in ameliorating and nationalizing the rival loyalties of the Antioqueño, the Bogotano, and the Costeño.

Then, in 1946, Colombia's democratic reputation was shattered, and the apparent workability of its political system was seriously called into question. From that date until 1958, the nation was immersed in a state of chronic civil strife that was to cause, by the most conservative estimates, over two hundred thousand casualties among a population of some 14 million. It is a bit difficult to find an appropriate term to describe this phenomenon. Its causes were too complex and intricate, its political objectives too inchoate, to define it simply as a rebellion against constituted authority. The lack of any overall strategy or organization prevents us from calling it a revolution or a civil war. Colombians themselves use the term *la violencia* – "the violence" – to describe the total phenomenon of civic breakdown, savagery, bloodshed, and chronic guerrilla warfare.

Conventionally, the period of the most acute and characteristic incidence of *la violencia* may be dated from the ill-fated election of 1946 until the establishment of the civilian National Front government in 1958. However, although our discussion will concentrate on the phenomenon during this decade, it is a most arbitrarily set definition. Sporadic outbreaks of violence were an undercurrent of Colombian history throughout the twentieth century, particularly during the early 1930s. Furthermore, although the problem has ameliorated somewhat in the years since 1958, it has continued, taking new and in some ways more critical forms, up to the present time.

In the 1950s, therefore, a reappraisal of Colombia's political system seemed to be in order. What had happened to the Colombian tradition of political civility and stability? Why had our assessments of Colombian politics been so mistaken? Why had we failed to foresee this eruption of civic disorder?

Quite predictable and conventional explanations are inevitably proffered for widespread resort to political violence anywhere in the present-day world. For many, *la violencia* in Colombia represented a mass uprising against the rigidities of an oppressive and unjust social order, the inevitable consequence of a system of marked inequality, in which political and economic advantage were monopolized by a small "oligarchy" while the great bulk of the population subsisted in dire poverty.[4] For others, the guerrilla movements reflected a campaign of subversion inspired and directed by Communist elements.[5] Both explanations have some bearing on the problem, the first infinitely more than the latter, and both must be taken into account in a final assessment of the phenomenon. However, neither explanation is totally satisfying. To a very great extent, the causes of *la violencia* were rooted in the nature of the Colombian political system itself. In good measure, the factors that brought about civic turmoil were the dark side of the same web of political forces that had enabled Colombia to achieve political stability and democratic process during the first half of the century. There was one question that was not asked of the Colombian political process during the period of its democratic reputation that might serve as a key in unraveling the complex phenomenon of *la violencia*. Why did Colombia, almost uniquely among nations of its type in Latin America, have a system of politics geared to nationally organized, mass-based political parties?

A critical distinction must be made between the character of the Colombian party system when viewed from above, as a component of the national political process, and when viewed from below, as an institution that, with others, made up the fabric of life of the small town or rural community. Viewed from above, at the level of national politics, the Colombian party system looked like a means of ordering power, of establishing consent within a democratic context, and as an institution contributing to the integration of the Colombian nation. However, at the local level, in many areas of Colombia, the same party system prevailed, but its significance and characteristics were different. In the countryside, party identification tended to reinforce other social cleavages — of community, family, and region — cleavages that had a component of conflict about them as part of the legacy of the civil wars of the nineteenth century. The characteristic rural community in Colombia is almost completely composed of adherents of one party or the other. Generally, party competition at the local level is found only where there is some background of recent population mobility. Orlando Fals Borda, the Colombian sociologist, describes the effect of party as a local institution in his discussion of rural life in the Department of Boyacá:

> Politics as action and not as ideology gives personality and cohesion to many *veredas*... Since the local people are actively brought together in a policy of self defense (this seems to be a heritage of the civil wars) it would be suicide for a known Liberal to try to enter Conservative *veredas* like Chulavita, for example, and *visa versa*. In

[4] See, for example, the argument of Vernon Fluharty, *Dance of the Millions* (Pittsburgh: University of Pittsburgh Press, 1957).

[5] This was the initial explanation of the *Bogotazo* offered by Secretary of State Marshall, in Bogotá at the time of this incident as representative to the Inter-American Conference of that year.

the same way, a Conservative renter seeks out a Conservative landlord, and a Liberal renter a Liberal landlord. At times, *veredas* separate from *municipios* for political reasons. . . . In many cases, politics is inherited with the honor of the family, and the violence that results is simply a matter of vendettas.[6]

To a large extent, the peculiar party system of Colombia was a heritage of the nineteenth-century civil wars. At the national level, the postindependence period was characterized by a running debate between the adherents of the Liberal and Conservative ideologies of that day. While these battles were fought at the doctrinal and policy level by intellectuals and politicians in the cities, landowners and the leaders of local *caudillo* bands took sides in terms of them in the country. Should a marauding band under a Liberal chieftain pillage a rural community, its inhabitants might seek out the protection of a Conservative landowner and his armed retainers. Identification with the Conservative party and a seething hatred for the Liberals, emerging out of such an incident, became institutionalized and perpetuated in the local community, passed down from father to son.

Endemic rural violence, reaching something of a climax in the first years of the twentieth century, threatened to destroy the national society that the men of the cities sought to create. By 1906, during the administration of Rafael Reyes, the partisans of the cities, of the middle and upper classes and the intelligentsia, agreed to a political truce. Colombian politics in the twentieth century was, to a large extent, something of a "gentleman's agreement" between the political elites of the warring factions to treat each other in a civil fashion so that the violence stirred by party strife in the countryside would not destroy their world. For more than forty years, the system worked. The cleavages of class, property and wealth, region, and family remained and occasionally erupted in violence, but as long as the critical factor of party conflict was held in check, civic disruption remained a countertheme in a Colombia that was apparently achieving economic and political sophistication.

In the twentieth century, the Colombian parties grew large and aggregative. They became coalitions of quite diverse ideologies. This was particularly true in the Liberal party, where the classic liberalism of the nineteenth century, espoused by landowners and the newer industrial and commercial interests, came into conflict with the doctrines of social reform preached by a new generation of political leaders. Almost everywhere else in Latin America, the advent of this younger group of political leaders, touched by such disparate inspirations as Marxism, continental socialism, Peruvian *Aprismo,* and the New Deal in the United States, led to party fragmentation. However, in Colombia, this heterogeneous set of political attitudes was held in uneasy equilibrium within the Liberal party, both for reasons of the generic futility of third-party

[6]Orlando Fals Borda, *El Hombre y la Tierra en Boyacá* (Bogotá: Ediciones Documentos Colombianos, 1957), p. 191.

movements in well-established two-party systems and, more importantly, because of the potentially ominous consequences of a breakdown in the party equilibrium that had been established. Hence, within the party, there was a substantial effort at accommodation of diverse opinion, the costs of give-and-take among quite diverse political factions always to be measured against the potential threat should partisan fragmentation upset the delicate balance that had been achieved.[7]

The critical factor that shattered this system was perhaps the emergence of the movement for reform throughout Latin America that came with the end of World War II. This widespread mood of change and unrest was born of the idealism of the wartime "struggle for democracy," the very real economic and social changes that affected Latin America during the war years, and a complex of other factors. From 1944 to 1948, major political transformations took place in many of the Latin American nations. Long-term dictators were replaced by younger, idealistic, civilian leaders. The characteristic political phenomenon of the period, particularly in the Caribbean region, was the emergence of democratic reform movements, of the style of José Figueres's *Liberación Nacional* in Costa Rica, and Rómulo Betancourt's *Acción Democrática* in Venezuela. In most nations, these movements emerged as new and distinctive political formations. However, in Colombia, due to the recruiting capabilities of the existing party system, this force did not emerge as a separate movement. Rather, it destroyed the existing structure of politics by attempting to remain as part of it.

Jorge Elíecer Gaitán was, in political style and political ideology, quite compatible with the other leaders of the democratic reform movement of the postwar period. Long a leader of the more radical reform wing of the liberal party, he emerged as a popular hero and national leader at the end of the World War II. The emergence of Gaitán, and the reformist mood of the period, was finally more than the system's resources of political accommodation could handle. The Liberal party split in the elections of 1946, the more radical elements supporting Gaitán, the more "established" factions in the party endorsing the moderate Gabriel Turbay. The Conservative party, under the leadership of Mariano Ospina Pérez, won the presidency with a minority of the popular vote and returned to political control for the first time since 1930.

At this point, political violence became a national problem. In a pattern that is not unusual for Latin America, it was difficult, when a political party returned to power after years in opposition, for its opponents to peacefully accept the electoral test or for the victors to deal generously with the

[7]On the development of the modern Colombian political system, see Vernon Fluharty, *Dance of the Millions;* Eduardo Santa, *Sociología política colombiana* (Bogotá: Editorial Iqueima, 1955); Jesús María Henao and Gerardo Arrubla, *Historia de Colombia* (Bogotá: Librería Voluntad, 1952); José A. Bermúdez, *Compendio de la historia de Colombia* (Bogotá, 1960); Milton Puentes, *Historia del partido liberal colombiano* (Bogotá: Editorial Prag, 1961).

vanquished. After the transition of government in 1930 there had been a flurry of sporadic bloodshed and conflict in the countryside. Again, in 1946, after the Conservatives returned to power on the basis of a most uncertain mandate, the level of political polemic grew much more vituperative and combative, threats of insurrection were heard in the legislative chambers and in the press, and national party leaders goaded on their followers in the villages.

That the transition of 1946 led to violence more persistent and tragic than that of 1930 may be traced to a number of causes. In the first place, greater political awareness had developed by the later date, and the desire to "tap" mass political support was a more important ambition of political leaders throughout Latin America. Second, renewed ideological ferment and the aspiration for sweeping economic and social reform complicated the task of the "democratic aristocrats" in maintaining the structures and techniques of party competition that had prevailed since 1900. Third, for a complex of situational reasons, the national police force and, to a lesser extent, the army had become the partisan instruments of the victorious Conservatives and were often used vindictively against affiliates of the Liberal party.

Thus, the built-in hatreds, the potential for violence, involved in the heritage of partisan identification at the local level, which had so long been held in check by the "gentleman's agreement" at the national level, were now released as national leaders sought to mobilize mass support for a contest no longer bound by the historic rules.

There is a tendency toward the polarization of political positions in Latin America, toward excess, and a tone of strife and of the macabre in political oratory that has been explained in many ways. Some attribute it to a lasting flaw in Hispanic character, others to the high stakes of the political game in Latin America, still others to the frustrations of an imperfect social order. None of these explanations seem to fit the problem with any precision. In any case, the phenomenon is evident. In most countries, most of the time, the exorbitant tone of political discourse and the frequent incitements to rebellion that it contains do not result in holocaust, owing to the residual political indifference, skepticism, tolerance, and innate good sense of the citizenry. However, in Colombia, circa 1947, an oratory of appeal to violence apparently fell on receptive ears. The political polemic of the day seemed to release latent aggressions and conflicts. The following examples, only two among many contained in Monseigneur Guzmán's collection, illustrate the character of political communication taken up by both parties after 1946. That both examples emanate from Liberal forces is merely coincidence. Equally combative statements can be found on the Conservative side.

> Fellow Liberals ... We must maintain faith and our spirit of combat.... But we must be ready and attentive to orders. The extermination must be complete. Every estate and business of a

Conservative will have to pass permanently into Liberal hands. The same must be done with public offices. No Conservative must remain alive.

Liberal Agrarian Directorate[8]

Liberals: the advance command posts of the party order: Use all means to impede the government and its employees. Burn and destroy the houses of the Conservatives, and if they are obstinate, sack them. Their goods must pass by whatever means into the power of the Liberals. Down with the police. In the army we have copartisans that can help us in case of need. Steal the guns of the police and dress in their uniforms so as to pass as government agents, to find out what is going on in the Conservative ranks, and the plans of the government. This government must fall. Do not hesitate if Conservatives are in your family because they are sworn enemies of the Liberals and must be destroyed. Blood and politics do not mix. One must unfrock priests and enter the convents to ascertain if arms are hidden there.

Committee of Liberal Democratic Action[9]

The initial incident of violence varied greatly from locale to locale. In some cases, the assassination or imprisonment of local Liberal party leaders by Conservative police led to retaliation against the police or Conservative leaders. Or an attack of unknown origin on a Conservative village or estate might cause reprisals to be taken against the nearest available Liberal adherents. Once set in motion, such patterns of blow and counterblow were often recurrent.

Most authorities agree that partisan conflict, unleashing long dormant social, community, and family cleavages, "triggered" *la violencia* in Colombia. However, the phenomenon soon became complicated by a complex chain reaction of secondary causes. Prominent among these, particularly after 1954, was the role of the military.

Ospina Pérez was succeeded in the presidency by the more reactionary and heavy-handed Conservative Laureano Gómez in 1950. Gómez sought to bring an end to the civil strife by strong-man tactics, dismissing Congress, imposing tight censorship, and severely restricting political activities. His methods both failed to reduce the incidence of violence and also alienated the urban political elites. In 1953, he was overthrown in a military coup. In July 1954, General Gustavo Rojas Pinilla became president, and the military returned to Colombian politics for the first time in fifty years.

Rojas instituted a campaign of "pacification" in the countryside which began auspiciously but soon degenerated into a further stimulus to political violence itself. Often, at the local level, the army chose to fight violence with

---

[8] Mg. Germán Guzmán Campos, et al., *La Violencia en Colombia* (Bogotá: Ediciones Tercer Mundo, 1962), p. 244.

[9] Guzmán et al., *La Violencia,* p. 245.

violence. In some cases, a complex pattern of retaliation was involved. Should an army patrol be attacked by a guerrilla band identified with the Liberal cause, let us say, the army might respond by using heavy weapons against a nearby Liberal village. Their homes destroyed and families dead, the survivors might take to the mountains to join a guerrilla operation, the "enemy" now identified as the army.

In the 1950s violence had become "institutionalized" in Colombian politics. The guerrilla bands, which for longer or shorter periods of time controlled large sections of the country, were in many instances quite self-sustaining, many of them possessing intricate systems of organization, law, and logistics of supply.

In the period of institutionalized violence, the initial political causes of the turmoil became less apparent. The phenomenon was increasingly complicated by motives of revenge, self-defense, or sheer desperation. The preeminence of such factors in comparison to political objectives is well revealed in the biographies of guerrilla leaders collected by Guzmán.[10] Reaction to violence had become a major cause of continued violence. Those who had seen their homes, villages, and families destroyed would organize for defense or attack. In some cases their actions were directed against a specific assailant, the army, a rival party or band. In others, armed force was primarily used as a means of survival, through theft and looting. In still others, violence was indiscriminate, without motive or hope.

Another "secondary" factor of the chain reaction of violence was simple gangsterism, which fed upon, was concealed by, and emerged out of the whirlwind of civic disruption. In some areas, the threat or fact of violence was used to drive down property prices and force sales. Hijacking and theft were also blended with the more general breakdown of civic order.

Most tragic was the "heritage of violence" felt by young men who were in their early twenties at the end of the decade of the 1950s, who had joined the guerrilla bands in early adolescence upon the death of their families, had grown up with *la violencia,* and knew no other way of life.

Certainly there was a component of social strife in *la violencia,* of revolution against an archaic social order, and something of true class conflict. Unquestionably Communist and, in the early 1960s, Castroite agitation was a factor in the turmoil, and foreign direction and assistance probably does account in some good measure for its recent reemergence. But these appear as phases of the whole, as factors that were true at some times and some places, or as elements inextricably interwoven with other patterns of motivation and behavior.

Several characteristic features of the incidence of violence in Colombia should be noted. First, this was primarily a rural phenomenon. After the dramatic incident of the *Bogotazo,* when, on April 9, 1948, the capital city of Colombia erupted in uncontrollable rioting, pillage, and arson following the

---

[10]Guzmán et al., *La Violencia,* p. 245.

assassination of Gaitán, the major cities of the nation were relatively immune from violent outbursts, almost islands in the tumult that was afflicting the rural areas. This was true despite the fact that the urban population increased enormously during the period of the violence, placing severe strains on housing, urban facilities, and possibilities of employment as refugees streamed to the urban areas from the country.

Second, violence was concentrated in the highland areas of Colombia. The Caribbean coastal areas in particular were virtually unaffected by the problem. Some have attributed this to the more easygoing quality of the racially heterogeneous coastal culture. However, a more likely explanation probably is to be found in the absence of the divisive heritage of party conflict in this area. The legacy of the nineteenth-century civil wars was nowhere as pronounced in the Caribbean area as in the highlands.

Third, *la violencia* remained a localized, fragmentary phenomenon throughout the period. No national leadership emerged to meld the isolated rebel groups into a cohesive national movement with defined political objectives. That this did not occur may have something to do with the geographic fragmentation of Colombia itself. Or it may be attributed to the capacity of national authorities to prevent the emergence of any potentially effective national revolutionary movement. But, to a large extent, the fact that *la violencia* remained as a frustrating and inextinguishable peat fire, rather than breaking out as a full-scale conflagration, is probably due to the very diversity of motives that led to resort to violence itself.

Why did *la violencia* persist so long? In part, the answer to this question may be found in the chain reaction of secondary causes that built on the original political conflict. Incident, followed by retaliation, followed by counter-retaliation, provided always fresh motives for terror. But it is also clear that *la violencia* was a war that no political decision could end. The capabilities of the national government were not sufficient to put an end to the civic disorder, and the rebels lacked any suggestion of the organization or cohesiveness that would have been necessary to ultimately overthrow the national order.

In 1958, one year after the downfall of Rojas Pinilla in a military coup, the "gentleman's agreement" on which the Colombian political system had been based through most of the twentieth century was reinstated. The Conservative and Liberal parties agreed to divide the responsibilities of government equally between them for a period of sixteen years. The parties would alternate the presidency every four years. (We have now concluded the second period of this arrangement. Alberto Lleras Camargo, a Liberal, was president from 1958 to 1962. The term of the Conservative, Guillermo León Valencia, expired in 1966. He was succeeded by the Liberal, Carlos Lleras Restrepo. In 1970 Misael Pastrana Borrero, Conservative, was elected, completing the arrangement.) Cabinet posts and legislative seats are divided equally between the parties, as are local government offices.

This National Front government appeared as the last chance for the civilian political elites to restore order and civility to Colombian politics. It is true that with the establishment of this government, the partisan warfare that was the initial cause of *la violencia* diminished. However, the secondary causes of violence, violence as a political and social institution, proved more difficult to eradicate. Only slowly and gradually in the early 1960s did the Colombian military eliminate the remaining guerrilla bands, one at a time. And by the middle of the decade, the instances of rebellion came more to take on the character of a National Liberation Front, with support and assistance to some rebel groups from Cuban sources demonstrated. In this latter period also, a wave of kidnapping for ransom of members of wealthy and prominent families became a new form of civic terror.

Thus violence, its causes and effects, but most often its bewildering presence, were a prominent part of Colombian political life from the later 1940s to the mid-1960s. Despite the various studies, speculations, and analyses, there is a great deal that remains mysterious about the origins of this problem and the reasons for its persistence. To this day, it is difficult to assess the claims on the state that the political use of violence represented. We assume that *la violencia* was related to the unrest and agitation for reform that is characteristic of Latin America in this period, but the extent to which this is true is hard to ascertain unless we are willing to subscribe to the notion that all revolt must be something of a class revolution. The reasons for resort to violence were to such a large extent localized that to understand them fully would be to know the detailed social histories of hundreds of Colombian villages and regions.

However, despite the complexity of the phenomenon of violence, the role of partisan conflict was a central factor throughout the period. And this is indeed the tragic irony of modern Colombian political life: the pattern of nationwide party identification and cohesion that seemed for so long to be the basis of political maturity and democratic practice became ultimately a major cause of political breakdown.

CHAPTER 9

*Domestic Violence
in Africa:
Zaire*

As a candidate for Africa's leading laboratory of violence, the Zaire (formerly Congo/Kinshasa) faces competition only from Algeria. Algeria is probably the winner in duration and intensity (eight years, one million casualties) but Zaire in its brief life as an independent state is rapidly catching up in all categories and already leads in the range and eclecticism of its disorders. An exploration of post-independence violence in Zaire, and above all the rebellion of 1964, seems relevant to the quest for comprehension of internal warfare.

The adventure in instant decolonization in 1960 left in its wake a wave of disorders. The most important types can be grouped into five partially overlapping categories:

Army Mutinies. Violence incident to the revolt of the troops against their European officers, beginning July 5, 1960, is the touchstone for all others. The new state was deprived of its effective monopoly of force, and therefore an environment peculiarly favorable to perpetrators of violence was established. In the short run, a number of clashes occurred, sparked by fears of the mutinied troops that they were to be attacked by "Belgian paratroopers." In the long run, the inability of Zaire authorities ever to reestablish full control and discipline over all units meant that army units were frequently a participant in violence not relatable to the normal functions of maintenance of order.

A second wave of mutinies occurred in 1966 and 1967 in the aftermath of the rebellions. These resulted from the creation of mercenary units of white adventurers in 1964 to help subdue the insurgents. Once in existence, these units proved difficult to disband. Although there were only a few hundred white

147

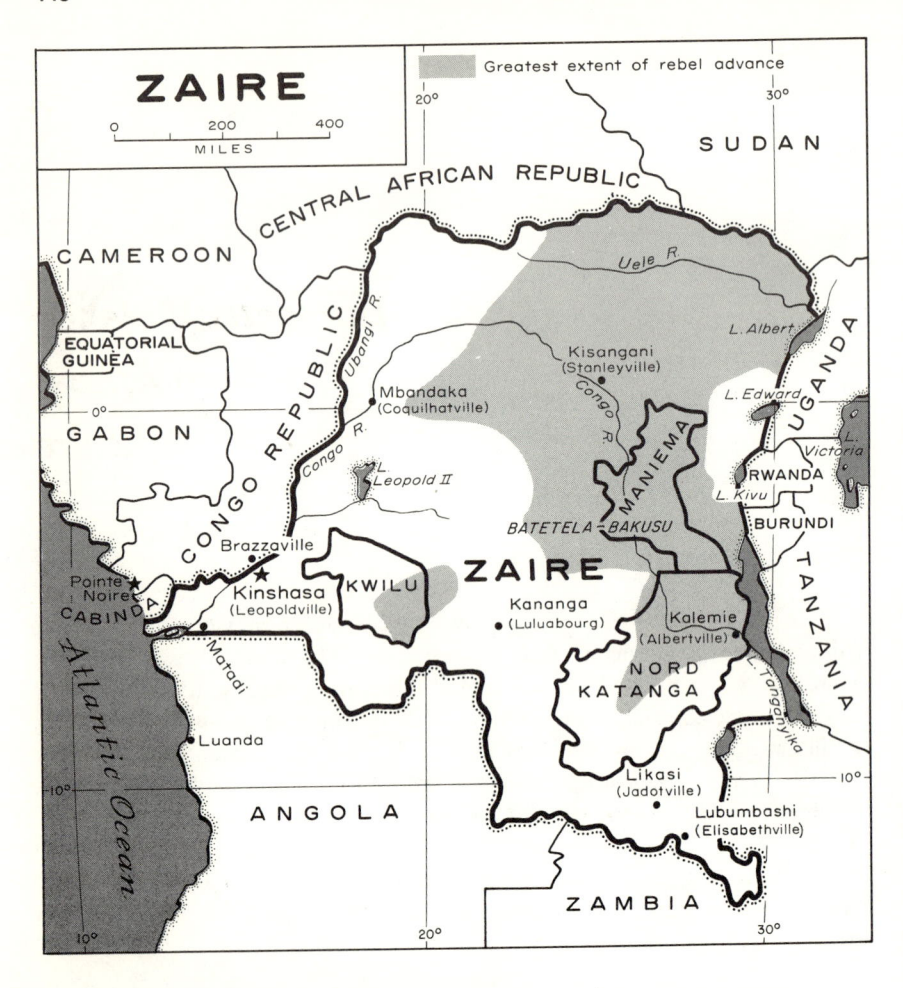

mercenaries, their capacity for troublemaking went far beyond their modest numbers. They were able to control some units and officers of the Zaire army. In the more serious 1967 mutiny, a surprise attack virtually exterminated a whole battalion of Zaire troops at Kisangani in their barracks. The mutineers established a redoubt for themselves in Bukavu and were driven out only after four months had elapsed from the beginning of the mutiny.

Anti-European Manifestations. In the immediate aftermath of an independence gone awry, a series of assaults against Europeans took place in widely scattered parts of the country. For the most part, the assailants were mutineers, often fearful that the Belgians were about to attack them. Much of the violence was aimed at humiliation rather than destruction of the victims; Belgian women were raped in the presence of their children or husbands, priests were paraded naked, men were required to perform barefoot dances. The number of fatalities at this stage was quite small, numbering no more than two dozen.

Ethnic Disorders. Although these were widespread, the greatest concentration of ethnic hostility was in former Kasai province. The vortex of conflict was the confrontation between Kasai Buluba, who had dispersed throughout the province and held a privileged position in the modern sector, and other ethnic groups, especially the Bena Lulua (who themselves were culturally Baluba and had never regarded themselves as a distinctive group until the colonial period). The Baluba were forced to retreat to their ethnic homeland of Sud-Kasai in a bloody exodus involving approximately five hundred thousand persons. Central and provincial authorities were neither willing nor able to protect them from their enemies. Comparable enforced departures of "stranger" groups, who enjoyed social and economic rank similar to that of the Baluba, can be seen in the riots against "Dahomeans" in Ivory Coast in 1959 and against Congo-Brazzaville citizens in Gabon in 1962.

Religious Uprisings. The leading example of this type was the revolt by several hundred followers of Mpeve, a syncretic movement in Kwilu province, in March 1962. The group simply refused to recognize the authority of the state and killed or captured those sent to enforce it. Military operations to suppress the movement resulted in seventy-five casualties. The Mpeve affair suggests comparison with the Lumpa Church clashes with the new African authorities in Zambia just prior to independence. Lumpa refusal to accept nationalist authority, because it was irrelevant to the world of Lumpa prophetess Alice Lenshina, made the bloody confrontation inevitable, leaving over six hundred dead.[1]

Warfare between Fragments of Zaire. Eleven days after independence the Katanga secession began the process of splintering Zaire. In August 1960, a second fragment declared itself independent: the Baluba province of Sud-Kasai. In November 1960, the Lumumbist groups, ousted from power in Kinshasa (Leopoldville),[2] established their own version of a "legal" national government in Kasangani (Stanleyville). Kinshasa and Kisangani each fell heir to part of the Armée Nationale Zairoise (ANZ, alias Force Publique), while Katanga and Sud-Kasai rapidly created their own armed forces. In 1960-61, these four armies engaged in a delicate dance of the cranes, circling each other but only rarely clashing directly. However, populations unfortunate enough to be in the path of these maneuvers suffered heavily. At most stages, military movements were the counterpoint to shifting patterns of negotiation. The ultimate military superi-

[1] James W. Fernandez, "The Lumpa Uprising: Why?" *Africa Report,* 9, No. 10 (November 1964), 30-32.

[2] Beginning in 1966, the names of Zaire cities were Africanized. Leopoldville became Kinshasa, Stanleyville Kisangani, and Elisabethville Lubumbashi, to cite the three most important.

ority of the United Nations restricted the possibilities of full-scale conflict, as did the poor discipline and inefficiency of all of the armies involved.

Inter-provincial Warfare. The total recasting of internal boundaries in 1962, breaking down six provinces into twenty-one, and the control by provincial authorities of armed police forces, led to several small-scale engagements between provinces. Conflict grew out of disputes over boundaries and territory; the acceptance of ethnic self-determination as a criterion for province formation led to inextricable difficulties in marginal zones, where two or more groups were mixed.

Insurrection in North Katanga. The Katanga secession produced in its turn a revolt of a large part of Baluba and other ethnic groups in the northern part of Katanga (recently renamed Shaba) province, who felt unrepresented in the Tshombe government and feared a regime where they would be subject to the unrestrained domination of the Lunda, Batabwa, Bayeke, and other southern Katanga ethnic groups. This insurrection is closest to the 1964 rebellion in terms of structure and goals. The Katanga Copperbelt towns were much too efficiently policed for urban Baluba to take the lead; a rural uprising broke out in August 1960, and despite brutal repressive campaigns by the Katanga gendarmery, large zones were never brought under administrative control. Some soldiers from the Kisangani Army took part, but the insurrection was mainly manned by rural youths. The rebellion was not only directed against Tshombe; the youths assassinated several leading Baluba chiefs.[3] The use of magic and drugs also appeared on a large scale. The youth bands, once established, could not be controlled by the leadership and were a source of terror and disorder both to the Katanga gendarmes and the local population.

Several conclusions emerge from this catalogue of political violence in the first three years of independence.[4] Most of it was related to the immediate disequilibria created when power was transferred before any clearly defined set of power relationships had emerged within the Zaire polity. The immediate breakdown of the instruments of coercion and the ineffectiveness of the administrative structure made dissidence relatively easy and created the expectation among many dissatisfied groups that their position could be

---

[3]The most prominent was Kabongo, ruler of the second largest Baluba traditional grouping. The circumstances of the assassination were both atrocious and clinically interesting. The murder was carried out in exaggerated violation of traditional norms of a chiefly death. Normally, a Baluba chief must die without blood; in this case, Kabongo was chopped to pieces – a blow against both chief and chieftaincy, sharply differentiating this rebellion from those Max Gluckman analyzes in developing his interesting hypothesis that many traditional revolts have had the function of sustaining the system, as the blow is struck against a chief in the name of chieftaincy. See Max Gluckman, *Custom and Conflict in Africa* (New York: Free Press of Glencoe, Inc., 1959).

[4]The three rounds fought between UN forces and Katanga gendarmes in September and December 1961, and December–January 1962–1963, are not included in this list, as they are not strictly internal warfare; also omitted are clashes between Belgian forces and Zaire units in 1960, especially at Matadi and in Katanga.

improved through violence. In the extreme case, groups sought to withdraw from the system, through claiming international sovereignty — as in the Katanga and, to a lesser extent, Sud-Kasai cases — or simply withdrawing internally, as with Mpeve. Only in North Katanga did internal warfare take on the dimensions of a full rebellion against postcolonial authority. The loss of monopoly of force by the central authorities permitted the proliferation of armed bands by which subgroups sought to enforce their claims. For the most part, these were in the hands of "states," and operated as regular armies; the North Katanga insurgents were alone in resembling a sustained force. The goals of internal warfare were relatively limited. Groups fought for differing interpretations of what power transfer settlement had been (or should have been), not yet to overthrow it.

We may also note in passing that the large towns were not the focus of violence, despite the massive migration to the city and vast unemployment. In 1959-1960, urban rioting had played an important part in the surge to independence; major disorders occurred in Kinshasa (January 1959), Luluabourg (July 1959, and sporadically thereafter), Kisangani (October 1959), Lubumbashi, Jadotville, and Kolwezi (March 1960). Urban violence predominated in the terminal colonial period; conflict shifted to the countryside after June 1960, and towns were relatively calm. This can be explained by the greater effectiveness of governmental coercion in the cities and the proliferation of armed groups in the countryside.

With the restoration of central authority over the entire country in January 1963, by UN armed intervention in Katanga, the first phase of violence came to a close. A new political equilibrium had emerged, and violence diminished to small-scale interprovincial skirmishing. Internal warfare of a new kind emerged in 1964, with the appearance of local guerrilla forces whose leadership proposed not just to alter the equilibrium, but to effect a radical social transformation — to achieve, in the words of the insurgent leaders, a "second independence." The rebellion succeeded in the latter half of 1964 in eliminating government authority from the northeast quadrant of the country and very nearly toppled the entire structure; it is by far Africa's largest postcolonial uprising. Our purpose is to examine its causes, goals, skill groups, participant groups, and effects.[5]

[5]The analysis of the rebellion is drawn in part from interviews in Kisangani (Stanleyville) and Kinshasa (Leopoldville) in January 1965, with Zairiens and expatriates who lived under rebel administration, and examination of a portion of the documents captured in Kisangani. Other sources include the excellent study of rebellion in Kwilu by Renée Fox, Willy de Craemer and Jean-Marie de Ribeaucourt, "La deuxième indépendance-Etude d' un cas: La rébellion au Kwilu," Etudes Congolaises, (Jan.-Feb. 1965), 1-35; the major Congolese newspapers, *Courrier d'Afrique, Le Progres, L'Etoile du Congo, Essor du Katanga, La Presse Africaine* (Bukavu), *Le Martyr* (published August–November 1965, in Kisangani). *Courrier Africain* (CRISP), *Etudes Congolaises*, and *Remarques Congolaises et Africaines* also have published valuable documentation on the rebellion. For a superbly documented account, see Benoit Verhaegen, *Rébellions au Congo*, Vols. I, II (Brussels: CRISP, 1966, 1969). One of the co-authors has put forward a more extensive analysis, "Rebellion and the Congo," in Robert I. Rotberg and Ali I. Mazrui, eds., *Protest and Power in Black Africa* (New York: Oxford University Press, 1970), pp. 968-1011.

The emergence of an insurrectional potential in the Congo has two intimately related aspects: a sense of relative deprivation creating a mobilization potential, and perspective of violent action as a feasible political response. The decline of material well-being of most areas, both urban and rural, since 1960, combined with the gross inequities in distribution of the rewards of independence, has produced a social polarization between "intellectuals" and "mass." Symptomatic of this were the appeal for a general strike by leading trade unions in March 1962, against the high level of remuneration for politicians, the widespread assassinations of "intellectuals" in rebel-occupied areas, and the formation of intellectual associations to defend corporate interests in Kisangani and elsewhere. The "intellectuals" are joined in the pillory of the deprived by the external enemy – above all, Americans, who protect the "exploiters" and in return allegedly receive untrammelled access to the riches of the country.

Resentment is also directed at those seen as the brutal hirelings of the parvenue ruling class, the police and soldiers. The army units, in continuity with colonial tradition in Zaire, have been in good part deployed throughout the countryside, not simply garrisoned in a few military camps. Excessively harsh repression of local incidents was frequent; the temptation to plunder proved irresistible to many soldiers when sanctions were absent and schooling in civic responsibility had been minimal. Even the privates received wages many times the average rural revenue.

Although these grievances were general, it is vital to note that perception of them was fragmented and passed through an ethnic-regional prism. Deprivation was relative in both time and space. All those who had not shared the spectacular promotions of 1960 were aware of the deterioration of their situation since independence. But the spatial referent was also crucial; the immediate point of comparison was the status of neighboring groups. If one group became persuaded that another was faring relatively well under the new rules, or that the "intellectuals" were predominantly recruited from a given ethnic community, the social enemy became objectified in ethnic terms.[6] In Kwilu, for example, the Bapende and Bambundu saw their unhappy condition as related to the domination of the Kwilu provincial government by Bambala, Bangongo, Bayanzi, and other north Kwilu groups, as well as the long imprisonment of their most prominent political leader, Antoine Gizenga. In Sankuru and Maniema, the Batetela-Bakusu saw the national government as controlled by groups hostile to them, who had participated in the assassination of their ethnic hero Patrice Lumumba. Politicians in the capital exacerbated their poverty by systematic and malevolent neglect. In the process of fragmented perception of deprivation, then, generalized grievances became fused with

---

[6] For further elaboration on this point, see the chapter on "The Politics of Ethnicity" in Crawford Young, *Politics in the Congo* (Princeton: Princeton University Press, 1965) and the bibliographic references cited therein.

entirely local ones. The behavior of a given territorial administrator, the removal of a given chief, inadequate ethnic representation in a given provincial government became absorbed into the antigovernmental syndrome.

Grievance alone is a necessary but not sufficient condition for the activation of sustained violence; to embark upon the adventure of insurrection, a man must see some prospect of success. A very dim spark of hope may suffice for the insurgent leadership, who have the most to gain from triumph, but recruits for partisan bands must be shown that they are not lemmings marching into the sea. In Zaire, there were both rational and supernatural reasons that success seemed possible.

In much of the eastern zone, the administration had been severely disorganized by repeated changes of regime at the provincial level. For example, in Maniema Province, cradle of the rebellion, there had been since 1960 seven changes in government, which usually involved purges extending downward to the rural capillaries of administration. Government authority had been virtually destroyed; what remained was capable neither of solving the problems of the local population, nor of suppressing revolt. Army ineptitude against other armed groups had been clearly shown in several humiliating encounters with Katanga gendarmes in 1960-62; few, however, suspected it would be so vulnerable to rural warriors without firearms. But the first outbreak of rebellion in Kwilu, January-April 1964, saw some of the ANZ's best units held at bay by guerrillas with spears and the ANZ chief-of-staff killed by a poisoned arrow. The next encounter, when two ANZ battalions were routed by a few hundred Bafulero warriors in the Ruzizi plain in May 1964, on the Burundi frontier, was an even more spectacular display of the impotence of the ANZ — both to potential rebels and to ANZ troops themselves. From then until the stiffening of the ANZ with mercenaries in August, the army simply melted away, and there were very few encounters. No more than 150 rebels seized Kisangani. The weakness of the ANZ was compounded by the persistence of divisions within it surviving from the period 1960-61 when the ANZ had been split between Kinshasa (Leopoldville) and Kisangani (Stanleyville). Outbreak of the rebellion in the east strained the loyalties of officers and men who had fought for Kisangani in the immediate post-independence confusion. The Armée Populaire de Libération (APL) was a small rebel force expanding into a power vacuum.

But this could not explain the initial enlistments or the spectacle of "simbas"[7] marching against ANZ positions. For this, the manipulation of magical beliefs was crucial. The material superiority of the ANZ was recognized, but it could be overcome by supernatural means. The deadly weapon of the army — bullets — could be rendered harmless by a magical protection that turned bullets into water. This is one of the most persistent themes in the folklore of African revolt, dating back to the earliest primary resistance movements, when Africans first faced the challenge of an enemy with firearms.

[7] As the APL troops referred to themselves; Swahili for "lion."

From Maji-Maji in Tanganyika through the Mad Mullah of Somalia to the Bakumu 1944 uprising in eastern Zaire and the North Katanga insurgency in 1960-62, village warriors have been rendered intrepid by the conviction that they have obtained invulnerability to bullets, which became as harmless as raindrops.

The utilization of magic was well-developed and ritualized. Each recruit went through an initiation ceremony, including light incisions in his chest and forehead and baptism with "Mulele water" (later "Lumumba water"), which conferred invulnerability upon the new simba. The continued potency of this protection depended upon the observation of certain taboos, which were also related to the control and discipline of the Popular Army. Touching an impure person spoiled the "dawa."[8] Women were included in this category, rendering this taboo a prescription for a celibate army. Rural warriors were not saints, of course, and absolution could be purchased from the unit witch doctor for dereliction from this harsh injunction. In battle, simbas had to walk straight forward and keep their eyes to the front to avoid loss of invulnerability. This tactic not only precluded unpremeditated retreats but also provided a plausible explanation for any casualties that did occur – they had turned their heads.

The idea of "dawa" as a bullet-proof shield melded easily with traditional views of causation, with the material and the supernatural intricately interwoven. The deadly power of a bullet was fully appreciated; at the same time, a more potent force could act upon this lethal agent and render it harmless. The material bullet is still present but transformed into water.[9] Social reinforcement of this belief derives not only from the ceremony, but also from general acceptance of the reasonableness of the proposition.[10] Pierre Mulele, leader of the Kwilu insurrection, demonstrated the power of his magic by firing blank cartridges at himself; it was widely reported that similar demonstrations were conducted in eastern zones, either with blanks or with rounds that had nearly all the powder removed, so that they limped feebly out of the barrel. Magic was made doubly effective by its persuasiveness to the ANZ as well as to the APL. Time after time, regular army units simply abandoned their weapons and fled because they believed it was pointless to fire.

In their expansive phase, simbas always concealed their casualties and claimed that they had suffered no losses in battle – and indeed they often did

---

[8] Swahili for "medicine"; in coastal Swahili, it is used to designate modern medicine, but in the Zaire dialect, Kingwana, it refers to various charms, talismans, and amulets used to ward off evil.

[9] This would appear to contrast with superstition often mildly present in Western soldiers, who wear good luck charms to secure the more impersonal intervention of divine fate, to keep them from the path of a bullet but not to transform the agent of death.

[10] An anthropologist at Lovanium University once inquired of his class how many believed in the efficacy of magic; 105 of 107 responded positively. J. C. de Ridder has shown that belief in magic remains general even in the well-established industrial centers of South Africa, through a series of psychological tests applied to a sample of 2500 adult African men in Johannesburg; *The Personality of the Urban African in South Africa* (London: Routledge and Kegan Paul, 1960), pp. 105-6, 160.

not. The need to maintain popular confidence in "dawa" helps make comprehensible some of the extravagant statements by APL leaders to explain defeats. General Olenga maintained his army was fighting thousands of "Americans" (i.e., mercenaries); he claimed that the "cowboys" had suffered ten thousand casulties in the defense of Bukavu.[11] By implication, even invulnerable simbas might have insufficient supernatural resources to cope with Yankee hordes; Olenga promised that this deficiency would be overcome by the imminent arrival of hundreds of thousands of Chinese. Aircraft presented another problem for "dawa"; invulnerability beliefs did not seem to extend to bombs and strafing. The central government made use of rather indiscriminate psychological air raids against Albertville, Kindu, and Boende. The bitter resentment these raids caused is perhaps partially understandable in terms of a violation of the rules of warfare within which the simbas were prepared to compete.

The acute weakness of governmental structures and coercive instruments, compounded by the potency of magic as a rural (and urban) mobilizer are both crucial to understanding the spread of the rebellion. Grievance predisposed certain populations to rebellion; the frailty of authority and the protection of the supernatural made the appeal to insurgency seductively free of risk.

The goals of the insurgent movements were diffuse. Post-overthrow programs remained undefined; clarity of purpose extended only to the elimination of the Adoula (and subsequently Tshombe) governments in Kinshasa and the uprooting of the baneful expatriate (American) influences associated with it. Diverse persons and groups in the rebel entourage aspired to displace incumbent power-holders at different echelons, but with a handful of exceptions there is no indication of concrete intent to exercise political authority roles in a different fashion. The most notable ideologue, Mulele, propounded an intellectually more elegant analysis of present discontents but was less specific on how he proposed to restore prosperity to the countryside. Thus, in contrast to Communist revolutions, the acquisition of a "liberated area" was a pyrrhic victory, as the absence of economic or social content to the rebellion became exposed. Kisangani was the most dramatic example; its capture was a momentous psychological triumph but a political disaster. The rebels were unprepared and unable to take administrative responsibility for such a large urban center. Such governmental functions as were performed merely perpetuated existing routine.

The rebellion took place on many levels and indeed was really a series of uprisings rather than a single, coherent movement. Flowing from its dispersed character was a wide range of leadership roles, related to the diverse functions at

---

[11] Kindu radio, October 2, 1964. There were no American casualties at Bukavu, and only a handful of American military personnel from the military advisory group were present. The successful defense of Bukavu against an estimated 6000 simbas was essentially the work of the ANZ itself reinforced by some Katanga gendarmes. This was one of the few battles in which the ANZ actually fought well.

different levels, Externally, the rebellion had its diplomats and its exile plotters; internally, one can distinguish rural organizers, local conspirators, military leaders, and wizards. Each skill role required markedly different kinds of actors, who often had little in common with each other. The gap between the leading diplomat, suave, sophisticated Thomas Kanza, and the most prominent fetish priestess Maman Marie Onema, incorporates the whole spectrum of acculturation in Zaire society.

Kanza was the prototype of the handful of rebel diplomats; examination of his functions illuminates their role. He had been one of Zaire's first university graduates, in 1956, and was the only significant person associated with the rebellion who held a university degree.[12] Since February 1960, the Kanza family had been embroiled in a bitter feud with the political movement representing their ethnic group, the Abako; this struggle foreclosed any possibility of a mass constituency for Thomas Kanza. He had represented the Kisangani regime at the United Nations in 1960-61, then served as Adoula's Ambassador to London from mid-1962 until December, 1963. During this period, he became well known in African leadership circles; his fluency in English, rare for a Zairien, greatly facilitated his ramifying network of Africa-wide contacts. He thus acquired an international constituency, reinforced by high prestige in university milieux in Zaire but without any popular domestic base. He negotiated with Tshombe in the weeks prior to the latter's spectacular reentry into Zaire politics and nearly became foreign minister in the Tshombe government. Shortly thereafter, he rallied to the rebellion and became its leading external spokesman.

The role of the external diplomat was in inverse proportion to the internal success of the rebellion. Kanza and his collaborators had virtually no capacity for influencing the internal dynamics of insurrection; he spent only two or three days in Kisangani, found himself unable to moderate the excesses of the rebel administration, and returned to his external post. When rebel fortunes ebbed inside Zaire, and there ceased to be even a relatively coherent internal structure, the sustenance of external support from other African states, both in arms and status, became more critical. In the phase of insurgency when a major tactical element is international pressure on the existing government to accede at least partially to rebel demands, the diplomats play an important part. Algerian experience suggests that if the rebellion triumphs, those whose only function had been diplomatic are rapidly demoted in favor of skill groups whose role was internal and whose political resources included access to domestic power factors.

The exile plotters tended to focus their hopes upon a power seizure in the capital. This group was composed of persons who had nearly all been associated

[12] Laurent Kabila of Nord-Katanga, also a diplomat, had received some university training in France. Toni Nyate, who headed Kisangani radio during the rebel occupation, had studied for two years at Moscow. Adrien Lakumukasi, briefly *chef de cabinet* for Kanza, and Saidi, temporarily on Gaston Soumialot's staff, had both flunked out of Lovanium; neither held his post for long. But university graduates now number in the hundreds, and their absence in rebel leadership ranks is striking.

with the Kisangani regime in 1960-61. After the Lovanium reconciliation, they had moved to Kinshasa, where since early 1962 they had been actively seeking to overthrow the Adoula government. They had abandoned their rural constituencies and were naturally driven to the strategy of capital opposition. When the possibility of parliamentary action ended in September 1963, they moved across the river to Brazzaville, where in October 1963, the establishment of the *Conseil* (sometimes *Comité*) *National de Libération* (CNL) was proclaimed.

The effectiveness of the exile groups was diminished by the constant divisions over tactics, leadership, and sources of external support. The cleavage tended to follow the Gbenye-Gizenga split, which had been a muted but crucial political theme in Kisangani in 1960-61. On the one side was Christophe Gbenye and most of the other exiles from Lumumba's party, MNC/L; on the other were leaders from Gizenga's wing of the Kwilu party, PSA, led by an apostate from the Gbenye group, Egide Bocheley-Davidson. The latter, although his mother came from the same ethnic group as Gbenye (Babua, in western Uele; his father was an immigrant from the West African coast), had become his bitter adversary.

Indicative of the level of animosity was a communique issued by the Bocheley-Davidson group after Gbenye had published a statement of "revolutionary objectives" in May 1964. "The CNL," the statement began, "which has imposed upon itself the discipline of intensive work in complete silence, is obliged to shed its customary discretion to unmask your [Gbenye's] true and hideous political visage." At the OAU emergency summit meeting on Zaire in September 1964, which took place simultaneously with Gbenye's proclamation of a revolutionary government in Kisangani under his direction, potential support by radical states was made impossible by public statements by the accredited CNL delegation in Addis Ababa, from the Bocheley-Davidson faction, that Gbenye had been "expelled" from the movement.

Exile plots foundered on the error of striking in Kinshasa itself, where the government was relatively strongest. The commando squads trained in a string of military camps in Congo-Brazzaville were ineffectual; an urban terrorism campaign launched in May 1964, was a pathetic failure. Assassination plots aimed at members of the Binza Group[13] (November 1963) or at President Joseph Kasavubu and Prime Minister Adoula (April 1964) fizzled, although the first nearly succeeded. But only a small proportion of the Kinshasa population came from areas represented in the Brazzaville coterie; the fragmented perception phenomenon operated to cast the rebels in the role of alien power-seekers, rather than social revolutionaries.

The rural organizers were the crucial figures in the rebellion. Without them, the insurrection would never have been more than a parlor conspiracy. The

---

[13] A political clique in Leopoldville which was the core of the Kinshasa "power structure" from 1961–64, including ANZ Commander-in-Chief Joseph Mobutu, former Foreign Minister Justin Bomboko, National Bank director Albert Ndele, and some others.

two most important were Mulele and Soumialot; the former organized the Kwilu uprising, and the latter was the central figure in sparking insurgent action in eastern Zaire. Although Mulele was considerably more ideological, they had much in common. Both had been important party organizers in 1960, Mulele as secretary-general of PSA in Kwile and Soumialot as Lumumba's top lieutenant in Maniema. Neither had been involved in capital opposition politics; Mulele had been abroad during most of the period 1960-63, and Soumialot had been constantly circulating through the provinces of Maniema, Nord-Katanga, and Kivu Central, building local alliances founded upon the ineitable web of conflict in rural politics. In both cases, the residual structure, especially youth committees, of political parties that had briefly achieved a relatively high degree of mobilization in 1960, were valuable accessories. Although parties atrophied everywhere, nuclei remained that could function as contact points. And both were committed to a tactic of rural organization; their political base was the village and small roadside town, not the large urban center. In Mulele's case, the ideology itself was peasant-oriented. The superior virtues of rural life were extolled, and the evils of administration by rootless men from the cities were excoriated.

An explicitly military skill group emerged in the eastern Zone. Rumors of the imminent formation of a "popular army" were current in Kisengani in May 1964; at the same time, guerrilla leaders of Bafulero bands in the Ruzizi plain, on the Burundi border, began using military titles. Nicolas Olenga first came to public notice in Albertville at the end of June 1964, as a "general"; in early July, he left for southern Maniema, where the core of the APL was organized. Olenga's ascent from utter obscurity could not have been forecast by anything in his earlier record. He had only a primary education, had been merely a messenger before independence, and had supported the pro-administration Parti National du Progrès (PNP) in the elections of May 1960. However, Olenga proved to be a brutal but effective organizer of a military force. As the APL took form, it became a power factor of its own in the rebel equation, and Olenga assumed a pivotal role in Kisangani.

Olenga assembled an officer corps heavily dominated by men from his own group, the Batetela-Bakusu, which was also the ethnic group of Lumumba and Soumialot.[14] A number of his officers, such as "Colonel" Joseph Opepe, military commander of Kisangani in August-November, were veterans of the Force Publique or ANZ. Olenga controlled the selection process and assured the personal loyalty of his lieutenants, reinforced by ethnic solidarity. Its discipline and cohesion at the command level, added to the knowledge of small-unit tactics

[14]The Batetela-Bakusu are a part of the larger Mongo culture cluster. They dominate Sankuru district and form an important part of Maniema's population. Soumialot's ethnic identity is in fact somewhat ambiguous. He was born at Samba, near Kasongo, a zone of cultural transition between Basongye and Batetela-Bakusu. Although he is listed in Belgium records as Basongye, he was considered in Kisangani to be a Bakusu.

by a portion of its officers, rendered it a relatively viable force in face of the feeble opposition it encountered from the ANZ in the early stages.

The APL took on the formal structure and nomenclature of the ANZ; in contrast in Mulele's partisans, who always operated as small guerrilla bands, Olenga's army increasingly tried to operate as a regular military rapidly became armed with modern weapons abandoned by the fleeing ANZ. An impressive logistical capability was acquired through the confiscation of all vehicles in the hands of companies, traders, and expatriates as the APL advanced and the utilization of the communication network of the eastern railroad. The officers wore uniforms identical to the ANZ, although often supplemented by monkey-skin caps, feathers, or other local headdress.

Recruitment of troops was indiscriminate, in contrast to the relative homogeneity of the officer corps. At each new locality, large numbers of young men were enlisted as simbas. A portion remained with the detachment left to garrison the town; the rest moved on with the advancing columns. The result was that simba units were ethnically heterogeneous in the enlisted ranks. Many of the recruits were very young boys. Twelve-year-old and even younger sambas were common; the APL was almost a children's crusade. A pay scale substantially higher than the wages of an ordinary worker, when jobs were to be had; the appeal of marching in Lumumba's memory; and no doubt the intrinsic attraction of marching off with an apparently triumphant army all swelled the APL ranks.

The local conspirators were those in each locality who had served as contact men for Soumialot's emissaries and had seized power in their town or chieftaincy in the wake of the rebel army. In few cases were these groups capable of eliminating central government authority by themselves. Only in Kindu was a town captured by internal insurrection. Isiro (formerly Paulis) and Likasi (formerly Albertville) were briefly seized by local youth groups, but the ANZ restored tenuous control; the warriors from without produced a durable rebel victory. In the towns, this leadership role was often played by pathological young men who had headed party militia in 1960. They were often youths with little education and dim prospects in the modern world, who had already come into sharp conflict with traditional authorities, missions, employers, and administration and had accumulated prison records.[15] In a social situation where violence suddenly becomes a critical skill and other political leadership to control its use is lacking, it seems likely that a "tsotsi"[16] element will rise to the

---

[15] Victor Benanga and Alphonse Kingis, the Kisangani diumverate in the wake of rebel conquest, were characteristic examples. Kingis was head of the Kisangani Kitawala community, a syncretic sect which in Zaire had a record of violence. Benanga had headed terrorist youth gangs in 1960 and has spent much of the time in prison since. Both were violent and sanguinary, and equally devoid of ideology.

[16] South African slang term for members of juvenile delinquent gangs in African townships.

surface. The leading role of tsotsis in the disorders that swept East London (South Africa) in 1952, once police fire on African demonstrators converted a disobedience campaign into a violent riot, is an interesting parallel.[17] A similar sequence appears to have taken place during the Kinshasa riots of January 1959.

In the countryside, local allies for the rebellion were often found among rival chiefs. For example, in Opala territory, southwest of Stanleyville, a local chief who in 1960 had been a leading MNC/L organizer found in the rebellion an opportunity for seizure of traditional office. With simbas at his disposal, he assassinated eight of the nine other recognized chiefs in Opala territory, which largely coincides with the Bambole ethnic group (the ninth fled to safety). He then proclaimed himself Bambole paramount chief, an office that has no sanction in history and to which in any case his claim was flimsy. Similarly, in Bafulero territory, the long-standing desire of a rival claimant to the chieftainship was a crucial dimension of the Ruzizi plain revolt.

The perspectives of this echelon of leadership were entirely local; they sought grass roots power. Upon seizure of a locality by the APL, a local youth leader emerged to claim his office as territorial administrator. Final arbiter of the situation was the commander of the simba garrison, almost invariably an outsider and generally from the Batetela-Bakusu group which officered the APL. Rebel local administrators owed their power to the popular army and were in touch with the rural organizer echelon. However, they owed nothing to the exile plotters and were not responsive to control from them.

Specialists in magic were the final element in the rebel leadership. Witch doctors had played an important role in the Balubakat uprising in North Katanga in 1960-62; indeed, there was some continuity of personnel. Joseph Amisi-Mahumedi, of Bakusu origin, was prominent in both insurrections. Fetishers were present in the Kwilu uprising as well but played a less prominent role; magical powers were attributed to Mulele himself. But in the eastern rebellion, witch doctors were accorded an institutionalized role and became a partially autonomous skill group. Each simba unit had its witch doctor, who used the title of "doctor" and often wore a Red Cross armband.

Witch doctors conducted the simba initiation ceremonies and were charged with maintenance of magical protection. Sanctions for gross negligence were severe; a number of cases were reported of witch doctors executed by their units if the "dawa" appeared to fail consistently. But the successful ones achieved great prominence. Maman Marie Onema, whose support Olenga had personally solicited immediately after conquest of Kindu, held court in regal fashion in Stanleyville during the rebel administration. Although they had no specific political goals, they were an autonomous, uncontrollable, unpredictable factor in the power arena, whose influence was magnified by the weakness and incapacity of other levels of leadership.

[17]D. H. Reader, *The Black Man's Portion* (Cape Town: Oxford University Press, 1961), pp. 26-27.

The parallel with the Maji-Maji uprising in Tanzania in 1905-06 is interesting. In this case, invulnerability came through baptism with water from springs in traditional Ngindo shrines. The transformation of a peaceful water-cult into a rebel army entirely altered the role of the fetish-priests associated with the shrines. Political leadership was eventually assumed by one of the cult leaders, whose skill was magic rather than fighting prowess. Similarly, in Zaire a situation where magical protection was far more critical than in normal times inevitably amplified the role of those believed to control it.

With few exceptions, leadership at all levels bore the stamp of mediocrity. No charismatic personality was thrown up by the movement to incarnate the rebellion. All leaders had a limited orbit of potential effectiveness, bounded both by the nature of their function, and the region of their constituency. Kanza had only an international base and no capacity for constructing a domestic machine. Mulele won the overwhelming commitment of Bapende and Bambundu; by this very token he circumscribed his radius of action, as neighboring groups perceived Mulelism as an ethnic threat. Soumialot could uproot central authority in Maniema but lacked political resources in Kisangani, which led to his eclipse once the old Lumumbist capital became the vortex of rebellion. Gbenye arrived in Kisangani a month after its capture and tried to assume leadership without control of either the APL or the youth. Olenga's command of the APL made him a central figure, but he lacked the will and talent to assume political leadership. Authority was fragmented and fluctuating. The rebellion was a headless horseman.

Active participants in the rebellions were above all drawn from a certain age set, the post-war generation, the "youth," both urban and rural. This group had grown up at the time of rapid generalization of rural primary education; it was briefly exposed to the broader perspectives of social promotion in the modern world, then quickly cast aside by the truncated educational pyramid, with only a handful able to find places in secondary school. The prospect of independence had appeared to offer dazzling opportunities to them; the disappointment was correspondingly intense.

Subaltern workers of the state harbored acute grievances against the new ruling elite. This is a very large category, numbering some three hundred thousand for Zaire as a whole. Legally, they are "sous-contrat" and thus not entitled to the generous salaries and other benefits enjoyed by those with civil service status. Not only have they received little pay advance since independence, unlike their superiors, but they have tended to be the first victims of arrearages in wage payments. In the towns, the "sous-contrats" were an important source of rebel support.

Townswomen also provided a surprising number of rebel activists. "Femmes Nationalistes" formations sprang up in a number of places; in Bunia it was the women who joined forces with the rebel columns from Kisangani to eliminate what tenuous central authority remained. Adult Zaire women are almost entirely illiterate, and very few speak French. Ample cause for frustration can be seen in an urban environment from whose modern social roles women are largely excluded through absence of education.

Ethnic identity was an important determinant of reaction to the rebellion. Ethnic communities that could find their own image mirrored in the insurrection were disposed to participate. Peak support came from groups that could most totally identify with the symbols of the rebellion. In Kwilu, the Bambundu and Bapende both could see the Mulelist guerila struggle as "their" uprising. Mulele was a Mumbundu; the prolonged imprisonment of Bapende favorite son Gizenga was a leading theme of protest. For the Batetela-Bakusu, the rebellion was in the name of Lumumba, was led by "their" army, supported by "their" party, and reinforced by "their" magic and witch doctors. For the Lokele, largest group in Stanleyville, the symbols of Lumumba, MNC/L, and Stanleyville itself served to relate the group to the movement.

For other groups, however, the symbols associated with the rebellion repelled rather than attracted. Most Bakongo (in western Zaire) recalled Lumumba as an adversary rather than a hero. The up-river leadership and Kisangani base also identified it as an alien movement. Although many of the same grievances existed and the social groups that rallied to the rebellion in the east were also to be found among the Bakongo, this particular movement could not draw Bakongo support. Antigovernment feeling was tempered by the presence of eminent Bakongo at all levels of authority in Kinshasa, beginning with Chief-of-State Kasavubu. Although rural Bakongo were also cruelly disappointed by the "system," it was in part "their" system. Another vital group, the Kasai Baluba, still bitterly recall Lumumba's political alliance with their Lulua adversaries and hold him partially responsible for their 1960 expulsion from areas into which they expanded during the colonial period. For similar reasons, Katanga copperbelt populations identified more closely with a Tshombe regime in Kinshasha than a Gbenye-Soumialot-Olenga rebel government in Kisangani.

THE LIMITATIONS OF REBELLION

The 1964 Congo rebellion, when added to other African evidence, suggests that overthrow of regimes sustained by internal warfare is an exceedingly difficult enterprise. Coups have been successful in Zanzibar, Congo-Brazzaville, Dahomey, Sudan, Nigeria, Ghana, Central African Republic, Togo, Somalia, Uganda, Mali, and Upper Volta; no doubt this list will grow. But insurrection that must depend upon protracted insurgent action has numerous liabilities as a tactic. Zaire rebels did have in their favor both a widespread hostility to the central government and the weakness of its repressive instruments. The ANZ had twenty-four battalions available to contain the rebellion; in the Cameroons, UPC dissidence is easily contained by three battalions, plus a Bamileke guard of eighteen and twenty-five hundred gendarmes. But despite the fragility of central authority in Zaire, five hundred mercenaries, some air logistical support from the United States and Belgian military advisors, and a few aging fighter-bombers were able to turn the tide. The rebellion had either to sweep the country immediately or fail in its central goal of overthrowing the regime.

The built-in regionalism of revolt is a logical concomitant of the historical artificiality of most African states. In the terminal colonial period, mobilization on a national scale was possible for political opposition to colonial rule; however, nowhere in tropical Africa was a colonial regime overthrown by guerrilla warfare. Sustained violence against colonial rulers, even though on behalf of a national objective, became in all cases regionally circumscribed. In the Cameroons, the UPC revolt, although in the name of a radical ideology, drew guerrilla fighters only from Ruben Um Nyobe's Bassa, the Bamileke country, and adjoining Mungo district.[18] In the 1947 Madagascar uprising, although it was massive in scale, only one-third of the island was affected, with the Betsimisiraka and Tanala groups the major participants.[19] The Mau Mau movement in Kenya was limited to Kikuyu and Meru. Political commitment to the extent of enlistment in a guerrilla army requires a loyalty more compelling than that which the present African political units can command as a symbol even when the enemy is as sharply demarcated and easily recognized as the alien colonizer.

The guerrilla wars of liberation against Portuguese colonial rule which began in 1961 in Angola, and by the mid-60s had begun in Mozambique and Portuguese Guinea (or Guiné-Bissau) as well, have been beset by these same tensions. The most effective insurrection, in Portuguese Guinea, has come closest to achieving complete unity, aided by the small scale of the polity and exceptionally able leadership of Amilcar Cabral. However, even in this instance, the Portuguese have been able to exploit Fulani reticence toward the liberation struggle, especially that of the still-influential chiefs. The Angolan liberation movement has been particularly hard hit by persistent regional and ethnic rivalries, although hopes rose in 1972 when the two most important movements formed an alliance.

Post-independence insurgency has not yet taken place elsewhere in Africa on a scale comparable to the Zaire, although guerrilla activity was still extensive in the first post-independence years in the Cameroons. But it seems axiomatic that the revolutionary enemy after independence cannot be as clear, because it is partly internal. In ethnically fragmented Yugoslavia, only the highly unifying experience of the German occupation, with the alien able to serve as vortex for all social hostility, enabled the nearly-decimated Yugoslav Communist move-

[18] Victor T. LeVine, *The Cameroons from Mandate to Independence* (Berkeley, Calif.: University of California Press, 1964), pp. 153-71.

[19] Raymond Kent, *From Madagascar to Malagasy Republic* (New York: Frederick A. Praeger, Inc., 1962), pp. 35, 43-44, 95-109.

ment to transcend nationality differences. For Zaire, the colonial enemy was clear enough in the diffusion of nationalism period, 1959-60. But the external enemy today is much less obvious to the rural villager. "Americans" are seldom seen outside a few large towns, except for Protestant missionaries. Yankee exploitation can have a mobilizing appeal in Cuba, but is beyond peasant cognition in Zaire. And once internal enemies are defined more closely than simply "politicians," stones are inevitably cast at somebody's native son. Secessionist rebellions, as in the southern Sudan Eritrea (Ethiopia), or eastern Nigeria, belong to a quite different category of conflict, which we have discussed in Part I.

Lacking transcendent unifying symbols, the rebellion is forced between the millstones of fragmented perception of grievance and spatial relativity of deprivation. Its orbit of effective action is confined by the radius of its symbols and leaders. Where it extends beyond that point, as Olenga's army did in August-September 1964, the rebellion is a hostile occupation rather than a liberating force. When these zones of potential effectiveness lie too far from the political capital or critical economic centers to really threaten the system, the regionalization of rebellion is a critical weakness.

Secondly, there are serious liabilities to a rural insurrection. Although it can rapidly create a local base, a village army is unlikely to be capable of administering large urban centers, nor are the pathological youth who are the town allies. Responsibility for rural zones places only minimal requirements on rebel leadership; governing Kisangani led to maladministration, an undiscriminating and self-defeating policy of assassination, conspicuous ethnic favoritism for Batetela-Bakusu, and eventual alienation of people initially favorable to the rebellion.

In the Zaire case, with the top level of leadership mainly confined to diplomatic or other exile functions, the dialectic of rural insurgency threw up a leadership incapable of implementing the social revolution in whose name the appeal to arms was launched. Popular army officers were relatively homogeneous ethnically, not ideologically; Olenga hardly bears comparison with Colonel Houari Boumedienne in Algeria, General Vo Nguyen Giap in North Vietnam, or even Gamal Abdel Nasser as a social revolutionary military specialist. He is more readily compared to "Marshall" John Okello, the Ugandan who commanded the Zanzibar coup, then was hastily bundled off by the more ideological Zanzibari leaders, presumably mistrustful of his penchant for brutality and incendiary statements. Youth leaders like Benanga and Kingis gave no evidence of a political vision extending beyond liquidation of "counterrevolutionaries," and local rural leaders had narrow, parochial, and limited objectives. Power gravitated into the hands of those whose behavior defeated the purposes of rebellion, at least as proclaimed by the exile diplomats.

The nature of the APL also probably renders it incapable of prolonged insurgency, except in the Maniema heartland and a few scattered areas of peak rebel support. Both the heterogeneity of the ranks and the ethnic homogeneity of the officer corps make it an alien force in the countryside outside of Maniema. As long as the garrisons were posted in towns, this did not matter. When it was forced into rural refuges, it was unable in most areas to be as fish in water, following the Maoist metaphor. Olenga's decision to form a military force organized like a regular army, rather than a guerrilla band in the Mulele pattern, rendered it vulnerable to progressive isolation by counterattacking government forces. In Kwilu, on the other hand, where the partisans were entirely drawn from the area in which they operate, they sustained activity outside the towns for a long period.

In November 1965, General Joseph Mobutu (who in 1972 renamed himself Mobutu Sese Seko) seized power by military coup and gradually built up a strongly centralized regime. His regime initially benefited from a fatigue and disillusionment with disorder and rebellion as pervasive as the animosity toward "politicians" that had fueled the rebellions. Although a few pockets of dissidence lingered for a time, by 1969 tranquility had been restored throughout the country. In 1968, the GNP surpassed preindependence levels for the first time, and the Mobutu regime produced a period of relative stability and even prosperity. However, the renewed momentum of development was particularly strong in the zone around the capital of Kinshasa, the copperbelt of Katanga, and, roughly speaking, the southern axis which joined them. Much of the northeast, badly disrupted by the rebellions, recovered only very slowly and lagged far behind the economically expanding zones. Secondary schools in particular, key to social mobility for the new generation, faced great handicaps in this region.

PART THREE

THE PURPOSE OF POLITICAL ORDER:

Development and the Problem of Political Ideology

CHAPTER 10

The Meaning of "Revolution" in the Developing World

Whether the mood be one of eager anticipation or ominous foreboding, there is a widely held opinion in the advanced, industrialized parts of the world that the emerging regions are destined to pass through a period of turmoil, violence, and radical political experimentation on the road to maturity. To some extent, this sense of an impending sharp break from the political values and practices of the West is due to the very statements of the leaders of the developing nations. During the past generation, the public voice of the developing nations has often been one of frustration, resentment, and condemnation of the past and the presentation of a vision of the future that often sounds imprudent or at least unorthodox to Western ears.

The complacent sense that the idea of revolution was peculiar to the developing world, that industrial Western societies had transcended their conflicts and outgrown ideology was shattered by the events of the latter 1960s. Earlier, one spoke of an "end to ideology" in the West, noting that an increasing consensus was being achieved on the purposes, goals and institutions of the established order. At one level the classic conflicts of conservatives and liberals, capitalists and socialists, appeared to dissipate into qualified commentaries on whether a little more or a little less government direction was appropriate to the commonly accepted going concern. Yet by 1971 a book could be published titled *Decline of Ideology?* and articulate sectors of the societies of Western Europe, the United States, and Japan were seriously questioning the assumptions of the establishment.[1]

---

[1] M. Rejal, ed., *Decline of Ideology?* (Chicago: Aldine-Atherton, 1971). On the "end of ideology" thesis, see: Seymour Martin Lipset, *Political Man* (New York: Doubleday & Company, 1960), pp. 403–17; Daniel Bell, *The End of Ideology* (New York: Free Press of Glencoe, Inc., 1960); Edward Shils, "The End of Ideology?" *Encounter,* 5 (November 1955), 52–58. For a rejoinder, see Joseph LaPalombara, "Decline of Ideology: A Dissent and Interpretation," *American Political Science Review,* 60 (March 1966), 5–16.

The depth of black anger in the United States was starkly revealed by the wave of massive, spontaneous riots in a number of urban ghettos. In the aftermath of these disorders, a mood of radical confrontation crystallized among the predominantly middle-class youth of the universities of the Western world. In the United States, hostility to the war in Vietnam was one major grievance, but there was also radical dissatisfaction with the culture and values of the affluent society. Even without the catalyst of the Vietnam war, grave disorders occurred in European universities – with the culminating point coming in May 1968 in Paris, when an atmosphere of revolutionary euphoria momentarily prevailed and it seemed for a time that the very fabric of society was coming asunder. In the new industrial giant of Japan, several elite universities were closed for months at a time by student revolutionaries. The idea of revolution could no longer be viewed as an infantile disorder associated with underdevelopment.

After 1970, the energies unleashed by the ideological outbursts of the late 1960s appeared to subside in the Western, industrial world. Political ideology continues to appear a more enduring theme in the emerging nations, although we assert this with far less confidence than a decade ago.

The developing world in the postwar period was often seen as a battlefield in a war of ideas. The raw materials of new societies and new states would be molded to the shape of either Western democracy or Soviet Communism. As the heterogeneity of both the "East" and the "West" has become obvious to even the most dogmatic, the rather mechanistic world-view that the developing nations were inexorably drawn toward either the Communist or the liberal-democratic ideal type of the nation in development has become increasingly untenable. (This strange position, that all that does not conform to one of these static models is in a state of disequilibrium and must eventually tend toward one of the polar opposites, was no doubt logically absurd from the outset.) Nonetheless, there remains a strong undercurrent of opinion in the advanced sector of the world that the political practice of the emerging nations is to be judged by the affinity of the pronouncements of their leaders to the ideological commitments and political institutions of the major powers. And given the propensity of the more vivid leaders of the developing nations to cast their political ideas in terms of the language of Western radicalism, it appears to the least sanguine that the "third world" generally is moving away from a politics that is compatible with that of the West.

There are several important reasons for us to expect that ideological politics will be more important in the developing nations than it is at present in Europe and North America. After all, in many of these nations, the place and purpose of government in the society, the role of religion, the social goals to which developmental effort should be directed – all the great issues of Western history – are as yet unresolved.[2]

[2] Seymour Martin Lipset emphasizes this explanation for the salience of ideology in developing nations in *Political Man.*

In many emerging nations, ideology may perform important functions in the process of development. David Apter, for example, stresses the role of ideology in binding a community together.[3] Ideology defines the things we have in common, the purpose of our "togetherness," which may be peculiarly necessary in culturally plural societies where the answer to such questions is not immediately apparent. Closely related to this is the problem of the legitimation of a new and generally unprecedented order of authority. For new states, seeking to replace more traditional forms of political life, ideology seeks to provide a rationale for a new pattern of political obligations, to answer the question of why one should obey this new group of leaders.

In the process of devlopment, ideology may be essential to transform traditional values, to establish a "mental environment" conducive to change. J. J. Spengler, in particular, has emphasized this function of ideology in emerging nations.

> It is my thesis that the state of a people's politico-economic development, together with its rate and direction, depends largely upon what is in the minds of its members, and above all on the content of the minds of the elites, which reflects in part, as do civilizations, the conception men have of the universe. The content of men's minds is looked upon as the potentially dynamic element, as the source whence issue change and novelty, in a world or universe that is otherwise passive. Accordingly, transformation of an underdeveloped society into a developed one entails transformation of the contents of mind of the elite who direct and of the men who man such underdeveloped society.[4]

And closely related to this, the "disorientation" of rapid change may create a need for what Clifford Geertz calls "a new symbolic framework in which to formulate, think about, and react to political problems."[5]

In the preceding section of this book, we discussed some of the reasons that some of the people of the developing world choose to act as revolutionaries in certain contexts and situations. In this section, we will consider why many of the leaders of these nations choose to think as revolutionaries, why they so often employ the symbols, myths, concepts, and ideals of Western radicalism and dissent to legitimize their political systems, define the purposes of their communities, and justify the economic, social, or foreign policies that they adopt.

We will do this by examining two words that appear over and over again in the ideologies of new nations: "revolution" and "socialism." In various combina-

---

[3] David Apter, ed., *Ideology and Discontent* (New York: Free Press of Glencoe, Inc., 1964). pp. 18ff.

[4] Ralph Braibanti and J. J. Spengler, eds., *Tradition, Values, and Socio Economic Development* (Durham, N.C.: Duke University Press, 1961), pp. 4-5.

[5] Clifford Geertz, "Ideology as a Cultural System," in Apter, *Ideology and Discontent*, p. 65.

tions and permutations, these words have come for many to characterize the quality of ideology in the developing world. We will try to understand the various things that leaders in the emerging nations mean when they use these terms and why they so often clothe their ideologies in this language.

Some may raise the objection that while "revolution" certainly connotes dissent in the Western context, "socialism" is, by this time in the history of the West, hardly a radical concept. Perhaps that will prove to be precisely the point of our analysis. In any event, we write primarily for a North American audience, and in this political culture, to identify as a "socialist" is to adopt a radical position, to take serious exception to the going concern. Furthermore, as we shall learn, many leaders of developing nations do identify as "socialists" to distinguish their position from alternative socioeconomic systems. Hence, our effort will be to clarify the various meanings of the term as it is used in the developing world and to distinguish these connotations from the various assumptions present in the West concerning the position and the degree of radicalism that the term "socialism" connotes.

We will inquire into what the leaders of the developing world mean when they define themselves as "revolutionaries" or as "socialists." But we must also ask whether such concepts really characterize the ideologies of the developing world. Again, we turn to the heterogeneous substance of the developing continents to ascertain the extent to which such generalizations hold true. Is the age of ideology really more alive in the newer states than in the older ones? Do the ideologies of the emerging nations really envision a major departure from the political and economic practice of presently industrialized societies?

THE RHETORIC OF REVOLUTION

Revolution has long been an ideological theme of new states born of violent conflict. Today revolution, along with democracy and socialism, are basic concepts in the political rhetoric of the majority of the lesser developed countries. Although contemporary America tends to distrust the connotations associated with the term, the symbolic meanings of revolution need not connote violence or radical political and economic policies. Our basic area of inquiry is the rhetoric of revolution, and no effort is made to provide a definitive meaning for the term. The word has been used by secularists and sectarians, Marxists and non-Marxists, modernists and traditionalists, newly independent states and ancient monarchies. Each has defined its respective revolution, but the authors can find no mutually satisfactory definition that encompasses the multitude of situations called "revolutionary." If revolution means an abrupt and major change in the political and social structure, should we say that a revolution took place in Germany in 1933 under Hitler and in 1945 under the Allies, or in Japan under MacArthur, or in all newly independent states where a new elite took over from the colonial administration? The *Webster's Dictionary* definition would fit many of these — "A fundamental change in political organization, or in the government or constitution; the overthrow or renunciation of one government or ruler, and substitution of another, by the governed." This entire definition would not fit the continuing revolutionary model of China, Mexico, and similar systems. It must be admitted that the authors dodged this very difficult question by discussing what the participants called revolution without evaluating whether a "real revolution" had taken place or not.

TYPES OF REVOLUTION

The rhetoric of revolution varies to a remarkable degree from one state to another, from the position of the Daughters of the American Revolution to the Chinese Communist Party's assertion, "There must be a revolutionary party able to interpret the universal truth of Marxism-Leninism with the concrete practice of the revolution in its own country."[6] The vagueness and vagaries of the concept as used in the developing countries, therefore, necessitates a careful delineation of its meaning on various levels. An initial way of clarifying the concept of revolution as an aspect of national ideology is to classify the lesser developed countries according to the importance of revolution as a national symbol. Is acceptance of revolution necessary for legitimacy of the regime? Is there permanency to the concept in the national ideology? Is revolution articulated only by those out of power?

REVOLUTION AS SYMBOL OF LEGITIMACY

In some countries, revolution is a continuing and permanent symbol, furnishing legitimacy to an established regime in which, by itself or with other vital symbols, it provides the foundation of national identity. These countries include Algeria, Bolivia, Burma, China, Cuba, Mexico, North Korea, North Vietnam, and the Egyptian Arab Republic.

In these states, revolution is a central facet of the continuing ideology of the nation, not a rhetorical symbol of any single administration or individual. Every new government that attains power must retain "the Revolution" as a central ideological identification if it is to maintain legitimacy. "The Revolution" is constantly used in speeches and public documents to display the continuity of new acts with past ideology, to control disparate elements, or, perhaps, as an actual guide to decision making. Ultimately, "the Revolution" sanctions the system and has a continuing immediacy in politics not readily

---

[6] Quoted in John W. Lewis, *Major Doctrines of Communist China* (New York: W. W. Norton, 1964), p. 275.

apparent in other systems. The difficulty in using this category in the Afro-Asian states is that most are so new that it is often not easy to ascertain whether "the Revolution" has attained a position where it will be necessary for future regimes to accept it as a necessary part of the national ideology. To illustrate this category, three examples are given — Mexico, one of the oldest cases; Algeria, a recent test of the continuing legitimacy of a symbol; and China, probably the most articulate and extreme of contemporary revolutionary regimes.

The Mexican Revolution

Mexico provides a particularly vivid example of the use of the concept "revolution" not only to refer to an historic period of violence and rebellion, but to identify an established political order.[7] In Mexico, the symbol "revolution" is used to consecrate a political system based on the dominance of a single party which claims lineal descent from the uprising of 1910. Furthermore, the idea of "revolution" to a very large extent provides the basis for the Mexican sense of nationhood.

As an episode of civic insurrection, "the Mexican Revolution" refers to the events of 1910-1917. During this period, the long dictatorship of Porfirio Díaz (1876-1910) was overthrown. The initial constitutionalist aspirations of Francisco I. Madero were quickly expanded as nationwide rural revolt led to demands for social reform, the restoration of lands to Indian communities, and a termination of foreign economic influence within the nation.

By 1917, stable government had been restored, but the leaders of the later period described their governments as a continuation of the "revolution," as the realization in public policy of the aspirations and objectives unleashed in seven years of civic turmoil. From 1917-1934, the approach of Mexican governments was essentially moderate, a matter of ratifying the changes that violence had wrought and cautiously rebuilding the fiscal and economic structure devastated in the years of rebellion. After 1934, with the administration of President Lázaro Cárdenas, the reform objectives of the Revolution were reasserted with greater vigor. And after 1940, when industrialization was the major emphasis of Mexican policy, policies favorable to the new middle class and entrepreneurial elites were also described as a matter of working out the implications of the Revolution. Mexicans have never been very concerned about the paradox of using the term which usually connotes a violent political upheaval to describe a quite stable, continuing order. The present period of Mexican history is officially known as the "institutionalized revolution."

The contemporary relevance of the symbol of Revolution may be seen in the dominance of the official party (P.R.I. — the Party of the Institutionalized

---

[7]See Robert Scott, *Mexican Government in Transition* (Urbana: University of Illinois Press, 1959) and Frank Tannenbaum, *Mexico: The Struggle for Peace and Bread* (New York: Alfred A. Knopf, 1950).

Revolution) which regularly wins from 80 to 90 percent of the vote in national elections. The legacy of the Revolution is constantly invoked in political oratory and political symbolism. Mexican literature (Azuela), art (Rivera and Orozco), music (Chávez) and cinema all deal heavily with the theme of the Revolution. In social science and social commentary, the process and objectives of the Revolution are the predominant point of reference. Identification with the mystique of Revolution is in fact quite widespread in the Mexican population. Almond and Verba found this to be a substantial factor in building positive mass support for a political system whose performance is frequently imperfect.[8]

Does the ideology of revolution provide a real guide to decision-making in modern Mexico requiring that government endorse certain policy alternatives and repudiate others? The Revolution is most frequently identified with agrarian reform, social and welfare legislation, the nationalization of such basic economic enterprises as oil and railroads, and the secularization of the church. However, in its long history, the revolutionary regime has also endorsed large agricultural enterprise, domestic capitalism, a renewal of foreign investment, and a *modus vivendi* with Roman Catholicism. In fact, the Mexican Revolution today connotes everything that has happened in this nation since 1910. Public policy thus includes every component that has gone into the process of modernization, and the contemporary Mexican policymaker can justify as "revolutionary" quite diverse and contradictory policies. The continuity of the symbol of "revolution" legitimizes virtually every policy alternative available to the modern statesman, and different patterns of policy may be emphasized and others underplayed depending on the needs of the moment. In one period, the focus may be on industrialization in the name of "revolutionary nationalism"; in another, on agrarian reform in fulfillment of the goals for which Zapata and Villa originally fought.

Of course, the mystique of revolution is not without its dissenters and skeptics. To many citizens, the symbol of "revolution" is but a propaganda tool cynically manipulated by political elites. For many radical intellectuals, the "Revolution" is said to have ended in 1940, with the close of the reformist administration of Cárdenas. However, for the greater part of the population, "revolution" remains a viable symbol of the growth to modern nationhood of the Mexican nation and the process of economic and social change that has taken place in the twentieth century.

Algeria

From the beginning of the Algerian insurrection on November 1, 1954, the idea of revolution has played a prominent rhetorical role. As the armed struggle wore on, the centrality of the "revolution" increased; although the term is

[8] Gabriel Almond and Sidney Verba, *The Civic Culture* (Princeton: Princeton University Press, 1963).

invoked a number of times in an early manifesto of the FLN (May 1955) to describe the goals of the movement, the accent is clearly on "liberation." Revolution is described in this document as "the annihilation of all vestiges of corruption and reformism, the causes of our present regression." In August 1956, a clandestine conference at Soumman, inside Algeria, proclaimed the formation of a *Conseil National de la Révolution Algérienne,* thereby embodying the revolutionary title in the supreme organ of the struggle.

The strategy followed by the FLN leadership, compounded by the bitterness engendered by the prolongation and intensification of the combats, led ineluctably to increasing stress on the revolutionary objectives of the movement; the peasant base of the guerrila army resulted in a mystique of rejection of the entire structure of colonial society rather than simple displacement of the colonial elite by the assimilated modern elite which was the pattern of decolonization elsewhere in erstwhile French Africa. The "peasant Revolution" found its philosopher in the West Indian psychiatrist Frantz Fanon, who became the leading intellectual publicist for the FLN. For Fanon, everything tainted with the poisoned touch of colonial society had to be consumed in the purifying fire of violence, which would simultaneously liquidate the ancient regime, demolish the psychological shackles of the all-pervasive colonial mentality which permeated so much of indigenous society, and forge the revolutionary national consciousness upon which the new society was to be built.

By the time independence was achieved in 1962, the cult of revolution was far more deeply rooted in Algeria than in any other African polity. The prolonged struggle tended to reinforce a leadership committed to revolution rather than compromise, the "purs et durs." This attitude was reflected in the constitution adopted in March 1963. In the words of one commentator:

> The Constitution must be above all the framework and one of the instruments of a revolution, of which the conquest of independence is only the first step. The preamble declares: "After having attained the objective of national independence which the *Front de Libération Nationale* assigned itself on 1 November 1954, the Algerian people continue their march down the path of a people's democratic revolution."

Article 3 of the constitution specifies that the official slogan is "Revolution by the people and for the people."

An attempt to formulate a thorough revolutionary and socialist ideology was made at the FLN Congress of April 1964, where a "charter" was adopted. Traces of the Fanon suspicion of intellectuals and the mentally colonized were reflected in one interesting passage:

> The bourgeois class, properly speaking, does not exceed 50,000 persons, or 1/40th of the active population. The petite bourgeoisie,

much stronger, represents 1/8th of the population. But, to determine the real force of these bourgeois and petite-bourgeois strata within the dynamic of the social struggle, one must consider not only their economic weight but also their ideological, cultural, and political influence, in a particularly handicapped worker and peasant milieu. Since Independence, a new social class in accelerated development threatens to intervene. That is the bureaucratic bourgeoisie, which is developing in the apparatus of the administration, the state and the economy, thanks to the sentiment of power which the exercise of authority gives it. This force, by its position in the state machinery, can be considerably more dangerous for the socialist and democratic evolution of the revolution than any other existent social force in the country; this is due to the fact that the Algerian state has maintained the administrative structures established by colonialism.[9]

The degree to which the idea of revolution had become a crucial legitimator for the regime was illustrated by the celerity with which Colonel Houari Boumedienne assured the world that he was preserving the revolution by destroying the cult of personality. The following excerpts from a speech made on June 30, 1965, illustrate this point:

... The fact, brothers, is that Algeria has found its true personality.... This fact must be realized and understood by the revolutionary forces of this country, for, as we have already said, this revolution was the revolution of the people and must and will remain the revolution of the people. This revolution will never deviate, even if the deviator is a person called Ben Bella.

Brothers, these are some of the facts. It was my duty to unmask them, for in the past three years many adventurers entered our country — persons who acted as advisors and counselors entered our country, persons who failed in other countries and who wanted to undertake new experiments in our country. To all these we say that Algeria, the Algeria of 1 November 1954 took advice from nobody. This revolution is still the same, and needs no advisor from abroad....

The fact is that there had been deviations which aimed at separating the revolution from its past.... This socialist line and this revolution were the outcome of huge sacrifices, the outcome of one and a half million martyrs, and the outcome of the revolutionary and vanguard forces in this country.[10]

One interesting interpretation, suggested by this and other pronouncements of Boumedienne, is that Ben Bella had seen the "revolution" consisting of two distinct phases: the liberation struggle, for which warriors were needed, and

---

[9] Jean Francois Kahn, "L'Algérie Nouvelle," *Le Monde,* Edition Hebdomadaire, February 11–17, 1965.

[10] Algiers Radio, June 30, 1965.

the social transformation, for which ideologically refined and technically competent technicians were needed (the pieds-rouges or French Communist and far-left advisors who flooded into Algeria after independence). For Boumedienne and the moujahids, the revolution was one and inseparable, and those that had carried out the first phase should carry on with the second.

With the passage of time, Algeria has taken on an increasingly technocratic hue, but the rhetorical commitments by no means have disappeared; indeed, it appears that they have grown stronger and more persistent. Some argue that the linguistic style of Arabic has a deeply rooted propensity for extravagance, of dissociation between verbal expression and practical action. One of the ablest studies of postindependence Algerian politics offers a persuasive interpretation of the deepening rhetorical commitment.

> In fact Boumedienne, lacking in personal appeal, relies more than Ben Bella upon "revolutionary" or ideological legitimacy to justify the power his military forces supply.... In fact revolutionary rhetoric has tended to hinder the "economic battle." But Boumedienne's concern for ideology, shared by most active Algerian politicians since 1962, connoted a search for legitimacy that the circumstances of independence had rendered so elusive.[11]

China

The Chinese example has been chosen as an extreme case. Not only does the official ideology of China maintain that the revolution against the Kuomintang and the old order was and is its central core, but the revolution as such must be a center of all other "correct" ideologies. In the words of a member of the Politburo of the Chinese Communist Party, "Revolution is the soul of Marxism-Leninism ... revolution is the locomotive of history." In the case of the Chinese revolution, although its immediate and middle-range character and goals have changed according to the vicissitudes of the party, the ultimate aim has been to establish a socialist society along the lines of Marxism-Leninism. The revolution has used and still uses other parties in achieving that goal, but the leadership must be under the Communist party, for, according to Mao. "without the party's leadership, no revolution can succeed." The Chinese revolution is, thus, similar to those of other communist states, although it does not look back to one climactic moment, such as the October Revolution in the Soviet Union. It is not just the coming to power of the

---

[11]Clement Henry Moore, *Politics in North Africa* (Boston: Little Brown and Co., 1970). Elsewhere, Moore gives an interesting analysis of the unusual rhetorical traditions of the Arabic language; see his "On Theory and Practice among Arabs", *World Politics,* 24 (October 1971), pp. 106–26.

Communist party, but a continuing act which terminates only with the attainment of a Communist society.

Mao dramatically displayed his continued adherence to the spirit of revolution during the Great Proletarian Cultural Revolution when he called for renewed revolutionary zeal throughout the republic. In those chaotic years, the need to revive the fire of revolution took precedence over economic development, party organization, and internal order.

What makes the Chinese case unique among our examples is the importance that her ideology gives revolution itself as a necessary road to the goals toward which she believes all nations should strive. Arguing against both the Soviet Union and the capitalist states, she declares that in no case have the latter given way peacefully, and thus revolution is inevitable if "the people" are to succeed. In answering Soviet criticisms of her policy, the official Chinese Communist reply asserted,

> On the question of transition from Capitalism to Socialism, the proletarian party must proceed from the stand of class struggle and revolution and base itself on the Marxist-Leninist teachings, concerning the proletarian revolution and the dictatorship of the proletariat.
>
> Communists would always prefer to bring about the transition to socialism by peaceful means. But can peaceful transition be made into a new world wide strategic principle for the international Communist movement? Absolutely not... the old government never topples, even in a period of crisis, unless it is pushed. This is a universal law of class struggle.[12]

These three examples have a number of interesting differences. In Mexico, revolutionary doctrine rose out of the political experiences and difficulties of the postindependence era; in Algeria it was associated with the long and bitter struggle for independence, whereas in China the rhetoric of revolution is derived from an international ideology, recast by civil war. Mexico's revolution has tended to become institutionalized and less emotional in tone, but Algeria and China are too close to their period of national struggle to expect a diminished fervor. Both China and Mexico have political parties that are closely tied to a specific doctrine of revolution and consider themselves inheritors of "the Revolution." Ironically, in Algeria and Mexico the revolutionary doctrine is not considered the handiwork of one individual, whereas in China, the adherent to a universal dogma, a personality cult surrounds the leader of the revolution, Mao Tse Tung. Finally, although all three are sympathetic to revolutionary movements elsewhere, only China is making active moves to proselytize and to export its particular brand abroad.

[12] Lewis, *Doctrines of China*, pp. 251–52.

REVOLUTION AS SYMBOL OF POLITICAL PURPOSE

In some countries, revolution is a symbol adopted by the present government, to indicate reformist intent, but has probably not been established as a permanent component of the regime or as a basis for national identity. These countries include Chile, Congo-Brazzaville, Guinea, and Syria.

This category must necessarily be speculative. It cannot be stated with certainty that Congo-Brazzaville, Burma, or a variety of African revolutions have not attained permanency as ideological symbols. The individual observer will probably have his own assessment, which only time can vindicate. Two examples of the perhaps transitory nature of revolution as a symbol of reform are Latin America and Indonesia.

Latin America

The word "revolution" has always been prominent in Latin American political rhetoric. Historically, movements and governments across the entire ideological spectrum – from extreme conservatism to militant radicalism – have described themselves as revolutionary in character. The term is used in connection with a variety of political phenomena, from the simple *coup d'état* to full scale political and social transformations, as in Mexico and Cuba. The symbolism of revolution is a constant of Latin American political culture. The most recent period of the continent's history is no exception.

In the 1950s and 1960s, a variety of moderate and conservative governments in Latin America described their program and aims as revolutionary in character, primarily to suggest that rapid development and crucial social change could be brought about without massive political upheaval. Thus, Rómulo Betancourt's *Acción Democrática* party in Venezuela described the policy they pursued from 1945-1948 and again from 1958-1969 as one of "democratic revolution." The term implied that modernization and change could come about within the framework of democratic elections and representative institutions. Agrarian reform, the universalization of health and education, and basic social services could be achieved in an atmosphere of free political debate and electoral competition. A violent overthrow of the existing system was not necessary to development.

Fernándo Belaunde Terry also appealed to this idea of democratic revolution in Peru from 1963 to 1968. It is interesting to note that the political rhetoric of the government of General Juan Velasco Alvarado, which overthrew Belaunde, while also pressing strongly for fundamental agrarian and nationalistic reforms, has made much less frequent use of the word "revolution" in describing its aims. They have tended to follow the current intellectual fashion in Latin American political discourse by describing such measures as "structural reform."

In Chile, Eduardo Frei, the Christian Democrat who served as president from 1964 to 1970 offered a "revolution in freedom," again suggesting a development strategy alternative to Communism or Castroism, one compatible with the maintenance of democratic institutions that long have been strong and legitimate in Chile. His elected successor, the Marxian socialist Salvador Allende also made prominent use of the rhetoric of revolution in describing a program of development toward the goal of socialist society, but again, one that would be accomplished within the context of electoral politics and democratic institutions.

The Brazilian president João Goulart (1961-1964) described his somewhat more flamboyant program of reform as "revolutionary," but so did the military group that overthrew Goulart. Their "Revolution of 1964" was designed to move Brazil toward advanced industrialization through a starkly capitalist program, with stress on foreign investment and incentives to rapid industrial growth. Social and agrarian reforms were decidedly played down. The political context of this "revolution" was one of military authoritarianism and an attempt to build a corporate state bearing a vague resemblance to Franco Spain or Fascist Italy.

Indonesia

Indonesia, at the height of the Sukarno era, proclaimed revolution as one of its most vital elements in its continually growing ideology. Slogans such as USDEK-MANIPOL and RESOPIM extolled revolution, and President Sukarno personally exalted it, proclaiming, "Read the Political Manifesto, read all my previous speeches, the bright thread which runs through all my speeches is: struggle, struggle, once again struggle, and that Revolution is struggle."[13]

In the Indonesian rhetoric, there were really two revolutions in one. "*The* revolution" was that of 1945, when the nationalists declared their independence from the Dutch and then fought for it until the legal transfer of sovereignty to the new Indonesian state in 1949. This revolution tended to lose its place in the Indonesian ideological lexicon during the 1950s. In 1959, in one of his most famous speeches, Sukarno demanded, "Where is the spirit of the Revolution today? The spirit of the Revolution has been almost extinguished, has already become cooled, without fire ... all failures, all jammings and deadlocks are at the bottom caused because we, deliberately or not, consciously or not, have

[13]From Sukarno's August 17, 1963, speech. USDEK-MANIPOL, RESOPIM, and other words in Sukarno's ideological lexicon are among the slogans that arose in Indonesia during this regime. MANIPOL means the Political Manifesto presented in 1959 which called for a return to the Constitution of 1945, antiimperialism, and a better society. USDEK, which is married to MANIPOL, was a five-point program including the Constitution of 1945, Indonesian Socialism, Guided Democracy, Guided Economy and Indonesian Identity. RESOPIM is from his speech of 1961 and stands for Revolution, Socialism, and National Leadership.

deviated from the Spirit, from the Principles, and from the Objectives of the Revolution.[14]

The continuing revolution supported by Sukarno and the Indonesian Communist Party quietly faded away with the death of the former and the virtual elimination of the latter. The basic ideology of the Indonesian Revolution of 1945, the Panjasila, remains an important part of the nation's ideology. There is no question that the Revolution of 1945 will remain a clear-cut break from the Dutch colonial past, although even that has dimmed over the past as epitomized by the successful visit to Indonesia by the Queen of the Netherlands. Continued economic and political stability may be the necessary prerequisites to the dampening of revolutionary zeal as future instability may revive past ideological struggles. Meanwhile, the nation is led by pragmatic, nonrevolutionary military officers and bureaucrats who pay the proper obeisance to the symbols of the past.

REVOLUTION AND MILITARY REGIMES

Sometimes revolution is a symbol adopted by a military regime as part of its ideological paraphernalia. Such is the case in Brazil, Burma, El Salvador, Iraq, Turkey, and Egypt.

A growing number of military regimes have come to use both social welfare goals and the rhetoric of revolution to effectuate and legitimize their regimes. Rarely do these military governments successfully establish permanent revolutionary ideologies, as they have found it difficult to obtain long-term voluntary acceptance of their views. In other cases, what has taken place was more a coup than a deep-seated, ideologically-oriented revolution. Exceptions have been Egypt, Turkey, and perhaps Burma, where action and the ideologies behind it have emphasized major political and economic change, and a discernable ideology has emerged. In Zaire, the Mobutu regime has proclaimed itself the enactor of the "Zaire Revolution." When a regime-sponsored single party was created in 1967, it was named the "*Mouvement Populaire de la Révolution*"; the precise policy imperatives deriving from the revolutionary commitment, however, are difficult to identify. The military leadership that took power in Panama in 1970 has also used the term "revolution" lavishly, though with programmatic implications that are far from clear. However, in the more important cases cited above, emphasis on reformist policies has been part of a changing set of values of the new military which has risen in Africa, Asia, and Latin America.

[14]From the Political Manifesto.

Egyptian Arab Republic

Although the rhetoric of the Egyptian revolution has changed somewhat over the years, its general goals have not.[15] The four horsemen of imperialism, Israel, Britain, United States, and France, are the rhetorical enemies (although France has been a diminished target since the end of the Algerian war). Concomitantly, a restoration of Egyptian greatness, at times converging with Arab or Muslim grandeur, has been defended. According to Nasser, "I myself shall struggle for the grandeur and dignity of Egypt until the last drop of my blood, because these are the principles for which I have risen." At another time, he described the liberation of the citizen and the "Motherland" as the first meaning of the revolution.

In order to achieve this liberation and revolution, it has been necessary to end the old corruption and feudalism which were believed to open the door to imperialist intervention. The elimination of the old ways demands self-sacrifice and discipline, so Nasser coined the motto, "unity, discipline, and work." The central theme has been social and economic advancement through land reform, education, and the elimination of the feudal structure and way of thinking. The 1956 constitution asserted that the role of the state was to ensure its citizens a decent standard of living, to protect their health and old age, and to guarantee their right to work. As time has passed, this theme of social revolution has been equated more and more with socialism and nationalization. "Arab Socialism" became more a part of the rhetoric, along with the slogan "socialism in which a state of well-being prevails." Yet socialism and anticapitalism do not mean proletarian revolution or European Marxism; they are termed Arab in nature and reformist in intent. Arab Socialism becomes tied to other elements of the revolution — antiimperialism, Arab unity, Egyptian-Arab greatness, and an end to the old ways. Parenthetically, the privileged groups in old Egypt were in large part aliens or minorities, such as Copts, Jews, Greeks, Ottoman Turks, and Europeans. Here lay the nexus between Arab nationalism, revolution, and socialism.

Burma

The Burmese military came into power by coup in March 1962, and proclaimed the establishment of a revolutionary government.[16] Burma had experienced one "revolution" when it gained its independence from the British

---

[15] For information on Egypt's ideology see Leonard Binder, *The Ideological Revolution in the Middle East* (New York: John Wiley & Sons, Inc., 1964); Robert St. John, *The Boss* (New York: McGraw Hill Book Company, 1960); and Nasser, *The Philosophy of the Revolution* (New York: Smith, Keynes and Marshall, 1959).

[16] See Fred R. von der Mehden, *Religion and Nationalism in Southeast Asia* (Madison: University of Wisconsin Press, 1963).

in 1948, but in the ensuing years the rhetoric of Burmese politics had centered upon nationalism, socialism, and Buddhism, with a decreasing use of the word "revolution." A review of the literature of the controlling party, the Anti-Fascist People's Freedom League, and of the military caretaker government of 1958-60 shows a striking absence of revolutionary terminology. This pattern changed markedly with the coup of 1962.

The new government was headed by a "revolutionary council" whose doctrine articulated a comparatively well-organized theory of revolution. The revolution rejected the old parliamentary political order, the evils of capitalism, and the disintegration of the Burmese Union from internal insurgency. Positively, the revolution called for the establishment of a socialist system, national unity and self-discipline, the formation of a new "socialist society" and political system, and the control of "the evil tendencies of man" in order to bring forth a spiritual improvement of the people. The revolution remains led and controlled by the military, and no major civilian group or individual has been capable of heavily influencing its leadership in its headlong effort to establish a socialist society more Marxian in its values and far-reaching in its policies than any other non-communist Afro-Asian state. Yet this revolution is indigenous in its concepts and terms itself "the Burmese Way to Socialism." Its Marxism is impregnated by indigenous Burmese values, and every effort has been made to distill out of it foreign elements unsuitable to what are felt to be national needs.

REVOLUTION AS HISTORIC SYMBOL

In some countries, revolution was an historic act which, although a national symbol, has little place in contemporary ideological rhetoric. This is the case in the Philippines, Thailand, and many African states.

A number of countries have as one of their national symbols "the Revolution," the act of independence, an experience that is still honored but that is little used in ideological rhetoric. An example close to home would be the United States, a nation born in revolution but whose ideology no longer emphasizes the fact except on the Fourth of July or in efforts to impress the newly independent states. Similarly, most Latin American states refer to the historical fact of the independence movement, terming it a revolution, but the concept does not have the same emotional connotations as the latter-day concept of social revolution. In Latin America, and particularly in states such as Cuba, Mexico, and Bolivia, there has been more than one revolution since independence, and we have something of a layer cake effect with one revolution atop another, each accompanied by its own ideological paraphernalia. The original "revolution" brought independence from Spain, to be followed by palace uprisings of one sort or another and finally, in a few cases, a major economic and political upheaval. The final revolutionary concept may be an amalgam of some or all of these experiences.

In Asia there are two examples of this concept of revolution as historic symbol – the Philippines and Thailand. In the former, reference is made to the revolution of 1896 and the wars against Spain and the United States, but the passing years tended to dim the emotions wrought by these events and the idea of a continuing revolution did not have a part to play in the national rhetoric. In the 1960s, as Philippine nationalism grew, there appeared to be a revitalization of these historic events, epitomized by the decision to change independence day from the date upon which the country received independence from the United States (July 4) to a date in line with her earlier revolutionary experience.

Thailand is an even more interesting case, for its "revolution" took place as late as 1932, when the absolute monarchy was overthrown by coup. Today the country's ideology centers primarily upon Buddhism, the monarchy, democracy, and the Thai nation. The "revolution" was primarily a peaceful readjustment which made comparatively minor changes in the power structure. The concept of the 1932 revolution has little apparent ideological vitality, although from time to time the term is used to hark back to the earlier period. For example, the coup by Marshal Sarit Thanarat in 1958, which scrapped the constitution and established martial law, was led by an elite group called the Revolutionary Party (Khana Pathiwat, which had earlier been called the Khana Thanan or Military Party).

FAILURE TO LEGITIMIZE REVOLUTION AS CONTINUING POLITICAL SYMBOL

Some governments in the recent past have used the symbol of revolution as a prominent part of their ideological rhetoric, but the symbol did not become permanently legitimized. Among these have been Colombia (Alfonso López), Costa Rica (Figueres), Ghana (Nkrumah), Guatemala (Arévalo, Arbenz), Venezuela (Betancourt), and Peru (Belaunde).

Most Latin American states have enjoyed the problems and luxuries of independence longer than the majority of their Afro-Asian counterparts. In these nations various military and civilian leaders attempted to found new systems built upon doctrines with revolutionary themes. However, due to personal inadequacy, military, Church, or other opposition, or the myriad forces that can destroy a Latin American regime, they failed to solidify their power. This failure also ended the paramountcy of their ideology, and succeeding governments did not find it necessary to accept the former revolutionary doctrine.

Guatemala provides an interesting problem in assessing the relative "permanence" of the symbol of revolution.[17] The movement that overthrew the dictator Jorge Ubico in 1944 described itself as "revolutionary" in character, and the concept became central to the subsequent administrations of Juan José

[17] Ronald M. Schneider, *Communism in Guatemala: 1944–1954* (New York: Frederick A. Praeger, Inc., 1958).

Arévalo and Jacobo Arbenz. Whan Carlos Castillo Armas overthrew the Arbenz government in 1954, he initially made a substantial effort to identify himself with the objectives of the Revolution of 1944, claiming that he intended to restore the "Revolution" to its proper direction, purged of Communist influences. However, since 1957, invocation of the Revolution of 1944 has fallen into disuse under the military governments of Generals Idígoras and Peralta. In one sense, then, we may say that the symbol of revolution failed to become permanently legitimate in Guatemala, a critical component of national or regime identity. On the other hand, political dissidence in Guatemala continues to cluster around the figure of Arévalo and the events and policies of the 1944-1954 period. For most Guatemalan opposition groups, both within the country and in exile, the Revolution of 1944 continues as a prominent part of their ideological equipment. Should one of these groups return to power, it might claim lineal descent from the leaders of the uprising of 1944. In this case, a certain continuity to the postwar history of Guatemala might be established, with the Idígoras-Peralta period identified as something of a Thermidorian phase of an ongoing revolutionary process. On the other hand, a successful rebel movement in Guatemala might wish to establish its own distinctive identity, apart from the antecedent movement of the 1940s. In such a case, the Revolution of 1944 would appear as no more than a brief, completed phase in Guatemalan civic life, without peculiar pertinence or significance for the process of national development.

REVOLUTION AS POTENTIAL POLITICAL SYMBOL

In many countries, significant political movements, rather than regimes, now out of power adopt revolution as a prominent ideological symbol for the nation.

Latin America	Asia	Africa and the Middle East	
Argentina	Burma	Angola	Morocco
Bolivia	Cambodia	Ethiopia	Mozambique
Brazil	Ceylon	Guiné-Bissau	Muscat and Oman
Colombia	Laos	Iran	Rhodesia
Guatemala	Philippines	Iraq	South Africa
Panama	South Vietnam	Jordan	Sudan
Peru	Thailand	Lebanon	
Uruguay			

In a variety of countries throughout the developing world, there are groups attempting to overthrow the political system. These groups may espouse Communist ideology, as in the Philippines or South Vietnam; attached to a particular leader or an indigenous philosophy, as among the various guerrilla movements of contemporary Latin America; desirous of regional autonomy, as in Northern Borneo; or a combination of several of these forces, as in most of the countries listed. The Pathet Lao mixes Communism with resentment by hill tribes of Mekong Lao domination; Malaysian Communist leaders have long had a strong element of Chinese chauvinism; and in the Middle East there have been Communist efforts to play upon Kurdish nationalism, which is split between the nationalist (Barzani) and Communist-dominated (Kurd Democratic Party) elements. The point of differentiation here is that none of these groups has succeeded in toppling the political apparatus.

Latin America

Guerrilla movements played a prominent and much-discussed role in Latin American politics in recent years. While often markedly different in objectives and strategy, most shared a common world-view and a common conception of the significance of revolution. Generally, they perceived the continent as dominated by oligarchic elites who presided over a system based on the economic and social exploitation of the mass of the population. The power of the oligarchy derived from and was dependent upon the structure of international capitalism. "Imperialism," and particularly the power of the United States, was the underpinning of the system of control. Peaceful, evolutionary reform could not fundamentally change this system. What was required was massive change, which must be brought about by revolutionary means. With the exception of Cuba, nowhere did these movements succeed. By the early 1970s, their influence and prominence seemed to be waning. However, during the mid to late 1960s, their presence was a significant and controversial factor in the politics of the region.

Che Guevara's effort to recreate the Cuban Revolution in Bolivia in 1967 perhaps exemplifies the aims and strategy of this form of revolutionary appeal. In a situation where the dominance of existing elites is well-established but where there are significant weaknesses in their power, the indicated strategy for the revolutionary is to establish a base among the peasantry, a small cohesive guerrilla army, that can promote and dramatize the message of revolution, demonstrate the limits of the government's coercive power by carefully selected aggressive actions, and gradually expand the movement by recruitment and conversion in rural areas.[18] A further implication of the strategy is that the solidarity, cohesion, and "participatory democracy" practised by the guerrilla band will serve as a model for the political organization of society once power is won. Both Maoist and Castroite inspiration and precedent are apparent.

---

[18] Regis Debray, *Revolution in the Revolution* (New York: Monthly Review Press, 1967); John Gerassi, *Venceremos! The Speeches and Writings of Che Guevara* (New York: Monthly Review Press, 1967).

The basic model and vision took different forms in different nations. One variation was the strategy of urban terrorism, the most-publicized example of which was the *Tupamaro* movement in Uruguay. They stressed hit-and-run violence and the kidnapping of prominent figures. The underlying premise of such activity seems to have been that mass uprisings do not occur in "exploitative" societies because of fear of the coercive power of the state. If the revolutionaries can dramatically demonstrate that insurgency can be committed with impunity, the potentially revolutionary mass will come to sense their capacity for effective political action, and overcome their fear of reprisal.

Not all the movements saw their prime objective as the capture and control of national political power. Some, such as the "peasant leagues" fostered by Hugo Blanco in Peru and Francisco Julião in Brazil were dedicated to an "agrarian revolution," to the organization of peasant farmers for the achievement of land reform and change in the political patterns of rural life. For such movements, long-run goals of national political transformation were more ambiguous and unclear.

The romantic appeal of revolution in Latin America in the 1960s was very strong. Much of the symbolism of revolution was embodied in the personalities of heroic leaders and martyrs. These ranged from the "professionalism" of Guevara to the drama of the Colombian rebel priest Camilo Torres who, frustrated in attempts to promote reform through established processes, joined a guerrilla movement and was killed by the Colombian army. A more subtle approach to the creation of "revolutionary consciousness" was exemplified by Paulo Friere of Brazil, who advocated the teaching of literacy using instructional materials that stressed radical political appeals.

The exploits of the Latin American guerrillas provided symbols and heros for other ideological radicals, most prominently students, not only in Latin America, but in the United States and Western Europe as well. The vision of revolution they espoused played a central role in the radical mystique of the late 1960s throughout the world.

By their own admission and self-analysis, the guerrillas failed.[19] They misinterpreted the nature of the "revolutionary situation". In Bolivia, Guevara tried to duplicate the Cuban experience and failed to win over a peasantry that, secure in land received in an agrarian reform in the 1950s, remained loyal to the established government. Elsewhere, failure is attributed to the counterinsurgency tactics of Latin American armies instructed and equipped by the United States, to the pervasive grip of traditional power structures, or simply to the failure of the masses to achieve "revolutionary consciousness." In the 1970s, the appeal to revolution is apt to remain persistent in Latin America — this is a consistent theme of the political culture, and the manifest inequities of the social order in

---

[19] For a general discussion of these movements, and a commentary on their own analysis of their failure, see John D. Martz, "Doctrine and Dilemmas of the Latin American 'New Left'," *World Politics,* 22 (January 1970), pp. 171–96.

many nations have hardly disappeared — but the aims and tactics, the nature of the revolutionary appeal, is likely to be different.

ABSENCE OF REVOLUTIONARY SYMBOLISM

The symbol of revolution is not particularly salient in political life or rhetoric within the following countries:

Latin America	Asia and Africa	
Costa Rica	Central African Republic	Niger
Ecuador	Chad	Nigeria
Haiti	Gabon	Pakistan
Honduras	Ivory Coast	Rwanda
Nicaragua	Kenya	Saudi Arabia
	Kuwait	Senegal
	Liberia	Sierra Leone
	Malawi	Somalia
	Malaysia	Togo
	Mauretania	Upper Volta
		Zambia

The apparent preoccupation of governments and movements within the lesser-developed countries with the rhetoric of revolution makes this category a fascinating one. Why has revolutionary doctrine not obtained a foothold in these states? What, if anything, is different about these nations? In a few new states of Africa a simple explanation might be that they received their independence without struggle and are too new to have developed ideologies. This, of course, does not explain the instance of revolutionary rhetoric in the older states, let alone among the new nations of Africa that have revolutionary elements, such as Tanzania or Guinea. It can be argued that conflict has taken place largely within a conservative or traditional pattern, dampening revolutionary rhetoric, as in Saudi Arabia or Nicaragua.

Nicaragua

The case of Nicaragua provides an interesting example of a country in which revolutionary appeals are curiously absent from the nation's political life, either as a key concept of opposition or as a means of justifying a certain technique of governance.[20]

[20] Charles W. Anderson, "Nicaragua: The Somoza Dynasty," in Martin Needler, ed., *Latin American Political Systems* (New York: Van Nostrand Reinhold, 1970), pp. 109–31.

It is interesting, but not terribly significant, that the Somoza family administrations and the intervening government of René Schick, which together constitute a political regime extending from 1937 to the present, never referred to their political intentions as revolutionary in character, despite persistent claims that their technique of rule was singularly propitious for the development and progress of the nation. What is more surprising is that the concept of "revolution" appears so seldom and is such a muted theme in the literature of opposition to the Somoza regime that we have been able to assemble.

Several explanations for the failure of the symbol of revolution to become salient in the political life of Nicaragua may be offered. First, it might be suggested that the abuses and imperfections of the Somoza regime, and the desirability of its termination, were sufficiently obvious as not to demand more extensive justification. Certainly, much of the literature of opposition to the Somoza government focuses on the quality of that government itself rather than on the promises or goals of the prospective replacement.

Second, the opposition to the Somoza government was in good measure an operation from exile, and the exile groups, scattered about the Caribbean area, never achieved the cohesion necessary for the creation of an organized rebel movement, with stated objectives, ideology, and program.

Third, much of the organized opposition to the Somoza regime identified with the historic Conservative party of Nicaragua. The Somoza themselves were identified with, and endorsed by, the historic Liberal party. For much of the Conservative leadership, and particularly its elder statesmen, the Somoza government was interpreted primarily as an episode in the traditional conflict between the two parties rather than a unique phenomenon of dictatorship requiring a revolutionary solution. The more persistent theme of the Conservatives throughout the Somoza period has been of the "it's time for a change" variety, as though the presence of a two-party system provided the basis for political change without the need for a revolutionary restructuring of the system itself.

"REVOLUTION" AS AN EXPRESSION OF POLITICAL GOALS

The goals set forth in the ideological rhetoric of the spokesmen for revolution among the lesser-developed states are often vague and fluid and at times appear irrational to the outside observer. Clearcut ideologies are the exception, not the rule. Fluidity is apparent to any student of the history of ideology of the new states and may reflect a competition of ideas, reaction to changing circumstances, or a variety of other forces. An assessment of the goals of revolution is also made difficult by the extent to which there are no clearcut priorities given to particular aspects of the ideology. Revolutionary doctrine within the general ideology may be part of a universal dogma such as Marxism-Leninism, an integrated national ideology such as was formulated over the years by Sukarno, or an element of a vague, ad hoc set of principles, badly articulated and lacking internal discipline. Presented below is an analysis of various revolutionary goals distilled from the rhetoric of revolution.

Revolution as an Anticolonial, Antiimperialist Struggle. The struggle to gain independence from the mother country has often been articulated in terms of revolution. The goal of the revolution is independence, but included are hopes for what independence will bring: economic and social betterment, the rebirth of national culture, psychological rejuvenation of the individual, an end to specific grievances against the colonial regime, and so forth. Thus, the goal of independence may be an umbrella for a variety of other desires, articulated and unarticulated, conscious and unconscious, modern and traditional. Regarding our own experience, Seymour Martin Lipset has commented in *The First New Nation*, "When Americans celebrate their national heritage on Independence Day, Memorial Day, or other holidays of this sort, they dedicate themselves anew to a nation conceived as the living fulfilment of a political doctrine that enshrines a utopian conception of men's egalitarian and fraternal relations with one another."[21] During Indonesia's struggle for independence one of her nationalist leaders asserted the aims of that country's national revolution:

> The aim is the unity of the Indonesian people and the realization of social justice and prosperity for our people. Therefore the abolition of the colonial system alone is not enough. We need an economic and political structure which can guarantee the realization of social justice, and this could not be realized in the Dutch time which was colonialistic and capitalistic in nature.[22]

Following the successful achievement of the revolution for independence, the place of revolution in the national ideology may vary. In some states, such as the United States and a number of Latin American countries, it may lose its immediate ideological vitality and become of primarily historical significance. The loss of impact may be revitalized later by those attempting to reinstate the glories of sacrifices of the revolutionary struggle. This tactic has been most obvious in Indonesia but is to be found to some extent in most countries with independence struggles (as Castro invokes the memory of José Martì, and Philippine leaders honor Rizal). Finally, the revolution may be considered a continuing struggle for independence from the last vestiges of neo-colonialism and imperialism, a goal still unfulfilled. This attitude is to be found in the more

---

[21] Seymour Martin Lipset, *The First New Nation* (New York: Basic Books, 1963), p. 75.

[22] Quoted in George Kahin, *Nationalism and Revolution in Indonesia* (Ithaca, N.Y.: Cornell University Press, 1952), p. 309.

radical states of Africa and most obviously in Algeria, Communist China, and several Latin American nations.

Revolution for Economic and Social Development. Inherent in most of the rhetoric of revolution is the achievement of short- or long-term economic and social goals. It is the rare revolutionary who, like Sukarno, would state, "Indonesia has NOT embarked upon a course of utilizing our newly won independence as the *capital for mainly economic development.*[23] More common would be the following demands of Mao Tse Tung:

> ...First, the present government must be remolded into a united front government in which the representatives of the people take part. Such a government should be at once democratic and centralized. It should carry out the necessary revolutionary policies. Secondly, people should be granted freedom of speech, press, assembly, association and of making armed resistance against the enemy, so that the war will take on a masked character. Thirdly, the living conditions of the people must be improved through such assessments, reducing rent and interest, raising the pay of workers, officers of lower level and soldiers, taking good care of the families of soldiers fighting the Japanese, and extending relief to the victims of natural calamities and of war refugees, etc.[24]

Again, the revolutionary statements regarding economic and social goals can be broken down into somewhat arbitrary divisions. They may be directed against specific grievances, such as the concentration of wealth and power in the tin industry and large land holders in Bolivia or the "feudal" structure in China. These demands may hide a broader range of targets, but the emotional brunt of the attacks are easily recognized "enemies." Again, the revolution may be directed against rather broadly defined enemies of the people such as capitalists and imperialists (Burma, Algeria) in terms of what might be called vulgar Marxism, i.e., broad demands for social reform and the destruction of the people's enemies without a strict acceptance of any doctrinal position. A third pattern of rhetoric centers on revolutionary goals tied to integrated ideological doctrines such as Marxism-Leninism. This form may be found today in North Korea, North Vietnam, and Communist China. There is, then, a basic difference between the early general statements of Nasser that "These... are the aims of the revolution: to end the exploitation of the people, to realize national aspirations and to develop the mature political consciousness that is an

---

[23] Special issue of *Le Monde,* May 1964, republished by the Information Division, Embassy of Indonesia, and entitled "Reflections Upon the Indonesian Revolution."

[24] Quoted by Jerome Ch'ên in *Mao and the Chinese Revolution* (London: Oxford University Press, 1965), p. 226.

indispensable preliminary for social democracy"[25] and the aims expressed by N. N. Pak of North Korea:

> The leadership of the toiling masses led by the working class, the core of which is a Marxist-Leninist Party, and the carrying out of the proletarian revolution in one form or another, and the establishment of the dictatorship of the proletariat in one form or another, the alliance of the working class with the peasantry and other strata of toilers, and liquidation of capitalist property and the establishment of public ownership for the basic means of production; the gradual Socialist transformation of Agriculture; the planned development of the national economy ... ; the realization of the socialist's revolution in the areas of ideology and culture and the creation of a numerous intelligentsia, devoted to the working class ... and the solidarity of the working class ... with the working class of other countries — proletarian internationalism.[26]

This difference is too obvious to be commented upon, although it should be noted that this sort of explicit statement by Communists is often not made publicly prior to the attainment of power.

Revolutionary Romanticism. A third set of goals of the revolution may fall generally under the rubric of romanticism or emotion. Revolution may be a reminder or demand for the return to past glories. This theme has a number of variations, such as the search for national identity in Indonesia, a return to traditional forms like the Mahdi complex in the Sudan, the rise of a particular ethnic or racial group such as the anti-"Arab" facet of the revolution in Zanzibar, the Hutu overthrow of the Tutsi "feudal overlords" in Rwanda, or the place of the Indian in Mexico. This cultural aspect is, to a degree, antimodern and traditional in its position and superficially may appear to be a demand for a reactionary revolution. However, this assessment would miss the other part of the goal, for the "chosen," whether they be the Indian, Indonesian, or Algerian peasant, is to be led to a better economic and social existence more compatible with "modern" Western material values than with traditional feudal ones. The purpose of the revolution is to overthrow ethnic- or colonially-oriented feudal groups that hinder modernization or usurp all its benefits. The harkening back to past glories is not a demand for a reinstatement of the precolonial regimes but a reminder of the greatness that is again possible with the successful achievement of the revolution.

There also may be an aspect of pure romanticism in the call for

---

[25] "The Egyptian Revolution," *Foreign Affairs* (January 1955), p. 208.

[26] Quoted in Philip Rudolph, *North Korea's Political and Economic Structure* (New York: Institute of Pacific Relations, 1959), p. 58.

revolution – a feeling of exhilaration with the prospect, best epitomized in Sukarno's confession:

> Well, frankly, I tell you: I belong to the group of people who are bound in a spiritual longing by the Romanticism of Revolution. I am inspired by it, I am fascinated by it, I am completely absorbed by it, I am crazed, I am obsessed by the Romanticism of Revolution. And for this I utter thanks to God Who Commands All Nature![27]

ACCEPTANCE AND REJECTION OF THE SYMBOL "REVOLUTION"

One of the most fascinating and frustrating questions to be asked is why some individuals or groups accept the rhetoric of revolution and others do not. In seeking an answer, it is necessary to analyze historical, cultural, and, particularly, personal experiences. This section will consider a number of possible factors that may be causally related to the presence of revolutionary doctrine, but it should be stressed that the particular combination of forces behind specific revolutionary doctrines may differ markedly from case to case. The following list of factors is not intended to exhaust all possible forces.

The Decolonization Experience. Certainly the experience of colonial rule has been blamed by many for the growth of revolutionary doctrine. For example, an Algerian statement during the struggle with France asserted,

> The Algerian problem is essentially a colonial one, and so long as the colonial regime continues to exist there can be no permanent solution and no permanent peace in Algeria, for it is in the nature of colonialism that it contains within itself the germs of continual conflicts and constitutes the greatest threat to peace.[28]

Yet this idea does not provide a ready explanation, given the number of ex-colonial people not led to violence and revolution by the colonial experience. It can, of course, be argued that the atmosphere of colonial oppression provided an environment for later revolutionary doctrine, but this begs the question. What particular situations related to colonial rule and decolonization aided that environment? A few tentative suggestions can be made.

When the colonial regime rules a society where there is a politically aware stratum but will not allow modern nationalism a legal place, extralegal revolutionary groups tend to replace the moderates. This fairly straightforward hypothesis can be supported by a variety of examples – Indonesia, Algeria, and,

---

[27] Independence Day Speech, August 17, 1960.
[28] See Fred R. von der Mehden, "The Role and Themes of Ideological Systems in Burma, Indonesia and Malaysia: A Comparative Study," USIA, Research and Reference Service, R–64–65 (May 1965), p. 9.

most forcefully, Vietnam. In the prewar Vietnamese case, the French administration suppressed modern nationalists and at times used violent methods to repress those who sought open, peaceful means of independence. The result was revolutionary doctrine. According to Ellen Hammer, "By declaring political opposition illegal and subject to police reprisals, the administration left nationalists who desired action no alternative but to operate clandestinely, as revolutionaries.[29]

It has been argued by some that the most dangerous course a colonial system can take is a fluctuating program of repression and concession, that this actual or perceived lack of continuity of policy leads to frustrations of a violent nature.[30] There can be some doubt as to the universal applicability of such a hypothesis. Colonial administration in general is notoriously lacking in continuity of policy, and there are cases where such discontinuity did not leave an appreciable legacy of revolutionary doctrine (Madagascar, Malaysia, India). At the same time there are examples of a changing colonial policy driving individuals into an acceptance of a revolutionary doctrine. A prime example would be the former Netherlands East Indies – Indonesia. After centuries of economically oriented policy, from the beginning of this century up to 1926-27, there was a major expansion of political liberties and responsibilities for the colonial peoples. A variety of political parties and ideologies arose, some revolutionary in doctrine (which may also illustrate the counter-argument that revolutions appear appropriate when the ties are loosened). After the 1926-27 abortive revolt the Dutch established more repressive controls over nationalist activities. Individual moderate nationlists found this vacillation policy a frustrating reminder of the lack of control that they had over their own destiny and turned to more revolutionary doctrines.

Is there a relationship between the presence or absence of violence in the decolonization process and the presence or absence of revolutionary doctrine? Of course, violence may be an effect rather than a cause of earlier colonial policies. A catalogue of colonial experiences where violence took place coincides remarkably well with the presence of revolutionary doctrine – Burma, Vietnam, Indonesia, Algeria, Syria. This is not to state that violence is necessary for the presence of revolutionary rhetoric, but certainly it opens the way for a greater anticolonial, antiimperialist attitude, for clandestine organization, aid (material or moral) from revolutionary-oriented states, and the development of a multitude of personal frustrations.

Within any colonial system there is the opportunity for the growth of systematic or chance insults and humiliations, actually perpetrated or erroneously perceived as perpetrated by colonial administrators upon the population. Instances of perceived oppression may sensitize an individual to later demands for revolutionary change.

[29] Ellen Hammer, *The Struggle for Indo-China* (Stanford, Calif.: Stanford University Press, 1954), p. 79.
[30] For example, this thesis is put forward by Robert A. LeVine, "Anti-European

The "Failures" of Independence. When independence did arrive, there were great hopes for what it would bring. The newly established governments were not always able to bring these hopes to fruition. This is not the place to discuss the reasons for the failures of many new governments in the lesser-developed countries, but we can analyze in greater detail three of the results of failure and their impact on the doctrine of revolution:

1. Inability of the government to achieve the political and social goals of independence or promises of the regime.[31] If we view the growth of revolutionary ideologies in the lesser-developed countries, we find these "failures" a stated reason for revolution by those immediately involved. Naguib and Nasser attacked the corruption and incompetence of the Wafd Party, General Ne Win argued that the civilian parliamentary system had not provided for the needs of the people and called for a revival of the concept of revolution in Burma, Sukarno of Indonesia proclaimed the need to revitalize the Revolution of 1945 and revolutionary concepts after the failure of the government to live up to the earlier revolution for independence. In Zaire, Congo-Brazzaville, and Vietnam, similar statements were made by those proclaiming revolutionary doctrine. These attitudes engendered by the "failure" of the revolution or independence movement are not new or primarily Afro-Asian. One Latin American writer complained, "We accepted the proposition that sovereignty or the power to command resided in the people, just as we had formerly been convinced that sovereignty of kings came from God. But we had only substituted one dogma for another." National independence was gained on "the last day of despotism and the first day of the same thing."[32]

2. Inability of the government to cope with the problems of ethnic, religious, or ideological disunity. Closely tied with earlier charges of inefficiency by the political governors of new countries is the claim that the unity of the nation itself is in jeopardy due to the conscious or unconscious acts of the ruling group. In Indonesia the return of the spirit of the 1945 revolution was deemed necessary because of internal strife in Java and the Outer Islands. In Burma, the belief of the military regarding the inability of the government of U Nu to cope with internal insurgency was seen by the Revolutionary Council as the first cause of the coup of 1962. Their desire was, according to the military, not to become another Laos or Vietnam.[33] Nasser has asserted that a major object of the Egyptian revolution was to unite a people divided by poverty and imperialism. Like the former point, this situation need not inevitably lead to the call for revolution and is but one variable among many.

3. The inability of the government to cope with outside aggression or war.

Violence in Africa: A Comparative Analysis," *Journal of Conflict Resolution,* 3, No. 4 (December 1959), 420–29.

[31] Fred R. von der Mehden, "The Role and Themes of Ideological Systems," p. 9.

[32] Quoted in Harold E. Davis, ed., *Governments and Politics in Latin America* (New York: The Ronald Press Company, 1958), p. 119.

[33] *Burma Weekly Bulletin,* 10 (March 15, 1962), 395.

This situation can lead to either frustration with the rulers, engendering demands for immediate change, or weakness within the system which allows for the formation of strong antigovernment power. Examples abound — the former case may be found in Indonesia, where the years of abortive negotiations over West Irian and, later, confrontation with Malaysia led to demands for a spirit of sacrifice like that of the revolution for independence from Holland. The best case is Egypt, where observers have pointed to the disaster of the Palestine War as a reason for the growth of revolutionary fervor within the officer class. With regard to the weakening caused by external strife bringing demands for change and a weakened central government unable to meet those demands, one need only point to South Vietnam. Similarly, the Bolivian revolution traces its roots to defeat in the Chaco War with Paraguay, and the "revolutionary" thought of the Peruvian Aprista Movement is in linear descent from the outraged pamphleteering of Manuel González Prada following Peru's defeat at the hands of Chile in the War of the Pacific.

The three aforementioned factors may account for dissatisfaction or even coup but not necessarily a doctrine of revolution. Two further points must be made. First, these failures normally must develop over a number of years, festering and frustrating those who choose revolution. Secondly, there must be a perception that the "normal" means of evolutionary change are not possible or beneficial. The revolutionary may feel that the closed nature of the political structure does not allow for evolutionary change. For example, there is little opportunity for a major change from the outside within a one-party state. Perhaps the social structure does not allow for sufficient change or upward mobility, as within Imperial China before the revolution of 1911.

However, it is also possible that "revolution" itself becomes the acceptable and normal process of political change, and election or cooption the "exception" to the rule. This may be the case in the "typical" Latin American revolution syndrome, where internal struggle and jealousies, personality cults, doctrinal differences, and regionalism within the small politicized stratum involved in politics has led to chronic "revolutionary" instability. At the extreme is Marxist-Leninist theory as expounded by Communist China, which states that a change in the present capitalist system cannot come without revolution. Finally, there are those who argue that a revolutionary doctrine is required, whether the system is open to change or not, as a purifying experience necessary to mobilize a people for action and sacrifice.

We are left with the modest conclusion that the most striking aspect of the idea of revolution in the developing world is the diversity of its usage. In many contexts, it can best be understood as ritualized rhetoric, divorced from policy decisions. In others, the symbol of revolution may be a surrogate for radical transformation of the system; in still others, revolution is a compelling guide to action. It remains for us to examine the closely related concept of developmental socialism, and to try to measure the relationship between ideology and action in the developing world.

CHAPTER 11

Socialism as a Program for Development

What precisely should political leaders do to achieve development? Economists, political scientists, and sociologists have constructed theories that attempt to capture the essence of the developmental process. Often these implicitly or explicitly contain advice as to how the statesmen of the third world should marshall their resources. However, the task of developmental statecraft is probably better understood if we look at the problem as the leaders of these nations themselves define it. What goals do they seek, and what measures do they plan to take to achieve them?

Of course, the spectrum of approaches to the problem of development is very broad. Some political elites are intent on maintaining the existing structures of their societies essentially intact, making only such concessions to change and modernity as are necessary to guarantee the continuity of the going concern. Others are in effect pragmatists. Tacitly, they may see the systems of the Western industrial nations as the long-run goal to be achieved, but they think and act in the present, taking such measures as they suppose will encourage economic growth and enhance the stability and effectiveness of the regime. There are many, though, who see development as something other than a repeat of the historical experience of the former colonial power or of the United States. Identifying capitalism as the distinctive developmental process of the Western industrial nations, they often use the term *socialism* to distinguish their vision of the future development of their own nations.

Some would argue that socialism is on its way to becoming the characteristic ideology of the developing world. Certainly, the theme is prominent in political rhetoric and argument throughout Africa, Asia, and Latin America. Even where leaders and movements do not identify themselves directly with socialism — as is often the case in Latin America — the pattern of belief and intention is remarkably similar to that of avowed socialists in other emerging nations.

But what specifically does socialism mean as a program for change? And do those who seek socialistic development see a common future for the developing world? There is a tendency to jump to conclusions here, to see a worldwide pattern where there may be the utmost diversity, unified only by a word. There are at least three problems in assessing the implications of the widespread interest in socialism in the developing world.

First, socialism may mean something quite different from the point of view of an industrialized and a developing nation. Socialism appeared as an ideology in the West after the industrial revolution was far advanced. Furthermore, socialism as a set of parties and movements has had a diverse history in the West in the twentieth century. Hence a European socialist of the 1970s, a Harold Wilson or Willy Brandt, may or may not mean the same thing by socialism as his counterpart in the developing world. The citizen of the Soviet Union, with his more rigorous conception of "scientific socialism" and his specific vision of Marxism-Leninism is apt to be totally baffled by the freewheeling unorthodoxy of socialists in the developing nations. In the United States, by a quirk of history, socialism inevitably connotes a radical position, to take serious exception to the going concern, quite unlike its contemporary connotations in Western Europe where the basic socialist position is not vastly different from that of the American Democratic party. The idea of the "trend to socialism" in the developing world is apt to have very different connotations depending on where one stands in the political tradition of the industrialized world itself.

Second, the leaders who identify with socialism in Africa, Asia, and Latin America may or may not have the same thing in mind. Is the ideology of socialism in the emerging world a coherent whole, or do we artificially link unrelated and potentially conflicting political purposes under a common rubric?

Third, does ideology make any great difference in what governments concretely do about political, economic, and social change? In practice, is there a discernible difference between a socialist program for development and one that is not labeled by this term? When sweeping and grandiloquent rhetoric is reduced to practical activity and accomplishment, what do we find?

It would seem worthwhile to put in perspective what the leaders of the developing nations mean by socialism and how they are using the state as an instrument of economic and social change. To do this, we should first examine the various meanings of socialism, the different trends and movements identified with the term, that exist in Africa, Asia, and Latin America. Beyond this, we should seek out the common elements in the pattern. Why has socialism seemed so uniquely plausible to leaders of nations so different in culture and heritage, with such distinctive developmental possibilities and problems? How does socialism in the developing world differ from its Western counterparts and why? To what extent are the "socialists" of the developing world in agreement, and to what extent are they marching to the sounds of different drummers? Then, we should assess the actual extent of the socialist mystique in the developing world. How widespread in fact is the use of the term "socialism" to describe a doctrine of governance? Finally, we should get some notion of the degree of correspondence between theory and practice. How different is an avowedly socialist policy from a nonsocialist policy in today's developing nations?

A SURVEY OF DEVELOPMENTAL SOCIALISM

Let us begin with a survey of the broad and rather colorful spectrum of movements, forces, and intellectual trends that might be identified with developmental socialism as a way of getting a feeling for the heterogeneity of the substance with which we are dealing.

Africa

African Socialism. One of the most interesting ideological phenomena to come out of the developing world in recent years is African Socialism. Considerable efforts have been made to delineate the distinctive features of this doctrine. In fact, a conference of African leaders at Dakar in December 1962, sought to arrive at a codification of this ideology. However, the differences between the ideas and approaches of those leaders who identify as African Socialists are perhaps more impressive than the fraternity of doctrine they have established or the commonality of their efforts.

Certainly, there are common themes in African Socialism. Friedland and Rosberg suggest that three main strands might be unwoven from the complex fabric of ideas and issues. These would include (1) "the problem of continental identity," the idea that African Socialism must be distinguished from other kinds of socialism and that socialism in Africa is to be modeled more on the communitarian roots of traditional African society than upon the problems that suggested socialist ideas in Europe; (2) "the crisis of economic development," the idea that only through state planning, stimulation, and social mobilization can the continent achieve the rapid economic growth that it seeks; (3) "the dilemmas of control and class formation," the search for a doctrine of common endeavor that will meld diversities into a dynamic nationalism and prevent the emergence of class divisiveness.[1]

---

[1] William H. Friedland and Carl G. Rosberg, Jr., eds., *African Socialism* (Stanford, Calif.: Stanford University Press, 1964), pp. 1-11. In the same volume Aristide Zolberg describes the main points to emerge from the Dakar Conference as follows: (1) the urgency of development; (2) rationality and planning; (3) the uniqueness of African Socialism; (4) economic modernization without alienation; (5) the dilemma of traditionalism and modernism; (6) mobilization of the masses; (7) the need for world solidarity. *Ibid.*, pp. 113-27. See also the special issue of *African Forum*, 1 (Winter 1966) devoted to African socialism. For a Marxist perspective, see Giovanni Arrighi and John S. Saul, "Socialism and Economic Development in Tropical Africa," *Journal of Modern African Studies,* 6 (August 1968) pp. 141-69.

A French scholar, L. V. Thomas, suggested a useful recapitulation of the salient differences between African Socialism and classical Marxism-Leninism.[2]

Theme	Marxism-Leninism	African Socialism
Atheism	Yes	No
Materialism	Yes	No
Alliance with capital	No	Yes, with independence
Internationalism	Yes	Yes, in African context
Specificity	No (dangerous)	Yes (necessary)
Historical determinism	Rigorous	Flexible
Class struggle	Yes (essential)	Avoid at all costs
Nationalization	Absolutely	Not necessarily
Single party, dictatorship of proletariat	Yes	Single party, not proletariat
Collective ideal	Yes	Communitarianism
New ethos	Yes	Yes

It is no accident that definitions of African Socialism begin to appear in the early 1960s; 1960 was the year of African independence, with no less than sixteen countries achieving sovereignty. Prior to that time, ideological debate focused on the goal of independence itself; whether this was to be achieved through revolutionary action, as in Algeria, or by electoral organization and negotiation, as in most of tropical Africa, the transcendent goal of independence dictated the tactic of the comprehensive national front. Aggregation of anticolonial grievances was thus the order of the day, rather than the potentially divisive task of defining the content of independence. When self-government had been achieved, it was necessary, even urgent, to move swiftly to a programmatic definition of the goals of independence. Many of the particular features of African Socialism become more understandable when set against the immediate background of the comprehensive nationalist movement. Unity was a paramount consideration; accordingly, aspects of socialist ideology – such as the idea of class struggle, or antagonism to religion as the "opium of the people" – that had strongly divisive implications had to be rethought. Further, nationalism in Africa asserted the rights of Africans (colonized subjects) against Europeans (dominating colonizers). From this followed logically the stress upon commonalities in African cultures, particularly the communitarian tradition, which required a uniquely African adaptation of the socialist intellectual heritage.

With more than a decade of independence passed, in most cases, the crucible within which socialist thought is forged has drastically changed. Most countries were in their second or third development plan by the second decade of independence. Ideological doctrine had been subjected to the corroding – and stimulating – impact of the concrete process of policy choice. By the mid-1960s, a pattern of instability, usually through military intervention, began

[2] L. V. Thomas, *Le Socialisme et l'Afrique* (Paris: Liore Africain, 1966) I, p. 58.

to be evident, affecting the perspectives of all participants in the political process. In many instances, the material benefits of independence were largely reserved for the political-administrative class; many, especially radical critics of African political development, argued that the crystallization of an "administrative bourgeoisie" was the dominant social fact. Students and young intellectuals, faced with less dazzling opportunities for swift promotion than were available to the independence generation, joined in the attack on African Socialism, with its flexibility and compromises, calling instead for a rigorous "scientific socialism." The specific personality of given leaders also entered the equation of differentiation. All these currents produced by the early 1970s a greater divergence in the ideological signposts and policy pathways to development than existed in the early 1960s. The interesting effort in 1962 to arrive at a common synthesis of what constituted African Socialism would have been unimaginable a decade later. Three fundamentally different approaches to the question of socialism in sub-Saharan Africa might be identified as follows.

Radical, Mobilization Socialism. Such leaders as Sékou Touré of Guinea, Kwame Nkrumah of Ghana (overthrown in 1966), the government of Congo-Brazzaville and the officials of the Union Soudanaise of Mali (both replaced by young officers in 1968) share with other African socialists a sense of the cultural distinctiveness of Africa and hence the need for a distinctive interpretation of socialism. However, each of them tends to place greater emphasis on socialism as a means of marshalling and ordering a society for the purposes of rapid modernization. All four looked on socialism as a "scientific" means of social engineering. Although none offers allegiance to any Communist power, each shows a greater identification with formal Marxism-Leninism and the Soviet and Chinese experiments than is characteristic of other African Socialists. The Marxist influence is especially strong in the three francophonic cases (Guinea, Mali, Congo-Brazzaville); this reflects, in part, the far greater significance of Marxism in the French intellectual tradition, and the important role played by *groupes d'etudes communistes"* (Communist study groups) in the World War II era as meeting grounds for the nascent nationalist elite. Here one finds the Marxist intellectual tradition as an encompassing framework for ideological debate. No total subservience to rigidly prescribed doctrine perhaps, many adaptations to local circumstance, but political positions require justification within the web of Marxist premises.

Traditional African values were not portrayed as antithetical to socialism. Touré, in particular, laid great stress on the communitarian heritage of rural society. Chieftaincy, warped and fossilized by manipulation of the colonial administration, was abolished in Guinea with independence, but otherwise internal class antagonisms were held to be absent. Both Touré and Modibo Keita of Mali made use of their descent from traditional heroes of the nineteenth century to enhance their legitimacy.

There have been shifts over time in the radical version of African Socialism. Nkrumah, whose first published work (*Toward Colonial Freedom,* 1942) was in the orthodox Marxist-Leninist mode, downplayed such themes as he guided Ghana to independence in the 1950s. In his final years in power, his socialist preferences became much more pronounced, and returned to the earlier Marxist stress, reflected in a sharpening hostility to what he saw as imperialistic forces abroad, and internally, to Ghana's relatively large commercial and professional classes and the prosperous cocoa farmers. In policy terms, socialism was implemented through the (costly) expansion of the state sector with the establishment of a number of state enterprises, rather than nationalization of existing firms. Touré, whose ideological statements now run to seventeen volumes, shifted his position on the purportedly classless structure of African society and began to attack the more prosperous classes of African traders and civil servants.

What happens to the radical socialist commitment when the initial leadership is overthrown? The Ghanaian experience is in sharp contrast to the other cases. The socialist rhetoric of the Nkrumah regime disappeared with his demise in 1966; many of the state enterprises he had launched, which generally proved to be expensive fiascos, were liquidated or sold to private interests. On the other hand, after the overthrow of Modibo Keita of Mali in 1968, the army junta which succeeded maintained a striking continuity in its ideological pronouncements.[3] In Congo-Brazzaville, despite several changes in leadership since the 1963 revolution, including a military coup in 1968, the socialist motif in regime ideology has remained stable. This suggests that radical socialism has now become so internalized in the value matrix of the political elite that, at least as rhetoric, a stable, institutionalized ideology exists.[4]

Communitarian Socialism. Julius Nyerere of Tanzania and Leopold Senghor, despite the considerable differences between them — a gap that widened in the 1960s — both represent a similar emphasis in African socialist thought. Here, stress is placed on the communitarian qualities of traditional African society, socialist society is to be achieved through building upon this communal tradition. Cooperative modes of production are held to be innate in African society; socialism therefore flows naturally from the uprooting of alien, imported values of individualism and materialism introduced by the colonizer.

Related to the communitarian theme is the strong conviction of the distinctiveness of the African tradition and a rejection of the premise that

[3] A careful content analysis of the speeches of Moussa Traore, who replaced Keita, over his two years in office (1968–1970) compared with public statements by Keita in the first two years of independence (1960–1962) showed a remarkable concordance. Michael Schatzberg, "The Coup and After: Continuity and Change in Malian Politics" (unpublished seminar paper, University of Wisconsin, 1971).

[4] Paul Beckett, "Revolutionary Systems: A Conceptual Model and Comparative Study of Four African Revolutionary Regimes" (Unpublished Ph.D. dissertation, University of Wisconsin, 1969).

socialism is a precast universal dogma. Nyerere expressed these thoughts vividly in a lecture at the University of Cairo in 1967:

> Unfortunately, however, there has grown up what I can only call a "theology of socialism." People argue — sometimes quite violently — about what is the true doctrine. . . . Frankly, this seems to me to be absurd. I am a Christian and it is part of my belief that the word of God is expressed in the Bible. To me, therefore, in spite of — or even because of — the contradictions of the Bible, it is quite sensible to try to get its full meaning, and, when I am trying to act in accordance with God's wishes, to refer to those who have given the Bible a detailed study. . . . But the books on socialism are different. They are written by men; wise and clever men perhaps — but still men. Consequently we should use their books as we use the work of living people — knowing that one individual may contribute greatly to the solution of a problem, but that no man is infallible. Indeed, I think that this idea that there is one "pure socialism" for which the recipe is already known, is an insult to human intelligence.[5]

Senghor, perhaps more self-conscious of his role as political philosopher, situates his appeal to the African communitarian tradition within a wide-ranging, subtle, and sophisticated framework. Because of the greater importance of Marxism in French-speaking circles, more attention is paid to a debate with the Marxists and selective borrowing from the Marxist tradition. At the same time, Senghor was greatly influenced by Teilhard de Chardin and argues the importance of the affirmation of African distinctiveness, summarized as "negritude," in the ultimate emergence of a universal human synthesis.

The practical implications of communitarian socialism by the early 1970s has become widely divergent in Senegal and Tanzania. In Senegal, Senghor faced not only strongly entrenched French interests and a substantial Senegalese middle class, but also a complex linkage of leaders of the Islamic brotherhoods, peanut producers, and marketing agencies, which greatly limited his freedom of action.[6] The groups most adversely affected by the implementation of socialist policies in Tanzania, the Asians and Europeans, were highly vulnerable socially and politically, and lacked the potent political resources of the Muslim notables in Senegal. In Senegal, the commitment to communitarian socialism has been primarily reflected in a cautious yet persistent promotion of cooperatives and rural community development and enlargement of the state role in peanut marketing. In Tanzania, measures inspired by *Ujamaa* have been much more far-reaching. Salary levels of the administrative class have been held to relatively

---

[5] Julius K. Nyerere, *Ujamaa: Essays on Socialism* (London: Oxford University Press, 1968). pp. 76-77. The main texts of Nyerere's thought are conveniently gathered in this volume.

[6] Lucy C. Behrman, *Muslim Brotherhoods and Politics in Senegal* (Cambridge: Harvard University Press, 1970). See also, for an excellent study of the relation of ideology and rural policy, Henri de Decker, *Nation et Developpement Communautaire en Guinée et au Senegal* (The Hague: Mouton, 1967).

austere levels, and elite consumption restrained. Civil servants and political leaders are not permitted to operate small businesses, rent urban housing, or serve as company directors, all of which are very widespread practices among top bureaucrats and politicians in Africa. A strong effort is being made to promote production as well as marketing cooperatives, particularly in central Tanzania. Large-scale farming, involving extensive hired labor, is being curtailed, and is slated for elimination.

Moderate, Welfare Socialism. Many African leaders understand socialism as a "middle way" between capitalism (by which they mean complete *laissez faire* or the "capitalism" that they associate with imperialism) and communism. Their approach is essentially pragmatic and developmental. They would have the state inspire and direct the process of growth, but within a pluralistic social and economic order. They would extend public services to improve the standard of living of their peoples, but they hardly plan on a total mobilization of the society for the purposes of change.

Such is characteristic of the Kenyatta government's identification with African Socialism. In a sophisticated document, *African Socialism and its Application to Planning in Kenya,* it states, "African Socialism must be flexible because the problems it will confront and the incomes and the desires of the people will change over time, often quickly and substantially. A rigid, doctrinaire system will have little chance for survival."[7]

Since the formulation of its official ideological position in 1965, socialism has become a muted theme in development politics in Kenya. It may be that its value from the beginning was mainly symbolic, a way of affiliating with a dominant African ideology rather than a distinctive program of government. In the period since publication of *African Socialism and its Application to Planning in Kenya,* the country has gone through a phase of rapid economic growth in which the national elites have fully shared. Foreign investment has been encouraged and Western economic assistance solicited. Rural policy has been based on encouraging individual land registrations, rather than on seeking cooperative villages as in neighboring Tanzania. Kenya's new elite is heavily involved in entrepreneurial activity, both in operating farms in the areas once restricted to European settlers and in diverse small businesses. Even the regime's best-known radical critic, Oginga Odinga is a prominent businessman.[8] Socialism in Kenya has come to be understood as a pragmatic doctrine not inconsistent with the vigorous encouragement of the private sector.

However, such welfare socialism is not at all a matter of merely exchanging the Soviet Union for Scandinavia as the model of the desired society. In spite of

---

[7] *African Socialism and its Application to Planning in Kenya* (Nairobi: Government Printer, 1965).

[8] Odinga has published a major critique of Kenya socialism as practiced by the Kenyatta regime, *Not Yet Uhuru* (London: Heinemann, 1967).

the fact that this stream of thought, as someone has put it, "is more apt to reflect the gospel according to Harold Laski rather than Karl Marx," it too stresses the unique grounding of socialism in the African environment, the special needs for state direction of the developmental process, the desire to achieve modernity without undue cost in terms of traditional values. However, for leaders like Kenyatta and Mboya, socialist doctrine appears more as a means of opening up flexible alternatives for action than for narrowing down social complexity through a rigid program for change.

Middle Eastern and Arab Socialism

Within the Arab world, there are at least four distinctive variations on the theme of developmental socialism that should be singled out for comment.

UAR and Military Socialism. Throughout the developing world, reformist military leaders have sought to stimulate development through organization, social mobilization, and a vigorous assertion of governmental power and economic activity. Ayub Khan's Pakistan, Rivera's El Salvador, Velasco's Peru, Ataturk's Turkey, Perón's Argentina — all in one way or another belong to this type. Only in Burma, Iraq, and Nasser's Egypt, however, has the military identified this activist role explicitly and consistently with socialist doctrine.

For Nasser, rapid economic development was to be the foundation for national power, to assure independence and to build a more satisfactory social order. To achieve this, disciplined and authoritative leadership was required. There is a Marxist tone to this doctrine, but it is a matter of using propositions and concepts as tools in the fashioning of an independent ideology rather than as a blueprint to be followed in detail. The following statement sums up quite well the major themes of Nasser's socialist approach:

> If the economic foundation of society which we inherited had been a strong one, it would have affected our new system positively. However, we inherited a backward economic foundation, and in our endeavor to build socialism, and to emerge from the stage of feudalism and capitalism to the stage of socialism we have first to establish a sound economic foundation. To do so we must mobilize all our efforts. Without laying down this sound basis we cannot possibly realize socialist transformation or build the new social relations we are advocating ... A sound economy should, of course, rest primarily on an industrial groundwork. Indeed, after the ourbreak of the revolution, we established this economic foundation. But does this mean that we have solved all contradictions? The answer is no. Contradictions will continue to appear, and they will be continuously fed by the forces of reaction. ... Can the state realize overnight or in a year or ten years all the demands of the masses? Clearly enough, the fulfillment of these demands depends on the potentialities at our disposal. And how can we increase these potentialities? By creating a sound economic foundation. ... [9]

[9] Gamal Abdel Nasser, Address to the Arab Socialist Union, May 16, 1965.

It is worth noting that the regime commitment to socialism in the UAR did not follow immediately on the heels of the military coup in 1952. Initially, the central ideological themes of the Naguib government (1952-1954) and the Nasser regime thereafter were simply those of nationalist revolution: anti-imperialism abroad, and animosity to the traditional symbols of the *ancien regime* — corruption, political parties, and the old ruling oligarchy — at home. The emergence of the socialist theme can be seen in three phases, with 1956, 1958, and 1961 as crucial dates marking ideological hardening of the regime. 1956 was the year of confrontation with the West. The abrupt American withdrawal of tentative aid proposals for the construction of the Aswam dam led to the Nasserite riposte of nationalization of the Suez Canal; this in turn produced the Anglo-French-Israeli invasion, which resulted in a new wave of seizures of British and French property. Two years later, the abortive fusion of Syria and Egypt into the United Arab Republic led to a further infusion of socialist content into Nasserite Arab nationalism. The intellectual father of Syrian Ba'ath socialism, Michael Aflaq, remarked at a press conference at the time of fusion that Nasser had good revolutionary instincts but lacked a refined socialist ideological perspective to accompany them. Although Nasser found the Aflaq statement impertinent, the fact remains that after the birth of the UAR, socialism came increasingly to the fore as an explicit ideology. Finally, the Syrian secession in 1961 led to a further radicalization of Nasserite ideology. Nasser blamed the rupture of the union with Syria on "reactionary forces" which would have to be crushed by sweeping measures that would enlarge the public sector and expropriate the propertied classes in Egypt (which retained the national designation of UAR).

With the death of Nasser in 1971, the future of socialism in Egypt entered a new and significant stage. Anwar Sadat inherited an order structured on socialist premises, but seemed inclined to moderate Egypt's commitment to this distinctive approach to development. Foreign capital was encouraged to enter the country, not to replace the established public industrial sector, but to flesh out the industrial structure of the country. Socialist structures, in particular the party organization and other vehicles of mobilization, were played down, radically refurbished, or in some cases abolished. The strategy did not seem to be that of undoing all that had been accomplished in the previous nineteen years, but rather of moderating the course of an established and going concern by introducing elements of economic pragmatism and political liberalism. In a recent statement of his philosophy, designed for foreign audiences, Sadat stressed a philosophy of socialism cast in terms of cooperation among the various sectors of Egyptian society rather than class conflict and emphasizing economic growth and education as achievements of socialism in Egypt, not, significantly, the expropriation of landlords or the nationalization of industries.[10]

[10] Anwar el-Sadat, "Where Egypt Stands," *Foreign Affairs*, 51 (October 1972), pp. 155-66.

Algeria and Peasant Socialism. Ben Bella's Algerian socialism differs from those doctrines we have considered so far in that it was based on a successful revolutionary movement, in which one class, the peasantry, played a predominant role.

Unlike other African independence movements, the FLN founded its strategy upon rural-based insurrection. The subtle game played in other colonial areas — that of exploiting constitutional mechanisms to formulate self-government demands, in which the skills of the urban-based elite in translating the independence desire into the vocabulary and cultural standards of the colonizer were crucial — was ruled out by the tenacious French conviction that Algeria was not a colony, but an integral part of France. Especially after the urban network of the FLN in Algiers was largely dismantled by the brutal but efficacious *parachutistes* of General Jacques Massu in 1957, the survival of the Algerian revolution depended entirely upon the loyalty of the countryside. Accordingly, there emerged an explicitly "peasant" emphasis to socialist programs set forth as the objective of the revolution.

In the countryside, land was a critical issue; Europeans, approximately 10 percent of the pre-1962 population, held approximately twenty-seven million hectares as opposed to seven million hectares owned by Algerians.[11] The pledge of land to the land-hungry Algerian peasantry was a major appeal of the FLN. On a more ideological plane, the unique virtues of a peasant revolution were extolled by the adopted philosopher of the revolution, the West Indian psychiatrist Frantz Fanon. Only the peasantry remained free of the corrosive taint of the colonial system; for Fanon, even the urban proletariat was disqualified from leadership in the task of regenerating a people along new lines. The peasant character of the Algerian revolution explains the special affinity that Ben Bella felt for Fidel Castro and, to a less pronounced degree, the interest in the Chinese model of socialism widely held among the Algerian elite at the time of independence.

In the first decade of independence, Algerian socialism underwent marked alterations as doctrine was transformed by practice. As the Algerian war came to a close, a strongly Marxist policy was enunciated in the Tripoli program of May 1962. In 1964, many of these ideological themes were confirmed in the Algiers Charter, product of an FLN party congress dominated by the more doctrinal wing.

However, actual policy was invariably more pragmatic than the rigors of official ideology might suggest. As early as 1964, Algerian and foreign Marxist critics began to question the socialist commitment of the regime.[12] Many of what appeared to be the most sweeping radical measures of the independent government were in fact inevitable adjustments to a new situation. The overwhelming majority of the Europeans left the country, abandoning farms and

---

[11] Charles-Henri Favrod, *L' F.L.N. et l'Algérie* (Paris: Plon, 1962), p. 172.

[12] Representative of this literature is Gérard Chaliand, *L'Algérie est-elle Socialiste?* (Paris: Maspero, 1964).

businesses. The formula of "worker's self-management" was employed to operate these properties. In part, there was no choice, as the farm workers in many instances had simply assumed control; the government was anxious to retain the economies of scale through managing these farms as large, market-oriented units rather than encouraging their subdivision into individual peasant plots. What might not be apparent at first glance was that this policy offered reasonable satisfaction to the approximately one hundred fifty thousand former farm workers, but made no dent in the plight of more than one million landless persons.[13]

Destourian Socialism. Tunisia is a fascinating variant of developmental socialism; it stands somewhat apart from most African examples in the close relationship between words and deeds. "Socialism" was not an ideological armor that the "Combattant Supreme," Habib Bourguiba, stepped immediately into when independence was first won in 1956; rather there was an almost imperceptible phasing into the commitment to socialism, culminating in the rebaptism of the ruling party, formerly known as the Neo-Destour, as the Destour Socialist party.

Initially, Tunisia talked officially neither of planning nor of socialism. Half a decade elapsed before Bourguiba chose the moment, with skillful disarming of his critics on the left, to proclaim 1961 the "year of the plan." Intellectual energies were to be mobilized in the elaboration of a ten-year plan. Six months after his speech announcing the conversion of Tunisia to planning, he went further with a major pronouncement on "Neo-Destourian Socialism." This was at once a new step, yet carefully linked philosophically to older themes in Neo-Destour nationalism. What was at stake was not the enactment of the class struggle on Tunisian soil, but a new phase of the struggle for human dignity that had begun with the drive for independence.

> A new conception of national solidarity is being born. . . . The struggle will not end in success unless there is full realization that what is at stake is human dignity, without which life is not worth living. Socialism, once adopted as an ideological label, was perfectly natural; even the companions of the Prophet . . . were socialists before the invention of the word, considering themselves members of the same family. They were not individualists; not one among them sought enrichment at the expense of the others. All worked for the common good. By turning back to the sources of Islam, we are to imitate them in their self-sacrifice, their love of their neighbors, and their sense of solidarity.[14]

---

[13]Thomas L. Blair, *"The Land to Those Who Work It:" Algeria's Experiment in Workers' Management* (Garden City, N.Y.: Doubleday and Co., 1969).

[14]Charles A. Micaud, *Tunisia: The Politics of Modernization* (New York: Frederick A. Praeger, Inc., 1964), pp. 142-43.

Bourguiba has frequently described his strategy as a "policy of steps," within the frame of a relatively constant long-run set of objectives. Destourian socialism seems to go through phases of sharp steps forward, followed by a period of quiescence and perhaps even of retreat. The clarity of doctrine and policy is evident only if viewed over a number of years. However, in 1969, Destourian socialism experienced a serious setback in the crisis over cooperativization in agriculture. Lands retaken from French settlers had been organized into state-run cooperatives after 1964. Suddenly, in 1969, it was announced that this program would be extended to large-scale Tunisian landholdings (about one-third of the arable land) and that small cultivators as well would be regrouped in production cooperatives. This reform — which had originated within the more ideological wing of the Destour Socialist party — encountered massive resistance. Within nine months it was abandoned, and its main architect, Ahmed Ben Salah, was jailed.[15]

Ba'ath Socialism. Ba'ath socialism is the intellectual product of an unusual confluence of currents of thought: Islam, Arab nationalism, French existentialism, romanticism, and, last but not least, socialism. This potpourri took on relatively coherent form through the brilliant polemics of a Syrian intellectual, Michel Aflaq; in his own career these diverse strands had flowed together. Aflaq had been a student in France during the mandate days and returned to be a school teacher in a provincial town. His doctrine had special appeal to students, intellectuals, and the administrative middle class made up of civil servants, teachers, and junior officers.

Article 4 of the Ba'ath constitution argues that socialism is the necessary means for fully developing the potentiality of the Arab people; for the Ba'ath, nationalism and socialism are therefore but two sides of the same coin. Only through socialism can the Arab genius find its full expression; socialism "will guarantee to the nation continuous growth in its spiritual and material development and strong fraternization among its individuals."[16] Socialism is much more than a matter of economic organization; it is a way of life, a key to comprehension of the whole cultural universe.

The Ba'ath program, as prescribed by its constitution, has a series of quite explicit demands. Rural exploitation will be ended by limiting ownership to the scale that can be personally cultivated. Workers are to participate in management, with state determination of wages. Banks are to be nationalized and credit supplied on an interest-free basis. Foreign and domestic commerce is to be subject to close regulation. As Leonard Binder has observed:

---

[15] Lars Rudebeck, "Developmental Pressure and Political Limits: A Tunisian Example," *Journal of Modern African Studies,* 8 (Spring 1970), pp. 173–98.
[16] Quoted in Leonard Binder, *The Ideological Revolution in the Middle East* (New York: John Wiley & Sons, Inc., 1964), p. 183.

> ... this series of proposals does not coincide with Marxist doctrine nor the policies of west European socialist parties. We may note briefly that these reforms will hardly touch the urban lower middle class and the peasantry.... Owners of large tracts of land, large-scale entrepreneurs, and foreign enterprises are the only ones to be seriously affected.... Ba'ath socialism does not lead to a dictatorship of the proletariat nor to a nationalization of production. Ba'ath socialism means the dictatorship of the lower middle class and the levelling down of all those who stand above them in the social and economic scale....[17]

Ba'ath socialism has been influential throughout the Arab world. However, its base of operation has remained Syria and Iraq. The Ba'ath party assumed power in Syria in 1958, was partly eclipsed by Nasserism during the 1958-1961 union with Egypt, then regained power in 1963. In that same year, a Ba'athist faction of the military seized power in Iraq. In retrospect, this seems to have been the high-water mark of Ba'ath socialism. Although successive military factions who have held power in Damascus and Baghdad since 1963 have laid claim to the Ba'ath banners, the intellectuals who once gave elan and vitality to the doctrine are no longer prominent. Yet the basic themes of Islam as secular Arab cultural heritage, nationalism and socialism appear institutionalized as basic postulates of ideological discourse.

Latin America

In Latin America, the problem of defining the varieties of developmental socialism is complicated by the fact that other symbols and ideas are often used to define ideologies and programs that would normally be described as "socialistic" in other parts of the emerging world. Thus, the "structuralist" school of economic development, which has been peculiarly prominent in the region, deriving much of its initial intellectual apparatus from the work of Raúl Prebisch and the group of economists associated with the Economic Commission for Latin America, provides a distinctive ideology of development; in its more radical formulations it can call for a program of nationalization, comprehensive agrarian and social reform at least as vigorous and sweeping as that associated with some of the more militant socialist movements in Africa, the Middle East, and Asia. Furthermore, radical Catholicism, of the type advocated by the Colombian guerrilla priest Camilo Torres or asserted by the left wing of Christian Democratic parties, as in Chile, is at least as vituperative in its condemnation of foreign imperialism and internal power structures and class systems as are

---

[17] Binder, *Ideological Revolution,* p. 184. For another useful discussion of Ba'ath socialism, see Manfred Halpern, *The Politics of Social Change in the Middle East and North Africa* (Princeton: Princeton University Press, 1963), pp. 235-48; and Kemal H. Karpat, ed., *Political and Social Thought in the Contemporary Middle East* (New York: Praeger, 1968), pp. 185-97.

avowedly radical or Marxist movements elsewhere. Finally, the "Democratic left" movements of Latin America feel an identification with the social democratic parties of Western Europe but rarely do they self-consciously use the term "socialism" in describing their ideology today (many espoused more self-consciously socialist ideologies until the late 1940s), although their vision of a gradualist, reforming road to development has much in common with moderate socialist movements in India, East Africa, and elsewhere.

Various explanations can be offered for the fact that socialism is not accepted as a unifying symbol for those who would invoke a vision of development different from that of Western industrial capitalism. One reason may be that until the election of Salvador Allende in Chile, the historic Socialist and Communist parties of the continent had little success in winning widespread support, and newer reform movements sought to avoid associating themselves with their failure. It may be that some Latin American leaders — the Prebisch structuralists and the Democratic left in particular — were influenced by the sensitivity of American opinion to the word "socialism" itself. (However, this does not mean that Latin American reformers have necessarily soft-pedalled their real objectives to avoid incurring the displeasure of audiences in the United States. The aspirations that Africans and Asians might describe as "socialistic" are likely to appear in Latin America under the rubric of "revolution." Such are the ironies of the etymology of development ideology in today's world.) However, the most likely explanation is that Latin America has a longer and more differentiated political history than the nations of Africa and Asia, its leaders can appeal to a variety of culturally legitimate ideological themes (as in the case of radical Catholicism), and its contemporary politicians are not so immediately conscious of the European socialist tradition as the obvious alternative to capitalism as are their counterparts in nations closer to the colonial experience.

For these reasons, describing the spectrum of socialist and quasi-socialist thought in Latin America is a somewhat delicate matter, for we must deal not only with movements that formally acknowledge socialist ideology, but also with groups that only occasionally use the term but whose total style of political argument closely parallels that of those in other parts of the devleoping world who formally and insistently claim socialism as their ideology.

Historic European Socialism. Virtually every ideological movement to appear in Europe in the nineteenth and twentieth centuries has made an impact on Latin American politics. Sequentially, Liberalism, Positivism, Anarcho-Syndicalism, Second International Socialism, Communism, and Fascism have been absorbed into the stream of Latin American thought and political conflict.

It might be suggested that, of all these transplanted doctrines, European socialism has been the least successful in Latin America. Although a Socialist party was established in Argentina as early as 1896, and although by 1940 such parties had been created in at least eight Latin American nations,[18] all remained as relatively minor factions, and none has ever been in a position to convert its program into public policy. Until 1970, the only nation to illustrate the direct impact of the European social democratic tradition was Uruguay, where a welfare state created by José Batlle y Ordoñez between 1903 and 1915 was preserved and extended by subsequent governments.

However, with the election of Salvador Allende to the Chilean presidency in 1970 the historic Socialist and Communist parties of that country had an opportunity to initiate a program that has some parallels to radical developmental socialism elsewhere. Allende was pledged to nationalize many of the major foreign- and domestically-owned enterprises, the banking system, most institutions of foreign trade, and to hasten the pace of the agrarian reform program initiated under his predecessor, the Christian Democrat Eduardo Frei. In addition, there were promises of sweeping programs for income redistribution and welfare, and a constitutional revision to bring about greater "direct democracy" by replacing Chile's bicameral legislature with a single-house popular assembly. One of Allende's first accomplishments was the nationalization of the American-owned copper companies which dominated Chile's foreign trade. This project was carried out during his first year in office.

Until it was overthrown in 1973, this was described as the first freely-elected Marxist government in the world. Allende himself was a Socialist though he governed through a complex coalition of forces including Communists, left-wing splinter groups, and radical Christian Democrats. Elected as a minority president, without control of the Congress, the initial radicalism of his program was considerably tempered by the limitations of his power. Interestingly, Allende's roots were deep in the Chilean parliamentary system. For twenty years he served as opposition leader in the nation's Senate, and he remained committed to achieving the transformation of Chile into a socialist society by constitutional means. Although in program and overall ideological temper Allende's government had much in common with more militant, radical forms of developmental socialism elsewhere, in eschewing revolutionary means he departed from the approach and style of Castro or Ben Bella and had more in common with the Latin American democratic left of the Christian Democrats. In the matter of ends, he is properly classified as a radical mobilization socialist, but in regard to political means, he belongs with the moderate reformist groups.

The Democratic Left. This category includes a loosely united but self-consciously similar group of parties. The acknowledged ancestor of most of these movements was Víctor Raúl Haya de la Torre's APRA party, which emerged in Peru in the 1930s. The movement spread in the postwar period to

---

[18] Argentina, Chile, Peru, Ecuador, Colombia, Panama, Cuba, Brazil. See Robert J. Alexander, *Labour Movements in Latin America* (London: Fabian Publications, Ltd., 1947) and *Communism in Latin America* (New Brunswick, N.J.: Rutgers University Press, 1954).

include José Figueres' *Liberación Nacional* of Costa Rica, Rómulo Betancourt's *Acción Democrática* of Venezuela, Fernándo Belaunde Terry's *Acción Popular* in Peru, and at least half a dozen other groups of some political significance.

Although many of these parties can trace their origins to Marxist student groups and similar organization in the 1930s and 1940s, they became militantly anti-Communist by the postwar decade. Today their closest ideological affinity is probably with European social democracy and the more liberal element of the Democratic party of the United States. Cautiously but not uncritically pro-American, they identified closely with the Alliance for Progress program of John Kennedy in the early 1960s. They seek to bring about change and development by evolutionary means, through democratic processes.

Their programs are flexible and pragmatic. Generally, they prefer regulation and taxation to nationalization as means of controlling foreign enterprise and directing its activities toward the needs of national development. They seek to raise the standards of living of the poorer part of their societies, less by a radical redefinition of the social and economic order than by extending to the rest of the population the services and institutions presently available to the middle and upper classes. Hence, emphasis is on education, public health, transport, and social welfare services. Agrarian reform does not imply "communalization," but usually the universalizing of private property through encouragement of family-sized parcels.

While quite undogmatic in their economic and social programs, these parties are almost militant in their conviction that economic development can be brought about through democratic process and that development itself implies democratic maturity. In any event, the commitment of such movements to democratic process is on the whole far more rigid and — if one will accept a somewhat surprising use of the term — doctrinaire than their economic and social objectives.

Although such parties were prominent in Latin American politics in the early 1960s, with the end of the Alliance for Progress they became less significant as major contenders for power. Today important Democratic Left groups exist only in Venezuela and Costa Rica. Some feel that events have passed them by, that they have become relatively more conservative with the passing of time, and that their approach to change has been superceded in the changing fashions of Latin American politics. However, their general philosophy is one that has considerable appeal in many sectors of Latin America, and the approach to change that they represent may one day become predominant again.

Christian Democracy and Radical Catholicism. In basic policy orientation, the Christian Democrats have a great deal in common with the Democratic Left. They are committed to an evolutionary approach to development, eschewing means that are incompatible with democratic and constitutional principles. Some may doubt the propriety of including the Christian Democrats in a catalogue of socialist movements. Certainly, they owe little of their political philosophy either to Marxism or to the broader socialist tradition. Rather, the ideological foundations of their programs are to be found in the social teachings of the Catholic Church, particularly the encyclicals of Leo XIII and John XXIII. In the Chilean case particularly, the inspiration of Jacques Maritain and Teilhard de Chardin is significant. Interesting parallels and comparisons may be drawn between the theological foundations of the political thought of Eduardo Frei and Leopold Senghor of Senegal.

Christian Democratic parties have been particularly prominent in Chile and Venezuela, where under the leadership of Frei and Rafael Cáldera respectively, they controlled the government in the late 1960s and early 1970s. Similar parties exist in most of the nations of Latin America, although they are quite small.

Political Catholicism in contemporary Latin America is hardly a monolithic force. Whereas the Christian Democrats may be identified in global terms with moderate reform socialism, another sector of political activity that ideologically identifies with Catholicism has a greater affinity to radical, revolutionary socialism. For many intellectuals and some proportion of the younger priests, the Christian Democrats are not sufficiently militant and forceful in their approach to change. As noted above, some elements in the Chilean party supported the government of Salvador Allende. Elsewhere, priests and Catholic laymen have collaborated with revolutionary and guerrilla forces.

Institutionalized Revolutionary Socialism. Doctrinal socialism played a role in the regimes that followed from the Mexican Revolution of 1910 and the Bolivian Revolution of 1952, but it was no more than one ingredient in a complex set of aspirations and circumstances. The impact of socialist thought can be seen in the dictum of the Mexican Constitution that "education be free, universal and socialistic" and in the famous labor code contained in Article 123 of that document. The ideology of the *Movimiento Nacional Revolucionario* of Bolivia also contains prominent components of socialist orthodoxy.

However, the basic reforms with which these two revolutions are identified, thoroughgoing land redistribution and economic nationalism including the expropriation of basic industry (tin mines in Bolivia, oil resources and transport facilities in Mexico), arose more out of specific circumstances than ideological imperatives. The actual presence of wide-spread peasant revolt in both nations no doubt served to give greater centrality to the issue of agrarian reform than might otherwise have been the case. Nationalization in both countries has been directed at quite specific enterprises, for quite specific reasons.

The brand of "socialism" represented by these two nations might be described as follows: The specific agrarian and economic objectives identified with each revolution were pursued with constancy and ideological rigor. However, to be effective, these experiments required that the health and vigor of the rest of the society be enhanced. Here, the ideology of revolution specified no particular techniques. Hence, nationalistic economic development in Mexico has been accompanied by the growth of a substantial domestic and foreign private enterprise sector, and Bolivia, to protect its agrarian and mining reforms, has been required to pursue a policy of fiscal orthodoxy and close association with the United States.

Today, especially in Mexico, socialism is less an ideology and more an institutionalized aspect of the going concern. Modern Mexico is in many respects an industrial society — many would describe it as a capitalist society. Yet the historic legacy of socialist programs is evident, not only in nationalistic symbols but in a continuing concern for agrarian reform, social welfare, and the maintenance of a substantial nationalized industrial sector.

Structuralism. Today, when change-oriented Latin American elites criticize the status quo and call for a general overhaul of the institutional life of their societies, they are as likely to talk in terms of "basic structural change" as "socialism." Deriving from the work of Raúl Prebisch, Argentine economist and director of the United Nations Economic Commission for Latin America, "structuralism" has in the past generation become a distinctive variant of development ideology. The approach is compatible with fairly conservative conceptions of the development process when it is taken to mean that Latin America requires a change in the institutional character of its economies, toward greater self-sufficiency and industrialization through import substitution and export diversification, often to be accomplished by encouraging foreign investment and domestic enterprise. However, structuralism can imply a far more radical position when the failure of reform is attributed to the power of entrenched elites and interests. Structural change then comes to imply a sweeping reconstruction of established institutions, wresting power from those who control large landholdings, corporate enterprise, and the government bureaucracies, and establishing institutions more responsive to popular needs. It is a position that could readily be identified with militant, nationalistic socialism elsewhere in the world.

Although such ideas are widespread among Latin American intellectuals, the best example of a government founded on this philosophy is probably that of General Juan Velasco Alvarado, who came to power in Peru in October 1968 through military coup. Velasco's program represents an interesting combination of both the moderate and more radical themes implicit in the structural approach. Although he has imposed measures of strict control on foreign investment, required compulsory profit-sharing in all firms, and taken actions to insure that eventually workers will own 50 percent of all companies and that Peruvians will hold 51 percent of the stock in foreign corporations, and although early in his administration he presided over a much-publicized nationalization of the properties of the International Petroleum Corporation, he has at the same time actively courted further foreign investment in Peru. His policy seems to be one not of ideological condemnation of foreign enterprise and its dominance in the Peruvian economy, but of setting more stringent conditions for its operation so as to assure a more socially-conscious contribution to national development. Velasco also put into effect a sweeping agrarian reform, one of the most comprehensive in Latin America outside of Cuba, which particularly affected the highly commercialized large farms of the coastal regions.

In the early 1970s, there was some expectation that this form of reformist military government would spread widely in Latin America. Some governments based on the Peruvian model were formed, most notably in Bolivia, but none had the staying power of the Velasco administration. Generally, in the early 1970s, Latin American military governments were more prone to a conservative approach, as exemplified by the cases of Argentina and Brazil.

Revolutionary Socialism. Fidel Castro's Cuba remains the single Latin American example of radical mobilization socialism in power. Castro took power in January 1959, with a program that very much resembled the Democratic Left position — restoration of the Constitution of 1940, elections, moderate agrarian reform, control but not comprehensive nationalization of foreign enterprise. Estrangement from the United States and radicalization of the movement followed, and within a few years Castro proclaimed that he had adopted the Marxist-Leninist position.

Cuba represents an extreme form of socialism in global perspective. Nationalization of the economy is almost complete, including not only foreign enterprise and basic industry, but small shops, housing, and virtually all means of production and trade. Political competition, and all forms of "bourgeois democratic" practice, including elections, freedom of speech and of the press, freedom of association and organization, have been eliminated. Political mobilization — as in the campaigns to eradicate illiteracy and the motivation of "voluntary labor" to bring in the sugar harvest — is a prominent aspect of political organization.

A striking redistribution of wealth has taken place. Although food rationing and an absence of many of the amenities of life persist, their absence is more apt to be noticed by the middle-class city dweller. An "equality of sacrifice" seems to have been imposed, and peasant life probably has improved markedly in nutrition, education, and housing. Generally, in basic reforms, preference has been given to the rural citizen rather than to the people of the cities. New housing, services, roads, and schools are more evident in the countryside, whereas the cities have been permitted to decay.

Although the Cuban model remains central to many radical movements in Latin America both as exemplary of the technique of revolutionary capture of power and as an incarnation of the effort to build a new order on militant socialist principles, some of the attractiveness of the Cuban experiment was noticeably fading by the early 1970s. In terms of economic development, Cuba has not been an outstanding success. The economy has stagnated, registering negative rates of growth in the revolutionary period. The promised diversification of the economy, away from monocultivist dependence on sugar, has not been achieved. At the end of its first decade, the Cuban revolution was in many ways quite as "dependent" internationally as it was at the beginning. Some felt that all that had been accomplished was the exchange of the hegemony of the United States for that of the Soviet Union. Nonetheless, the Cuban system is stable and established, and it continues to evolve internally. As the decade of the 1970s goes on, the reputation and characteristics of this distinctive experiment in development are apt to take on new shadings of meaning and significance for those attracted to the utopian version of the message of developmental socialism.

The essence of the distinction between the Democratic Left and the Castroite position on Latin American development could perhaps be distilled as follows: For the Democratic Left, the existing modern sector in Latin America, with its conventions concerning property and contract, its industrial organization and forms of commercial transaction, its important private foreign and domestic business sector, is something of value. The problem of development is that the rewards of the productivity generated through this modern sector have not been diffused widely enough through the rest of the population. However, for the Castroite, the modern sector is precisely the problem of development. It exists not to generate productivity, but to exploit the productivity of the remainder of the society. The destruction of the corrupt network of transactions and influences is an essential precondition of socialist development. Close trade and economic linkage with the United States is necessarily exploitative, in this view, because the United States is the heartland of world capitalism. Seizure of American assets in Cuba and reorientation of trade patterns were indispensable prerequisites for ending Cuba's status as an appendage of the capitalist system, according to Marxism-Leninism-Castroism.

Asia

The range of implications that the word "socialism" bears and the contextual frameworks within which socialist movements appear are perhaps broader in Asia than in any other part of the developing world. The ideological spectrum runs from the Maoist version of Marxism-Leninism practiced in China and its Korean and Vietnamese variants, through the European-oriented, relatively orthodox socialist parties of India and Malaysia to the indigenous variants of Sukarno, U Ba Swe, and Nehru. The context varies from mature, industrial socialism, as in Japan, where the arguments and appeals of socialism are quite similar to those that attended the growth of the socialistic mystique in Europe, to the most vivid versions of a socialism that takes its meaning from the problem of incipient economic development. The following are among the more distinctive patterns of socialist thought to be found in the less-developed nations of the Asian continent.

If any one characteristic can be said to be common to Asian socialism, it is the effort of its national spokesmen to describe their particular brand as unique to the country and particularly suited to the peculiar environment of their nation. Thus, we have the "Socialism à la Indonesia," the "Burmese Way to Socialism," the Maoist-Chinese reinterpretation of Marxism-Leninism, the "special" mixed economy of India, and former prime minister Sihanouk's very personal effort at national development. As might be expected from this drive toward national socialism, Asia is the home of a wide variety of socialist alternatives; but, ironically, the attempt by the political leaderships to nationalize socialism has led to little competition among socialist alternatives within each country. Although each claims his socialism is unique, it is possible to establish a rough classification of socialist systems in Asia.

Marxist-Leninist Socialism. Some 800 million people of Asia either profess communism or are under communist control. Even here, in spite of a general respect for Mao Tse-tung held by most Asian Communist parties, each party describes itself as nationalist and within the political heritage of its nation. We can roughly divide Asian communist ideologies into three types.

Mainland China holds herself to be the major Asian communist state and her leader Mao Tse-tung as the last of the great Marxist theoreticians. This is not the place to describe Chinese Communism in full, particularly given the subtleties of the arguments in the Sino-Soviet dispute. We can, however, note a few salient facets of Chinese Communism as it differs domestically from the Soviet model.

Under the commune system China has gone further than any state in mass social organization and control of the peasants' land. Early in his career, Mao gave far more credit to the peasant than to the Soviet Union, although after 1949 primary emphasis was given to industry; the urban proletariat have been given eight times the electoral power of the peasants in a system of weighted voting. Finally, the rhetoric of Chinese Communism displays missionary zeal and is emotional, aggressive, and dogmatic.

North Korea and North Vietnam constitute a second type of communism. In many ways they form a halfway house between China and the Soviet Union. They differ from China in that they are not major spokesmen for communist theory or policy (although Ho and Giap had some pretentions) and economically they have not been willing to follow Mao in his policy of communes.

Communist parties out of power make up the third category. Although these parties differ widely in their policies, they share one common problem:

how to exist and grow within the particular political environment of the nation in which they are working. The difficulties of success by peaceful means have led many to accept the Peking line, but the danger of frightening away possible adherents has also led to public stands far more moderate than are the private policies. Thus they shy away from strongly antireligious views, from acceptance of the idea of the communes for their country, and from too strict adherence to dogma and an emphasis on the international aspects of the communist movement. They underline nationalism, unity, economic and social reform, and anti-imperialism.

As a side aspect of Marxism-Leninism we must note the existence of "Trotskyist" parties in Asia, particularly in Ceylon, Indonesia, pre-war Indo-China, and Burma. Compared to other communist organizations, these parties tend to be more nationalist and more dominated by personalities.

The 1960s marked the emergence of splinter groups standing to the left of the orthodox Communist parties. The most prominent examples are the Naxalites in West Bengal, India, and the youthful insurgents in Ceylon (Sri Lanka) whose brief uprising in 1970 required the deployment of the entire army and thoroughly unsettled the socialist government of Mrs. Bandaranaike. Although such groups are loosely designated as "Maoist," it would be misleading to interpret them as disciplined followers of any internationally inspired movement. They appear, rather, analogous to the "Weatherman" faction of the SDS in the United States and the "gauchistes" in France, committed to revolutionary immediacy, sharply critical of orthodox Marxist-Leninist movements, mostly of a young, alienated generation, anarchic in style and manners. Much of their critique derives from Marxist tradition and ideology however. Although it seems unlikely that they will swell into mass movements, they may well come to be a significant element on the left fringe of the socialist spectrum.

Doctrinal Socialism. Considering the national interpretations given socialist doctrine in Asia, this category may appear absurd. However, this type includes the various evolutionary, democratic socialist parties in Malaysia, Singapore, India, pre-1962 Burma, Indonesia (before their demise), and Ceylon. Each has its own special ideological variations. Socialism in Malaysia and Indonesia has emphasized Marhaenism, an often vaguely defined national socialism. Party Rakyat of Malaysia called it "socialism which is suitable with climatic conditions of this country . . . it is not Utopian nor scientific socialism, but practical socialism." The People's Action Party in Singapore is committed to more formal socialist doctrine although its policies tend to be practical, moderate, and tolerant of "necessary capitalism." Both the PAP and the Congress Party of India uphold a "mixed economy" although it is far more an ideological commitment for the Congress Party. Burma under U Nu supported evolutionary, parliamentary socialism but gave it an added facet through his injection of traditional Burmese and Buddhist values. Yet all were at least publicly committed to democracy, moderation, a place for some capitalist enterprise, and to what they described as "socialist principles."

We must consider recent Burmese and Indonesian systems quite separately. Socialism as practiced in Burma was to be peculiarly Burmese, patterned to fit the Burmese environment (called the Burmese Way to Socialism, similar to Indonesia, where Sukarno liked to speak of "socialism à la Indonesia"). The Burmese Way to Socialism was not considered to be evolutionary or devoid of class inferences. Also, like the Sukarno brand, it was to cover all aspects of Burmese life, not just the economic. Both the Burmese military and Sukarno spoke of the spiritual attributes of socialism (in the philosophy of the "Environment," it is stated that man is naturally egotistical and self-seeking by nature and that self-interest and social interest must be correlated). In the strictly economic field, the Revolutionary Council has called for and implemented nationalization of vital means of production, distribution, communication, external trade, and education. Gaps in income are being closed as far as possible. There has been full awareness that physical and intellectual differences affect the quantity and quality of services an individual can render. The general plan reads much like the early writings of Mao Tse-tung, such as his "new Democracy," although there appears to be no causal relationship. Sukarno gave socialism an important role in his ideology. NASAKOM had communism in it, RESOPIM presented the trilogy of Revolution, Socialism, and National Leadership, and USDEK had as one of its five principles "Indonesian Socialism." Indonesian Socialism was viewed as a special harmonious blend of Western socialism with Indonesian elements such as gotong-rojong (cooperation).

The Indonesian concept was not as well-defined as the Burmese. In fact, the Indonesians denied that Indonesian Socialism was "a definite system, the full details of which are already known." Indonesian Socialism was explained in terms of planning a division of the economy of state enterprises, cooperatives, and the private sector, and there has been constant repetition of the need for a socialist society. In recent years Sukarno talked less of planning and specific goals and more in ideological terms, emphasizing the eradication of the "exploitation of man by man" and the importance of the spiritual rather than material aspects of life. The successor military regime seems far less ideological, far more pragmatic, in its outlook on Indonesian development.

PATTERNS OF DEVELOPMENTAL SOCIALISM

The preceding survey suggests the rich variety of uses of the term "socialism" in the major regions of the developing world. Let us now suggest a single typology which classifies the range of socialist thought in the third world.

Doctrinaire Marxist-Leninist Socialism. Despite the increasing tendency toward heresy in the Communist world, it is possible to distinguish from other forms of developmental socialism those movements that: (1) formally accept Marxism-Leninism as a definitive explanation of the reasons for underdevelopment and of the "scientific" program required of a nation that would develop: (2) endorse some communist state as a desirable developmental model; (3) count some group of communist nations as their primary allies and the developed nations of Europe and North America as their primary enemies. In this category, we would include the People's Republics of China, North Viet Nam, and North Korea, as well as the formal Communist parties and National Liberation movements present in other parts of the developing world.

Radical, Mobilization Socialism. For these movements, "socialism" connotes primarily the techniques of mobilizing and organizing a total population for the purposes of rapid development. Socialism implies the unqualified commitment of a people to the purposes of national development, as directed and marshaled by political authorities. Political control through a single monolithic party and a total reorientation of economic and social institutions under state auspices are characteristic ideological imperatives. This category is to be distinguished from the preceding in that strict ideological adherence to Marxism-Leninism is not present, there is no total commitment of alliance to the Communist blocs, nor are the Soviet Union or Mainland China exclusively adopted as appropriate models for the developmental process. Rather, the process and imperatives of radical mobilization are equated with a unique and militant nationalism, rejecting dependence on any set of presently developed nations. This category would include Castro's Cuba, Sékou Touré of Guinea, Nkrumah of Ghana (1957-1966), the governments of Congo-Brazzaville and Mali (at least until 1968), as well as Sukarno in Indonesia, Nasser in the U.A.R., and Burmese Socialism since 1962. The Allende government in Chile probably had a stronger affinity to this group than to the former.

Eclectic Socialism Based on Peasant Revolution. The category is distinguished by the fact of successful revolution, based largely on the rural lower class, which definitely reshaped the structure of power in the society and required specific policy priorities as a consequence. In such cases, socialism refers to agrarian reform and related programs and to quite specific objectives in the field of economic nationalism. Formal doctrine is generally loose and unrigorous, and in fields not included within the specific objectives of the movement, policy is apt to be flexible and pragmatic. Although the affinity of Ben Bella's Algerian revolution to the Cuban experiment has often been noted, it is interesting to observe that there is a much closer parallel to the Bolivian and Mexican revolutions. These three cases are the most pertinent examples of socialism thus defined.

Communitarian Socialism. Here socialism is identified with the vision of a harmonious social order, of development achieved without the dehumanizing consequences of radical individualism and the furious competitiveness that seem to characterize the presently advanced nations. In some cases, the model invoked is the social solidarity of the traditional peasant community. In other cases, this sense of socialist society is related to classic Eastern philosophy and religion.

One must be careful not to identify such aspirations too closely with specific movements. As we shall see, such attitudes are characteristic of socialist thought in much of the developing world. However, the theme is so central to the thought of some leaders and movements that it really identifies them as a distinctive variant of socialist doctrine in the developing world. In this category, one would include both Leopold Senghor and Julius Nyerere, as well as U Nu's Buddhistic socialism in Burma and the neo-Gandhian components of Indian socialist thought as well.

Moderate Reformist Socialism. This remaining category includes a wide variety of movements and leaders whose socialist philosophy is basically one of using governmental institutions to direct an essentially private and pluralistic economy and society toward developmental goals. The process of development is to be gradualist and democratic, achieved without cataclysmic upheaval or coercive regimentation. Although nationalism is an important value for these countries, they are not belligerent toward the presently advanced nations, and they seek either a policy of nonalignment or one of cautious and critical identification with the Western nations.

While major revision of existing economic and social institutions (such as the nationalization of industry or radical agrarian reform) are to be considered alternatives available to movements of this type, they are not ideological imperatives. Rather, such movements would select from the fullest possible arsenal of policy strategies those most appropriate to specific situations and circumstances. The Democratic Left, Christian Democratic, and orthodox Socialist parties of Latin America would be included in this category, as well as the Kenyan variant on African Socialism, Destourian socialism, and the Congress Party in India.

THE LOGIC OF DEVELOPMENTAL SOCIALISM

Many of the leaders of Africa, Asia, and Latin America have found in the word "socialism" a satisfying description of their political philosophies. This fact is apt to lead the observer in the advanced nations to erroneous conclusions. He may assume a uniformity of belief and intention that is not the case.

However, it is not only doctrinal heterodoxy that makes it difficult for the outsider to understand the appeal and implications of the socialist mystique in the developing world. What is even more at issue is that socialism, when viewed from within the context of a newly developing nation, bears very different connotations from those familiar to the American, European, or even to the Soviet mind. The classic arguments of European socialism, for example, mean something quite different when they refer not to the correction of the social evils that came with rapid industrialization, but to the initiation of the industrialization process itself.

Despite the bewildering variety of socialist ideas that exist in the newly emerging continents, there is a common core of meaning and a common thread of logic that distinguishes the appeal of the term "socialism" in the developing world from that familiar to the industrialized nations. To describe this phenomenon, we will try to pull together some of the similar features of socialist thought throughout the developing world, always being careful to distinguish the important variations on the central theme. We will also try to show why socialism has seemed to be such a plausible and natural position for so many of the leaders of these emergent nations.

Socialism and the Rejection of Colonialism

To most nationalists in Asia and Africa, colonialism and capitalism were inseparable phenomena. Historically, to many, capitalism had been the prime cause of colonial expansion in the first place. Nehru, for example, argued that the initial industrial revolution in the West, in Britain, was financed by looting the static wealth of India. He wrote:

> Bengal had the first full experience of British rule in India. That rule began with outright plunder, and a land revenue system which extracted the uttermost farthing not only from the living but also from the dead cultivators. ... The corruption, venality, nepotism, violence, and greed of money of these early generations of British rule in India is something which passes comprehension.
>
> But it was all in the cause of progress, and Bengal can take pride in the fact that she helped greatly in giving birth to the industrial revolution in England.

Nehru went on to quote approvingly from Brooke Adams' *The Law of Civilization and Decay:*

> ... the Bengal plunder began to arrive in London, and the effect appears to have been instantaneous, for all authorities agree that the "industrial revolution" began with the year 1770. ... Before the influx of the Indian treasure, and the expansion of credit which followed, no force sufficient for this purpose existed. ... Possibly since the world began, no investment has ever yielded the profit reaped from the Indian plunder. ...[19]

[19] Jawaharlal Nehru, *The Discovery of India* (London: Meridian Books, 1946), pp. 296-97.

Elsewhere, nationalists agreed that colonial partition of Afro-Asia had resulted from the competition of newly industrial powers in Europe for sources of raw materials — extracted by cheap labor — and for markets for their industrial products. Further, the pattern of economic development under colonial rule — usually based on large foreign-operated mines and plantations, with commerce dominated by large European trading firms, such as Unilever's United Africa Company, or the Compagnie Française d'Afrique Occidentale (CFAO), and with retail trade frequently dominated by pariah immigrant minorities who entered under the protective umbrella of the colonial powers (Asians in East Africa, Levantines in West Africa, Portuguese in the Congo, Indians in Burma, Chinese in Southeast Asia) — reinforced the identification of "capitalism" with colonialism.[20] Similarly, the idea of imperialist exploitation was a far more satisfying explanation for the difference in material well-being between the advanced and underdeveloped regions than the alternatives — climate, the lack of a Protestant work ethic, or a scientific outlook on life.

Hence, as Alex Josey puts it, "Socialists and nationalists generally — and in Asia a Socialist is first a nationalist — automatically opposed capitalism because they opposed colonialism with which it was associated.[21]

We may note a curious paradox in the equation of capitalism and colonialism. Classical economists would find colonial economic policies as repugnant as colonial nationalists, although for obviously different reasons. Especially in Africa, colonial regimes were thoroughly interventionist, imposed close controls over a wide section of the economy, opposed "wasteful competition," and were prone to promote public and private monopolies. Colonial policies were saturated with paternalistic assumptions about the proper method of promoting development, and were as distrustful of the invisible hand of the market mechanism and normal economic incentives as the most militant development socialists. Thus, from the standpoint of orthodox economic analysis, colonial economic policy could appear to be "creeping socialism" rather than "capitalism."

In discussing the relationship between socialism and anticolonialism, the peculiar place of Latin America should be noted. Here, independence and socialism are not identified, for the obvious reason that socialism did not exist as an important ideology at the time of Latin American independence. Rather, the rebellion against Spain and Portugal was fought under the aegis of the Enlightenment and liberalism. However, in the contemporary period, Latin Americans are increasingly prone to explain their distinctive problems in terms of the region's history of "dependence." Latin America's growth as a civilization coincided with the development of capitalism, and its unique institutions — large estate agriculture, production for a foreign market, dependence on raw material

[20] See, for example, Kwame Nkrumah, *Neo-Colonialism: The Last Stage of Imperialism* (New York: International Publishers, 1965).

[21] Alex Josey, *Socialism in Asia* (Singapore: Donald Moore, 1957), p. 2.

exports, weak governments more eager to meet the demands of foreigners than citizens — reflect the particular place that the region occupied in the growth of industrial, capitalist economies. As some have remarked, imperialism was not the last stage of capitalism, but, from the Latin American point of view, the first. Hence, socialist doctrine seems highly suggestive to many Latin Americans in explaining who they are and what they have become as a society, as well as pointing to both possibilities and constraints in building economies and polities more independent of "imperialistic" control. Here the perceived issues of colonialism and imperialism seem to be particularly economic ones, and thus especially pertinent for classical socialist analysis.

Socialism and the Political Socialization of New Elites

In understanding the breadth of the appeal of socialism in the developing world, it is crucial to examine the patterns of political socialization and, above all, the role of the modern educational system in the diffusion of new values. Especially in Afro-Asia, many of the present generation of political leaders have acquired their modern political values largely through the educational system. Family, a central factor in transmitting partisan identification and political values in Western systems, tends to be of less importance in implanting modern political orientations in the developing world because frequently the family will be locked into the little world of the traditional community, and accordingly will not be committed to a modern syndrome of values. For many of the new elite, therefore, the hunt for a modern ideology departs virtually from a blank tablet. And there is necessarily a hunt for ideology: the values of the traditional world simply do not address themselves to modernization and social change. Exposure to modern education will trigger the search. Socialism is a particularly satisfying answer for those brought up in the colonial environment because it is an ideology that unequivocally embraces modernization, while rejecting the colonial framework and the "establishment" ideology of the colonizer.

The family and traditional kinship solidarity group can be expected to inculcate a set of traditional values, especially in the religious sphere. However, in many developing states the new national political patterns are at least partly separate from traditional religious identity. Thus acquisition through the educational system or otherwise of a socialist orientation does not need to conflict with continued identification with a traditional religion, except in the case of Marxist-Leninist interpretations of socialism. But the key point is that the young student in a developing state is most unlikely to bring to his first confrontation with the idea of socialism a set of favorable orientations to a nonsocialist political and economic system, as does, for example, the American child.

Western universities, especially in Britain and France, have played an important role in transmitting a broadly socialist world view to their respective political elites. This was particularly marked in the French case, where various forms of Marxism are intellectual orthodoxy in many university faculties. Although British socialism was predominantly non-Marxian, many of the most influential university lecturers, such as Harold Laski at the London School of Economics, were socialists. In this respect, it is important to recall that many independence leaders were educated in the West in the 1920s and early 1930s, at that point when socialist ideas were most in vogue among European and North American intellectuals and when the future of capitalism was most in doubt. They belonged to an intellectual period in which there seemed to be only two choices of political economic system — socialism and capitalism — the latter inconceivable because, as Schumpeter mourned, nobody really loved it. Nehru's statement of 1934, "Whither India?" is most pertinent in this connection:

> Capitalism has led to imperialism and to the conflicts of imperialist powers in search of colonial areas for exploitation. . . . It has led to ever-increasing conflicts with the rising nationalism of colonial countries, and to social conflicts with power movements of the exploited working class. It has resulted in recurrent crises, political and economic, leading to economic and tariff wars as well as political wars on an enormous scale. Every subsequent crisis is on a bigger scale than the previous one, and now we live in a perpetual state of crisis and slump and the shadow of war darkens the horizon.[22]

Not only did the often powerful critiques of the Western economic system formulated from university rostrums leave a profound mark on the new elites, but also socialism became an orthodox pattern of thought amongst their peer group. European student associates with whom they were in close contact tended to come from the left of the political spectrum. Communist groups, especially in France, assiduously cultivated overseas students. It was on the left that support could be found in conflicts with the colonial power, whether it be over the specific issue of the arrest of one student, or the broad cause of colonial freedom. When all this is added to the fact that the new elites felt no identity with or interest in the Western economic system, the overwhelming appeal of "socialism," as distinguished from "capitalism," can be readily understood. To deny the socialist creed was to remove oneself beyond the pale of intellectual acceptability in the eyes of one's contemporaries.

Socialism, like revolution, contains a strong element of romantic appeal. In addition to a plausible critique of the present, there is a promise of prosperity within the grasp of the new elite. Socialism is an exciting, engrossing vision of

---

[22] Jawaharlal Nehru, *Nehru on Socialism* (New Delhi: Perspective Publications, Ltd., 1964), p. 21. For a useful discussion of this phenomenon, see Edward Shils, "The Intellectuals in Political Development," in John H. Kautsky, ed., *Political Change in Underdeveloped Countries: Nationalism and Communism* (New York: John Wiley & Sons, Inc., 1962).

the future. Socialism is an instrument by which a new tomorrow can be constructed out of innumerable cups of coffee in left bank cafes in Paris. The struggle of socialism, to the new elites from the developing world, is the struggle of new against old, poor against rich, generosity against greed, justice against iniquity.

Out of the orthodoxy of socialism as a world view of the new elites came a particular sensitivity of many to criticism from the left. Abuse from the right is of no concern, as it comes from a direction where hostility is to be expected. Denunciation from the left, on the other hand, comes from within the family and can have a humiliating impact. Thus, in defining public statements of ideological position, it is important to trim one's sails to the larboard winds.

Not only the universities, but also the secondary schools are important in the diffusion of ideological awareness; secondary school teachers are critical agents of politicization of the new generation. In a number of Latin American countries, secondary school teachers constitute an embittered, underpaid category, whose frustrations are frequently reflected in commitment to ideologies of the left. In former French colonial areas, where French nationals still make up a large percentage of the secondary teaching corps, many secondary school teachers, since the days of the Popular Front in 1936, range from mildly Marxist to rigorously Marxist-Leninist. In many parts of Africa, secondary schools are boarding schools. The importance of the teachers as vectors of new ideas becomes all the more important in this context.

Socialism and National Integration

The ideas of nationalism, independence, economic development, and socialism are intricately and subtly interwoven in the thought of new nations. Independence contains the formal presumption of nationhood, but the "people" in whose name the independence movement was fought are generally not yet aware of their distinctive national identity or of the implications of the Western idea of nationhood as an integrated and self-conscious community. The "goals" of the independence movement are not achieved with the establishment of independent self-government. For that status to be maintained, for the newly defined territorial entity to become a going concern, it is necessary to "build" the nation.

One can work the equation either way. On the one hand, social solidarity, a sense of the interdependence of the nation that would develop, is essential if economic growth is to be achieved. On the other hand, economic development is an essential means to the creation of an integrated society.

The ideal of social harmony contained in Western socialist thought is a useful component of a theory of nation-building. Western socialism posed an ideal of social solidarity and brotherhood as an alternative to the competition and divisiveness presumed to be the by-product of liberalism and capitalism. The situation is different in a new nation, but the appeal and the vision of a harmonious society has, if anything, an even greater significance and urgency. It is essential to create this sense of common endeavor if the new national community is to be successfully established, if it is to maintain its independence against outside threats, and if independence is indeed to bring in its train higher levels of productivity and more adequate general standards of welfare.

For the more militant socialists of the developing world, socialist unity is particularly critical and urgent, because the new nation is persistently threatened by a reassertion of capitalist and colonialist control. These themes are dominant in the socialist appeal to unity of the People's Republics, Castro, Nasser, and Kwame Nkrumah.

> Once this freedom is gained, a greater task comes into view. All dependent territories are backward in education, in science, in agriculture, and in industry. The economic independence that should follow and maintain political independence demands every effort from the people, a total mobilization of brain and manpower resources.[23]

Here, socialist solidarity is justified as the means to national power and the maintenance of independence. However, for the more moderate socialists of the developing world, the pursuit of social harmony is more often interpreted as the end to be sought through the developmental process. Hence, for Leopold Senghor, speaking of the problem of African unity in this instance:

> In the first phase of nation-building, we must organize the public powers of the federal state... to provide a structure to guarantee their authority and permanence. We must also define the program that will orient the action of these public powers.... For only this action can make of our various populations a *People*, that is to say, a *Community*, where each individual will identify himself with the collective whole and vice versa. But the *unanimity*, the *communion*, of souls is not enough. For the people to become a nation, the individual must grow as his standard of living and culture is raised.... Our program, inspired by our doctrine (African socialism), will permit the federal State to realize the *Negro-African Nation*.[24]

From such a perspective, the principles of social pluralism and limited government cherished in Western liberalism may still be valid goals for the long

---

[23] Kwame Nkrumah, "Background to Independence," cited in Paul E. Sigmund, Jr., *The Ideologies of the Developing Nations* (New York: Frederick A. Praeger, Inc., 1963), p. 199.

[24] Leopold Senghor, *On African Socialism*, trans. Mercer Cook (New York: Frederick A. Praeger, Inc., 1964), p. 25.

run, but in the immediate postindependence period, they are not particularly pertinent to the needs of the moment. Government in a new nation *is* limited, thwarted in its modernizing drive by traditional commitments of loyalty and social relationship. What is essential is not a doctrine of individuation, of social pluralism, but an ideology that encourages and justifies a new common loyalty to the nation. For some leaders of new nations, the vision of social solidarity that is part of the promise of Western socialism is an appropriate component of the myth of nationality.

The distinctive implications of the ideal of social solidarity in the various movements we are considering should be appreciated. Socialist "togetherness" means one thing in the mobilization regimes, where the effort is to galvanize the populace into a single-minded dedication to the development of the nation and a total responsiveness to the intentions of the modernizing elite. In the more moderate systems, the ideal of socialist harmony and brotherhood summarizes the good society to be achieved through development. Such leaders reject both the enforced, lock-step harmony of totalitarian system and what they believe to be the anomic individualism of Western capitalism.

The Democratic Left and related reformist parties of Latin America should be distinguished. Certainly, nation-building is a central goal of these movements as well as those of the newly independent states. For the first century of Latin American independence, the "nation" too often connoted merely the life of the capital city, with the rural dweller, the Indian, belonging to a most imperfectly assimilated hinterland of nationhood. However, for these reformist movements in Latin America, the effort is more often that of incorporating the Indian, the peasant, and the urban slumdweller into the modern sector than of creating a totally new social system. The value is more often one of universalizing liberal, democratic, pluralistic society than that of seeking a utopian socialist community.

Socialism and Economic Development

The idea of socialism in developing nations is intimately linked to the commitment to economic development. Indeed, it is striking that in many instances socialism did not become a salient ideological theme until independence came into view, or even after. In one sense, developmental socialism is a reorientation of nationalism to meet the challenge of independence. During the period of agitation for termination of colonial rule, the demand for self-government eclipsed all other issues. Once independence came, the purposes of nationalism required redefinition; it is at this juncture that explicitly socialist regime commitments were frequently taken. For example, socialism only begins to occupy a central place in official pronouncements in Egypt after 1956. Although Africa has had many socialist intellectuals, for two or three decades, the idea of African socialism only comes to the fore in the late 1950s; the first major statement was the Senegalese intellectual Abdoulaye Ly's *Les Masses africaines et L'actuelle condition humaine*, published in 1956.[25]

For many leaders of the developing world, socialism appears to offer a shortcut to development. Their argument is that it is both unnecessary and undesirable for their nations to repeat the slow and painful process of industrialization undergone by Europe and North America. Some would assert that the experiences of the Soviet Union and China prove that an underdeveloped nation can catch up with the industrialized powers in a short period of time. A far larger group, however, simply feel that the presently underdeveloped nations can learn from the experience of the advanced ones, need not repeat their errors, and can profit from the ideologies and social innovations that served as correctives to the inequalities and inefficiencies that attended early industrialization in the West.

The need for the state to vigorously assert its powers in the name of economic development is argued in many ways. In the first place, the state appears to many leaders of developing countries as the only really modern institution in the society. The state is the institution best suited to the accumulation of capital, to marshaling the initiative and resources necessary for major economic undertakings. Only the state has the organizational capability appropriate to the total task of modernization.

Furthermore, the state is the logical instrument of tutelage in a society which is not yet operating according to the rules and conventions of modern economic life. It is not political restraint that prevents the emergence of initiative and innovation. Far from feeling that state economic intervention is the "road to serfdom," the leaders of many new nations perceive "serfdom" as a long reinforced pattern of traditional life. To stimulate initiative, the state must act as the liberating and changing force.

Some leaders, most notably Kwame Nkrumah, have even asserted that capitalism is "too complicated" a system for the developing nations. Precisely what this somewhat startling assertion implies is unclear. It would seem that the market mechanism is a far simpler key to economic organization than the intricacies of centralized planning. However, it is probably the case that such a highly politicized leader as Nkrumah feels vaguely uneasy with a system of social regulation that is not directly responsive to political direction. It may seem "less complicated" to decree wage levels rather than to assume that bargaining between employers and organized employees will result in a level of compensation appropriate to the economy, even though the first mechanism is probably more subject to serious miscalculation than the second.

Above all, the faith in socialist techniques of transformation represents an almost supernatural persuasion of the capability of the state and its human armature, the public service, to order and control the economy. Militant

[25] Abdoulaye Ly, *Les Masses africaines et l'actuelle condition humaine* (Paris: Editions Présence Africaine, 1956).

developmental socialists appear to be unshakably convinced of the rationality of the political decision-making process and fail to reckon with unanticipated consequences of political choices — that institution of a nonconvertible currency would lead to large-scale smuggling, that nationalization of the retail trade would lead to a breakdown of the distribution system, or that import controls would lead to massive corruption.

Moreover, insistence on socialist development often rests on nothing more than a rather rigid understanding of what capitalism entails. Many developmental socialists are such merely to distinguish themselves from "capitalism," which they equate with thoroughgoing *laissez faire* policies. They describe themselves as socialists merely to indicate that they intend to follow the Keynesian and welfare state practices that have been characteristic of nearly all Western nations since 1930.

Thus, what a leader means by "socialism" often depends on his definition of "capitalism." José Figueres of Costa Rica and Jomo Kenyatta of Kenya have essentially declared that the argument is meaningless and have declared themselves to be advocates of a "mixed economy." Figueres writes:

> In practice, neither of the two systems have been effected anywhere in absolute form. . . . The nations that call themselves socialist have had to leave at least small commerce in private hands . . . and a good part of the land. . . . On the other hand, the great nations called capitalist, and particularly the United States, have organized their industry and large commerce in the form of enterprises whose capital belongs to the public who buy shares. . . . Presently, these very enterprises are helping their employees to buy stock. This is a new form of socialism, stimulated precisely by those men who most fear the word "socialism."
>
> What has happened is that, while men argue in the newspapers over words and phrases, over "directed economy" and "free enterprise," over "inviolable property" and "social necessity," events have been following, almost by themselves, the only possible road in present-day society: A *combination* of the two systems, capitalist and socialist, that tries to combine the advantages of both and reduce the defects of each. To that synthesis of the two historic tendencies the name *mixed economy* is now applied.[26]

And the government of Jomo Kenyatta repeats a similar theme:

> As predictive models of what would happen to factory system societies, both Marxian socialism and *laissez faire* capitalism have been failures. The economic systems in actual use throughout the world today bear little resemblance to either model.[27]

---

[26] José Figueres, *Cartas a un ciudadano* (San José: Imprenta Nacional, 1956), pp. 14–15.

[27] *African Socialism and Its Application to Planning in Kenya*, p. 7.

Hence, the term a leader applies to his development strategy depends a great deal on his perception of the alternatives. He may be a socialist because he believes that capitalism is no more than unrestrained free enterprise. He may also be a socialist to distinguish himself from communism, which he identifies with totalitarianism. Or he may reject all the orthodox labels, either because he feels they are meaningless, like Figueres, or because each has negative connotations, like Kayibanda.

All who identify as "socialists" or "social reformers" in the developing world might agree on the most rudimentary implications of socialism for economic development. Beyond that, diversity is the rule. Hence, both a Figueres and a Nasser might agree that the state must play a more assertive role in the economy of a developing nation than that recommended in classical liberal thought. However, for a Figueres, the implication will be that the state must direct, stimulate, and regulate an essentially private and pluralistic economic order, while a Nasser will insist that the state directly marshal and control the factors of production.

Similarly, "planning" is a common theme of all forms of developmental socialism and social reformist thought. However, for a Figueres or a Betancourt, planning essentially means that there should be a long-range design for the use of the conventional taxation, spending, and regulatory powers of the Western nation-state. For a Nehru, planning implied that the state should administer a comprehensive program for national development, which would be enforced on both the private and public sectors. For a Castro, planning implies the direct control and politicization of all the factors of production in the society.

Furthermore, the state is expected to play a direct role in productive enterprise throughout the developing world. However, there is great diversity of opinion on what the extent of that role should be. For a Figueres, state control of banking, some share of electric power generation, public housing, insurance, and wholesaling service for certain major commodities was about all that was required. For India or Mexico, the list would be extended to include basic industries, such as steel and petroleum. Only in such countries as the People's Republics, Cuba, Burma since 1962, and Guinea until 1962 does one see an intent to extend state control to the level of small commerce and craft manufacture.

With the exception of the Marxist-Leninist states, even the more militant socialist regimes in the developing world are far from seeking a total socialization of the economy. Hence, Nkrumah envisioned a complex economic structure for Ghana, in which transport, communications, energy, and cocoa production would be almost entirely in the public sector; a "mixed" sector, with public capital predominating, in banking, construction, engineering, large-scale agriculture, mining, and fishing; and a totally private sector of cooperatives and private business in small commerce, manufacture, and farming.[28] In his design

[28]Charles F. Adrian, "Contrasting Types of African Socialism," in Friedland and Rosberg, eds., *African Socialism,* pp. 269–70.

for a "socialist society" in Chile, the government of Salvador Allende stopped far short of total socialization. Control of banking and firms involved in foreign trade and specific basic industries was essential, but a substantial private sector including (when Chilean officials were speaking seriously of their program, other than for rhetorical effect) some latitude for foreign enterprise was anticipated.

It is interesting to note that many developmental socialists regard the private sector as an essential "countervailing force" to check on the performance of state economic activities. Notice the similarity in the following quotations:

> Moreover, the maintenance of the role of the private sector beside that of the public sector renders control over public ownership more effective.
>
> Gamal Abdel Nasser
>
> I think it is advantageous for the public sector to have a competitive private sector to keep it up to the mark.
>
> Jawaharlal Nehru[29]

The idea that the state should act forcefully to stimulate domestic sources of productivity and enterprise and that foreign enterprise should at least be regulated, so that it serves the interest of the development of the new nation, is hardly a unique contribution of socialist thought. Alexander Hamilton's *Report on Manufactures* is an excellent codification of many of the arguments advanced by "socialist" leaders in many nations of the developing world.

When the developing state comes into conflict with private enterprise, the operative principle is far more often nationalism, reinforced with socialist arguments, than the other way around. For much of the developing world, modern economic life – industry and commerce – is predominantly a foreign concern. The situation may be either one in which large foreign-based capitalist organizations control industry and the exploitation of raw materials, or it may be one in which local commerce is dominated by "foreigners" – as in the case of the Indian merchants of East Africa and Burma (until 1962), or the Chinese in Thailand. In either case, such visible foreign economic predominance is a source of nationalistic discontent. If the Indian merchants of Burma are displaced by state action, if the copper mines of Chile are expropriated, if the UAR assumes control of the Suez Canal, if Venezuela acts to subject foreign oil companies to a rigorous program of control and taxation, the argument generally hinges more on the imperatives of national interest than public ownership of the means of production. On the other side of the coin, the "national interest" may require that one adopt a definitively nonsocialist policy toward foreign enterprises critical to the national economy.

Thus arise the riddles and paradoxes that surround socialist economic policies in many nations of the developing world. In some countries – India,

---

[29] Paul E. Sigmund, ed., *Ideologies of the Developing Nations,* pp. 103, 134.

Costa Rica, Mexico, and Venezuela, for example – policies of state intervention in the economy are more designed to create a vibrant, dynamic, national system of private enterprise than they are to "socialize" the society. The intent is to create the physical infrastructure of transport, communications, and power; the financial intermediaries of banking and insurance institutions; the basic industries, such as steel and petroleum, that are essential to make possible and support domestic private economic initiative.

Finally, "socialism" or "social reform" implies that the state should actively intervene in the economy to create greater equality of opportunity and of welfare. Development should not result in the affluence of a limited minority, but should be reflected in the material betterment of the mass of the population and particularly the more impoverished sectors. Again, the implications of this objective vary greatly. For the "Democratic Left" of Latin America and their counterparts in Africa and Asia, what appears as a vigorous and innovative egalitarian drive is often no more than a desire to "universalize" those basic public services that are commonly accepted and beyond serious ideological controversy everywhere in the world. Hence, the goals are universal education, minimum standards of public health, support for labor organization and the cooperative movement, and access to suitable means of transport and power. In countries with high illiteracy rates, low life expectancies, and low employee bargaining power, the achievement of such objectives may require considerable militancy and a forceful assertion of state authority. However, the end in view is hardly radical or revolutionary. It is merely an attempt to achieve a social and economic system that would be quite conventional anywhere in the West.

The acceptance of socialism as a development ideology does have important implications for the future evolution of the idea. Historically, socialism was a philosophy of redistribution, not of development. Not until the inauguration of the Soviet Five Year Plans did the motif of economic growth become linked with any form of socialism. Today, growth has become a central objective in both socialist and liberal economies. In Europe, acceptance of a growth rate yardstick for evaluating economic choices has been a crucial factor in eroding traditional socialist dogma and converting it into a philosophy of peaceful social reform. For example, public ownership, once a key policy plank for most socialist parties, could perhaps be argued as a measure aimed at redistribution of wealth, or democratization of the economy. If it has to be measured by its contribution to the growth rate, it becomes simply an untenable proposition, except in special cases.

Similarly, in developing areas, a large part of the explanation of the pragmatic quality we often find in the application of socialism to policy derives from the growth measure. A given choice must be defended by its probable consequences for the growth rate, and not solely by its contribution toward achievement of a blueprint of a socialist society. In most new nations, it is pointless to redistribute poverty.

Socialism and Social Structure

Developmental socialism may become more comprehensible if it is situated within the context of its social structure. In many Afro-Asian new nations, and particularly in Africa, the most prestigious and largest employer is the state itself. The great majority of university graduates in many countries seek positions in the civil service. The private sector is frequently dominated by foreigners or immigrant minorities. A French Marxist writer, René Dumont, has cogently described the emergent social stratification in tropical Africa:

> Thus is created in Africa a new type of "bourgeoisie," which Karl Marx could hardly have foreseen: a bourgeoisie of the public service. It will perhaps make us nostalgic one day for that old West European bourgeoisie, to which we have directed so many reproaches.[30]

The middle class in the West was historically linked to mercantilism and subsequently industrialization. Its interests were rooted in the changing economy, not the state. For the new middle class in many developing nations, the state itself is the interest which it seeks to defend. If we were to stand Karl Marx on his head, we might suggest that an ideology that rationalizes and legitimates a central role for the state in the economy is as much a reflection of class interest as was the nineteenth-century *laissez faire* capitalism for the Western middle class. A recent study of social structure in Bameko, capital of Mali, illustrates this point:

> Out of the administrative and commerical development two "elite" groups have grown: The civil servants and the merchants. The fight for independence was mostly carried on by the civil servants, who expressed both their own aspirations towards self-government and the wishes of the workers' unions and peasantry for a bettering of their living conditions. . . .
> In opposition to the civil servants, the merchants were, for the most part, rich but illiterate and unable to assume the task of governing a modern state. . . . After the victory of the R.D.A., the civil servants took over the government. They had, however, no foothold in the economic structure of the country: hence their endeavor to create a state economic sector through the partial nationalization of banking, transport, and public services. By doing so, they pushed private business into more remote corners.[31]

The converse of this proposition is suggested by the cases of Nigeria and Japan. Nigeria has by far the largest indigenous business and commercial class in

---

[30]René Dumont, *L'Afrique Noire est mal partie* (Paris: Editions du Seuil, 1962), p. 66.

[31]Claude Meillassoux, "The Social Structure of Modern Bamako," *Africa*, 35, No. 2 (April 1965), 133-34.

tropical Africa. This is surely related to the subdued role of socialist ideology in Nigeria; the term has occasionally appeared in political rhetoric, but it would be difficult to point to any policy decision in Nigeria that has been motivated by a commitment to socialist ideology. In Japan, the process of modernization has been almost entirely carried out by Japanese entrepreneurs, business houses, banks, and commercial firms. Although Japan possesses a strong Socialist party and a significant, albeit fragmented, Communist party, socialism has never been a dominant world view. Latin America could also be cited in support of the proposition that socialism is unlikely to be an unchallenged social philosophy if a large segment of the private sector is controlled by local elites.

A final factor which has contributed to the appeal and plausibility of socialism in Africa and Asia particularly and, in a slightly different sense, in Latin America as well, should be noted. To a certain extent, to define oneself as "socialist" was to do no more than to recognize the character of the political economic structure that had been inherited with independence. Particularly in those nations that achieved independence after about 1950, "socialism" was, among other things, a way of rebaptising state capitalist colonial systems. Hence the "welfare colonialism" practiced with growing conviction by most of the imperial powers since the 1930s, and particularly after World War II, had left in its train a substantial public sector of basic social services, economic control mechanisms, and the like. Many of the prime features of state enterprise in Africa – for example, the commodity marketing boards, the education and health establishments, the public utilities – were legacies that the newly independent states were charged with maintaining the furthering.

Although Latin America did not participate in this work of "welfare colonialism," the adoption of Keynesian economic programs in the 1930s and, more markedly, hemispheric collaboration in the allied effort in World War II led the Latin American states to assume many new economic responsibilities and functions. Controls were imposed on the production and export of major commodities and on prices and wages. Inter-American economic cooperation led to innovative measures in technical assistance and development policy. Many of the present-day development banks of Latin America, for example, are the lineal descendents of World War II *fomento* agencies, structured with U.S. assistance and encouragement. Furthermore, confiscation or control of Axis properties in the Americas often led to direct state control of enterprise. Many of the national airlines of Latin America, most notably Columbia's AVIANCA, are the product of this process, as are some nationalized industries and the state farm system in Guatemala.

The Domestication of a European Ideology

We have noted the close, symbiotic relationship between socialism and nationalism in the developing world. The objective of socialist development is to make the new nation a going concern, to reduce economic and political dependence on the developed areas. Hence, it is not at all surprising that virtually all movements that identify with socialism assert their distinctiveness from European doctrinal antecedents. As there is a need for political and economic independence in the developing world, so there would seem to be an almost equally intense desire to declare ideological independence from the presently advanced nations.

Nearly all forms of developmental socialism are defined as "indigenous" or "nationalist" reinterpretations of Marxist-Leninist or European socialist doctrine. So universal is the theme that the self-proclaimed evolution of Fidel Castro from a personal revolutionary position to Marxist-Leninist orthodoxy is virtually a unique case.[32]

The work of differentiating developmental socialism from the classic texts and sources proceeds along a number of related lines. We will consider the basic themes one by one, although they are always interwoven in the thought of the leaders of the emerging nations.

First, there is the process of philosophical criticism, in which it is argued that the classic Marxist or socialist arguments do not apply to the conditions or cultures of the developing nations. Second, the developmental socialists argue that they have improved on the theoretical apparatus of socialism. They have the advantage of hindsight. They are aware of the unfortunate theoretical and practical consequences of Western doctrines and they seek to avoid them. They come to the task of development not as imitators, but with new and fresh ideas that will produce social structures superior to those that were the product of modernization in the West. Third, the developmental socialists assert that the distinctiveness of their approach to socialism is rooted in the historic cultures or the native philosophies of their peoples. They are in this sense conservative. Their effort is to find the uniqueness of what is their own and to preserve it against the onslaught of modernization by integrating the values of tradition with those of change.

The philosophic critique of classical socialism may be fashioned in a number of different ways. Within the immediate family of Marxism-Leninism itself, almost all roads seem eventually to lead to heresy. Most familiar, certainly, was the early Maoist doctrine, with its major premise of a revolutionary base in the peasantry rather than in the proletariat. The distinctive phenomenon of Castroism has provided Latin America with a new way of being a Marxist-Leninist.

Outside of the immediate Communist camp, the themes of Marxism-Leninism are selectively accepted or disowned in a variety of ways. Some accept the humanist message of the early writings of Marx and reject his later materialism. Others accept Lenin's interpretation of imperialism and virtually ignore the remainder of Communist canonical literature. Still others, most

---

[32]See Fidel Castro, "Soy Marxista-Leninista," in *El Pensamiento de Fidel Castro* (Bogotá: Ediciones Paz y Socialismo, 1963).

notably Nkrumah in his *Consciencism*, use the bare framework of Marxist logic as the organizational vehicle for a personalized interpretation of the developmental process.

Most interesting, however, are those who have systematically rejected both Marxist and Continental socialist orthodoxy in the name of a total, indigenous reformulation of the socialist message. Senghor, with his scholarly critique of both the Marxist program and the Marxist epistomology in the name of a more sophisticated notion of developmental process that relies heavily on the works of Teilhard de Chardin, is an outstanding and distinguished case in point.[33]

Of at least equal importance is the daring and imaginative rejection of orthodox socialism contained in the ideology of Víctor Rául Haya de la Torre and the APRA movement of Peru. In the early 1920s, Haya broke with his long-time ally, José Carlos Maríategui, when the latter insisted on doctrinal conformity to orthodox Marxism-Leninism. Haya argued that Communist doctrine, designed for the industrial societies of Europe, simply did not fit the circumstances of Latin America. Moreover, he asserted, classic Marxism represented an archaic form of philosophical analysis. The immutable laws, the inflexible process, contained in Marxism reflected a form of philosophic analysis based on the world-view of Newtonian mechanics. In the twentieth century, Marx's ideas must be interpreted in the light of the Einsteinian revolution. The Marxist message was not absolutely compelling but bore different implications depending on the position of the observer in the relativity of "historic space-time." Hence, from the perspective of Peru, imperialism was not the last stage of capitalism, as Lenin had argued. Rather, imperialism represented the *first* stage of capitalism in Peru. Furthermore, in a preindustrial society, class cleavage was not a matter of the conflict between the bourgeoisie and the proletariat. Rather, for Peru, what was at issue was a clash of cultures — the superimposition of a Spanish, Western "exploiting" class on pre-Columbian Indian society. This pattern of social conflict conformed to Marx's basic premises. It had resulted from a technological change (the possibility of exploration and empire) and rested on control of the means of production. The resolution of the problem was dialectical, but a dialectic emerging from the contradictions of cultural pluralism rather than from capitalistic society. The appropriate outcome would not be proletarian revolution, but the successful synthesis of Indian Western culture — the achievement of "Indoamerica."[34]

Both Senghor and Haya de la Torre are distinctive for the originality, depth, and detail of their philosophical criticism of Marxism-Leninism. However, the essential point of both is that it is inadvisable and unnecessary for the underdeveloped nations to slavishly follow either Western liberalism or classic

---

[33] See Senghor's *On African Socialism*. Also, *Teilhard de Chardin et le socialisme africain* (Paris: Editions du Seuil, 1962).

[34] Víctor Raul Haya de la Torre, *A dónde va Indoamérica?* (Santiago: Biblioteca América, 1936); *Espacio-tiempo histórico* (Lima, 1948); Harry Kantor, *The Ideology and Program of the Peruvian Aprista Party* (Berkeley: University of California Press, 1953).

socialism. These philosophies inadequately account for the full range of values important to man. Each has led to unfortunate social consequences. The newly developing nations can do better. Aware of the defects of the older doctrines of change, both in theory and practice, they can fashion a way to development that will be more appropriate to their own cultural context and more adequate and humane as a form of social order. In this, Haya and Senghor are not unique. They are representative of a general major premise of developmental socialism.

The distinctiveness of developmental socialism is put in many different ways, but across the three continents that we are considering there are striking similarities concerning what it is that the new nations must do better than the old, what assumptions of Western thought must be discarded or reexamined. Both Western liberalism and socialism have concentrated too exclusively on the material aspects of human life. They have neglected the humanitarian and "spiritual" side of life, which also can only be realized within the social order. The developing nations do not wish to choose between the anomic individualism, "the lonely crowd," which they identify with Western liberalism, and the regimented subordination of individual to society that is the consequence of communism.

It is in its concern for the *humanistic* quality of development (to borrow a word much used by Castro as well as by Senghor and others) that the uniqueness of developmental socialism is said to be found. Thus, to Juan José Arévalo of Guatemala, his own doctrine of spiritual socialism "signifies a true doctrinal innovation for our America, up to now debating between conservatism, liberalism, and Marxism." Arévalo distilled the essence of this spiritual socialism as follows:

> We are socialists because we live in the middle of the twentieth century. But we are not materialistic socialists. We do not believe that man is above all stomach. We believe that man is, before anything else, a being with dignity.... Our socialism is therefore not a matter of the ingenious redistribution of economic goods, the stupid leveling of economically different men. Our socialism is going to free men psychologically, to return them to that psychological and spiritual integrity that both conservatism and liberalism have denied them.[35]

---

[35] Juan José Arévalo, *Escritos políticos y discursos* (Habana, 1953), pp. 127-30. See also Marie Berthe Dion, *Las ideas sociales y políticas de Arévalo* (Mexico: Edit. América Nueva, 1958).

It is important to distinguish between two stages of Arévalo's thought. "Spiritual socialism" pertains specifically to his presidential administration, from 1945-1950. With the overthrow of the Guatemalan "Revolution" in 1954, Arévalo has been most identified in his writings with virulent anti-Americanism. This later period of Arévalo's thought may be studied both in his *The Fable of the Shark and the Sardines* (New York: L. Stuart, 1961) and in his *El AntiKomunismo en América* (Mexico: Edit. América Nueva, 1959).

The idea that the idealistic, or moral, goal of socialism is of equal or greater importance than its economic program is to be found in the ideologies of many other leaders of developing nations. For example, Sukarno has stated:

> ... Socialism in its essence is a morality, a morality of high standards which demands that men should not quarrel among themselves, that all men should live like brothers, that all men should taste happiness. That is the essence of socialism and that is the essence of our identity, the essence of our Constitution.... I could even say that this is the essence of the Message of the Sufferings of the People.[36]

Quite often, the moral goal of socialism is phrased as a rejection of European culture or perhaps of some of the more abrasive features of modernization and development.

> Come, comrades, the European game is definitely finished; we must find something else.... Europe has acquired such a mad, disorganized speed that it now is out of any control, beyond any reason, and is plummeting at a terrifying pace toward an abyss which we would do well to quickly avoid.... European achievements, European techniques, European style must cease to tempt and demoralize us.
> When I seek the man in the European technique and style, I see a succession of negations of humanity, an avalanche of murders.
> ... Two centuries ago, a former European colony decided to catch up with Europe. It has so well succeeded that the United States of America have become a monster where the sins, the sicknesses, and the inhumanity of Europe have reached frightening proportions....[37]

Often the "spiritual" quality of developmental socialism is linked to the religious or philosophic tradition of the particular culture. Thus, Sampurnanand writes of Indian socialism:

> I would like to begin by admitting that Indian Socialism is not a very happy choice as a name.... Sarvodaya is another name which I might perhaps have used. It is the name chosen by Mahatmaji for what he considered to be the goal of all effort in the field of public work. It means the *udaya* of all, *udaya* standing not only for material prosperity, but for spiritual good.

[36]Cited in Jeanne S. Mintz, *Mohammed, Marx and Marhaen* (New York: Frederick A. Praeger, Inc., 1965), p. 190.

[37]Frantz Fanon, *Les Damnés de la terre* (Paris: François Maspero, 1961), pp. 239–40; see also Seydou Badian, *Les Dirigeants africains face à leur peuple* (Paris: François Maspero, 1964).

Quoting Vinoba Bhave, he goes on to say:

> Sarvodaya is not content with the utilitarian doctrine of achieving the greatest good of the greatest number, nor does it believe that an inevitable historical process is polarising society into classes with nothing but conflicting interests.... Sarvodaya ... stands for the all-round well-being of all. It believes that institutions and relationships should be fashioned on the twin principles of Truth and Non-violence.[38]

In a very different religious setting, Manuel Sarkisyanz comments on the goals of U Nu's Buddhist socialism:

> ... His prewar essay "Kyan-dawbuthama" ... indicates that already at the beginning of his political career his image of capitalism referred to its underlying utilitarian primacy of the Self, the Self in which Buddhism sees the basic illusion and a cause of suffering.... In his election platform of November 16th, 1959, U Nu described his Buddhist socialism, reiterating (as in 1935) that acquisition economy had developed out of the Illusion of Self which Buddhism aims to overcome, and that it obstructs a social order which would make meditation economically possible for all, thereby permitting universal liberation from impermanence.[39]

And in the Western Hemisphere, José Figueres relates his social democratic ideology to a vision of Christian humanism.

> The Bible speaks of certain men who were *just*; that is, individuals well adapted to community life, being cooperative and not antagonistic, friendly and not aggressive, who cultivated love and not hate.... I do not want to say that we participate in the belief that the individual is the means to an end, that end being The State or Society. Completely the opposite. Our basic conception, philosophical and political, is that society ought to be the best possible means to [the development of] the most felicitous type of human – the Just Man.[40]

Certainly, the Western observer is entitled to maintain a certain scientific skepticism in the face of all this. For many leaders, such prophetic moments are an indulgence sandwiched in between detailed commentaries on a program for economic growth. Furthermore, as we have already noted, the ideal of socialist

---

[38] Sampurnanand, *Indian Socialism* (New York: Asia Publishing House, 1961), pp. 1–2.

[39] Manuel Sarkisyanz, "On the Place of U Nu's Buddhist Socialism in Burma's History of Ideas," *Studies on Asia: 1961* (Lincoln: University of Nebraska Press, 1961), pp. 59–61.

[40] José Figueres, "El Hombre Justo" (address before the Assembly of the Americas, Miami, Dec. 21, 1952). Mimeo. copy in the archives of the Partido de Liberación Nacional, San José, Costa Rica.

harmony has a certain utility in a new nation, which must seek a common unity out of cleavages of language, ethnicity, economic class, and regionalism. It is natural that the developing nations would seek to demonstrate their cultural superiority to the industrial powers. Also, a founding father is in some sense entitled to dream.

However, in many of its manifestations, there is a permanence, an insistence, and a sincerity about these affirmations of the moral or humanistic dimensions of socialism. It may all seem terribly lofty, vague, and impractical to the Western observer, but perhaps he is just too obsessed by the material dimensions of man.

Many leaders and movements assert that the values to be realized through socialism and the qualities that distinguish developmental socialism from its Western counterparts are to be found in indigenous culture. In traditional society, it is claimed, one finds a prescientific socialist community. Thus, for Kwame Nkrumah, the African village community "can only be described in its social manifestations as being socialist."[41]

Fenner Brockway describes a similar theme in the thought of Nyerere.

> Nyerere emphasises the basic idea ... that socialism is a natural expanding development of the traditional tribal system of Africa. Every individual was completely secure in African traditional society. Natural catastrophe brought famine, but it brought famine to everybody. Nobody starved, either of food or of human dignity, because he lacked personal wealth; he could depend on the wealth possessed by the community of which he was a member. "That was socialism. That *is* socialism."[42]

Leopold Senghor urged an "inventory" of African civilization, convinced that: "We would learn that Negro—African society is collectivist, or more exactly, communal.... We would learn that we had already achieved socialism before the coming of the European. We would conclude that our duty is to renew it by helping it to regain its spiritual dimensions."[43]

This search for the native roots of communitarianism is often identified specifically with African Socialism. However, it is in fact a universal theme of socialist thought in the developing areas. The same idea is found in Latin America wherever Indian cultures form an important part of the population. Thus, the Mexican Revolution was to restore the "lost" communal lands to the Indian communities. The agrarian reform was not an innovation derived from Western socialism. It was a distinctively Mexican remedy. The roots of the *ejido* system, which was to form the basic structure of the new agrarian system, were said to be derived from pre-Columbian, Aztec land ownership practices. A similar idea is to be found in Peruvian *Aprista* thought. Here again, it is not

---

[41] Kwame Nkrumah, *Consciencism*, p. 68.

[42] A. Fenner Brockway, *African Socialism*, p. 29.

[43] Leopold Senghor, *On African Socialism*, p. 49.

socialism that is the justification for communal landowning, but rather the Inca *ayllu*. In the lore of the Mexican Revolution and in *Aprista* ideology, indigenous socialism is a coefficient of national distinctiveness. To invoke "Mexicanness" is in some sense to invoke the *ejido*. And the entire complex structure of the Inca "welfare state" seems, for the *Apristas*, to suggest that socialism is peculiarly appropriate as a form of social organization for Peru.

In Asia, the notion that socialism is imbedded in traditional culture is also to be found. That is, of course, the basis of the distinctiveness of the thought of Gandhi as well as Bhave. U Nu's socialism was in some measure founded on the Buddhist tradition of "proper" kingship, of the ruler who was in some sense a potential Buddha, a benevolent and protective savior, guiding the society toward harmony and bliss. Both Sukarno's concept of "permusjawaratanperwakilan," or unanimity arising out of deliberation as a guide to political action, and "Gotong-rojong," or mutual self-help, are attributed to traditional principles of political and social organization in the Indonesian village.

Again, we see the intimate relationship between socialism and nationalism. To seek out the roots of socialism in traditional culture is not only to justify and legitimize an ideology; it is also an effort to find one's own national uniqueness. Nationalism in the West has always implied the existence of a people who shared a common culture and were aware of their distinctiveness in the world. In the new nations, the character of the "people," the culture of the "nation," is often far from clear. The leaders go in quest of the *Volk* that must be there to give meaning to that innocent act of nation-declaration and boundary determination. And, fortuitously, they often find that the *Volk* were socialists.

Furthermore, to assert the values of traditional communitarianism is to qualify the values of modernization and development. It is to suggest that the emerging nations do not wish to replicate in detail the experience of the West. It is also a way of describing the problem of a transitional society that would move toward modernity without wrenching social maladjustments or harsh breaks in cultural continuity.

However, it must be noted that the vision of traditional socialism often rests on extremely tenuous grounds. The idealized portrait of African communitarianism does not fully square with the social organization of most African villages.[44] The pre-Columbian socialism of Latin America, if it ever did in fact exist, has been so overlaid with Western influences that it probably has little meaning in the lives of the Indian populations of that continent and hardly constitutes an adequate basis for social reorganization. And village India is a far different thing when viewed in the harsh light of day than it appears to be in Gandhian philosophy. All civilizations have a myth of a primeval past that was more wholesome and happy than the existing social order. There is no good reason to expect the developing nations of today to be any different.

[44]See Igor Kopytoff, "Socialism and Traditional African Societies," in Friedland and Rosberg, *African Socialism,* pp. 53-62.

Thus, the developmental socialists insist that they are something new under the sun. African, Asian, and Latin American socialism is not merely the transplantation and diffusion of European thought. It has critically borrowed from the classic sources, but the ideological effort has been more creative than imitative. For the developmental socialists, the "technology" of social doctrine is not transferable as is the technology of road building or corn cultivation. Not only are they unconvinced that Western doctrine is right for their cultures; they are also unconvinced that Western doctrine is right in a universal sense. Since they are obsessed by the idea of nationalism and independence, they are no more eager to be ideological satellites than economic or political ones. (In fact, for many developmental socialists, "socialism" is a way of declaring Cold War neutrality, a way of affirming that one is neither a capitalist nor a Communist.) In short, by their own self-appraisal, the one characteristic that is common to all those whom we have chosen to describe as developmental socialists is that they have chosen to think otherwise about the indicated path to development.

THE EXTENT OF THE APPEAL OF DEVELOPMENTAL SOCIALISM

It has frequently been asserted that socialism is the characteristic ideology of the developing nations. However, it is perfectly clear that many statesmen in Africa, Asia, and Latin America choose to think otherwise. Raphael Saller, the minister of finance of the Ivory Coast, for example, recently said:

> We do not practice a policy of African socialism, for which no one, by the way, has been able to give us an exact definition, rather we try to resolve our economic difficulties by the least spectacular measures.... We have a certain amount of wealth, but not more than other African countries. Our success is essentially due to the fact that we have encouraged investments, and that we have also created a climate of political stability, absolutely necessary, for one cannot attract flies with vinegar.

Though few in Latin America, Africa, or Asia would describe themselves overtly as "capitalists," many do assert that they are liberals, or conservatives, or merely ignore the question of doctrinal labels altogether. And beyond those who are simply "not socialists," many regimes in the developing world are militantly opposed to socialism or communism.

Just how widespread is the ideological appeal of socialism in the developing world? To get at this question, let us distinguish the nations of the developing world in terms of the capacity of socialist movements or leaders to actually influence the formulation of public policy through control of political institutions.

TABLE 11-1
Socialism as Regime Commitment

Continent	Militant, Mobilization Socialism and Communism	Moderate, Reformist Socialism and Eclectic Institutionalized Socialism
Africa	Algeria Congo-Brazzaville Guinea Mali Tanzania	Kenya Senegal Somalia Zambia
Middle East	Egypt South Yemen	Iraq Syria Tunisia
Asia	Burma China North Korea North Vietnam	India Singapore
Latin America	Cuba	Mexico Uruguay

It should be remembered that our analysis is open to the widest range of ideological heterodoxy. We will accept at face value the self-assessment of anyone who chooses to call himself a socialist, no matter how far from any orthodox definition of the term his opinions may happen to be. We will also include in our typology certain leaders and movements who do not overtly and insistently proclaim their identity as socialists but whose total style of political argument and ideology closely parallels the themes, concepts, and intentions of leaders who formally claim socialism as their ideology. How close these parallels must be to warrant ushering a specific individual or movement into the fold is of course a matter of judgment, and each reader is entitled to think differently of the matter. For the moment, we are interested in a gross approximation that can suggest the magnitude of all forms of socialism in the policy format in the developing nations, and we have preferred to err on the side of inclusion of questionable cases.

Countries in which socialism is a commitment of the political regime. We include in this category those nations in which socialism has been acknowledged by all governments since independence or since the end of World War II in the case of older nations. Also included are nations in which a major political transition since independence or World War II established a socialistic regime commitment, which in our judgment is at this point firmly established. (See Table 11-1.)

TABLE 11-2
Socialism as Commitment of Some Government

Continent	Avowedly Socialist	Related Social Reform Movements
Africa	Ghana (Nkrumah, Numeiri) Sudan (Al Khalifah) Zaire (Lumumba)	Sierra Leone (Stevens) Uganda (Obote)
Middle East	Iran (Mossedeq) Yemen (Sallal)	
Asia	Ceylon (Sri Lanka) (Bandaranaike) Indonesia (Sukarno) Pakistan (Bhutto)	Bangladesh Thailand (Pridi)
Latin America	Chile (Allende) Guatemala (Arévalo-Arbenz) Guyana (Jagan)	Bolivia (Paz Estensorro) Brazil (Goulart) Costa Rica (Figueres) Ecuador (Arosemena, Velasco) Honduras (Vileda Morales) Peru (Belaunde Terry, Velasco Alvarado) Venezuela (Betancourt, Leoni)

Countries in which socialism has represented the ideological commitment of some government since independence or World War II but has not been endorsed by all governments in this period. This group of nations also includes cases where the present government is self-defined as "socialist" but where, in our judgment, the reestablishment of a nonsocialist government would be less than a revolutionary measure. (See Table 11-2.)

Countries in which no movement calling itself socialist has been effectively in control of government since independence or World War II but a socialist or related movement constitutes the principal source of opposition to the established regime and would be the logical alternative to the government presently in power. It should be noted that in many of the countries included in the previous category, the socialist movement is at present the primary opposition party. However, we have not counted countries twice, for we wish to establish a scale of decreasing salience of socialist ideology. (See Table 11-3.)

Countries in which socialism is not particularly important in the political process. The category includes nations in which socialism is effectively suppressed, those in which it has not emerged as a political force of consequence, and those in which socialist or related social reform movements are present but do not constitute an important or central source of opposition to the government in power. (See Table 11-4.)

TABLE 11-3
Socialism as Principal Opposition

Continent	Avowedly Socialist	Related Social Reform Movements
Africa	Cameroon Madagascar Niger	
Middle East	Jordan Libya Morocco	
Asia	Laos South Vietnam	
Latin America		El Salvador

Despite the admitted imperfections in such an analysis, the rough and always tentative judgments that must be made, the basic point is clear. We have tried to define socialism as broadly as possible, to include as "socialist" even the more questionable cases. Even so, it is evident that socialism is far from engendering complete unanimity in the developing world. Nonetheless, it is also

TABLE 11-4
Socialism not Important

Continent	Nation	Continent	Nation
Africa	Botswana Burundi Cameroon Chad Dahomey Ethiopia Gabon Gambia Ivory Coast Lesotho Liberia Malawi Mauretania Niger Nigeria Rwanda Swaziland Togo Upper Volta	Asia Latin America	Afghanistan Malaysia Nepal Philippines South Korea Taiwan Argentina Colombia Haiti Nicaragua Panama Paraguay
Middle East	Kuwait Lebanon Saudi Arabia		

TABLE 11-5
The Political Significance of Development Socialism

Situation	Militant, Mobilization Socialism and Communism	Moderate, Eclectic Socialism and Related Social Reform Movements
	(Cases)	*(Cases)*
1. Socialism as commitment of the political regime since independence or World War II.	12	11
2. Socialism as ideological commitment of some government since independence of World War II, but not endorsed by all governments during this period.	11	11
3. No socialist or related movement in power since independence or World War II, but such a movement is the principal source of opposition to the present regime.	6	3
4. Total of cases where development socialism has some political significance.	Cases (Sum of above) 54	
5. Socialism is not particularly important in the political process.	Cases 34	

clear that developmental socialism, in all its forms, is an important ideology in the contemporary period.

Thus, the *extent* of developmental socialism in the three continents of the emerging world might be analyzed as shown in Table 11-5.

Our effort, in this chapter, has been to discover the extent of the appeal of socialism in the developing nations. From Table 11-5 we find that if we define the term in the broadest, most inclusive sense possible (including not only Marxist and avowedly socialist governments and movements but also those that in some sense have an ideology or program that, however, moderate, has some affinity to forces that formally define themselves as socialist in character), developmental socialism has had an impact on the political life of slightly less than two-thirds of the nations of the developing world.

If we define socialism narrowly, including only those groups that present a vision of the development process markedly different from the Western liberal experience (militant, mobilization socialism and communism), then we would say that developmental socialism affects the political system in about a third of the nations we are considering. In this strictest sense of the term, developmental socialism has become the established and stable going concern in only about 15 percent of the cases.

Returning to the broader, more all-encompassing sense of the idea and ideal of development socialism, about one-quarter of the nations of the developing world have, in one sense or another, "institutionalized" an approach to development that could be described as socialistic in character. About half of all developing nations have had some experience with socialistic government in the past generation or since the date of independence. And development socialism, in one of its myriad varieties, is a live political option for about three-fifths of the nations of Africa, Asia, and Latin America.

By continent, the vitality of developmental socialism appears as shown in Table 11-6.

Militant socialism, it is apparent, is far more prominent in Asia, the Middle East, and Africa respectively than in Latin America. In Africa, the very newness of many states may account for the large number of cases where socialism is not an important alternative. More Latin American cases, proportionately, fall in the second category due to the peculiarities of political instability in that part of the world, but this may also be due to the longer time span being considered in that continent (these nations were independent prior to many of those elsewhere) and the greater complexity of an older political process. It is also apparent that the more moderate, social democratic movements are more characteristic of Latin America.

TABLE 11-6
Importance of Developmental Socialism by Continents
Number of cases

Situation	Africa Radical	Africa Moderate	Middle East Radical	Middle East Moderate	Asia Radical	Asia Moderate	Latin America Radical	Latin America Moderate
1. Regime commitment	5	4	2	3	4	2	1	2
2. Government commitment	3	2	2	0	4	2	3	7
3. Principal opposition	1	2	2	1	2	0	0	1
4. Socialism unimportant	Cases 19		Cases 3		Cases 6		Cases 6	

It appears that over half of the nations of Asia, Latin America, and the Middle East have had some experience with socialist government, whereas the number of governments so constituted in Africa is slightly less than half of the total. Socialism is a live political alternative in about three-quarters of the nations of Asia, the Middle East, and Latin America, but in only about half of the African states.

In the period since the first edition of this book in 1967 (although our analysis really reflected the state of the world in about 1965) the overall, global appeal of socialism and its particular forms has remained relatively constant. There is a general shift toward the incidence of more moderate forms of socialism, which confirms our intuitive sense of increasing pragmatism and a less "strenuous" outlook among the movements we are considering. The only pronounced trend is in the expansion of our second category (commitment of some government) at the expense of the "regime commitment" category, reflecting the demise of apparently well-established systems such as those presided over by Nkrumah, Sukarno, and others in the intervening period. The conclusion we would draw is that socialist movements, and particularly those of the more militant variety, are probably less likely to be permanent fixtures on the political landscape than they appeared to be at the time of our first analysis of this phenomenon.

CHAPTER 12

Political Ideology and Development Policy

So far, we have been considering the adoption of an ideological symbol among the leaders of the developing world. However, once we have defined the various meanings of a term like socialism and measured the extent of the appeal of these beliefs, it becomes apparent that we must ask further questions if we are really to gauge the distinctiveness of this approach to change.

Whatever else the term may imply, socialism would seem to connote an approach to the role of government in economy and society that is different from that of systems that do not describe themselves as socialist. To what extent is this the case? How different is an avowedly socialist policy from a nonsocialist policy in today's developing nations?

Of course, there is a categoric difference between mobilization systems such as China, North Korea, or Cuba and the more conventional political economies of the rest of the developing world. Where the private sector is radically attenuated, where most of the means of production are in the hands of the state, where there is nothing resembling an open market for the basic factors of production, we are dealing with cases where socialist ideology has obviously had a revolutionary impact. However, the more tantalizing and subtle question is whether socialist ideology makes a difference in the operation of a conventional political economic system.

Intuitively, one suspects that the role of government would simply be larger in socialist or reform-oriented systems, that the state would play a larger role in economy and society and governments would absorb a higher proportion of national product in taxation. The following tables provide some tentative evidence concerning these propositions.

TABLE 12-1
Role of Government in the Economy
Percentage of GNP consumed by the public sector;
classified by regime orientation in the late 1960s

Avowedly Socialist or Social Reform	About 1958	About 1968	Avowedly Nonsocialist	About 1958	About 1968
Algeria	35	–	Argentina	10	11
Bolivia	9	10	Brazil	12	11
Burma	6	7	Cameroon	13	16
Cambodia	19	16	Chad	–	14 (1963)
Ceylon (Sri Lanka)	15	13	Colombia	5	7*
Chile	10	12	Dahomey	–	18 (1966)
Congo-Brazzaville	23	–	Dominican Republic	13	13
Costa Rica	11	14	Ecuador	12	15
Egypt	–	24	El Salvador	10	10
Iraq	18	21	Ethiopia	–	10
Kenya	–	15	Ghana	9	18
Libya	–	14	Guatemala	7	8
Mexico	6	6*	Honduras	10	9
Peru	9	11	Indonesia	–	6
Sierra Leone	–	7	Iran	11	15
Syria	–	23	Ivory Coast	11	14
Tunisia	–	20	Jordan	26	30
Uruguay	11	13	Korea	13	11
Venezuela	16	14	Lebanon	–	10
Zambia	13	13	Madagascar	20	21
			Malawi	13	17
			Malaysia	16	19
			Morocco	12	14
			Nicaragua	–	11
			Niger	–	12
			Nigeria	6	6*
			Pakistan	7	7
			Paraguay	9	8
			Philippines	8	9
			Saudi Arabia	–	19
			South Vietnam	–	20
			Taiwan	20	18
			Thailand	9	9
			Upper Volta	–	10

Source: United Nations, *Statistical Yearbook: 1971.*
*Due to federal or quasi-federal structures, these figures are not strictly comparable.

The data, admittedly, is fragmentary. We include only those nations for which relatively comparable statistics are available. (Given the conventions of international accounting, to include more radical mobilization regimes in such a summary would very much misrepresent the comparison between these structurally distinct systems and the more orthodox, Western-styled political

TABLE 12-2
Role of Government in Extracting Resources from the Economy
Taxes as proportion of gross domestic product, about 1965; classification by regime orientation in that year

	Avowedly Socialist or Reform		Avowedly Nonsocialist	
	Nation	Percent	Nation	Percent
Over 15% of gdp in taxation	Chile	22	Ecuador	16
	Guyana	17	Zambia	21
	Peru	16		
	Tunisia	22		
	Uruguay	28		
	Venezuela	16		
Under 15% of gdp in taxation	Bolivia	12	Colombia	11
	Burma	14	Ghana	14
	Costa Rica	15	Honduras	10
	India	11	Jordan	11
			Nigeria	11
			Panama	14
			Philippines	12
			Taiwan	14

Source: United Nations, *World Economic Survey: 1967*.
Note: Classification of nations may not be precisely identical to earlier or later typologies. We have tried to match existing data with the orientation of the government presumptively responsible for policy formulation. Differences in the date of available data series account for different typologies of ideological orientation.

economies. For example, United Nations statistics report that the Cuban government consumed only 13 percent and the Guinean government only 11 percent of gross national product circa 1966-1968.)

However, a comparison such as this provides our first suggestion of the ambiguities that appear when one attempts to relate ideology and practice in the developing world. Certainly there is a tendency for socialist and reform-oriented governments to devote a higher proportion of societal resources to public purposes. However, the variation is not terribly great, and there are significant exceptions and problems. The Middle East oil-producing nations have large public sectors independent of ideological orientation. Many nonsocialist states, such as the Ivory Coast, Malaysia, and Taiwan, do have large public sectors, confirming impressionistic evidence of greater public assertiveness in such nations without socialist ideology. It is interesting to note that virtually none of the developing nations cited achieves rates of taxation comparable with those of the advanced welfare state systems of Western Europe.

Socialism, or a strong commitment to social reform, would seem to connote an intention to use government assertively as an instrument of economic and social change. Table 12-3 provides a measure of whether this

TABLE 12-3
The Socioeconomic Role of the State
Percentage proportion of government expenditures
devoted to economic and social functions, about 1968

	Avowedly Socialist or Reform		Avowedly Nonsocialist	
	Nation	Percent	Nation	Percent
Over 50% expenditures for socio-economic functions	India*	61	Argentina	68
	Peru	54	Ecuador	50
	Tanzania	52	Guatemala	50
	Uganda	55	Honduras	66
			Malaysia	55
			Nigeria	51
			Pakistan	57
			Philippines	69
			S. Korea	72
			Sudan	55
			Thailand	57
35-50% expenditures for socio-economic functions	Ceylon (Sri Lanka)	39	Brazil*	34
	Costa Rica	42	Colombia*	42
	Egypt	36	Dominican Rep.	47
	Iraq	47	El Salvador	49
	Kenya	48	Ghana	46
	Mexico*	40	Lebanon	38
	Zambia	39	Malawi	45
Under 35% expenditures for socio-economic functions	Burma*	33	Ethiopia	17
	Chile	25	Haiti	25
	Syria	22	Indonesia	7
			Jordan	37
			Liberia	35
			Panama	28
			Togo	25

Source: United Nations, *Statistical Yearbook: 1971.*
*These figures may not be strictly comparable due to governmental economic structure or national accounting techniques.

intention is fulfilled in practice, and whether socialist governments differ markedly from nonsocialist states in the proportion of government resources dedicated to developmental purposes compared to the proportion that go to meet the basic administrative and defense responsibilities of the state. If in fact developmental socialism implies a more assertive role for government in social and economic affairs, we would expect to find a larger proportion of public resources and energies devoted to the promotion of industry and agriculture, public works, education, and social welfare than to the basic functions of regulation, law enforcement, and security. This measurement is perhaps the strongest test available from international statistical sources on the distinctiveness in practice of different ideological orientations to the project of development. Despite the limitations of the data, the results are sobering. It is apparent that there is little overall difference between the socialist and reform-oriented nations and those of more orthodox — in some cases conservative or reactionary — inclinations. It is apparent that many nonsocialist states are as active, or more active, than socialist ones in directing the resources of the state toward developmental purposes.

In achieving perspective on the policy implications of socialist ideology in the developing nations, it is important to note that many of the things some states do in the name of socialism, others do simply in the name of development, without attaching ideological connotations to their programs. Particularly interesting in this respect is the role of the state as entrepreneur, as the builder, owner, and operator of productive enterprises.

State ownership of basic industries is a classic postulate of Western socialism. State initiative in the creating of such enterprises where they do not yet exist is a central imperative of contemporary developmental socialism. However, is the extent of public ownership or entrepreneurship really a distinctive mark of socialist policy in the developing world, or is our problem merely that certain forms of public ownership have ideological connotations in some states and not in others?

It would be deceptive and arbitrary to simply classify nations according to the presence or absence of certain forms of public ownership, for, outside the Communist world, most developing countries are experimenting with complex and subtle techniques of intertwining private and public economic effort. Various forms of capital mixing, either through the creation of a state enterprise alongside private firms in a particular industrial sector or through enterprises in which both private and public capital participate, are equally as characteristic as the state monopoly. Although the variations and combinations are too complex to be neatly reduced to chart form, it is possible to make some general observations on the relationship of ideology to the role of the state in economic enterprise.

Transport, power generation, and communications services are all areas in which the dominance of public enterprise seems to be without any particular ideological significance. In Africa and Asia, many such enterprises were inherited as going concerns from colonial administrations and passed naturally into the public sector of the new states. In Latin America, many of these basic services were initially constructed and operated by private, foreign capital, and in some cases their nationalization has implied ideological motivation, as in Mexico and Argentina. However, ideological considerations were never exclusive and not always paramount. For example, the nationalization of many Latin American railways after World War II owed much to the declining capacity or desire of foreign firms, preoccupied with global conflict, to satisfactorily maintain and capitalize the systems.

In Africa and Asia, public ownership of railways is almost universal where such services exist. In many cases, railways constitute one of the major components of the public economic sector, as in India, where the rail network is the largest state enterprise. The greater part of railway mileage in Latin America is today owned and operated by the state. Only in Honduras is the system entirely in private hands. In a few countries — Costa Rica and Chile, for example — both public and private networks exist. In other nations, including Colombia, the national network is state-owned, with a few short private lines supplementing it.

There may be some relationship between an ideology of militant nationalism and the willingness to invest in that expensive symbol of national pride, an overseas airline. The case of Ghana, with its excessive expenditure for modern jet aircraft of both Soviet and Western manufacture, comes immediately to mind. However, air transport is characteristically either a public or a mixed enterprise in the developing world and appears to be without ideological significance. Complete private control of internal air service is found in only a few nations — South Korea, El Salvador, and Honduras among them. While a state corporation may monopolize air service, as in Burma, more characteristic is the presence of both private and public lines, as in Colombia, Iran, Bolivia, and Venezuela.

In the generation of electric power, a great variety of relationships between private and public ownership may be found. At one extreme, nations like Indonesia and Burma have attempted to remove private activity completely from this field through an active policy of nationalization. In other nations, among them Ceylon and Thailand, public power generation is predominant, simply because the private sector was never of much importance. In a third set of states, new, large-scale undertakings, particularly in the hydroelectric field, are state-sponsored, while highly regulated private concerns continue to operate on a smaller scale. Such practice is characteristic of India, the Philippines, Malaysia, and much of Latin America. (The low relationship of this mixed system to the ideology of the political regime is perhaps indicated by the fact that public power generation accounts for 75 percent of output in Mexico, but also 85 percent in Peru, 75 percent in Colombia, and only 32 percent in Chile. Of these nations, only Mexico could remotely be defined as "socialist-oriented" in the relevant period.) Private power generation predominates in only a few states, including Cambodia and South Viet Nam.[1]

Perhaps, then, it is not in such basic infrastructure services, but in such areas as mineral exploitation and heavy industry that we can find a distinction in the entrepreneurial practice of avowedly socialist and nonsocialist states. Consistently, foreign exploitation of basic mineral resources has been prominent in the bill of particulars that socialist-oriented nationalist movements have issued against the colonial power. However, with a few prominent exceptions, such as

---

[1] For a good summary of the public-private mix in power generation in Asia, see United Nations, Economic Commission for Asia and the Far East, *Proceedings of the Regional Seminar on Energy Resources and Electric Power Development* (1961), pp. 237–38.

the 1952 nationalization of the tin industry in Bolivia and the subsequent expropriation of Gulf Oil or the 1971 takeover of copper mining in Chile, the developing nations have been, in fact, quite hesitant about nationalizing basic mineral exploitation industries. In Peru, for example, the much-discussed nationalization of the International Petroleum Company's assets in 1969 was one specific case, where the conduct of the private firm had been, by the most tolerant of standards, extraordinary, and the nationalization hardly represented a blanket policy. Each recent case has its distinctive characteristics. While Algeria in the early 1970s was taking over the oil industry with considerable skill and determination, Zambia's nationalization of the copper industry was conducted with great care and attention to businesslike proprieties, with the former owners still operating as minority shareholders.

Particularly in Africa, where costly mineral developments are beyond the operational capacity of the present governments, the foreign firm often enjoys great latitude and many advantages (tax holidays, repatriation of profits, and the like). Such programs are found in nations of quite diverse political ideologies, among them Congo-Brazzaville, Gabon, Liberia, Mauretania, Nigeria, and even Guinea, particularly with regard to the aluminum industry.

Two cases require particular attention: petroleum production, and the integrated iron and steel industry. Such spectacular cases as the ostensibly total nationalization of petroleum production in Mexico, Argentina, and the abortive effort in Indonesia (during the Sukarno government) have attracted wide attention in Europe and the United States. However, this practice is far from characteristic of the petroleum-producing regions of the developing world as a whole. More common is a system in which a national petroleum enterprise operates alongside highly regulated foreign concessionaires, as in Peru, Venezuela, and Bolivia, or one in which petroleum resources are formally nationalized and contractual relationships with private firms are used for exploration and exploitation purposes, as in Iran or, until recently, Argentina. This is not simply a matter of ideological choice, but again relates to the limits that economic reality places upon policy options for many developing states. Petroleum, like the mineral industries, requires high capital outlays which are unlikely to be available within a developing state. The high requirements for skilled managerial and technical personnel impose a second constraint. Thirdly, the international marketing of the product is likely to be beyond the capabilities of the majority of developing states. The fatal weakness of Iranian Premier Mohamed Mosadeq's efforts to nationalize Anglo-Iranian in 1951-1953 lay in his inability to market the oil. Similar problems may arise in connection with the nationalization of copper in Chile. Thus, in most cases, however ideologically desirable, nationalization in these sectors is often not practical.

State ownership of basic iron and steel production is often cited as an example of socialist developmental technique, as in the case of India. However, it should be noted that state ownership or participation is characteristic of such enterprise wherever it is found in the developing world, whatever the ideological auspices. For example, in northern South America, integrated iron and steel plants either partially or wholly in the public sector usually have been the creation of relatively conservative military governments, as in the cases of the originally public Paz del Rio works in Colombia, the Chimbote complex in Peru, and the mixed enterprise Guayana project in Venezuela.

It is against such a background that the socialist programs of many developing states should be read. "Public ownership of basic industry" may be a matter of ideological significance for some movements or governments. However, particularly in the more moderate, reform-oriented cases, it appears that the only real difference between a socialist and a nonsocialist policy is that the socialist government will put into ideological context that which the nonsocialist government will also do on purely pragmatic grounds.

It is only when we leave the field of such basics as transport, power, communication, mineral resources, and heavy industry that real differences in public entrepreneurship between some socialist and nonsocialist states become apparent. Thus, aggressive state entrepreneurship of diversified medium and light industry, such as is found in Egypt, Communist states, and to a lesser extent in Nkrumah's Ghana, India, and Mexico, has no real counterpart in nonsocialist states. Similarly, policies of sweeping nationalization of industrial enterprise, as in Burma since 1964, are clearly dictated by socialist ideological commitment. However, when one surveys the extent of state industrial enterprise across the developing world and eliminates such cases as Egypt from consideration, one finds that state industrial activity is more clearly related to the level of industrialization achieved by the nation as a whole than to the presence or absence of socialist ideology. To belabor the obvious, such moderately industrialized but nonsocialist states as Argentina, Colombia, and Peru have a more extensive and diversified state industrial apparatus than such militantly socialist but nonindustrialized states as Guinea, Mali, and Sukarno's Indonesia.

Perhaps the most distinctive characteristic of militant "mobilization-society" socialist systems is the desire to extend the principle of state entrepreneurship even to the level of small business and commerce. Cuba is perhaps the best example of the progressive extension of state control to incorporate even the smallest type of trade and commerce. Although most socialist movements in the developing world, even such relatively ambitious ones as those of Ghana and India, pointedly exclude the small shopkeeper from the public sector, a few experiments in such total socialization of enterprise have been attempted. Guinea was the first to attempt to bring small business and commerce under state control but, since 1962, has markedly retreated from this policy. Burma, since 1964, also has instituted such a policy, but appeared to recoil from its consequences in 1966. A similar experiment has been attempted in Mali since 1961.

It is worth noting that in some avowedly socialist states the central thrust of public ownership will be directed specifically at the alien groups or interests which symbolize "capitalism." For example, in Guinea the embodiment of capitalism was the *Compagnie Française d'Afrique Occidentale* (CFAO), the omnipresent French trading company which dominated commerce in colonial Guinea. Until the eve of independence, commerce was the main economic activity and certainly the most conspicuous one. It was generally believed that enormous profits were accumulated by the CFAO by exploiting the ignorance of the rural peasantry. The strength of this conviction was reflected not only in Guinea's swift move to nationalize CFAO, but also in the extraordinary decision to assume that "profits" from the new nationalized trading corporation would provide 40 percent of the finance for the ambitious three-year plan launched in 1960. Needless to say, the regime had greatly overestimated not only the real profitability of the CFAO, but also their capacity with a severe shortage of skilled personnel to manage the state trading corporation with any profit whatsoever.[2]

Another example is the drive to force Asians out of their control over cotton and coffee processing and marketing in East Africa. Government is actively intervening to force a transfer of cotton ginning and coffee processing to cooperative unions. Although this process can be, and occasionally is, rationalized as a fulfillment of socialist aims, the impetus behind it is clearly not ideological, but rather drives from the bitter resentments accumulated during the colonial period over alleged "cheating" by Asian (and European) buyers and processors. "Capitalism," in this context, meant the Asian ginner.

It may be that the distinguishing feature of a socialist development policy is not to be found in the area of public ownership and operation of enterprise, but in the use of the "economic jugular veins," the basic regulatory and stimulative devices of banking, commerce control, planning, and taxation policy. Certainly, there is a distinctive difference between a centrally planned and regulated system, such as that of India, and a less concerted effort to direct the process of growth, characteristic of such states as Malaysia, Peru, Thailand, and others. However, it must also be reported that the more closely one examines the techniques of economic regulation and control used in these different systems, the less sharp the distinction between them becomes. Thus, in many of the more avowedly liberal states of Latin America, such as Colombia, Ecuador, Argentina, and Peru, the combined impact of the Hispanic heritage of extensive state economic regulation, Keynesian policy devices, and characteristically Latin American techniques for the control of international trade and exchange has provided government with an arsenal of regulatory instruments comparable to those employed in centrally-planned mixed systems, such as that of India. Furthermore, in states ideologically committed to private enterprise, careful and rigorous regulation of basic public services such as transport and power is substituted for public ownership as a means of assuring that the "public interest" will be served. Such is the practice in Malaysia and the Philippines, as well as in many Latin American nations.

[2] See the illuminating article by Elliot J. Berg, "Socialism and Economic Development in Tropical Africa," *Quarterly Journal of Economics*, 78 (November 1964), 549–72.

At this point, we can do no more than to raise the question of whether centralized planning makes a major qualitative difference in the economic practice of the new states. We cannot yet answer the question. However, it is apparent that some states, such as Mexico, which have not engaged in centralized planning, nonetheless have found it possible to closely regulate the direction of economic growth through political coordination of the many regulative and stimulative devices available to modern government.

A suggestive indicator, expecially in Africa where virtually all states rely heavily on expatriate advisors in the technical tasks of plan preparation, might be the nationality and political values of the technicians recruited. For example, part of the difference between policies pursued in radical socialist states like Guinea and Mali and moderate socialist states like Kenya, or nonsocialist states like Nigeria, can be attributed to the type of advisors chosen. Guinea and Mali have relied heavily on French Marxist technicians, whereas Kenya and Nigeria have listened mainly to Western economic advisors.

Banking is one of the basic jugular veins of modern economic life. Public control of the supply of credit in a society is a basic means of directing the process of economic growth. In this field, the practice of the developing nations is extremely varied. An ideologically diverse group of states has attempted to nationalize all forms of banking activity. Among these are Costa Rica (1949), Burma (1962), Cambodia (1964), Indonesia (1965), Tanzania (1967), Chile (1971), and the Philippines (1972). A process of virtual nationalization has also taken place in South Korea, where government has acquired a controlling interest in most of the formally private banks. More characteristic of the practice of developing nations is public control of central banking and of a set of "development banks" in fields of particular interest to economic change, such as industry, small agriculture, and foreign commerce. The establishment of such systems would seem to have very little to do with the imperatives of a socialist approach to development. Chile was one of the pioneers in this field, its *Corporación de Fomento* dating from the 1930s. A similar agency, the Uganda Development Corporation, was established by the British colonial administration in 1952. Relatively liberal regimes have been assertive in establishing such systems — Colombia and the Philippines, for example — but they also have been part of more or less socialist designs for growth, as in India, Ceylon, and Mexico. Nor is such a system characteristic only of relatively "enlightened" capitalist states. Nicaragua, for example, has a quite efficient and substantial development institute.

Given the dependence of most developing nations on international trade, it is not surprising that government should exercise substantial regulation over the conditions of overseas commerce. Special monopolies to control the marketing of major export commodities are characteristic public institutions in much of the developing world. In many nations, such institutions are particularly important instruments for governmental regulation of the economy, not only because of the control they exercise over an important productive activity, but because the profits they have earned through their marketing activities are a major source of development capital. In West Africa, the economic importance of such commodity marketing boards is particularly apparent. Such agencies as Nigeria's Cocoa, Groundnut, Palm, and Cotton marketing boards, Ghana's Cocoa Marketing Board, and others play a major role in the political economy of the nation. Parenthetically, independent governments have had much more difficulty in generating surpluses from marketing boards in the present period of relative decline of primary commodity prices than did their colonial predecessors. During the immediate postwar period and the Korean primary commodity boom, marketing boards could accumulate huge reserves by failing to pass on to the peasant producers the new high prices. However, the days of windfall profits for marketing boards are over; more frequently they have encountered large deficits in recent years. It is politically difficult in developing states (as in the United States for farm products for which minimum prices are guaranteed) for governments to cut prices to producers.

Most of these agencies were established before independence. They form part of the "colonial legacy" of state economic actitivy, and their presence and role cannot be attributed primarily to the ideological inclinations of the new states.[3] However, such institutions are the property of no specific geographic area. For coffee in India, for rice in Burma, for timber in Malaysia, and for coffee again throughout Latin America, such agencies are characteristic policy instruments of the developing nations. In Latin America particularly, such institutions need not be exclusively agencies of government but may involve a subtle and complex intertwining of public authority and private control. Thus, the coffee control institute of Colombia, for example, is formally a private association of coffee producers, yet it receives its revenue from public taxes on coffee and is quite clearly an agency of "public" policy.

Whereas all developing nations exercise some degree of control over imports, primarily through customs controls, some states also have established state trading concerns in this field. The presence of such institutions is more likely to indicate a preference for public enterprise related to socialist ideology than in the case of export monopolies, which seem to be standard equipment for developing nations of different ideological inclinations. Thus, Ceylon has import monopolies for textiles, milk, newsprint, and other commodities, and Indonesia under Sukarno established six distinct institutions for import and export control.

Given the acute ideological sensitivity of many developmental socialists to the economic aspects of imperialism, it might be expected that one could distinguish the policies of socialist and nonsocialist states on the basis of their treatment of foreign investment. One would expect to find that socialist governments would be more wary of the foreign private investor as a central

---

[3]For an excellent survey of the operations of these agencies before independence, see David Carney, *Government and Economy in British West Africa* (New Haven: Yale University Press, 1961).

symbol of colonialist exploitation. On the other hand, one might expect that avowedly liberal states would attempt to establish a regime in which the free play of market forces could prevail, in which the foreign investor would be attracted by a relatively permissive policy concerning his entry and exit from the economy and the use he made of his resources while he was there. Using the reports of the International Monetary Fund on exchange restrictions, we have tried to arrange the countries of the developing world in three general categories: (1) those that actively seek to restrict the role of private foreign capital in their economies and place major limitations on the extent of foreign ownership that they will permit; (2) those that seek foreign investment but would carefully regulate the conditions of such investment; and (3) those that are essentially open and relatively unrestrictive in their approach to foreign investment – in short, those that apply basically the same type of public controls to domestic and foreign firms.

Given the difficulties of synthesizing and comparing the complex policies of the various nations, this presentation must be interpreted cautiously and critically. Furthermore, our rank order of the levels of regulative policy might not be acceptable to all observers. However, in general, one can see a repetition of the pattern we have previously observed. There are clearcut cases at either end of the spectrum where ideology obviously corresponds to practice, where the ardently socialistic regimes are more prone to delimit the sphere of operation of foreign private capital, and where those states dedicated to a liberal ideology are more permissive concerning the activities of foreign enterprise. And again, we note that in the largest number of cases, socialism as espoused ideology need not connote a distinctive policy orientation.

One fundamental question posed by developmental socialism is the relationship between the public and the private economic sectors in the task of change. Except for the most extreme, most versions of developmental socialism insist that private economic activity has some role to play in the design for progress. Conversely, there are no doctrinaire *laissez faire* states in the developing world. Even those nations most committed to a Western, liberal view of development find it necessary and desirable to allow government a substantial economic role. Furthermore, few ideologies of development offer clear, sharp *a priori* definitions of the appropriate roles of the private and the public. Rather, most prescribe that these relationships must be worked out over time, as experience and practical judgment dictate. Given such considerations, it seems pertinent to ask how the relationships between governmental and private economic activity have developed in Africa, Asia, and Latin America. What has been the process of conflict and accommodation between the public and the private economic sectors in these nations? How have the relationships between the public and the private economic spheres actually developed?

In assessing this question, we have tried to ask ourselves what the relationships between the private and public sectors have been *in fact* in the nations of the developing world since independence or the end of World War II,

TABLE 12-4

The Role of the State in Controlling Foreign Investment
About 1970; classification according to orientation
of government apparently responsible for policy

Policy Toward Foreign Investment	Avowedly Socialist or Reform-Oriented	Avowedly Nonsocialist
Restrictive		
Exchange inconvertibility, prohibitions on capital repatriation, marked limitations on foreign ownership	Burma China Cuba Guinea North Korea North Vietnam	
Regulative		
1. General restrictions on repatriation of capital and/or profits; stringent conditions on foreign investment	Algeria Cambodia Ceylon (Sri Lanka) Chile Congo-Brazzaville Egypt Mali Tanzania	Nepal Rwanda
2. Approval of foreign investment, terms and type of investment, conditions of repatriation of capital and/or profits.	Iraq Peru Uruguay	Colombia Ecuador El Salvador Ghana	Kuwait Morocco Nigeria Paraguay Philippines
3. Modest restrictions as in (1) and (2) above	Kenya India Senegal Uganda	Afghanistan Brazil Cameroon Central African Republic Chad Dahomey Gabon Haiti Iran	Ivory Coast Malagasy Mauretania Mauritius Niger Thailand Togo South Korea South Vietnam Upper Volta
4. Generally limited restrictions, stricter with regard to raw materials industries	Bolivia Libya Sierra Leone Tunisia Zambia	
Essentially Liberal		
	Costa Rica Singapore Venezuela	Argentina Burundi Ethiopia Guyana Honduras Indonesia Jordan Laos	Lebanon Liberia Malawi Malaysia Nicaragua Pakistan Panama Saudi Arabia

Source: Adapted from, International Monetary Fund, *Annual Report on Trade Restrictions,* 1971.

no matter what the ideological intentions of governments in power might have been. Our intention is to provide an overview of the total problem of the incidence of socialist practice and socialist ideology in the developing world. Hence, we related our findings to the conclusions on the significance of socialism as a political ideology, presented at the end of the first part of this volume. Of course, our classification is purely a matter of personal impression and judgment based on major policies and events in these nations. (See Table 12-5.)

The *caveats* that apply to a typology such as this are fairly obvious. We classify together nations whose economies are very dissimilar. It means one thing to constrict or eliminate the private sector in China or Cuba and quite another in Guinea or Mali. Similarly, a policy of basic permissiveness toward the private sector bears very different implications in Colombia and in Upper Volta. Furthermore, by concentrating on a relatively short span of time, we neglect problems of historical policy development. It is true that government has not markedly increased its role *vis-à-vis* the private sector in a number of Latin American nations in the postwar period, but the policy apparatus of each of these countries includes a good many controls that date from earlier epochs. Finally, some of these nations are far too young, others far too unstable, others too inchoate in their political economic arrangements for us to feel very confident in our judgments.

Nonetheless, an examination such as this, taken as a whole and in the light of all the uncertainties we must feel concerning matters of detail, does provide us with some understanding of the nature of the world of emergent nations. First, it is clear that total antipathy toward private economic activity and the desire to create totally state-controlled economies is far from characteristic of the political elites of the developing world. The number of cases in which the state has acted unsympathetically and aggressively toward the private sector is a very small proportion of the whole. What is far more evident is a pragmatic groping toward a developmental format in which both the state and private enterprise will play an important role, in which their energies will be interwoven in the process of economic growth. There is a certain skepticism about putting all eggs in either basket. Some leaders of developing states choose to call this socialism. Others prefer to call it something else. Whatever ideological rubric is chosen, it is quite apparent that a good number of the leaders of developing nations intend no orthodoxy.

Finally, it would seem that socialist inspriation is hardly a necessary condition for the more effective deployment of public powers in the interest of development, change, and reform. Among our nonsocialist nations (and we have defined "socialism" in the most inclusive fashion possible) we do find some regimes that are dedicated to the preservation of the privileges of a miniscule elite. However, we also find a very good number of governments that do not define themselves as socialist, and in some cases not even as reformist, but that nonetheless are using the powers of the state for the purposes of development in

TABLE 12-5
The Terms of Conflict and Accommodation Between the Public and the Private Sectors in the Economies of the Developing Nations General tendency during the period from independence of World War II to 1972

	Socialism as Regime Commitment		Socialism as Commitment of Some Government	Socialism as Major Source of Opposition to a Non-socialist Regime	Socialism Unimportant in National Politics
	Militant, mobilization socialism	*Moderate socialism and related reform movements*			
1. Radical effort to constrict or eliminate the private sector and incorporate it into the regime.	Burma North Korea China North Vietnam Cuba Tanzania Egypt South Yemen Mali	Iraq Syria	Chile		
2. Extension of public control over the operation of the private sector, domestic and foreign, without attempt to constrict or eliminate the private sector.	Algeria	Somalia Zambia	Ceylon (Sri Lanka) Iran Pakistan Peru Sierra Leone Sudan Zaire		Nigeria South Korea Taiwan
3. Increasing accommodation of the private sector into a regime which began with apparently greater socializing intent.	Congo-Brazzaville	India Kenya Mexico Senegal Tunisia	Bolivia Cambodia Ghana Indonesia Uganda Venezuela		

TABLE 12-5
(Continued)

	Socialism as Regime Commitment		Socialism as Commitment of Some Government	Socialism as Major Source of Opposition to a Non-socialist Regime	Socialism Unimportant in National Politics
	Militant, mobilization socialism	*Moderate socialism and related reform movements*			
4. Private sector dominant and legitimate.		Singapore	Brazil Costa Rica Ecuador Guatemala Guyana Honduras	Laos Lebanon Libya Madagascar Malaysia Morocco South Vietnam	Afghanistan Argentina Cameroon Central African Republic Colombia Chad Dahomey Ethiopia Gabon Haiti Ivory Coast Kuwait Liberia Malawi Mauritania Nepal Nicaragua Niger Nigeria Panama Paraguay Philippines Rwanda Saudi Arabia Togo Upper Volta

very much the same way as some regimes that insist on the distinctiveness of the socialist design for change.

In any event, the conclusions of an essay such as this must be suggestive rather than definitive. There is much that we did not answer and did not know how to answer. The patterns of public policy in the developing world are far too rich in experimentation and innovation to be easily classified. The hard statistical data of comparison are unavailable for most countries, and even where such data are to be found, one quickly becomes aware that one is apt to be measuring what the statistical officials think the outside world ought to think is occurring in their nations rather than what is actually going on. We could find no convincing way of comparing the relationship between developmental socialism and the goals of the welfare state throughout the developing regions.

However, despite such reservations and limitations, the basic point of the essay still remains. One searches in vain for that ideological commitment that characterizes the developing nations or the doctrinal trend that unifies the aspirations of the "third world." Socialism does have a strong attractiveness in some nations, but in others it does not. And within the group that would define itself as socialist, we find great diversity of intentions and performance. Some socialist states have used government in a distinctive way as a tool of development, but other avowedly socialist states appear to pursue public policies that are not particularly different from states that are avowedly nonsocialist.

There are patterns in the developing world, but none of them can be said with certainty to characterize that world. There appeared a "trend" toward the revolutionary socialization of economy and society in the early 1960s in some regions and some nations. There continues to be a "trend" toward comprehensive planning and regulation of the economy in some of the societies of the developing world. Also apparent is a "leveling off" of socialist aspiration with the inclusion of certain basic utilities and industries in the public sector, as there is in some nations a tendency for the private sector, domestic and foreign, to be increasingly accommodated to a fundamentally socialist design for development. One also notes the extension or reassertion of conventional, liberal economic systems in some places and a movement of capitalist regimes to accommodate some measure of "socialist" demands and aspirations.

But it would be premature to forecast an end of ideology in the developing world. The logic of developmental socialism remains compelling for many political leaders, however diverse the policy implications may be. At this moment, in looking back over the first generation of what might very well be called the "age of development," no single pattern is dominant. What we have fundamentally confirmed is heterogeneity. Given the diversity of peoples and cultures with which we are dealing and a liberal appreciation of creative difference, that is probably all to the good.

Index

Abako, 156
Abernathy, David, 83
Acción Democrátic (Venezuela), 141, 180, 214
Acción Populaire (Peru), 214
Action Group (Nigeria), 84, 86
Adams, Brooke, 224
Aden Protectorate, 73
Adoula, C., 155, 156, 157
Afghanistan, 19, 106*t*, 248*t*, 264*t*, 268*t*
Aflaq, Michael, 207, 210
African National Congress, 35
African Socialism and its Application to Planning in Kenya (Kenyatta), 205
Afrique Equatoriale Française, 71*t*, 75
Afrique Occidentale Française, 71*t*, 75
Algeria, 23, 107*t*, 164; economic development in, 253*t*, 258, 264*t*, 267*t*; expatriation from 105, 107; and France, 183, 194, 195; political violence in, 114, 116; revolution in, 173, 174, *175-78*, 179, 192, 210; socialism in, 208-9, 222, 246*t*
All-Ceylon Buddhist Conference, 58
Allende, Salvadore, 181, 212, 213, 215, 222, 234, 247*t*
Alliance for Progress, 214
Almond, Gabriel, 5, 175
Ambonese, 39, 70*t*, 75, 77
Amin, Idi, 108
Amisi-Mahumedi, Joseph, 160
Anderson, Charles W., 8-9
Andhra (India), 42, 44
Anglo-Burmese War, 127
Anglo-Iranian Oil Company, 258

Angola, 37, 71*t*, 163, 186
Anti-Fascist People's Freedom League (Burma), 184
Anyanya, 75
Aprismo, 140, 197, 243-44
Apter, David, 171
Arabs, 19, 26, 67, 74, 119; irredentism of, 71*t*, 73, 74; socialism of, 183, 206-11; in Sudan, 75, 105
Arakanese, 70*t*, 134
Araucanians, 46
Arbenz, Jacobo Guzmán, 185-86, 247*t*
Arévalo, Juan Jose, 185, 186, 240 and *n,* 247*t*
Argentina, 49-50, 78, 186*t*; economic development in, 253*t*, 255*t*, 256, 258, 259, 260, 264*t*, 268*t*; pluralism in, 24, 70, 70*t*, 72, 106*t*, 109
Armas, Carlos Castillo, 186
Armee Nationale Zairose (ANZ), 149, 153, 154, 155*n,* 157*n,* 158-59, 162
Armee Populaire de Libéation (APL), 153, 154, 155, 158, 159, 160, 161, 164-65
Armenian Catholics, 60, 73
Armenians, 71*t*
Arosemena, Carlos Julio, 247*t*
Ashanti, 71*t*
Assam (India), 44
Ataturk, Kemal, 206
Austro-Hungarian Empire, 41
Avianca, 237
Awami League, 92, 96, 97
Awolowo, Obafemi, 82-83, 84
Ayllu, 51, 244

Azerbaijan, 71*t,* 73*n,* 77
Azikiwe, Nnamdi, 82-83, 85
Aztecs, 18, 243
Azuela, M., 175

Baamba-Bakonjo, 71*t*
Ba'ath Socialism, 207, 210-11
Bafulero, 158, 160
Bahrein, 73
Bahutu, 76, 108
Bakongo, 32-33, 37, 71*t,* 162
Balew, Abubakar Tafewa, 85, 87
Baluba, 149, 150 and *n,* 162
Balubakat, 160
Bambala, 152
Bambole, 160
Bambundu, 152, 161, 162
Banderanaike, S. W. R. D., 58, 220, 247*t*
Bangala, 31-33
Bangladesh, 44, 70*t,* 73, 77, 106*t,* 247*t;* war of independence for, 79, *92-100*
Bangongo, 152
Bapende, 152, 161, 162
Barotse, 21
Batabwa, 150
Batak, 26, 39
Batetela-Bakusu, 152, 158 and *n,* 160, 162, 164
Bayanzi, 152
Bayeke, 150
Belaunde, Terry Fernándo, 180, 185, 214, 247*t*
Belgium, 16, 76; and former Congo, 31-32, 33*n,* 147, 148, 150*n,* 163
Bella, Ben, 177-78, 208, 213, 222
Bello, Ahmadu, 87
Bemba, 35
Benanga, Victor, 159*n,* 164
Bengal (India), 40, 44, 57, 77, 92-100, 70*t,* 224. *See also* Bangladesh
Betancourt, Rómulo, 141, 180, 185, 214, 233, 247
Bhave, Vinoba, 242, 244
Biafra, 75, 79-91, 98-100. *See also* Nigeria
Bihar (India), 44
Biharis, 96, 98, 99
Binder, Leonard, 5, 210-11
Blanco, Hugo, 52, 188
Bocheley-Davidson, Egide, 157
Boer Republics, 18*n*
Boer War, 114
Bolamba, Antoine-Roger, 34
Bolikango, Jean, 33
Bolivar, Simon, 72
Bolivia: economic development in, 253*t,* 254*t,* 257, 258, 264*t,* 267*t;* Indians of, 45, 51, 55-56; pluralism in, 24, 106*t,* revolution in, 173, 184, 186*t,* 187, 188, 192, 197, 215-16; socialism in, 215-16, 217, 222, 247*t*
Bombay University, 41-42
Bomboko Justin, 157*n*
Borda, Orlando Fals, 139
Borneo, 24, 187
Borrerro, Misael Pastrana, 145
Botswana, 18, 123, 248*t*
Boumedienne, Houari, 164, 177-78
Bourguiba, Habib, 209-10
Brahman caste, 43, 92
Brandt, Willy, 199
Brazil, 48, 50, 78; economic development in, 253*t,* 255*t,* 264*t,* 268*t;* pluralism in, 24, 25, 106*t;* revolution in, 181, 182, 186*t,* 188; socialism in, 213*n,* 217, 247*t*
British Guiana, 18
Brockway, Fenner, 243
Buddhism, 22, 185; in Burma, 57, 127, 129-31, 134, 184, 220, 223; and socialism, 220, 223, 242, 244; in Sri Lanka, 23, 26, 57-59
Buddhist Committee of Inquiry, 58
Buganda, 71*t,* 103, 110
Bunge, Carlos Octavio, 117
Burma, 26, 78, 102, 105, 108; colonialism in, 18, 19, 225, 234; economic development in, 253*t,* 254*t,* 255*t,* 257, 259, 261, 262, 264*t,* 267*t;* pluralism in, 38-39, 67, 106*t;* political violence in, 113, 116, 117, 122, 123, 125-35; religions in, 23, 26, 57, 58; revolution in, 173, 180, 182, 183-84, 186*t,* 192, 195, 196; separatism in, 70*t,* 72, 76; socialism in, 206, 219, 220-21, 222, 223, 233, 246*t*
Burundi, 18, 107*t,* 248*t,* 264*t;* political violence in, 113, 153, 158; separatism in, 71*t,* 75-76, 77
Bhutto, Ali, 247*t*

Cabildo, 72
Cabral, Amilcar, 163
Cady, John, 129, 130
Cáldera, Rafael, 215
California, 70*t,* 72
Camargo, Alberto Lleras, 136, 145
Cambodia, 18, 23, 38, 106*t,* 119, 186*t;* economic development in, 253*t,* 257, 261, 264*t,* 267*t*
Cameroon, 71*t,* 103, 107*t,* 162-63, 248*t;* economic development in, 253*t,* 264*t,* 268*t*
Canada, 15, 114
Cao Dai, 23
Cárdenas, Lázaro, 174, 175
Casamance Province (Senegal), 24
Caste system, 22-23
Castro, Fidel, 191, 208, 213, 217, 222, 229, 233, 238, 240

Index

Castroism, 144, 181, 187, 218
Catholics. *See* Armenian Catholics; Roman Catholics
Celebes Islands, 26
Central African Republic, 67, 71*t*, 107, 162, 189*t*, 264*t*, 268*t*
Central American Federation, 18, 70*t*
Ceylon, 186*t*, 220, 247*t*; economic development in, 253*t*, 255*t*, 257, 261, 262, 264*t*. *See also* Sri Lanka
Chaco War, 197
Chad, 57, 71*t*, 78, 106*t*, 189*t*; economic development in, 253*t*, 264*t*, 268*t*
Champassak (Laos), 24
Chavéz, Carlos, 55, 175
Chibcha language, 47
Chicanos, 16
Chile, 50, 195; economic development in, 253*t*, 254*t*, 255*t*, 257, 258, 261, 264*t*, 267*t*; Indians in, 45, 46; pluralism in, 24, 106*t*, 109; revolution in, 180, 181; socialism in, 211, 212, 213 and *n*, 215, 222, 234, 247*t*
China, 18, 44, 73*n*, 105, 107*t*; and Burma, 127, 132; as colonial power, 225, 234; Communist Party in, 119-20, 132, 178-79, 219; economic development in, 252, 264*t*, 267*t*; and Malaysia, 20, 66, 73, 187; political violence in, 113, 116, 119; revolution in, 79, 173, *178-79*, 192, 197; socialism in, 202, 218, 219, 222, 231, 246*t*
Chins, 102
Christian Democratic Party, 211, 213, 214-15, 223
Christianity, 22, 23, 48, 242; in Africa, 23, 32, 33, 35, 57, 64, 81, 164; in Asia, 26, 39, 131; Catholic-Protestant cleavage in, 15, 23, 64, 84; Lebanese sects of, 60, 73
Cofradias, 53
Coleman, James S., 5
Colombia, 18, 50, 68, 78; economic development in, 253*t*, 254*t*, 255*t*, 257, 259, 260, 261, 262, 264*t*, 268*t*; Indians in, 45, 47; pluralism in, 24, 25, 106; political violence in, 113, *136-45;* revolution in, 185, 186*t*, 188; separatism in, 70*t*, 72; socialism in, 211, 213*n*, 237, 248*t*
Colson, Elizabeth, 35
Committee on Emotional Integration (India), 41, 43
Communism, 44, 77, 119-23, 178, 186*t*, 187, 237; Asian, 219-20, 222; in Burma, 72, 133, 135; in China, 116, 119-20, 132, 173, 174, 178-79; French, 122, 202; in Indonesia, 113, 182; in Latin America, 144, 181, 186, 212, 213; in Malaysia, 115-16, 120-22, 187; and revolution, 170, 192-93. *See also* Marxism-Leninism; Socialism

Compagne Française d'Afrique Occidentale (CFAO), 225, 260
Condorcanqui, Jose Gabriel, 46-47
Congo, 71*t*, 225
Congo-Brazzaville, 37, 71*t*, 104, 107*t*; economic development in, 253*t*, 258, 264*t*; political violence in, 149, 157, 162; revolution in, 180, 196; socialism in, 202, 203, 222, 246*t*
Congo Free State, 31, 68
Congress Party (India), 40, 44, 220, 223
Consciencism (Nkrumah), 239
Conseil National de Libération (Zaire), 157
Conseil National de la Révolution Algérienne, 176
Copts, 183
Coquilhat, Camille, 31
Corporación de Fomento (Chile), 261
Costa Rica, 70*t*, 106*t*, 141; economic development in, 253*t*, 254*t*, 255*t*, 257*t*, 261, 264*t*, 268*t*; and revolution, 185, 189*t*; socialism in, 214, 232, 235, 247*t*
Creoles, 20, 110
Cromwell, Oliver, 115
Cuba, 50, 106*t*; economic development in, 252, 254, 259, 264*t*, 267*t*; revolution in, 173, 180, 184, 187; socialism in, 213*n*, 217-18, 222, 246*t*
Cyprus, 113

Dacca University, 96
Dahomey, 71*t*, 107*t*, 149, 162, 248*t*, 253*t*, 264*t*, 268*t*
Dako, 36-37
Darcy, Robert, 109
Darfur, 71*t*
Dār ul-Islam (Indonesia), 23
Dawa, 154-55
Decline of Ideology? (Rejal), 169
Democratic Left, *213-14*, 218, 223, 230, 235
Democratic Party (U.S.), 199, 214
Destour Socialist Party, 209-10, 223
Deutsche, Karl, 5, 16
Díaz, Porfirio, 174
Diem, Ngo, 58
Dioula, 38
Dominican Republic, 46, 106*t*, 113, 253*t*, 255*t*
Dravidian language, 42, 104
Druze, 60, 73
Dumont, René, 236

Ecuador, 68, 189*t*; economic development in, 253*t*, 254*t*, 255*t*, 260, 264*t*, 268*t*; Indians in, 45, 51; pluralism in, 24, 25, 106*t*; separatism in, 18, 70*t*, 72; socialism in, 213 and *n*, 247*t*
Efiks, 80

Egypt, 60, 74, 115; colonialism in, 18, 19; economic development in, 253*t*, 255*t*, 259, 264*t*, 267*t*; revolution in, 173, 182, 183, 196, 197; socialism in, 206-7, 230, 246*t*
Ejido system, 55, 243-44
El Salvador, 45, 70*t*, 106*t*, 182, 206, 248*t*, 253*t*, 255*t*, 257, 264*t*
Eluwa, B. O. N., 83
Emerson, Rupert, 60
Encomienda system, 51
English language, 41, 58, 104, 105, 127
Eritrea, 71*t*
Ethiopia, 19, 26, 71*t*, 75, 78, 106*t*, 248*t*; economic development in, 253*t*, 255*t*, 264*t*, 268*t*; revolution in, 164, 186*t*
Ethnicity: in Africa, 29-33; in Asia, 38-40; as cultural differentiator, 21-22; in Latin America, 46-56; transterritorial, 44-45; and violence, 149
Ewe, 71*t*
Expatriation, 105-8

Facing Mount Kenya (Kenyatta), 38
Fanon, Frantz, 176, 208
Fedequalac, 33
Federalism, 102-3
Federation of Rhodesia and Nyasaland, 71*t*, 75
Figueres, José, 141, 185, 214, 232-33, 242, 247*t*
Fiji, 18
First New Nation, The (Lipset), 191
Fitzgibbon, Russell, 136
Flemings, 16, 33*n*
France, 16, 113, 133; as colonial power, 18, 60, 183, 194, 207, 208; socialism in, 202, 220, 226-28
Franco, Francisco, 181
Freedom Party (Sri Lanka), 58, 66
Frei, Eduardo, 181, 213, 215
Friedland, William H., 200
Friere, Paulo, 188
Front de Liberation National (FLN, Algeria), 176, 208
Furnivall, J. S., 125, 127

Gabon, 71*t*, 75, 107*t*, 149, 189*t*, 248*t*, 258, 264*t*, 268*t*
Gaitán, Jorge Eliecer, 141, 145
Gambia, 248*t*
Gandhi, Mahatma, 115, 223, 244
Garcia-Calderon, F., 117
Gbenye, Christophe, 157, 161, 162
Geertz, Clifford, 28, 171
Germany, 41, 105, 117, 163, 172
Ghana, 71*t*, 89, 107*t*; economic development in, 253*t*, 254*t*, 255*t*, 257, 259, 262, 263*t*, 267*t*; federalism in, 78, 102; social-

ism in, 202-3, 222, 233, 247*t*; violence in, 162, 185
Giap, Vo Nguyen, 164, 219
Gilan, 71*t*, 73*n*
Gizenga, Antoine, 152, 157, 162
Gluckman, Max, 150*n*
Gomez, Laureano, 143
Goulart, João, 181, 247*t*
Gowon, Yakubu, 80, 88, 91
Gran Colombia, 18, 70*t*, 72
Great Britain, 18, 226-27; as colonial power in Burma, 102, 125, 127-29, 131, 133, 134, 183; in Egypt, 115, 183, 207; in India, 40, 41, 92-94, 224; in Nigeria, 64, 80; in Uganda, 110, 261
Greek Catholics, 60, 73
Greeks, 105, 183
Guaraní, 22, 46, 48-50, 51, 102
Guatemala, 70*t*, 106*t*; economic development in, 253*t*, 255*t*, 268*t*; Indians in, 45-46, 53-54, 78; revolution in, 185-86, 186*t*; socialism in, 240 and *n*, 247*t*
Guevara, Che, 56, 187, 188
Guinea, 71*t*, 102, 107*t*; economic development in, 254, 258, 259-60, 261, 264*t*; revolution in, 180, 189; socialism in, 202, 222, 233, 246*t*
Guiné-Bissau, 186*t*
Gujaret (India), 42, 44
Gulf Oil Company, 258
Gunther, John, 136
Gurr, Ted Robert, 124
Guyana, 113, 247*t*, 254*t*, 265*t*, 268*t*
Guzmán Campos, Germán, 142-43, 144

Hagen, Everett, 117-18, 125
Haiti, 18, 106*t*, 110, 189*t*, 248*t*, 255*t*, 264*t*, 268*t*
Hamilton, Alexander, 234
Hammer, Ellen, 114-15, 195
Harar, 26
Harrison, Selig S., 44
Harvey, G. E., 125
Hashemites, 20
Hausa-Fulani, 64, 78, 80, 84-85, 88-90, 103, 104
Haya de la Torre, Victor Raul, 51, 104, 213, 239-40
Hindi language, 40, 42, 67, 95, 104
Hinduism, 22, 26, 58, 131; and caste system, 43, 92-93; vs. Islam, 41, 57, 92-96, 99
Hitler, Adolf, 105, 116, 172
Hoa Hao, 23
Ho Chi Minh, 219
Hodgkin, Thomas, 115
Honduras, 45, 70*t*, 106*t*, 189*t*, 247*t*; economic development in, 253*t*, 254*t*, 255*t*, 257, 265*t*, 268*t*
Huks, 123*n*

Index

Hungary, 113
Hutu, 193

Ibibio, 80, 81
Ibo, 22, 64-66, 75, 78; in Nigerian civil war, 80-85, 87-91, 99-100, 103
Ibo Federal Union, 82-83
Ibo State Union, 64, 82
Idígoras, Miguel, 186
Idris, Mohammed, 59
Ijaws, 80, 81
Incas, 18, 21, 46-47, 51, 244
India, 18, 26, 70*t*, 77, 105, 113, 195; and Bangladesh, 77, 92-96, 98-100; and Burma, 108, 131-32, 225, 234; caste in, 23, 43-43; economic development in, 254*t*, 255*t*, 257, 258, 259, 261, 262, 264*t*, 267*t*; ethnicity in, 40-44, 106*t*; government in, 68, 78, 103, 104; languages in, 22, 67; nationalism on, 29-30; socialism in, 218, 220, 223, 224, 227, 233, 241-42, 246*t*
Indians, American, 16, 18, 20, 21, 26, 29, *45-56*, 105, 117, 193, 239
Indigenismo, 45, 54-55, 102, 104
Indonesia, 68, 78, 102; colonialism in, 19, 125; economic development in, 253*t*, 255*t*, 258, 259, 261, 262, 265*t*, 267*t*; language in, 67, 104; pluralism in, 24, 39, 46, 106*t*; political violence in, 113, 114, 116; religion in, 23, 26, 57; revolution in, 180, *181-82*, 191, 192, 193, 196; separatism in, 70*t*, 75, 76, 77; socialism in, 220-21, 222, 247*t*
Indonesian Communist Party, 113, 182
International Monetary Fund, 263
International Petroleum Corporation, 217, 258
Iran, 19-20, 26, 186*t*; economic development in, 257, 258, 264*t*, 267*t*; irredentism in, 71*t*, 73*n*, 77; Kurds in, 44-45, 71*t*, 77; pluralism in, 38, 67, 106*t*; socialism in, 247*t*, 253*t*
Iraq, 20, 113; economic development in, 253*t*, 255*t*, 264*t*, 267*t*; irredentism in, 71*t*, 73; pluralism in, 22, 44-45, 67, 106*t*; revolution in, 182, 186*t*; socialism in, 206, 211, 246*t*
Ireland, 15
Ironsi, J. T. U. Aguiyi, 87-88, 91
Irredentism, 69-78
Islam (Muslims), 22-23, 26, 57, 70*t*, 115; and Ba'ath socialism, 210-11; in Central and East Africa, 26, 38, 57, 64, 204; vs. Hinduism, 40, 92-96, 99; in Lebanon, 60, 73; in Middle East, 20, 22, 45; in North Africa, 20, 23, 59; in Pakistan, 20, 41, 57, 92-96, 99, 108; in Southeast Asia, 23, 57, 131; in Sudan, 22, 75, 105

Israel, 20, 74, 116, 183, 207
Israeli Communist Party, 119
Italy, 59, 122, 181
Ivory Coast, 71*t*, 75, 107*t*, 149, 189*t*, 248*t*, 253*t*, 254, 264*t*, 268*t*

Jagan, Cheddi B., 247*t*
Jamaica, 18, 70*t*, 106*t*
Japan, 23, 170, 172; invasion of Burma by, 128, 133, 134; political violence in, 113, 117; socialism in, 218, 236-37
Jati, 43
Java, 24, 39-40, 76, 102, 119, 196
Jefferson, Thomas, 115
Jesuits, 48, 50
Jinnah, Mohammed, 95, 96
John XXIII, Pope, 215
Jordan, 20, 74, 106*t*, 186*t*, 248*t*; economic development in, 253*t*, 254*t*, 255*t*, 265*t*; irredentism in, 71*t*, 73
Josey, Alex, 225
Juárez, Benito, 55
Judaism, 20, 22, 74, 105, 183
Juliana, of the Netherlands, 182
Julião, Francisco, 188

Kabila, Laurent, 156*n*
Kabonga, 150*n*
Kachins, 70*t*, 102, 134
Kader, Abd-el, 23
Kanza, Thomas, 156
Karens, 26, 39, 70*t*, 76, 102, 133-35
Kasavubu, Joseph, 157, 162
Kashmir, 61*n*, 70*t*, 97
Katanga (Zaire), 24, 71*t*, 75, 76, 77, 149, 150-51, 153, 154, 160, 165
Kayibanda, G., 233
Keita, Modibo, 202, 203 and *n*
Kennedy, John F., 214
Kenya, 38, 107*t*, 163, 189*t*; economic development in, 253*t*, 255*t*, 261, 264*t*, 267*t*; federalism in, 78, 102; irredentism in, 71*t*, 75, 77; socialism in, 205, 223, 232, 246*t*
Kenyatta, Jomo, 38, 205, 206, 232
Kerala (India), 44
Khalifa, Ser el Khatim, 247*t*
Khan, Ayub, 97, 206
Khan, Syed Ahmad, 93
Khan, Yahya, 97, 100
Khana, Pathiwat, 185
Khatmia, 22
Khorosan, 71*t*
Kikongo language, 33
Kingis, Alphonse, 159*n*, 164
Kinshava Island, 76
Korea, 73*n*, 106*t*, 218, 253*t*. *See also* North Korea; South Korea
Kotelawala, John, 58

Kru, 36-37
Kshatriya caste, 43
Kuomintang, 132, 178
Kurdistan, 71*t*
Kurds, 44-45, 71*t*, 73 and *n*, 77, 187
Kuwait, 74, 107*t*, 189*t*, 248*t*, 264*t*, 268*t*
Kuzistan, 71*t*
Kwilu (Zaire), 24, 149, 152, 153, 154, 157, 158, 162, 165

Ladino, 53-54
Lagos, 80-82, 86-87
Lakumukasi, Adrien, 156*n*
Language: as cultural differentiator, 21-22; and ethnicity, 38-40; policy, and conflict, 66-67
Laos, 18, 23, 24, 38-39, 72-73, 78, 106*t*, 119, 186*t*, 248*t*, 265*t*, 268*t*
Laski, Harold, 206, 227
Lasswell, H. D., 118
Law of Civilization and Decay, The (Adams), 224
Lebanon, 59-60, 73, 75-76, 103, 107*t*, 186*t*, 248*t*, 253*t*, 255*t*, 264*t*, 268*t*
Lenin, V. I., 115, 238, 239
Lenshina, Alice, 23, 149
Leo XIII, Pope, 215
Leopold, of Belgium, 31
Lesotho, 18, 248*t*
Levantines, 225
Liberación Nacional (Costa Rica), 141, 214
Liberia, 20, 36-37, 78, 107*t*, 189*t*, 248*t*, 255*t*, 258, 264*t*, 268*t*
Liboke-lya-Bangala, 33
Libya, 107*t*, 248*t*; economic development in, 253*t*, 264*t*, 268*t*; federalism in, 78, 103; irredentism in, 71*t*, 73, 74; Senussi power in, 20, 59
Lingala language, 32-33
Lipset, Seymour Martin, 191
Lobobangi language, 32
London School of Economics, 227
López, Alfonso, 136, 185
Lovanium University, 154*n*
Luang Prabang (Laos), 24
Luckham, Robin, 88
Lucknow Resolution, 94
Lumpa Church, 23, 149
Lumumba, Patrice, 149, 152, 157, 158, 159, 162, 247*t*
Lunda, 21, 150
Ly, Abdoulaye, 231

MacArthur, Douglas, 172
MacDonald, Austin, 136
Machismo, 118
Macridis, Roy, 3
Madagascar, 19, 107*t*, 163, 248*t*, 253*t*, 268*t*; colonialism in, 18, 19, 195

Madariaga, Salvador de, 117, 118
Madero, Francisco I., 174
Madhya Pradesh (India), 44
Maharashtra (India), 42, 44
Mahdi, 22, 193
Maji-Maji uprising, 154, 161
Malagasy, 264*t*
Malawi, 26, 67, 71*t*, 107*t*, 189*t*, 248*t*; economic development in, 253*t*, 255*t*, 264*t*, 268*t*
Malaya, 73, 119, 120
Malayan Communist Party, 120, 121, 122
Malays, 20, 22, 66, 73
Malaysia, 23, 24, 103, 106*t*, 187; economic development in, 253*t*, 254, 255*t*, 257, 260, 262, 265*t*, 268*t*; races in, 20, 66; and revolution, 189*t*, 195, 197; separatism in, 70*t*, 75-76, 77; socialism in, 218, 220, 248*t*; violence in, 78, 115-16
Mali, 23, 38, 71*t*, 107*t*, 162; economic development in, 259, 261, 264*t*, 267*t*; socialism in, 202-3, 222, 236, 246*t*
Malinke, 38
Mao Tse-tung, 115, 178-79, 192, 219, 221
Maoists, 187, 218-19, 220, 238
Marhaenism, 220
Mariátegui, José Carlos, 239
Maritain, Jacques, 215
Maronites, 60, 73, 103
Marshall, George, 139*n*
Martí, José, 191
Marx, Karl, 206, 236, 238, 239
Marxism-Leninism, 10, 72-73, 199, 226-28, 233, 238-40; in Africa, 201, 202, 203, 204, 261; and Arab socialism, 206, 208; in Asia, 184, 218, 219-20, 221-22; in Latin America, 212, 213, 215, 217-18; and revolution, 172-73, 178-79, 191, 192-93, 197. *See also* Communism; Socialism
Masjumi, 23
Masses africaines et l'actuelle condition humaine, Les (Ly), 231
Massu, Jacques, 208
Mau Mau, 163
Mauretania, 71*t*, 107*t*, 189*t*, 248*t*, 258, 264*t*, 268*t*
Mauritius, 18, 119, 264*t*
Maya, 46, 53-54
Mboya, Tom, 206
Merina, 19
Mexico, 50, 78, 106*t*; economic development in, 253*t*, 255*t*, 256, 257, 258, 259, 261, 267*t*; Indians in, 45-46, 54-55, 193; national identity of, 102, 104; regionalism in, 24, 72; revolution in, 55, 173, *174-75*, 179, 180, 184, 193, 215, 243-44; separatism in, 70*t*, 72; socialism in, 215-16, 222, 233, 235, 246*t*

Mobutu, Joseph, 34, 64, 157n, 165, 182
Moguls, 40
Mohammed, 115
Molucca Islands, 26
Mongo, 22, 33-34, 46, 48, 62-64, 80, 158n, 163
Mongolia, 23
Mons, 134
Morley-Minto reforms, 93
Morocco, 18, 19, 107t, 116, 186t, 248t, 253t, 264t, 268t
Mossedeq, Mohammed, 247t, 258
Movimiento Nacional Revolucionario (Bolivia), 215
Mozambique, 163, 186t
Mughal Empire (India), 92, 95
Mulele, Pierre, 154, 155, 158-59, 160, 161, 162, 165
Mumbundu, 162
Muscat, 186t
Muslim League (India), 40, 92, 93, 94-95, 96
Muslims. *See* Islam

Naga, 70t, 76
Naguib, Mohammed, 196, 207
Nasser, Gamal Abdel, 74, 77, 115, 164, 183, 192, 196, 206-7, 222, 229, 233, 234
National Convention of Nigeria and the Cameroons (NCNC), 82, 84, 85, 86
Naxalites, 220
Ndele, Albert, 157n
Nehru, Jawaharlal, 29-30, 42, 94, 218, 224, 227, 233, 234
Nepal, 18, 23, 106t, 248t, 264t, 268t
Netherlands; as colonial power, 77, 102, 119, 181-82, 195, 197
Ne Win, 196
Nicaragua, 45, 68, 70t, 106t, 248t; economic development in, 253t, 261, 265t, 268t; and revolution, 189t, 189-90
Niger, 71t, 78, 107t, 189t, 248t, 253t, 264t, 268t
Nigeria, 22, 38, 64-66, 68, 71t, 104, 107t, 162, 189t; civil war in, 75, 76, 79-91, 92, 98-100, 103, 106; economic development in, 253t, 254t, 255t, 258, 261, 262, 264t, 267t, 268t; federalism in, 78, 103; socialism in, 236-37, 248t
Nigerian National Alliance (NNA), 86
Nigerian Youth Movement, 82
Nkrumah, Kwame, 185, 202-3, 222, 229, 231, 233, 239, 243, 247t, 251, 259
Nkumbula, Harry, 35
Northern People's Congress (Nigeria), 84, 85, 86
North Korea, 252, 264t, 267t; revolution in, 173, 192-93; socialism in, 219, 222, 246t
North Vietnam, 58, 108, 164, 264t, 267t; revolution in, 173, 192; socialism in, 219, 222, 246t
Nu, U, 196, 220, 223, 242, 244
Nueva Granada, 72
Nyanja language, 67
Nyasaland, 71t
Nyate, Toni, 156n
Nyere, Julius, 104, 203-4, 223, 243
Nyobe, Rubem Um, 163

Obote, Apollo, 247t
Odinga, Oginga, 205
Ogadan, 71t
Ogundipe, B. A. O., 88
Ojukwu, Odumegwa, 80, 88, 89-90
Okello, John, 164
Olenga, Nicolas, 155, 158, 160, 161, 162, 164, 165
Oman, 73, 186t
Onema, Maman Marie, 156, 160
Opepe, Joseph, 158
Ordoñez, José B. y, 213
Organization of African Unity (OAU), 75, 157
Orissa (India), 44
Orozco, José Clemente, 55, 175
Orthodox Churches, 60, 73
Orwell, George, 122
Ospina Pérez, Mariano, 141, 143
Ottoman, Empire, 20, 58, 183

Pak, N. N., 193
Pakistan, 23, 105, 106t, 131, 189t; and Bangladesh war, 79, 92-100; economic development in, 253t, 255t, 265t, 267t; excision of, from India, 41, 44, 77; relition in, 57, 107-8; separatism in, 70t, 73, 77; socialism in, 206, 247t
Pakistani Communist Party, 119
Palestine, 74, 197
Panama, 18, 70t, 72, 106t; development in, 254t, 255t, 265t, 268t; revolution in, 182, 186t; socialism in, 213n, 248t
Panchayats, 43
Paraguay, 106t, 197, 248t; economic development in, 253t, 264t, 268t; Indians in, 22, 45-46, 48-50; national identity of, 102, 105; separatism in, 70t, 72
Partai Surekat Islam Indonesia, 23
Pathans, 70t
Pathet Lao, 72, 119, 187
Paz Estensorro, Victor, 247t
People's Action Party (Singapore), 220
Peralta Azurdia, Enrique, 186
Perón, Juan, 206
Persian language, 40
Peru, 24, 50-53, 106t; *aprismo* policy, 140, 197; economic development, 253t, 254t, 255t, 257, 258, 259, 260, 264t, 267t;

Indians in, 21, 45, 46-47, 78; revolution in, 180, 185, 186*t*, 188; socialism in, 206, 213 and *n*, 214, 216-17, 239, 243-44, 247*t*
Philippines, 19, 57, 104, 106*t*, 248*t*; economic development in, 253*t*, 254*t*, 255*t*, 257, 260, 261, 264*t*, 268*t*; revolution in, 184, 185, 186*t*, 191
Phongyis, 130
Pilipino language, 104
Pizarro, Francisco, 46-47, 49
Poland, 105
Politics of the Developing Areas, The (Almond and Coleman), 5
Portugal, 45, 48, 163, 225
Portuguese Guinea, 163
Prado, Manuel González, 197
Prebisch, Raúl, 211, 212, 216
Pridi, 247*t*
Protestants, 57, 60, 225; vs. Catholics, 15, 23, 64, 84; missionaries, 26, 32, 164
Punjab (India), 42, 44, 57, 95, 99
Pye, Lucian, 5, 78, 116, 117-18, 120, 121, 122, 125

Qadafi, Muammar, 59, 74
Qadiriyya, 23
Qashqais, 71*t*
Qatar, 73
Quebec, 15
Quechua language, 46, 47, 51-52

Rahman, Mujibur, 97
Rajasthan (India), 44
Rakyat Party (Malaysia), 220
Reducciones, 51
Report on Manufactures (Hamilton), 234
Restrepo, Carlos Lleras, 145
Reyes, Rafael, 140
Reza Shah, 26
Riel Rebellion, 114
Rivera, Diego, 55, 175
Rivera, Julio Adalberto, 206
Rizal, José, 191
Rhodesia, 18, 19*n*, 34-35, 71*t*, 186*t*
Rhodes-Livingston Institute, 30
Robespierre, M. F. de, 115
Rojas Pinilla, Gustavo, 143, 145
Roman Catholics, 15, 22, 57, 58, 60; in Latin America, 23, 57, 175, 185, 211, 212, 214-15; vs. Protestants, 15, 23, 64, 84
Rosberg, Carl G., 200
Ruanda-Urundi, 71*t*, 75, 76
Rwanda, 68, 107*t*, 248*t*, 264*t*, 268*t*; colonialism in, 18, 19; revolution in, 189*t*, 193; separatism in, 71*t*, 75-76, 77; Watusi in, 19, 76, 108

Sabah, 24, 70*t*
Sadat, Anwar, 207
Salah, Ahmed Ben, 210
Sallal, Marshal Abdullah, 247*t*
Saller, Raphael, 245
Sampurnanand, 241
San, Aung, 128
San, Saya, 129-30
Sanga language, 67
Sanskrit, 40, 42, 43
Santos, Eduardo, 136
Sanur, 71*t*
Sao Thien G. C. B. A., 130
Sarawak, 24, 70*t*
Sarkisyanz, Manuel, 242
Sarmientos, Domingo, 117
Saudi Arabia, 20, 74, 107*t*, 189*t*, 248*t*, 253*t*, 265*t*, 268*t*
Saya San Rebellion, 129-30
Scandanavia, 205
Schick, René, 190
Schumpeter, 227
Scotland, 125
Senegal, 23, 24, 57, 107*t*, 189*t*; separatism in, 71*t*, 77; socialism in, 204-5, 215, 246*t*, 264*t*, 267*t*; Wolof in, 19, 23
Senghor, Leopold, 10, 57, 77, 203, 204, 215, 223, 229, 239, 243
Senussi, 20, 59
Shans, 70*t*, 102, 134
Shastri, Lal Bahadur, 104
Shays Rebellion, 114
Shi'ites, 22, 45, 60, 73, 103
Sierra Leone, 20, 107*t*, 189*t*, 247*t*, 253*t*, 264*t*, 267*t*
Sihanouk, Norodom, 219
Sikhs, 26
Sindhis, 57
Singapore, 18, 66, 70*t*, 77, 220, 246*t*, 264*t*, 268*t*
Sinhalese, 23, 26, 58-59, 65-66, 67
Sinkiang, 70*t*
Siquieros, David Alfaro, 55
Sklar, Richard, 85
Socialism: in Africa, 200-6; appeal of, 245-51; in Asia, 218-21; Ba'ath, 200-11; and colonialism, 224-26; Destourian, 209-10; in Latin America, 211-18; logic of, 223-45; in Middle East, 206-11; patterns of, 221-23. *See also* Communism; Marxism-Leninism
Socialist Party, 44, 212-13, 223, 237
Somalia, 154, 162, 189*t*, 246*t*, 267*t*; cultural pluralism in, 107*t*, 110; irredentism in, 71*t*, 75, 77
Somaliland, 20
Somozo family, 190
Soumialot, Gaston, 156*n*, 158 and *n*, 159, 161, 162

Index

South Africa, Union of, 18 and *n*, 21, 107*t*, 109, 119, 154*n*, 186*t*; political violence in, 114, 119, 123-24, 160
South Korea, 248*t*, 255*t*, 257, 261, 264*t*, 267*t*
South Vietnam, 23, 58, 113, 186*t*, 197, 248*t*; development policy, 253*t*, 257, 264*t*, 268*t*
South Yemen, 73, 246*t*, 267*t*
Soviet Union, 16, 178-79, 218; irredentism in, 71*t*, 73*n*, 77; socialism in, 199, 202, 205, 219, 222, 231, 235
Spain, 16, 181, 185; as colonial power in Latin America, 18, 45, 46, 47, 49-51, 56, 78, 105, 184, 225, 239; political violence in, 113, 117, 118
Spengler, J. J., 171
Sri Lanka, 23, 26, 38, 65-66, 67, 106*t*, 247*t*, 264*t*, 267*t*; Buddhism in, 23, 26, 57-58; colonialism in, 18, 19
Srinivas, M. N., 43
Stanley, Henry, 31
States Reorganization Committee (India), 42
Stevens, Siaka P., 247*t*
Struggle for Indo-China, The (Hammer), 114-15
Sudan, 22, 107*t*, 162, 247*t*; development policy of, 255*t*, 267*t*; irredentism in, 71*t*, 73; languages in, 67, 105; separatism in, 75, 76
Sudra caste, 43
Suez Canal, 74, 207, 234
Sukarno, Achmed, 102, 181-82, 191, 192, 194, 196, 218, 221, 222, 241, 244, 247*t*, 251, 258, 259, 262
Sumatra, 24, 26, 70*t*
Sunnites, 22, 45, 60, 73, 103
Swahili, 22, 67, 104, 154*n*
Swaziland, 18, 248*t*
Swe, U Ba, 218
Switzerland, 16
Syria, 44, 60, 71*t*, 74; 107*t*, 116; development policy, 253*t*, 255*t*, 267*t*; revolution in, 180, 195; socialism in, 207, 210-11, 246*t*; and U.A.R., 74, 77, 207

Táchira (Venezuela), 24
Tagalog language, 104
Taiwan, 73*n*, 106*t*, 248*t*, 253*t*, 254 and *t*, 267*t*
Tamils, 26, 58-59
Tanganyika, 154
Tanzania, 75, 102, 104, 107*t*, 161, 189, 203-5; development policy, 255*t*, 261, 264*t*, 267*t*
Teilhard de Chardin, Pierre, 204, 215, 239
Teluga language, 42
Texas, 70*t*, 72
Thailand, 19-20, 23, 26, 38, 67, 70*t*, 105, 106*t*, 108, 119, 127, 247*t*; Chinese in, 66, 234; development policy of, 253*t*, 255*t*, 257, 260, 264*t*; revolution in, 184, 185, 186*t*
Thanarat, Saret, 185
Thomas, L. V., 201
Tibet, 23, 70*t*
Toba Bataks, 39
Tobago, 18, 70*t*, 106*t*
Togo, 71*t*, 107*t*, 162, 189*t*, 248*t*; development policy in, 255*t*, 264*t*, 268*t*
Tombalbaye, Pierre, 57
Tongo, 34-36, 46, 80
Torres, Camilio, 188, 211
Touareg, 71*t*
Touré, Sékou, 202-3, 222
Toward Colonial Freedom (Nkrumah), 203
Traore, Moussa, 203*n*
Trinidad, 18, 70*t*, 106*t*
Tshombe, Moise, 150, 155, 156, 162
Tubman, William Shadrach, 37
Tunisia, 18, 19, 107*t*, 116, 209-10, 246*t*, 253*t*, 254*t*, 264*t*, 267*t*
Tupac Amarú, 46-47, 50, 53
Tupí, 47-48
Turbay, Gabriel, 141
Turkey, 44-45, 71*t*, 105, 182, 183, 206
Tutsi, 193

Ubangi, 71*t*
Ubico, Jorge, 185
Uganda, 23, 37, 71*t*, 108, 247*t*; coup in, 162, 164; cultural pluralism in, 107*t*, 110; development policy of, 255*t*, 164*t*, 267*t*; federalism in, 78, 103
Uganda Development Corporation, 261
Ujamaa, 204
Unilever Company, 225
Union des Mongo, 34
United Africa Company, 225
United Arab Emirates, 73
United Arab Republic, 71*t*, 74, 77, 107*t*; socialism in, 206-7, 222, 234
United Grand Progressive Alliance (Nigeria), 86
United Kingdom, 15. *See also* Great Britain
United National Independence Party (Zambia), 35
United National Party (Sri Lanka), 58
United Nations, 59, 74, 150 and *n*, 151, 156, 254; Economic Commission for Latin America of, 211, 216
United States, 103, 140, 170, 183, 185, 187, 218, 262; political violence in, 113, 114; racial conflict in, 16, 170; revolution in, 184, 191; socialism in, 199, 220; and Zaire, 155 and *n*, 163, 164
University of Cairo, 204

Untouchables, 43
Upper Volta, 71*t*, 107*t*, 162, 189*t*, 248*t*, 253*t*, 264*t*, 268*t*
Urdu language, 42, 95-96
Uruguay, 18, 50; cultural pluralism in, 106*t*, 109; development policy in, 253*t*, 254*t*, 264*t*; revolution in, 186*t*, 188; separatism in, 70*t*, 72; socialism in, 213, 246*t*
Uttar (India), 44

Vaisya caste, 43
Valenicia, Guillermo León, 145
Vanderkerken, Georges, 33
Vasconcelos, José, 55
Velasco, Alvarado Juan, 180, 206, 216-17, 247*t*
Velasco Ibarra, Jose Maria, 147*t*
Venezuela, 18, 24-25, 70*t*, 72, 78, 106*t*, 113, 141; development policy if, 253*t*, 254*t*, 257, 258, 259, 264*t*, 267*t*; revolution in, 180, 185; socialism in, 214, 215, 234, 235, 247*t*
Verba, Sidney, 175
Viet Cong, 119
Vietnam, 23, 38-39, 73*n*, 79, 106*t*, 108, 119, 123, 170, 218; Buddhism in, 23, 57-58; colonialism in, 195, 196; political violence in. *See also* North Vietnam; South Vietnam
Vileda Morales, Ramón, 247*t*
Villa, Pancho, 175
Violencia, la, 138-39, 143-44, 145-46
von der Mehden, Fred R., 8-9

Wafd Party (Egypt), 196
Wahabi, 20
Walloons, 16
Wang Shou-tao, 120
Watusi, 19, 76, 108
War of the Pacific, 197
West Cameroons, 71*t*
West Indies Federation, 70*t*, 103
Whiskey Rebellion, 114
Why Men Rebel (Gurr), 124
Wilson, Harold, 199
Wolof, 19, 23
Wriggins, Howard, 59

Yao, 26
Yemen, 19-20, 22, 71*t*, 107*t*, 113, 247*t*
Yoruba, 64, 78, 80-82, 84-85, 88-89, 103
Young, Crawford, 8-9
Yugoslavia, 16, 163

Zaire, 24, 38, 68, 71*t*, 102, 107*t*, 122, 247*t*, 267*t*; federalism in, 78, 103; political violence in, 113, *147-65*; and revolution, 75, 77, 182, 192; tribes in, 21, 22, 31-34, 37, 63
Zambia, 21, 23, 30-31, 34-36, 71*t*, 75, 107*t*, 189*t*, 246*t*; development policy, 253*t*, 254*t*, 255*t*, 258, 264*t*, 267*t*
Zanzibar, 18, 19, 68, 149, 162, 164, 193
Zapata, Emiliano, 175
Zipa, Chibcha Emperor, 47

DATE DUE

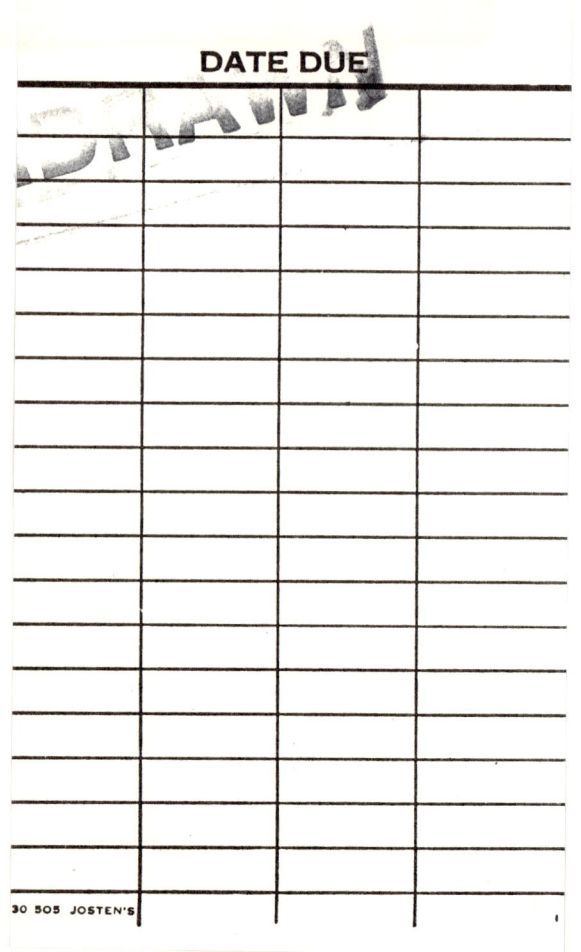

WITHDRAWN

30 505 JOSTEN'S

MONTGOMERY COLLEGE LIBRARIES
germ, circ   JK 60.A53 1974
Issues of pol

0 0000 00131541 5